.GETTING THERE.

GETTING THERE.

The Epic Struggle

between Road and Rail

in the American Century

STEPHEN B. GODDARD

BasicBooks
A Division of HarperCollins*Publishers*

Designed by Jessica Shatan

Library of Congress Cataloging-in-Publication Data
Goddard, Stephen B., 1941–
   Getting there : the epic struggle between road and rail in the American century/ by Stephen B. Goddard.
      p. cm.
   Includes bibliographical references and index.
   ISBN 0–465–02639–7
   1. Transportation, Automotive—United States—History—20th century. 2. Automobiles—Social aspects—United States—History—20th century. 3. Roads—United States—History—20th century. 4. Railroads—United States—History—20th century.
I. Title
HE5623.G63 1994
388.3'0973—dc20   93–50543
                                                                                              CIP

94 95 96 97 ❖/RRD 9 8 7 6 5 4 3 2

To the memory of my mother,

ELIZABETH O'CONNOR GODDARD,

and my aunt,

MARY C. O'CONNOR,

who taught me to love words

CONTENTS

PREFACE

●────────────────────────────────●

A century ago, hard-topped roads leading from the industrial downtowns of America stopped at the city lines. There, as in ancient cities, another world began. Amid weeds and cornfields, dirt paths snaked outward. During dry weather, people ventured forth in their horse-drawn wagons, but in rainy seasons those foolish enough to brave the mud soon found themselves mired up to their hubs. And as they sat and fumed, smoky locomotives and electric interurban trains streaked by, carrying passengers and produce in to the bustling depots.

In the early twentieth century, bicycles and automobiles changed all that and caused a national clamor for good roads. Railroad depredations had poisoned the well of public opinion, and rail owners came to view angry governments as, at best, an obstacle in their path. The motor industry, which the public embraced as an alternative to the hated rails, viewed government as a partner in progress. This contrast spelled doom for the iron horse and untold prosperity for the horseless carriage.

By the 1920s, a powerful force had evolved, wedding road builders and the motor industry, in which government and business joined happily in promoting as a national policy one mode of travel over all others. The highway-motor complex coalesced automakers, cement, asphalt, and steel producers, and petroleum companies into a common purpose. Along the way, it added such diverse groups as road contractors, insurance companies, banks, and motel operators, to name but a few. The highway advocates became so dominant in American life that they were instrumental in changing the character of cities and helping to suburbanize the nation. And as the highway-motor complex eventually came to employ one of every six American workers, it became self-perpetuating by making the economy dependent on its continued health.

The belief that in the march of progress, railroads simply yielded to a more advanced form of transportation is a myth. In fact, the highway-motor complex nearly killed off the American railroads. How its members went about that is a saga filled with high ideals and craven conspiracy, ambition and inertia, vision and myopia, inspiration and intrigue, opportunism and stupidity, greed and lust for power. This panoramic struggle displays the American character at its worst and at its best—showing how a fearful, fledgling democracy took on forces larger than itself and came to control some and become controlled by others during the golden age some have labeled "the American century." Our story is an epic, beginning with the Grangers, who first moved to harness the rapacious railroads, and ending with the data superhighways, which will become the interstates of the twenty-first century.

I use the term *highwaymen* repeatedly, to refer to the many and diverse members of the highway-motor complex. The term's gender designation is deliberate; practically all members who built the complex in the decades leading up to and including the interstates were men. The highwaymen of old robbed travelers on the open road. The new highwaymen robbed the world's most affluent nation of a choice how to get from here to there. Today, the term highwaymen is inappropriate and anachronistic, as women have joined their ranks. But the highway advocates continue to exert their influence. They manifest themselves daily in rush-hour traffic jams on superhighways running next to abandoned railroad tracks, in smog that overlies urban centers, in much larger government subsidies for those who drive to work than those who take the bus or train, and in America's dependence on oil and the resultant need to keep a military presence in foreign lands so petroleum will flow freely. But while some highway advocates have been avaricious manipulators, others have not. The thousands of engineers who built America's unparalleled road system, for example, were often men of high principle, engaged in what they saw as a noble mission. Yet as participants in creating an auto-dependent society, they must accept responsibility as well for the outcome.

To keep things in perspective, cars and superhighways have brought great joy and prosperity to America. I fondly remember my own adolescent days spent cruising the brand-new interstates in a 1953 Studebaker Starlight coupe, with such rock and roll hits as "Chantilly Lace" blaring from its radio. But a mature society, like a mature person, should recognize and correct overindulgence. For driving is inexpensive only when we neglect to include such social costs as polluted air, rush hour gridlock, illness from breathing gas fumes, huge government subsidies for highways and parking, and maintenance of an expensive military presence in oil-producing countries. For in fact, Americans pay a hidden cost of $2.25 per gallon each time we fuel up, over and above what we pay at the pump. Obviously, a nation with overcrowded, crumbling highways and under-used railways ought to strive for a greater balance between the two modes.

Today an information revolution is changing America with blinding speed. The same emotions that gave life to the epic struggle between road and rail will drive this movement and determine whether society harnesses it or is harnessed by it. During the last century, government failed to promote effectively the public interest—first in allowing railroads to exploit the people they served, then in breaking the railroads' spirit, and finally in overbuilding America's superhighways. We may be forgiven our mistakes of the past; we were naïve and untested then. Sadder but wiser now, we have at hand a century of experience with such commercial hurricanes. If we fail to bring these lessons to bear on twenty-first-century challenges, we have only ourselves to blame.

Hartford, Connecticut
February 1994

·GETTING THERE·

PROLOGUE: 1917

There can be no turning back. . . .
We are provincials no longer.

—President Woodrow Wilson,
Second Inaugural Address

Monday, March 5, 1917, dawned raw and gloomy after a weekend of heavy rain, but by mid-morning thousands of people had lined the broad thoroughfare, huddled against an angry northwest wind, which curled Old Glory around its flagpoles as far as the eye could see. Armed plainclothesmen stalked the rooftops of office buildings, peering down on two neat rows of national guardsmen, rifles at the ready, lined ten feet apart all the way to the Capitol. Just at eleven this March morning, the clip-clop of four horses' hooves punctuated the whoosh of the stiff breeze, as the open black carriage turned from the White House onto Pennsylvania Avenue.[1]

The weather matched perfectly the mood of Woodrow Wilson's White House.[2] Inauguration Day belonged to the people, and the President would wave and flash his toothy smile to the crowds, but he could be forgiven if his mind was elsewhere. A cordon of thirty-two Secret Service men framed the presidential carriage, as it entered what the *New York Times* called a lane of steel, stretching neatly to the Capitol dome.[3] Fear for Wilson's safety from both foreign and domestic foes was such that greater security surrounded this presidential inauguration than any since Lincoln's.[4] As damp onlookers watched from waterlogged grandstands erected alongside, Wilson's carriage-driver straddled the steel tracks of the city's ubiquitous electric streetcars, which had yielded their bustling role to this historic affair of state.[5]

The thought of greeting senators at noon could not have cheered the President. For much of his first term, as conflict raged across the Atlantic, Wilson had parried the conflicting entreaties of agitators: Stay out of the European war! Send American boys abroad before it's too late![6] Actually, no one had championed neutrality more than Woodrow Wilson.[7] Yet since Germany threatened to attack U.S. shipping, fearful American ships huddled in port, unwilling to move their commerce across the ocean and potentially strangling the economy. To project American solidarity to the Germans, the President asked the Senate to support him in arming those ships. But a dozen pacifist senators the day before vehemently filibustered the plan. Wilson lashed out in response, condemning "this little group of wilful men, representing no opinion but their own." Last evening, 3,000 agitated people massed for a pro-war rally in New York's Carnegie Hall, shouting "Hang them!" at the very mention of the obstructive senators' names.[8]

AN ADOLESCENT NATION

America, on which Europe had come to rely desperately for wartime supplies, was still a gangling adolescent—all arms and legs. Wilson knew in his heart that events would soon suck the nation into the vortex of this hated war.[9] Yet moving a couple of million men and thousands of tons of materiel to the European front in time to help would be a nearly impossible task.

Building what the world needed had proved easy for brawny smokestack America; getting it there had become the problem. Railroad leaders had so poisoned the well of public opinion in their headlong quest for monopoly power that a popular groundswell arose to straitjacket their operations. By 1917, the nation's overworked, underfinanced, overregulated, underinspired, and ineptly managed railroads couldn't even haul the goods that a mighty consumer revolution had spawned—let alone carry military transport. Its cargo now clogged railyards in the big cities, as boxcars of tomatoes and turnips rotted on sidings while waiting days to unload.[10]

And while motorized vehicles—the wave of the future—churned off midwestern assembly lines by the millions, more than 90 percent of America's roads were muddy, rutted, dirt paths, threatening to mire motor vehicles up to their hubs. So long-distance military truck transport seemed quite out of the question. The enemy apparently had factored this American Achilles' Heel into its calculations. By the time the United States could amass a military force from its vast expanses, Germany calculated, it would have delivered the coup de grace to the Allies.[11]

A Crusade for Good Roads

The last horse-drawn vehicle ever to carry a President to his Inauguration now crept along the white asphalt of Pennsylvania Avenue,[12] past the honky-tonk storefronts that lined its lower end. Horse and wagon teams were becoming rare of late and on a normal day, trolleycars linked to swaying overhead lines monopolized the center of the Avenue. But increasingly, a crush of motorized delivery wagons and open roadsters with drivers in scarves and goggles forced streetcar drivers to slow down or stop in frustration, as motorists asserted their new-found freedom from rigid rails.

Wilson's carriage now passed close to the imposing Willard Building, where soon would begin the greatest roadbuilding program the world had ever known.[13] Producers of automobiles, rubber tires, asphalt, cement and road machinery had sensed great profits in promoting vehicles not tied to steel rails. During the President's 1916 reelection campaign, they helped prod him into signing a modest "good roads" bill, designed to "get the farmer out of the mud" and to deliver the mail.[14] A Wilson stump speech marveled that America's enthusiastic new car owners "use them (roads) up almost as fast as we make them" and noted prophetically, "It is perfectly obvious that you have got to have an intricate and perfect network of roads throughout the length and breadth of this great continent before you will have released the energies of America."[15]

News that smoother roads were on the way steered Wall Street investors towards the auto industry, as Detroit now joined the railroads in courting the money markets. As bystanders along Pennsylvania Avenue flipped through the daily newspaper while awaiting a glimpse of President and Mrs. Wilson, ads beseeched them to buy stock in Pierce-Arrow "pleasure cars" and in Chevrolet, which trumpeted proudly that it had spent four times its net earnings to buy up smaller automakers. Competing for their attention were come-ons by the St. Louis Railroad, which sought money to buy new boxcars; and the New York Central, which took pains to stress—somewhat defensively—railroads' social responsibility.[16]

THE HATED RAILROAD—AMERICA'S ONLY HOPE

As the cortege turned onto the Capitol grounds, the President could see to his left the cavernous white marble Union Station, whose steam trains had disgorged car after car of guardsmen to protect the life of their commander in chief.[17] Thousands of wellwishers had paid three dollars apiece for a round trip to the festivities aboard New Jersey Central's Royal Blue Line. Yes, for better or worse, the nation still moved by rail; the inevitable network of good roads was still years away. If America had a prayer of helping hold Germany at bay, Wilson knew he would have to see to it that railroads did the job.

Forty thousand people had gathered on the West steps of the Capitol to hear the President deliver his second inaugural address. More than a dozen huge American flags hung lengthwise from the West Portico, blowing in unison with the chill, stiff breeze.[18] The mood of the crowd was sober and foreboding. "The inauguration was not a festival," the *New York Times* observed, ". . . it was a momentary interlude in a grave business, and it must be got over with as briefly and simply as possible."[19] Then someone in the anxious crowd began to spontaneously sing "America," and others picked up its strains until it became a mighty refrain.[20]

Behind Wilson sat the "little group of willful men": such senators as "Fighting Bob" LaFollette of Wisconsin and Albert Cummins of Iowa, fervid adherents of the popular Progressive movement. Committed to fundamental social and political change, the Progressives had played a major role in bringing the arrogant railroads to their knees, retaliating for their depredations in helping build the American West. They, together with business leaders across the country, now sought in Wilson's words some hint of how their lives were about to change. Railroad moguls, reduced to a reactionary and unimaginative lot by the hammerlock of ruthless regulation, greeted any news from government with great suspicion. And in Detroit, a clutch of entrepreneurs still young—men named Buick, Chrysler, Nash—wondered whether they could trust an Eastern-dominated government to protect their fledgling industry.[21]

The President's address stopped just short of the declaration of war Wilson knew he was fated to make. He summoned America to "stand together" amid European events that "have drawn us more and more irresistibly into their own current and influence."[22]

Within a month, Woodrow Wilson would declare war, at which point all his worst fears came true in a clash between free enterprisers, who had generated both industrial growth and wretched excesses, and the Progressives, who saw such growth as running roughshod over the rights of the average person.

Wilson Seizes the Rails

Railroad leaders held the key to effective mobilization. Feeling the public's angry glare upon them, they created a war board, to gather their independent lines into one massive network. But asking bitter rivals to cooperate in servicing each other's customers predictably produced only bickering and backbiting. And the smothering restrictions upon them by the Interstate Commerce Commission compromised their efficiency. By December, Wilson knew that the time for jawboning and conciliation had passed. The President seized control of the nation's railways but left their ownership untouched.[23]

To relieve the overwhelmed railroads, the military had little choice but to order trucks bound for the European front to drive from midwestern plants across narrow, frozen dirt roads to the Atlantic Coast, during a winter that turned out to be one of the most severe on record. Thirty thousand trucks bumped along as crews worked around the clock to clear heavy snowdrifts.[24] Throughout 1918, America's shackled and antiquated railroads and its pitifully inadequate roads did their best to mobilize and supply an overseas force of two million men.[25]

A Fateful Contrast

Abroad, the sophisticated road and rail networks of the grateful Allies sped the American relief quickly to the front lines. But at home, the experience exposed just how militarily and commercially vulnerable the largest Western nation was, simply because it couldn't move quickly from point A to point B. The lesson was not lost on the American people.

And so, in 1917, American road and rail entered the modern era. Railroads by then had existed for nearly a century, motor vehicles for barely two decades. The railways considered cooperation with government beneath them, akin to socialism, and policymakers returned their contempt. The motor industry and government, by contrast, reached out to each other eagerly and created an enduring, symbiotic partnership. Such starkly contrasting philosophies found their roots in the evolution of the two modes of transportation, and this basic difference would set the tone for the epic struggle that lay ahead.

· 1 ·

THE FIRST BIG BUSINESS

We hear no more the clanking hoof,
And stage-coach rattling by;
For the steam-king rules the traveled world,
And the pike is left to die.

—Rev. John Pierpont Morgan, the grandfather
of rail titan J. P. Morgan

IN THE FALL OF 1829 THE "STEPHENSON ROCKET," SPEWING THICK clouds of black smoke, raced along the new iron tracks of the Liverpool and Manchester Railway and hurtled over the finish line at the unheard-of speed of twenty-nine miles an hour. A Britisher, George Stephenson, had vanquished all rivals this day, in a race so alluring that Americans crossed the Atlantic by steamship to watch it. Flush with victory, the illit-erate inventor invited Fanny Kemble, the darling of the London stage, for a ride, and she quickly accepted. Fresh from starring in *Romeo and Juliet* to packed houses at Covent Garden, the twenty-one-year-old actress wore a bonnet over her brunette locks as she stood behind the hulking locomotive, its vertical smokestack ascending from the front of its round horizontal boiler, like a giant black *L*. "The engine was set off at its utmost speed, thirty-five miles an hour, swifter than a bird flies," Kemble wrote later. "You cannot conceive what that sensation of cutting the air was; the motion as smooth as possible too. I stood up, and with my bonnet off drank the air before me." The trip made her fall "horribly in love" with both Stephenson and his locomotive.[1]

The United States would soon experience a similar enchantment, which would infect businessmen and the general populace with railroad fever. Nineteenth-century America was a nation of entrepreneurs, a fact crucial to understanding this watershed in the country's history. Raised in a land of individual opportunity, free from the whims of arbitrary authority, farmers and merchants for two centuries had earned their living by taking risks for the promise of profit. Before the Iron Horse, reliance on the flesh-and-blood equine had limited how people related to time and space. A rider could carry a small load five to ten miles a day over dirt paths, defining the radius within which a farmer could sell his produce before it rotted. So a farmer's market was a local market. His customers were his neighbors. The farmer usually carried his own crops to the point of sale. And if another entrepreneur agreed to carry the farmer's crops to market for him, they could haggle face to face about the shipping price and shake hands on it.

RAILROADS SPROUT LIKE DAFFODILS

That intimacy of one-to-one trading was about to end. The American engineers and mechanics who had traveled to England for Stephenson's celebrated race now scurried to their workshops, to apply the new technology. Merchants in Charleston, South Carolina, seeking to halt their city's economic decline, hired Horatio Allen to build them a six-mile railroad to draw business from the interior. In 1830, the "Best Friend of Charleston" became the first steam locomotive to haul a train of cars in America. Soon, eastern cities were vying to attract the new railroads, which began to sprout like daffodils in April. By 1835, eleven states had granted charters over a thousand miles of track to two hundred fledgling operators.[2]

The pulsating black beast had an arresting effect on both sides of the Atlantic. The editor of the *Cincinnati Enquirer* returned from an 1846 excursion on a new section of railroad, to report seeing "herds of cattle, sheep and horses, stand for a few seconds to gaze at the passing train, then turn and run a few rods with all possible speed, stop and look again with eyes distended, and head and ears erect, seemingly so frightened at the tramp of the iron horse as to have lost the power of locomotion."[3] From London, Charles Dickens described an early locomotive's approach: "[A] dull light advancing, quickly changed to two red eyes, and a fierce fire, dropping glowing coals; an irresistible bearing on of a great roaring and dilating mass; a high wind, and a rattle—another come and gone."[4]

That this new mode of travel was literally unnatural unsettled some. One writer, describing the "Moral Influence of Steam," wondered whether by fostering effortless travel the railroad would "disturb the moral economy of the world, by opposing that great law of the universe, which makes labor the portion of man, and condemns him to earn his bread by the sweat of his brow." The French novelist Victor Hugo complained that "the flowers by the side of the road are no longer flowers but flecks, or rather streaks of red or white."[5] When a Vermont railroad began running trains on the sabbath in the 1850s, the state legislature made sure that conductors read a passage of Scripture to the riders.[6]

Yet few could help but marvel at the impressive display of engineering achievement the railroads represented and the promise they held for industrial growth. "Steam is annihilating space," one author gushed, in an oft-repeated theme.[7] But not everyone was so enthused. Henry David Thoreau warned darkly: "We do not ride upon the railroad; it rides upon us."[8] Yet few could disagree with William Makepeace Thackeray: "We who have lived before the railways were made belong to another world."[9]

THE EARLY DEVELOPMENT OF RAILROADS

Three phases mark the early development of American railroads. In the mid-nineteenth century, several major companies constructed basic routes, led by the New York Central, the Baltimore and Ohio, and the Pennsylvania. Then came the land-grant era, as the congressional bounty of free land led to westward expansion, overbuilding, and rampant competition, as rivals competed to buy up profitable feeder lines. By the mid-1890s, the third stage began, as the remaining titans sought to swallow up each other.

Rapid Expansion of Basic Routes

Long before land grants to railroads, canvas-covered Conestoga wagons had snaked westward over primitive dirt paths filled with settlers bent on charting a future that would be uniquely theirs. But some worried how a fledgling democracy could hold together while becoming so widely separated. Then came the railroad and the telegraph, which writers such as Walt Whitman, who called these innovations "the pulse of the continent," saw as the tie to unify the nation's far-flung people.[10] So the burgeoning early railroads seemed to have a nobility of purpose—a heavy burden to place around the neck of men who viewed themselves as mere capitalists. The railroad journalist Henry V. Poor set the idealists straight in 1852 by observing that railroads were "merely commercial enterprises, and are to be conducted upon commercial principles, which never sanction an enormous sacrifice for a contingent good."[11]

Before the Civil War, the railroads had their way with the American people, who were entranced by this invention that changed the way they lived. The railways' presence or absence caused major cities to rise or fall in relative prominence. Philadelphia's city fathers invested heavily in the Pennsylvania Railroad, fearing commercial competition from New York City, whose gentry had committed a stunning $23 million toward building the New York Central. So rapidly did the railroads grow that by the 1850s, the Pennsylvania employed more people than the state in which it was located.[12] Such relative size, together with government's hands-off attitude toward business, gave railroads greater power than that of the states to affect people's lives, thus making railroads corporate states unto themselves. Indeed, when the railways spread west, companies created states out of whole cloth and then, predictably, controlled those states' policies.[13] Such a railroad Ralph Waldo Emerson called "a judicial being, which has no judicial sovereign."[14]

For railroads offered the public more than the state could: wider markets for business, jobs for ordinary people, and dividends for stockholders. And where carriers sensed resistance, they had favors aplenty to dispense. In an age when hopping into the family car was not yet an option, traveling by rail had become hugely important. So a county assessor, surprised by a railroad gift of free rail passes for a family outing, might think twice before adding to that railroad's tax burden. Before long, anyone who was anyone—grain merchants, local legislators, opinion leaders—rode the rails for free. Rampant competition and free land had caused the railroads to overbuild, so they had plenty of excess capacity to give away.[15] And during each state's legislative season, some legislators seemed only too willing to consider railroad bills seriously once their palms were greased. The general counsel of the Santa Fe Railroad holed up at the Copeland Hotel in Wichita, Kansas, each session with instructions to dole out from $500 to $2,000 to each legislative leader—who earned three dollars a day—as a retainer if he was a lawyer, as expense money if he was not.[16] "Needy pastors were hurriedly converted to steam, and they presently could see God's hand on the throttle."[17]

By the start of the Civil War, thirty thousand miles of track crisscrossed the country, only the merest skeleton of the network that was to be built. But wartime necessity strengthened and improved the railroads, particularly in Union territory, proving "the supreme symbol of the gap between the industrial North and the largely agrarian South."[18] Yet the Great American Desert, as some called it, offered little incentive to rail entrepreneurs seeking a quick fortune. As uncharted territory, the West was worthless. Yet with a reliable way to get there, it could be a gold mine.

The Great Land Grab

So Congress embarked on a revolutionary course: to offer a way to get to a town before that town even existed. Many congressmen owned railroad stock, which made it that much easier to grant millions of acres of land to the eager railway companies.[19] During one Senate debate, Senator William R. King responded to those who charged that a grant to the Illinois Central was too large: "Well, sir, it is a great quantity (of land); but it will be there for five hundred years; and unless some mode of the kind proposed be adopted, it will never command ten cents."[20]

Overnight, railroads owned territories the size of states. While turning wilderness into bustling towns, some also misappropriated land for profit.[21] Historians have since debated bitterly whether the land grants were a government sellout or a foresighted strategy, and arguments on both sides abound. In either case, without the land grants, America undoubtedly would not have experienced either rapid westernization or the corruption that followed the West's unchecked growth. And the country might well have lost these vast western expanses to acquisitive foreign powers.[22]

Railroads rushed to gobble up the more than 130 million acres of land—collectively bigger than Texas—that Congress granted the fledgling rail companies and began spreading a steel capillary system throughout the uncharted West.[23] In return, the railroads agreed to open up the West to settlement and carry federal property and the mails at cut rates. Pioneers rode the rails into the wilderness and, seemingly overnight, built new towns with supplies manufactured in the East. Towns called Omaha, Tulsa, and Wichita grew from tiny settlements to cities overnight; from 1870 to 1890, Denver's population grew twentyfold.[24]

Then on a spring day in 1869, telegraphs clacked out the news that a four-hundred-dollar golden spike, driven in amid popping champagne corks at Promontory, Utah, had united the Union Pacific and Central

Pacific railroads into a transcontinental span.[25] The railroads had hauled in ramshackle three-story dormitories by flatcar along the route to house the thousands of men imported to complete the railway. Among them were Irish refugees from the potato famine and six thousand imported Chinese laborers with pigtails, wearing round straw hats, blue blouses, and pantaloons.[26]

Rail Titans Extend Their Power

Western settlers learned that good things came to a town fortunate enough to have a depot; to lack one was to be left behind. Their eagerness was not lost on the railroad men, who raised capital by convincing people who wanted the train to stop in their town to buy stock.

So virulent was the railroad fever that railroad promoters could often dictate their price for steering tracks into a town. When they called on the gentry of the fledgling town of Booneville, Iowa—demanding swamplands, $10,000, and twenty acres of town land before bringing their rails in—townspeople scurried to raise all but $1,200, for which they agreed to sign a note. Unacceptable, sniffed the promoters, who routed the line through a more cooperative town.[27] (One searches in vain for Booneville on a modern map.)

The land-grant railroads aggressively advertised in eastern newspapers for people to settle near the new lines. Land agents of the Illinois Central offered married men jobs at $1.25 a day, guaranteed for two years, seducing them away from teeming urban tenements to "a healthy climate, where land can be bought cheap... on long credit and low prices." Runners waited dockside in New York City to pounce on immigrants newly arrived from Europe, while Illinois Central agents scoured Germany and Scandinavia for potential settlers.[28]

RAILROADS TRANSFORM AMERICANS' LIVES

For settlements in nineteenth-century America, geography was destiny. Cities built near water, such as Chicago or New York, were already bustling trading centers, founded on waterborne commerce. Steamboats, which were slower than railroads but cheaper to operate, could ship for less. To compete, railways had to lower their rates. But if railroads could not undercut steamboats on price, they certainly could on speed, and railroads soon began to steal away bargeloads of business. States chartering railroads in such business hubs reasoned (correctly) that two competing railroads would offer cheaper rates than one, so these states often granted multiple charters.[29]

As urban competition forced railway companies to cut freight rates, their profits sank. Seeking to balance their books, the rails looked west— to the landlocked western towns they had created, which had no canals and a market small enough to justify only one rail line. The solution did not take much imagination: charge more in towns where they had a monopoly. Suddenly, farmers, who had to factor haulage costs into the price of their produce, were paying double to get their corn to market and found themselves underbid by farmers nearer the big cities, where competition held railroad rates in check. Depending on the location, it could cost more to ship wheat 100 miles than to another destination 200 miles away.

Monopoly Pricing Devastates Farmers

Some of the farmers whom the railroads were gouging had mortgaged their property to buy stock during the railroad fever. But then they discovered that many a railroad company had issued securities valued higher than the company's assets, which diluted the value of their holdings. On top of that, towns raised the farmers' taxes to cover their own bad railroad investments.[30] In a highly competitive market, the railroads' monopoly pricing made midwestern farmers' turnips and potatoes suddenly worthless. Some farmers, in frustration, shot their hogs and burned their corn for fuel.[31] In the prerailroad era, when all parties to commerce lived cheek by jowl, a businessman would have been reluctant to hurt the livelihood of a farmer with whom he worshipped on Sunday. But the eastern rail financiers could escape such forced intimacy, though not for long. For the railroads' simple business decision to charge what the market would bear would not go unanswered. From it would spring one of the most potent political movements in American history.

Free western land let America's pioneer railroaders experiment, setting down track one year, then rerouting it the next, until they figured out which route would generate the most business. European railroads, lacking the luxury of wide open spaces, often had to pay up to twenty thousand dollars an acre for land, which made the laying of track an irrevocable commitment. As the spiderweb of rail lines wove its way throughout

America, lower start-up costs helped carriers compete with one another. A railroad that would not agree to a price cut for a competitor might soon see that competitor building a parallel route elsewhere to siphon off business.[32]

In Volume Lies Profits

Trains and iron rails certainly cost more to build, even with free land, than did steamboats. But because a wheel riding a rail causes less friction than a boat moving through water, multiple railcars could easily be linked to a locomotive. Usually, adding an extra car meant no more expense than shoveling a little extra coal into the firebox.[33] The fact that each extra car cost less than the one before it soon drove the railroad industry, for in volume lay profits that would let men live like kings. So railways undercut each other in a withering rate war. To lessen its effects, carriers bid against each other to buy feeders to trunk lines, even if it meant paying far more than those were worth.

Locomotives hauling dozens of identical cars brimming with coal or wheat soon became commonplace. A rail center the size of Chicago typically received six hundred freight trains, or forty thousand loaded cars, daily.[34] Each added railcar not only would represent almost pure profit but also could be a competitive bludgeon. Some railways slashed rates to drive steamboat lines out of business, then raised the rates again after gaining a monopoly.[35]

By the 1880s, the nation's interconnected railroads formed a honeycomb of crisscrossing lines. At each juncture stood railway agents, paid by commission to use every means, fair or foul, to fill the snake of coal-black railcars waiting in the yard outside the depot. Shippers of livestock, produce, and coal stood in line outside their windows, haggling over rates, demanding discounts for volume shipments, and threatening to take their business elsewhere. Agents gained social stature at a time when the railway station had replaced the village green or general store as a social center. The railway agent not only planned customers' out-of-town trips and sold tickets but also operated the telegraph. In the days before radio, children pressed their faces against the window glass as they waited for the agent to post the latest sports scores from a thousand miles away—a scene tailormade for Norman Rockwell.[36]

Railroads Crusade to Standardize Time

A visitor entering Buffalo's railroad station in the early 1880s saw three clocks, each set to the time that cities had selected: a New York Central clock used New York City time; that of the Michigan Southern was set for Columbus, Ohio; and the third clock read local Buffalo time. In a day before standard time zones, when Chicago solar time was noon, it was 12:31 P.M. in Pittsburgh, 11:50 A.M. in St. Louis, and 12:07 P.M. in Indianapolis. Wisconsin, for example, maintained at least thirty-eight different local times.[37]

But during a decade in which hundreds of independent lines would build seventy thousand miles of track across America, the pressure for national standards became enormous. Spurred by national prosperity and a huge influx of investor money from Europe's financial capitals, a maze of steel rails knit the country together inexorably. The railways so widely influenced American life that they spearheaded a drive to standardize time throughout the country, in effect, making people march to their tune. In 1886, in a rare instance of cooperation among rivals, most American railroads agreed to place their tracks four feet, eight and one-half inches apart, allowing trains to travel anywhere.

The world had never known an entity more expansive or powerful than the railroad industry. Large local employers had existed before, but the very nature of rail transport allowed it to stretch into the most remote regions. From fifty thousand miles of track in 1870, American railways sprang to nearly two hundred thousand miles by the turn of the century. Attracting investment like a magnet, railroad capital soared from $2.5 billion in 1870 to $21 billion at its peak in 1916, when railroads were handing weekly paychecks to 1.7 million Americans. By contrast, in 1880—before the days of big government—the entire U.S. federal budget was a paltry $286 million a year.[38]

Railroads had caused an economic boom in Europe as well, and investors there now let their eye wander to the New World, where land was cheap and markets were big. German and Dutch speculators poured millions of dollars into American railroad schemes; Britons alone sank a staggering $2.5 billion into these enterprises.[39] By 1890, European investors owned majority control of such major lines as the Illinois Central, the Pennsylvania, and the Reading.[40]

CLASH OF THE TITANS

Inevitably, the no-holds-barred spirit of this golden age of railroading attracted those who enjoyed a brass-knuckles brawl. The rule book for American capitalism in the waning days of the nineteenth century was a tabula rasa, and that was just the way these free enterprisers liked it. Their fiercely independent natures have been embellished lavishly over the past century. There was semi-literate "Uncle Dan'l" Drew of the Erie Railroad, who as a cattle drover salted his steers, then let them drink their fill before weighing, but who piously said grace each day over his noon-time sandwich at Delmonico's.[41] One-eyed James Jerome Hill, whose rail lines opened up the West, could be mean and vindictive, but he was not above personally spelling his snow-shoveling crew for three hours in a driving snowstorm so his men could drink coffee and rest.[42] And there was "Jubilee Jim" Fisk, who owned a palace steamer upon which he toasted President Ulysses S. Grant; and the black-bearded ascetic Jay Gould, whose cold-blooded but effective business tactics reputedly drove an associate to suicide.[43]

These mavericks and others like them were now on a collision course. Adding to debt while pricing below cost can be a prescription for disaster in any business. Railroads soon realized that an effective way to end competition is to buy one's competitor. From 1880 to 1888, one-quarter of all railroad companies fell under the control of other lines. Price seemed no object; the titans felt that the volume of business won from their former competitors justified the debt.[44]

Given the thousands of individual transactions being bargained daily by salesmen on commission, price undercutting was hard to control. So the captains of competing lines pooled their business and agreed on rates, as they parceled shares out to each railway. The hope was to stabilize rates by removing any incentive to undercut another railroad's price.[45] But shippers used to dealing with a favored line might find a less cooperative railroad assigned to their freight. Like the farmers, the factories and warehouses began accumulating instances of "unfair treatment" by the carriers.[46]

Rockefeller's Rebates

But while a chorus of businessmen claimed that they were the victims of capitalism run amok, some exercised a market power greater than the lines over which their goods traveled. Large shippers, such as John D. Rockefeller's

Standard Oil Company, demanded rebates as the price of handling volume shipments. Oil traveled at that time for thirty-five cents a barrel, and Rockefeller not only got back twenty-five cents on each barrel but demanded and received a share of the income the rails earned from his competitors.[47] Rebates have earned the railroads disrepute, but few have blamed large shippers, who sometimes left the carriers little choice.

The railroads of the 1890s combined generous measures of eager investment money, corporate abuse, and avarice, stirred well; and America's financial community nearly choked on the resultant brew. Railroad moguls "watered" their stock by declaring that a line with $10 million of assets was suddenly worth $15 million. This allowed them to declare a $5 million stock dividend, amounting to instant profit for themselves and their cronies. Using this technique, the Erie Railroad quadrupled its capital shares in four years.[48] This, of course, diluted the holdings of all stockholders, so railroad boards declared cash dividends to keep them happy. Once the boards had exhausted all the stock they could credibly issue, they took the more perilous course of selling bonds. Unlike stock, which was just a slice of the ownership pie, bonds became a debt of the corporation.[49]

The Public Be Damned!

Chronicling the lifestyles of the rich and famous is an old American tradition, and the popular ten-cent magazines of the 1890s missed no chance to embellish tales of superrich railroad owners on their luxurious yachts and sumptuous Pullman cars—all of which made for good copy. Magazine readers gawked at color pictures of Marble House, William Vanderbilt's $2 million "summer cottage" in Newport. The same man, asked by the *Chicago Daily News* if his railroad would be willing to sustain a loss if the public interest demanded it, exclaimed, "The public be damned!"[50] Newspapers recorded the moguls' winter exodus to Miami Beach and Palm Beach, resorts built by their fellow rail magnate Henry Flagler.[51]

Yet, while their public image suggested wealth without end, the J. P. Morgans, Jay Goulds, E. H. Harrimans, and James J. Hills in fact now labored under crushing debt—a legacy of overbuilding and reckless bonding. Those obligations soon caught up with many and contributed to the financial panic of 1893, when many lines fell under the control of their lenders, usually eastern and European banks.[52]

ONLY THE STRONG SURVIVE

It was becoming clear that only the strong would survive, and a Darwinistic drive toward consolidating lines ensued that would leave only a handful of major systems still standing by 1900. In the East, the mighty New York Central and Pennsylvania lines held sway. In the South, Morgan forged a collection of short lines into the Southern, the Seaboard, and the Atlantic Coast lines. Harriman combined the Union Pacific, Southern Pacific, and Illinois Central in the West. Gould came to dominate the Southwest, and Hill merged the Great Northern with the Northern Pacific.

Eighteenth-century laissez-faire proponents, such as Adam Smith, could never have envisioned the U.S. free-enterprise context during the late nineteenth century. Unlike France and Germany, where statecraft was a visible hand in railway development, commerce alone drove the burgeoning American railroads, which grew like weeds while government leaders wondered how—and if—they could control these companies. European governments, surrounded by countries they perceived as hostile, took control of railroads early on, for military purposes. Such a prospect in laissez-faire America would have been unthinkable, and geography had made it unnecessary.[53]

J. P. Morgan—First among Equals

Stockholders control corporations, so eastern railroads gradually bought stock in each other's lines, forming "communities of interest," to defend themselves against one another.[54] But only one man had sufficient clout to pull all the others into line: J. P. Morgan, a formidable presence with piercing eyes and a bulbous nose that formed an exclamation point to his rotundity. The famed photographer Edward Steichen, when allowed a mere two minutes to photograph the famous magnate, said he "could think of nothing but the headlights of an express train bearing down on him."[55]

In 1889, Morgan summoned the heads of rival eastern lines to "one of the grandest, most solemn and momentous events" in American high finance, "bearing on nothing less than disposition of the supreme industrial power in the country." Meeting in his sumptuous library on Madison Avenue, amid paintings, ancient manuscripts, objets d'art, and glowing tapestries, the barons assembled on January 8, 1889. Letting it be known publicly that they were meeting in response to the public demand for reasonable rates, their hidden agenda was to "compose a

Magna Carta." Those who attended represented two-thirds of the nation's trackage.[56]

Morgan had gathered his fellow titans to induce them to form a nation-wide rate-making pool, which would secretly set fines and settle all disagreements over rates and service. As the nation's leading railroad financier, Morgan held a unique role among the assembled industry heads: he was the banker to many of his rivals. Morgan was unafraid to use his power to separate the railroads from the enervating competition and rate wars that were robbing the industry of profit. Choosing to rule with a velvet glove, Morgan assured his rivals that if they agreed to the rate-making compact, the bankers would starve their competitors of needed capital. The meeting ended in what came to be known as the Gentlemen's Agreement of 1889.[57]

Acting as banker and major stockholder for competing lines would give Morgan absolute control of twelve great rail systems covering fifty-five thousand miles of track by the turn of the century. In one celebrated power grab, he positioned his New Haven Railroad to take over the Boston and Maine, aiming to monopolize New England and control rates in this cargo-rich region. His New Haven line bought securities of little feeder roads, often at inflated prices. As one commentator observed, "Morgan made his money selling securities, not by running fine railroads."[58] While the railroad battles of the 1880s had been between powerful men, they were now waged among a few giant railroad conglomerates—"trusts," in the parlance of the time.[59]

A NATION TRANSFORMED

America's first big business, by opening up mass markets, made other large enterprises possible. A comparatively few people engaged in mechanized agriculture could raise the food to feed the city dwellers, who made the machines that mechanized agriculture. Moving goods quickly over large distances let small factories produce more, creating economies of scale, which made their rapid growth inevitable.[60] This, of course, gave railroads tremendous leverage. Farm produce was worthless, for instance, unless it could be shipped. So railroads dictated terms while shippers danced to their tune.

In the 1890s, American life was changing with breathtaking speed. Rail travel opened new vistas beyond the horizon. Photography now allowed magazines such as *McClure's*, *Munsey's* and *Cosmopolitan* to run pictorials profiling life in other countries.[61] Waves of European immi-grants increased Americans' everyday contact with strange new faces and cultures. Rural free delivery created a nationwide mail-order industry overnight, as Sears and Roebuck's catalogs led the way.[62]

Technology only intensified the process of change. The new open-hearth process to refine steel meant hauling ore from the Lake Superior region and coal from the Alleghenies. And where money was to be made, Morgan was to be found, as he and his associates formed U.S. Steel, America's first billion-dollar company, at a time when the average worker earned less than a thousand dollars a year. The telegraph and tele-phone had created a national communication system. Together with the railroads, they created one vast coast-to-coast free-trade zone, unim-peded—unlike Europe—by trading barriers.

Struggling to absorb the new industry demand, railroads began double-tracking their systems. They also developed more powerful locomotives, by enlarging their fireboxes and increasing the number of railcars they could carry. The invention of the electric locomotive, the Westinghouse air brake, and the Janney automatic coupler boosted efficiency and safety.[63]

Americans on the Move

Although readers hungrily devoured the latest tales of railroad abuses, they did not hesitate to line up at the depot, as the turn of the century ushered in the golden age of passenger trains. As color printing came into vogue, national magazines lured tourists west, with illustrated articles about such vacation spots as Yellowstone and Grand Teton national parks. The thought of emerging from an open wooden railcar, covered with soot from the spewing of spark and ash from a coal-fed steam loco-motive, had theretofore inhibited travel. But the advent of sturdier steel cars and cleaner-burning anthracite coal was promoted in popular ad campaigns like that of Lackawanna Railroad, whose fetching poster girl Phoebe Snow proclaimed, "My dress stays white though I ride all night, when I take the road of anthracite." In 1902, New York Central unveiled the "Twentieth Century Limited," which streaked the 960 miles from New York to Chicago in a mere twenty hours.[64] Between 1896 and 1916, the number of rail passengers would triple.

The epitome of luxury for those who could afford it was to travel first class on a Pullman car, surrounded by porters, waiters, maids, and bartenders to gratify every whim. Such bonuses as library-observation cars, sun parlors, barbershops, and buffet club cars made the Pullman the place for the successful family to be seen. The Twentieth Century Limited featured potted ferns adorning walls of Santiago mahogany in its dining room. But many were left outside looking in. Sinclair Lewis's *Main Street* contrasted the Pullmans with everyman's train, with "no porter, no pillows, no provisions for beds. . . . [A]ll today and all tonight they will ride in this long steel box" with an "aisle of bare, splintery, grease-blackened wood."[65]

A COLD SHOULDER FROM THE WHITE HOUSE

In the first few years of the new century a grand chess game, with America as the board, was under way. Edward H. Harriman, a minister's son whose physical presence suggested a bookkeeper rather than a titan, sought no less a goal than capturing the entire western railroad market. James J. Hill, approaching the end of his career, moved to block Harriman from controlling the Chicago, Burlington, and Quincy road, thus gaining a gateway to Chicago. Harriman countered by going after the Northern Pacific, which held half of Burlington's shares, knowing Hill's hold was insecure.

With the new century, time had eclipsed Morgan and the earlier generation of railroad titans, leaving Harriman as the industry's acknowledged leader. While all the rest were nearing retirement age, Harriman was not yet fifty. "A man of elemental force," he had scraped together the three thousand dollars needed to buy himself a seat on the New York Stock Exchange at age twenty-one. This small, slight man with thinning hair, "myopic eyes and droopy bookkeeper's moustache" wed the daughter of a small railroad owner and soon learned, as J. P. Morgan had before him, how the marriage of railroads and securities to finance them could make a man a millionaire.[66]

Harriman had raised impressive sums to help Teddy Roosevelt win election in 1904 to his first full term as president. In his letter of congratulation, Harriman told the president that job one for the railroads in the years ahead was to double-track their systems across the country, to meet the seemingly bottomless national demand. Harriman knew that both federal and state officials were talking about setting ceilings on what railroads could charge. This could not be allowed to happen, Harriman argued, if his industry was to pour its "so-called surplus earnings" back into such improvements. Perhaps expecting a reassuring, appreciative response, Harriman instead received a cold shoulder from Roosevelt with good reason. A grassroots movement of monumental proportions was beginning to make itself felt in the nation's capital, and the canny Republican was too good a politician not to know which way the wind was blowing.

· 2 ·

THE RUNAWAY IRON HORSE

I am so skeptical as to our knowledge of the goodness or badness of laws that I have no practical criticism except what the crowd wants. Personally, I bet that the crowd, if it knew better, wouldn't want what it wants.

—Supreme Court Justice Oliver Wendell Holmes, 1910

WHEN OLIVER KELLEY RESIGNED HIS SECURE POST OFFICE CLERKSHIP IN Washington, D.C., in 1868 and set off for the hinterlands with a missionary gleam in his eye, his colleagues shook their heads. His beard already gray in his early forties, Kelley's high forehead and wide-eyed eagerness bespoke dignity to some, zealotry to others. "An engine with too much steam on all the time," one friend characterized him. Kelley was unusually sensitive to things around him and, returning from a trip to the South, he was visibly shaken by the post–Civil War squalor, poverty, and apathy he had witnessed on southern farms. Although Boston-born, he took on the problems of rural farmers as his own and came to believe that the improvement of their lot lay in collective action. Enlisting six other men, Kelley created the National Grange of the Patrons of Husbandry and set out, nearly penniless, to change the country.

Dispensing charters to his new organization to help pay his expenses, Kelley swept into the Midwest, spreading his message through local newspaper articles and speeches. He had intended his Grange to offer social and intellectual uplift, but soon Kelley found himself tapping into a deeper vein of discontent. Farmers in the heartlands did not hesitate when Kelley asked whom they blamed for their economic woes: the railroads! Having mortgaged their farms to buy railroad stock based on promoters' inflated promises, they now found themselves doubly victimized. Slick railroad promoters not only had diluted farmers' investment by watering company stock but also had used their monopoly power to charge the midwestern farmers more than those near the cities, where railroads faced more competition.[1] Historically dependent on no one, farmers felt self-sufficiency slipping away as they became beholden to faceless tycoons in distant corporate boardrooms.[2]

Kelley, in agitating for change, was preaching to the choir, and his movement spread like a midwestern prairie fire. By 1875, twenty thousand chapters of his Grange dotted the heartland, having enlisted eight hundred thousand zealous members.[3] Not content to be a chowder and marching society, the Grangers by the 1870s had galvanized into a political force, riding wooden wagons into their state capitals to lobby against what they saw as railroad depredations. Joining them were merchants and small-factory owners, fearing their businesses could be wiped out if the rails did not treat them equally with their competitors.[4] Capitalism was about to confront a key challenge in the era of big business it had helped create: Did a private industry owe any responsibility for its actions to the society it served?

A BEHEMOTH IN FETTERS

State legislatures soon rang with debate over whether the runaway iron horse should be—or could be—reined in. Britain had regulated business for centuries, and American government had set caps on rates that inns and turnpikes could charge. But those agitating wanted even greater control. Soon most states responded by setting up railroad commissions, whose powers varied widely. Many eastern legislators—themselves rail officials, attorneys, or investors—held enough sway to keep their state commissions largely toothless. But the typical pioneer state legislature angrily voted to tinker with all aspects of rail operations, even telling the carriers what rates they could charge—a prospect the railroads considered unthinkable under a free-enterprise system.[5] Yet railroads were powerful enough in some western states to cause strong commissions to be disbanded. The railroads were a mighty Gulliver, but now thousands of Lilliputians threatened to hold this writhing behemoth in fetters. What had twenty years before been a partnership in progress between business and government had now become a war for survival.

Thus, less than a decade after the Civil War ended, a new civil war began, its sides trading just as much passion and hatred as had the slaveholders and the abolitionists. Virtually no American would be untouched by this struggle, which would wage unabated for a half century—a battle over man's relation to capital. The national struggle would be joined in Chicago, Carl Sandburg's "City of the Big Shoulders.... Player with Railroads and the Nation's Freight Handler."[6] There in the 1870s and 1880s a no-holds-barred engagement was waged over freedom, class, and money.

Seizing the Invisible Hand

In 1870, the state of Illinois prescribed rates that grain warehouses—often owned by railroads—could charge. The U.S. Supreme Court in 1886 upheld the statute, over the indignant protests of warehouse owners, who argued that the law interfered with their property rights. In the landmark *Munn v Illinois* ruling, the Court held, "When the owner of property devotes it to a use in which the public has an interest, he in effect grants to the public an interest in such use."[7] A century earlier, the economist Adam Smith had counseled that if the marketplace were left to its own devices, an "invisible hand" would guarantee that the results would benefit the populace.[8] With this Court ruling, America had now started to chip away at such laissez-faire thinking, which had guided its economy's meteoric growth during the nineteenth century.

As soon as the news came off the telegraph, state legislatures sprang into action, eagerly imposing new rate limits. Some carriers, caught in a vise between regulation and competition with other lines, went under the table, secretly rebating part of the fare to shippers on whom their business depended. Railroad lawyers burned the midnight oil, searching for an escape from this regulatory half-Nelson. Their resourceful counsel repaired for inspiration to the U.S. Constitution. Soon they were arguing that Article I, Section 8—which allowed Congress to regulate commerce "among the several states"—forbade states to interfere with railroads that passed through their jurisdictions *on the way to other states.*[9] Since 75 percent of rail travel at the time was interstate, great jubilation reigned behind the mahogany doors of railroad boardrooms when the U.S. Supreme Court sided with the carriers.[10]

Their celebration was short-lived. The Court had held that only Congress could tinker with such "commerce among the states." Until that time, Washington had been a benign presence in the world of business, but now the Grangers and their allies marched up Pennsylvania Avenue to the Capitol. Freedom to conduct one's livelihood had helped colonists to form a new Union, and Congress was reluctant to disturb this basic right. But no one had dreamed of enterprises as big or powerful as the railroads. A deluge of citizen complaints would soon swamp the courts, and congressmen knew they were generalists who understood little about this complex industry.

An Attack Dog with No Teeth

So in 1887, Congress created a new kind of entity to oversee the railroads and called it the Interstate Commerce Commission (ICC)—but seemed unsure of what it should do.[11] President Grover Cleveland signed the bill but voiced serious doubts about its clarity.[12] For such a landmark in American economic thought, the four-page Interstate Commerce Act is spare and modest of vision. Congress thought of regulation in those early days not as creating a workable harness for a runaway horse, but rather, as erecting a series of small hurdles. It prescribed "thou shalt nots" without any guidance how and in what manner the industry *should* operate.[13] The act's thrust was to make railroads post their rates publicly and charge them to all customers. But in a monumental passing of the buck, Congress directed its new child only to make sure railroad charges were "reasonable and just," without guidelines or punishment if the haughty railroads failed to comply. Moreover, by holding that no one who had worked for a railroad could be a commissioner, it banned most of those who really understood how this intricate megabusiness operated.[14]

Had David carried an empty slingshot, he would have been no worse prepared to deal with Goliath than was the fledgling ICC to shepherd the mighty railroads. By the end of its first year, the five new commissioners appointed by President Cleveland had a staff of only twenty-seven to deal with the world's largest industry, which was then moving seventy billion ton-miles of freight coast-to-coast over 150,000 miles of rail.[15] Powerless to act on its own, the ICC could only react to complaints from farmers or shippers. Many railroads simply sneered at ICC orders or fought them in the federal courts, where *laissez-faire* was not yet a dirty word.[16] Rail stocks actually advanced on word of the act's passage, as the Cleveland administration assured rail executives that the toothless measure simply satisfied "the popular clamor for government supervision of railroads."[17]

Railroads Rebuff Controls

Congress, in passing the Interstate Commerce Act, was hesitantly dipping a toe into icy water. While heeding the populist outcry from the Midwest, it feared dampening the competitive impulse that had fired the engine of national economic growth.[18] Not only did Congress feel the sense of maneuvering in uncharted waters; the railroads did as well. Insecure and indignant about this invasion of what they considered a God-given right to run their business, the rail owners soon came to regard government and the ICC as the common enemy. While the ICC had little real power, some railroads "fought, harassed, obstructed, and delayed at every possible point." Some railroads simply refused to post their rates publicly.[19] Yet, in spite of their angry protests, enough railroads complied that rail rates actually did fall for several years.[20]

In the mid-1890s, antirailroad fervor became pervasive. Steamships carried stacks of "ten-center" magazines back and forth across the Atlantic, cross-fertilizing the nations' quest to find an acceptable way to harness railroads without choking them to death. In Britain, Parliament moved to freeze railway rates, in part because English railroads reportedly gave cut rates to American imports.[21]

A HOLY UNION

If the railroads felt their friends were slipping away, at least they could still count on President William McKinley's friendly administration and the U.S. Supreme Court, if not for long. Congress had passed the Sherman Act in 1890 to ban monopolies, but five years later, the Court held that railroads could restructure their industry as they saw fit, even if competition fell by the wayside.[22] Indeed, of sixteen ICC rulings that the railroads appealed during the 1890s, the Supreme Court reversed fifteen.[23]

But the immediate threat to the industry came not from a hostile public but from within its own ranks. For the draining battles among railroad owners threatened to rock Wall Street and even endangered the financial health of European capitals, whose money men had sunk hundreds of millions of dollars into American lines. In May 1901, rail antagonists met at the Metropolitan Club in New York to hammer out one more peace pact, again under the stern gaze of their godfather, J. P. Morgan. The treaty would create a holy union controlling half the continental transportation network, a clear repudiation of the Interstate Commerce Act. They relaxed in the certainty that if the agreement turned out to be not quite legal, the newly reelected, genial President McKinley would look the other way.[24]

The Rough Rider Saddles Up

Less than four months later, when an aide brought his boss the news, Morgan "wheeled like a man stricken; . . . cursed and staggered to his desk while his face flamed red and then turned ashen."[25] President McKinley was dead, an assassin's victim. Malleable, benign McKinley. The vice-president succeeding him was the Rough Rider, the reformer Teddy Roosevelt, who as the governor of New York had repeatedly supported labor over capital—a traitor to his own class.[26] Morgan and his industry colleagues braced themselves for what they feared would be a rough ride indeed.

But Roosevelt's crusading rhetoric as governor outpaced his own inclinations. A critic had complained that McKinley was all that stood between "that madman" and the White House, but Roosevelt spoke for the nation now and moved to distance himself from bearded anarchists and red-shirted socialists, whom he saw as seeking to cripple the railroads by any means possible. But neither did he forget that his strength lay in his image as a crusader, as his public utterances would underscore.[27]

Even as Roosevelt tempered his critiques, the press more aggressively assailed the railroads, which by 1900 were merging with bewildering speed. Small local lines that had defined local communities now found themselves folded into systems with owners named Morgan and Harriman and Hill and Gould—men as far distant from common citizens in class and lifestyle as in miles. With the advent of a new century came a breed of investigative journalist known as the muckraker, dedicated to turning the spotlight on societal abuses caused by runaway economic growth. Popular magazines such as *McClure's, Collier's, Everybody's,* and *Cosmopolitan* inveighed against big business, "the System," monopolies, and special privilege and seemed to validate citizens' discontent. While Ida Tarbell railed against big oil and Upton Sinclair vilified the Chicago stockyards, Ray Stannard Baker wrote a blistering series entitled "Railroads on Trial."[28]

THE RISE OF "HANDSOME ALBERT"

Losing control of railroads' interstate trips only intensified state governments' zeal to control journeys within their own borders. "Progressive" governors such as Robert LaFollette of Wisconsin mounted populist campaigns to clamp down on escalating railroad rates, through new laws and investigations. Railroads complained that climbing labor costs and more sophisticated physical plants justified higher rates, but an angry public was in no mood to give the industry the benefit of the doubt.[29]

Iowa, whose 9,824 miles of track ranked fourth in the country in 1904, was fertile ground for antirailroad sentiment. For thirty years, two thousand chapters of the Grange had waged a seesaw battle with the rail industry. The carriers retaliated by putting on retainer in every major town a lawyer and a doctor—respected and influential citizens—to influence local politics. "Passes were distributed with shocking extravagance." Newspapers fallen on hard times could count on railroads' financial help, as long as they refrained from supporting "negative" laws and editorialized against passage of antirailroad laws.[30]

Onto this stage set in 1878 walked a young lawyer, Albert Cummins, drawn to Des Moines to find his fortune. As an inexperienced youth of twenty-one, Cummins had hired on as "chief engineer" to build a new rail line across Michigan, and he had entered law school when it was finished. Like the young Abe Lincoln, Cummins and so many other attorneys of his day earned much of their livelihood representing railroads. As the general counsel for the Chicago, Great Western Railroad, he earned a solid reputation as a corporate lawyer. Because Des Moines was then not yet a generation old, Cummins quickly became a member of the local establishment. But by 1890, agrarian Iowa, like much of the Midwest, was in desperate straits, in part because monopolistic railroad freight rates had devalued its farm produce.

Defending the railroads in Iowa was becoming impossible for anyone, such as Cummins, who aspired to political office. Tall and handsome, he cut a fine figure, with wavy graying hair, a bushy moustache, and expressive eyes. Supporters soon implored the man some called "the Des Moines

Apollo" to run for the U.S. Senate in 1893 as a Republican. No reformer at the time, Cummins called only for a few tepid curbs on railroads. He lost the election but gained the appetite for another campaign in 1901, by which time he still remained friendly enough with the railroads to ask them for free rail passes for his campaign. Some refused, for along the way Cummins had advocated letting rail workers sue their employers for on-the-job injuries. Workers were commonly crushed between trains when trying to couple them manually or were falling from ice-slicked roofs in the days before safety devices, and Cummins's position drew organized labor to his side. That friendship would endure throughout his career.[31]

From Retainer to Reformer

Cummins's ascendancy to the major leagues became apparent on November 20, 1901, when the glitterati turned out in force for a Chamber of Commerce dinner at Delmonico's in Manhattan. Sharing the dais with President Roosevelt, Andrew Carnegie, and J. P. Morgan was the recently elected Iowa governor, whose thoroughly mainstream speech exalting competition ruffled no feathers. But the new chief executive would not remain uncontroversial for long. Two months later, in his inaugural address in Des Moines, Cummins decried the corrupting power of corporate wealth, railroad stock watering, and the danger that railroad mergers would lessen competition. Before the year was out, publications such as *Harper's Weekly* heralded him as one of the country's leading reformers, even though his success in moving progressive legislation through the Iowa General Assembly was modest.

Gradually, Cummins realized that his continuing friendship with the carriers was blunting the force of his reformist zeal. In 1905 he declared independence from the railroad interests by returning free passes he had received from a dozen railroads, then asking the Iowa legislature to outlaw them and to cap passenger rates at two cents per mile. Soon thereafter, the governor boarded the train for Washington, where he would deliver a strident message: No longer was it enough for the ICC to veto unjust rates. From now on, it must actually *set* the charges railroads could make for the thousands of commodities rails shipped. To the outraged railroads, their former loyal retainer had become their implacable enemy.[32]

THE ICC FEELS ITS WAY

Administrative law, in which a legislated code guides specialists overseeing an industry, today pervades American society, and regulatory agencies abound. But the ICC was the pioneer in harnessing free enterprise when it was yet raw and untamed. Were the five ICC commissioners to legislate, to administer, or judge? The act creating the commission really did not say. So lawyers all, they soon fell back on what they knew. Choosing not to set down their own rules or to superimpose an overall plan for the industry to follow, the commissioners decided to judge each complaint case by case. And by what mathematical method could the ICC decide whether a rate to ship timber from Seattle to Denver was fair and reasonable? Commissioner Judson Clements, sharing the frustration of his colleagues, declared candidly, "There is absolutely none."[33]

The attempts of such a puny commission to regulate a huge industry would soon create an impossible bottleneck. A railroad that wanted to increase what it charged for shipping washboards and that was trying to comply with the law would have to wait months for an ICC okay. In a day when railroads competed mainly against one another, such a delay was at best inconvenient. Later, when they vied with unregulated truckers—who could steal away rail business by changing rates at will—such a time lag would prove catastrophic.[34]

In 1903, a crescendo of public pressure prompted Congress to outlaw any rate a shipper or carrier charged other than the one it filed with the ICC. The bill's sponsor, Senator Stephen Elkins, ran a West Virginia mine that shipped huge quantities of coal. He made no secret about the industry with which his sympathies lay: "My interest on the side of the shipper is ten times greater than on the side of the railroads."[35] But railroads, sapped by the internecine rate wars, agreed to his Antirebating Act to gain a truce, assure themselves stable rates, and avoid what they feared might be an even more radical measure.[36]

TESTING TEDDY

It is difficult to overemphasize the importance of such railroads as the Santa Fe or the Pennsylvania in American life during the preautomobile era. Steel, lumber, coal, grain—the elements that built and nourished the nation—all traveled mainly by rail. The activist Teddy Roosevelt knew that the country's predominant industry was at a crossroads, and he intended to help steer its future. Yet each path open to him was fraught with practical and political danger. He could let the free market work its will, but unfettered free enterprise had brought America to this crisis. Conversely, he could follow the lead of Europe, where governments nationalized railroads, or of England and Canada, which had worked out public-private partnerships, but these would be politically unpalatable to a freedom-loving business community. The Rough Rider decided to choose a trot over a gallop: he would seek to dampen railroad rates somewhat, to curb public agitation for more radical steps. Roosevelt spoke loudly and carried a big twig.[37]

But such an uneasy standoff did not slake the railroad barons' thirst for empires of steel. Edward H. Harriman and James J. Hill—with Morgan as conciliator—declared a truce in their quest to control the nation's rails (see chapter 1) and agreed to form a new entity they called the Northern Securities Company. Their two railroads' tracks paralleled each other for nine thousand miles. That they would stop competing and bind themselves to one joint rate was bad news to their shippers and to American consumers.[38] They soon telegraphed their displeasure to the White House, where an angry president dispatched his attorney general to court to block the "monster trust."[39]

Morgan, who learned about the president's action only after the fact, had been used to McKinley's more gentlemanly practice of sending warnings when he felt railroads had stepped over the line. Visiting the White House, the imposing titan implored Roosevelt: "If we have done anything wrong, send your man [Attorney General Philander Knox] to my man [naming one of his lawyers] and they can fix it up." Roosevelt stood his ground; his reformer's image was on the line.[40] In 1904 the theretofore railroad-friendly Supreme Court, in a five-to-four decision stunning in its precedent, ordered the moguls to break up their megatrust.

But sound and fury aside, the 1904 Northern Securities decision changed little. While the partners formally dismantled their combination, few shares of stock actually changed hands.[41] Financiers continued to buy stock, to gain control of competing railroads serving the same general area.[42] But if Roosevelt felt frustrated at being unable to restrain those he called the "malefactors of great wealth," he also feared "tyranny by the labor unions."[43] Born to wealth and enterprise, Roosevelt reacted viscerally to socialists and demagogues "who raved against the wealth which . . . embodied thrift, foresight, and intelligence." Between the two, the president would side with the country's engine of growth. But he sought to send the railroads a conciliatory message, that they could no longer afford to ignore public opinion, to which he would not hesitate to pander. As time went on, many railroad men would come to regard Roosevelt as their best friend, even while he campaigned and won election in 1904 on a wave of reformist sentiment.[44] But elemental forces beyond his control were building toward a fateful showdown.

THE LINES ARE DRAWN

Even rail defenders admit that by 1906, the carriers were financially overextended and the market for their stocks overinflated. Reports that laws and court decisions had failed to curb railroad abuses led the ICC to look into Harriman's operations. During public hearings on the subject, Harriman was brutally candid about his imperial designs. A questioner asked why he had recently bought a lot of Santa Fe Railroad stock:

> HARRIMAN: If you will let us I will go take the Santa Fe tomorrow.
> QUESTIONER: Then it is only the restriction of the antitrust law that keeps you from taking it?
> HARRIMAN: I would go on as long as I live.
> QUESTIONER: You would also take the Northern Pacific and Great Northern, if you could get them?
> HARRIMAN: If you would let me.
> QUESTIONER: And your power which you have would gradually increase as you took one road after another, so that you might spread not only over the Pacific coast but over the Atlantic coast?
> HARRIMAN: Yes.[45]

The "little giant's" lines were among the best operated in the industry. But the same country that exalted the virtues of competition feared the specter of monopoly. The politically sensitive ICC, alarmed by the expanding tentacles of Harriman's empire, asked Congress to outlaw *any* combination of lines that reduced competition.

Brandeis the Bête Noire

The Progressive movement, denouncing commercial "bigness" as inherently evil, had found an able spokesman in an intense young Boston lawyer, who would leave his fingerprints on railroad issues for several decades. Louis Debnitz Brandeis, a descendant of European Jewish liberal intellectuals, was a far cry from the Yankee rail tycoons, who moved easily in social circles from which men of his background were excluded.[46] He now began an assault on Morgan's drive to unite all New England lines under his control. In so doing, Brandeis showed an inkling of the zealous antirailroad advocate he would become during the next decade and later as a U.S. Supreme Court justice.[47]

Progressive diatribes did not faze Wall Street investors, but once signs grew that the rail interests could no longer prevent Congress from tinkering with railroad rates, stockholders began quietly unloading their holdings while prices still remained high.[48] Roosevelt had campaigned in 1904 only to cap rates, but the magazine exposés by muckrakers and Roosevelt's public actions against rebaters in 1905 and 1906 had deepened the public craving for letting the ICC set actual railroad rates. Rail leaders blanched when Roosevelt named to a 1905 ICC vacancy Franklin K. Lane, a California Democrat and its first clean-shaven commissioner, who vowed to teach corporations they were "not the creators, the owners, and the rightful managers of the government." The rails had had to deal with stern but reasonably fair ICC taskmasters, but they now were up against a genuine antirailroad crusader.[49]

Railroads Take the Offensive

As public hostility against them had grown from whispers into a deafening roar, most railroads had suffered in haughty silence. Some say they felt it beneath them to reply. But now a matter of principle—too basic to be ignored—was at stake: whether the state could tell businesspeople what they could charge for their products. The industry decided that the time had come to respond. It created a "reckless publicity campaign" headquartered in Washington, with branches in leading cities. While some public relations men fanned out to stage bogus prorailroad conventions, others set up card catalogs of newspapers, noting local editors' hobbies, prejudices, and personal weaknesses. Small newspapers, short of help, welcomed free articles, setting forth "good railroad doctrine." The Chicago publicity office alone employed forty "highly paid experts." One writer has described the campaign as "a most astounding demonstration of lengths to which organized corporate power would go to defeat regulative legislation."[50]

THE SHOWDOWN

A pluralistic democracy is a simmering cauldron in which ideologies and prejudices meld from time to time into movements, based on class, race, or philosophy, creating greater or lesser currents in the democratic soup and occasionally bubbling to the surface. Now and then, two ideologies may clash—sometimes on the street, other times within a legislative forum or a courtroom. Seldom in American history have two opposing philosophies clashed as fundamentally as did the Progressive movement and the captains of enterprise when Congress convened in 1906 to decide what to do about the railroads.

The chief battle raged in the Senate chamber, where two antagonists came to symbolize the mighty contending forces. On one side was the Republican Nelson Aldrich, who had risen from humble Rhode Island beginnings to wealth in the grocery business. "Disdainful of the powerless and lesser mortals, he identified the interests of the nation with possessors of wealth and power, who often returned the courtesy." But for the Progressives, the debate was a crusade for justice. Cummins's Iowa colleague Jonathan Dolliver saw the issue as nothing less than a battle between "The Great Republic and the Money Power."[51]

Congress Tightens Its Grip

But the railroads' most prodigious efforts fell short of swaying Congress. In the end, they lost the greatest battle in their history and, with it, the right to control their own industry. Congress armed the ICC with the power to set "just and reasonable" maximum rates for the future, rather than just vetoing "unjust and unreasonable" rates.[52] For the first time, the ICC's basis thrust was positive, not negative. From that day forward, public interests would dominate private interests in American railroad operations. The ICC, after two decades of powerlessness, began its effective life on June 29, 1906, when the Hepburn Act took effect. In 1907, the act's first full year of application, formal complaints filed by shippers increased sixfold.

So virulent was the antirailroad fever in the heartland that constituents of Senator William Peters Hepburn, the bill's sponsor, turned him out of office in his next election for not restricting railroads even more. Reflecting a prevailing view in the railroad industry, the *Commercial and Financial Chronicle* denounced the act: "The whole movement against the railroads is predicated . . . on the idea that they are extremely prosperous and that some of their profits might as well be taken from them and appropriated for the benefit of the shippers and the general public."[53]

An Impossible Job?

Consider the complexity of the job that Congress had delegated to the ICC. Railroads of the day set rates by commodity and class. Commodity rates alphabetically categorized six thousand specific products—"bark extract, oak; barley forks, wooden; barn door hangers"; and so on—and accounted for the most freight. Class rates grouped items into a few broad categories based on value, bulk, fragility, perishability, or the need for special handling. Regional rate bureaus within the industry sorted out the commodities into one of six rate levels.[54] After thirty years of hearing ad hoc complaints from grain dealers and poultry farmers, the ICC should have learned the futility of trying to decide "just and reasonable" rates one case at a time. What was needed was an overall framework of rates, to use as a guideline for each complaint.

Several factors may have prevented the ICC from developing such a framework: the industry's labyrinthine maze of rates; its commissioners' training as lawyers, not administrators; and the antirailroad fervor that inhibited the president from appointing anyone to the commission who, in fact, knew very much about railroads, since such a person would have had to come from within the hated industry. Indeed, the very complexity of the rate system is what best insulated the railroads from the government rate setters. Railroad agents had learned to be resourceful. For example, if the ICC had prescribed a rate to be charged for billiard cues at one rate level, the railway may in turn have moved that commodity into a higher category, thus giving itself an automatic rate increase. Conversely, a railway could give a favored shipper of beer bottles a rebate by placing them in a cheaper classification—in effect, creating a giant shell game, which the ICC was sure to lose.[55]

Vested Interest in Inequities

Yet lining up against predictable calls for the ICC to impose some order on chaos were not only railroads but some shippers, who had "vested interests in existing inequities."[56] The cornerstone of the railroads' rate system was to charge by the value of the item transported rather than by what it cost railroads to transport it. So to ship an ear of corn cost a farmer a small fraction of what it cost a manufacturer to ship a small piece of machinery the same size and requiring the same handling. Farmers railed against being charged more for short hauls than long hauls and against the common person being charged more than the gentry, but "value-of-service" pricing was a form of discrimination the farmers were only too happy to live with. Decades later, when this method had become an encrusted tradition, it would help doom the rails in competing with truckers, who charged only what it cost to transport an item.

However, if the ICC had thrown out the old way and instead abolished rate discrimination across the board, the dislocation in American life would have been remarkable. Potatoes and corn would have inevitably cost the urban consumer far more, and steel refineries would have had to move nearer their iron ore, which no longer would have been shipped cheaply in bulk.[57]

SHAPING AMERICAN LIFE

The first important case brought under the Hepburn Act illustrates the profound effect railroads had in shaping America. The city of Spokane, Washington, alleged that the Northern Pacific Railway Company and other railroads charged less to travel to western coastal cities such as Seattle than to inland Spokane. The counsel for the Union Pacific argued fervidly that only seventeen years before, Spokane had been a small town of nineteen thousand people with only water transportation and "could not do business if it wanted to." He credited railroad traffic managers for evolving a balanced system of competitive rates that he proudly acclaimed had allowed Spokane to grow to ninety thousand people. Challenging individual rates, he charged, would destroy the entire rate-making system of every railroad on the Pacific Coast.

Spokane's attorneys saw it quite differently. Far from being free agents, they argued, the railroads were "trustees of the public and responsible for the monies that came into their hands through the imposts they [were] empowered to levy by the government." Commissioner Charles A. Prouty, an acerbic and short-tempered Vermont lawyer, had been historically tough on the railroads. So when a railroad counsel argued that transportation costs usually add "an infinitesimal amount" to the cost of a consumer good, Prouty shot back: "So that when you impose a tariff high enough to check the consumption, you are a philanthropist?" Undaunted, the Union Pacific attorney replied, "Well, we may be."[58]

Archaic Progressives?

The rail industry had just lived through the longest period of stable prices in world economic history. Traffic was high and technology had cut costs, so losing control of their rates actually generated less angst than it might have in leaner times.[59] But by 1907, railroads seemed increasingly unable to attract the Wall Street investors they needed, to expand. State legislators' hostility, the clamor for labor wage hikes, and the Northern Securities decision all caused financiers to ask whether other industries might have brighter prospects.[60]

The Grangers had sown the seeds of resentment against the monied interests, and the resulting crop was well-organized lobbies in midwestern state capitals against the privileges of big business, which at the time largely meant railroads. But until 1909 these state movements were largely independent of one another, with little cross-fertilization of ideas. Then Wisconsin elected Governor Robert LaFollette to the U.S. Senate in 1907, and Iowa voters sent soulmate Governor Cummins to join him two years later. Rail interests had stymied Cummins's two previous tries for a Senate seat.[61] Now in Washington, he would become the arch-villain of a group that has been called the "archaic Progressives," who weakened—some would say destroyed—the railroads. Together, Cummins and LaFollette, spearheading a group of Republican insurgents, would give the Progressive movement national scope.[62]

But railroad magnates such as James J. Hill scoffed at blanket indictments of the railroads' alleged power and malevolent motives: "A barnraising is a combination," he said, calling the trend toward railroad mergers—"combinations"—a logical response to the demand for service at lower rates.[63] By 1906, a mere seven powerful groups controlled nearly two-thirds of the 225,000 miles of national rail lines, with their banker-creditors calling many of the shots.[64]

A Belated Change of Heart

Yet little by little, opinion leaders began to sense that the railroads' drive for increased rates might be justified after all, as a more balanced national discourse arose over the nature of bigness. Freight revenues had dropped in 1908 and 1909 from their high in 1907, and dividends had fallen sharply. Railroads argued that bankruptcy, reorganizations, and growth of property values had squeezed most of the water out of railroad stocks and that carriers now needed new capital desperately if they were to grow with the economy.

By 1910, twin forces were massing toward a showdown. Those who would put a straitjacket on the railroads called for even stiffer curbs than found in the Hepburn Act. But some in the media and government and even some shippers were contending that the carriers deserved higher rates. A clash of the two forces would dominate Washington's front pages that year, as reformers asked Congress for stronger laws and the railroads petitioned the ICC for a general rate increase for the first time.

William Howard Taft rode an even bigger wave of reformist sentiment into office in 1908 than had Roosevelt four years earlier. However, many politicians had come to understand belatedly that the railroad rate system was far too complex to control in detail, so Taft conceded that Congress should legalize the theretofore invidious pools, whereby railroads worked out their own rates. But the Progressive insurgents, led by their single-minded belief in the engine of competition, voted angrily against the pools as collusive.

Cummins Filibusters

Cummins, now the Senate's ICC overseer, took to the Senate floor for a blistering four-day speech and demanded that Congress let the ICC change rates on its own initiative and end railroads' right to appeal from ICC decisions. Sporting a shock of white hair and a moustache the shade of tobacco, the man Washington society dubbed "Handsome Albert" declared passionately that the railroads were now more prosperous than ever before. Cummins's victory was less surprising than the railroads' passive reaction to the resulting legislation. In 1906, the rails had raised an indignant furor. In four short years of living under the ICC's stifling edicts, the stuffing had gone out of them, and their demoralized leaders had become resigned to being under the government's thumb forever.[65]

Thwarted by Congress, the $14 billion industry, seeking an across-the-board rate hike, turned to the ICC in 1910 and found the deck stacked against it.[66] For Congress that year had demanded that the carriers who were seeking higher rates prove the reasonableness of not only the new rate but also the *old* one.[67] When Santa Fe President Edward P. Ripley admitted candidly that railroads charged "what the traffic [would] bear," the nation's daily newspapers gleefully recorded his quote, which also helped seal the fate of the rails' application.[68]

The railroads' inept counsel did not help their clients' cause, particularly when they were up against the likes of Louis Brandeis and Iowa's Henry C. Wallace, who later as the secretary of agriculture would spearhead the national program to build roads that would compete with the rails. Brandeis's strategy was to paint railroad leaders as not merely corrupt but inefficient and insensitive to public needs. Railroads suffered from "giantism," he said. If they used "scientific management"—a state-of-the-art tenet of the Progressive movement—they could eliminate the need for higher rates by cutting costs. Recent innovations had, in fact, cut railroad costs, but the dispirited carriers did not even bother to respond. The ICC decided, in effect, that the railroads had never had it so good.[69]

STATES PILE ON

The carriers, having now lived under both federal and state regulation, were coming to realize that it might be easier to deal with one hostile dog than with a swarm of bees. To the railroads, the ICC now represented the lesser of two evils, as state regulation ran rampant. In 1913 alone, forty-two state legislatures passed 230 railroad laws, which dealt with extra crews, length of the workday, grade crossings, signal blocks, and electric headlights. In 1912, the state of New Jersey required that all grade crossings be eliminated, as the "auto age [had] burst upon a society that was totally unprepared for it."[70] In Alabama, angry lawmakers provided that any railroad appealing from state law to federal court would forfeit its license to operate in that state.

While railroad deliveries ended at the depot, express companies were springing up to speed cargo to its final destination. While the ICC still regulated the nation's largest industry case by case, it ironically chose to create an overarching system to regulate the express companies. Chairman Franklin Lane in 1912 divided the nation into 950 blocks bounded by each degree of latitude and longitude and held that class rates would no longer be set from point to point but from block to block. Thus, the possible number of rates was cut from over 600 million to less than 345,000. The system was deemed so promising that the U.S. Post Office adopted the same method when it launched parcel post.[71] Whether such a blanket approach could have been adapted to the railroads is open to debate; what is not, is that such an industrywide approach was never tried.

THE ICC STANDS FIRM

Mounting costs and rigid rates sank railroad profits during 1913 and 1914. Shippers as large as Armour's meats and opinion leaders as influential as the *New York Times* began agreeing that the carriers were long overdue for a raise. Shippers, who had purposely located next to rail lines, saw capital slipping away from railroads and realized how dependent they had become on the rails. To make matters worse, Washington had shorted the railroads some $415 million in payments for carrying the mail. The government paid them a flat rate based on weight to haul the mail but weighed it only once each four years during a time of growth, when the new parcel post service was proving immensely popular.

But in 1913, the ICC again turned away eastern carriers' bid for an across-the-board 5 percent increase. In the minority was Commissioner Prouty, who had come to believe that the rails' poor service resulted simply from a lack of money. Recent federal support of the fledgling "good roads" program had convinced him that the railroads might do better financially if Washington took them over. When government-owned roads were needed, he said, Congress would simply vote whatever money was required. Prouty's comment would prove prophetic.[72]

By 1914, eastern railroads had laid off a hundred thousand men and were threatening to cut back service, but the ICC rejected yet another plea for higher rates. Tellingly, the commission minority now included a Woodrow Wilson appointee, Winthrop Daniels—the ICC's first and only economist at the time—who argued passionately that worldwide prices had risen 30 to 50 percent since 1906, when the ICC had assumed control of and had effectively frozen railroad rates.

THE RAILROADS IN WARTIME

A bullet fired in Sarajevo in August 1914 suddenly changed the complexion of the railroad problem. The First World War European allies relied on prompt shipment of arms and supplies from American shores, yet the railroads were hard-pressed to meet domestic demand, let alone wartime needs. President Wilson wrote in October 1914 to Daniels, his former Princeton colleague and ICC appointee, warning that "a concession to the railroads [was] absolutely necessary." But Cummins, wrathful as ever, called the modest hike the commission granted a "victory" for the railroads, as a result of railroad wealth "spent in behalf of a continuing conspiracy of money power."

Railroads, in spite of the vitriol being heaped on them, were still America's people movers. On a Saturday afternoon, the New Haven Railroad could carry 33,500 passengers to the Yale/Harvard football game at Yale Bowl within four hours.[73] But on September 22, 1915, one newspaper's business pages carried a passing comment that should have made American business sit up and take notice: "There was not a single transaction in St. Paul Railway stock [but] extraordinary activity of motor issues."[74]

After seizing the railroads in 1917, the wartime government eliminated state regulation for the war's duration. The rules of the game had changed. "Efficiency was the only criterion that mattered; maintaining competition did not."[75] Treasury Secretary McAdoo put traffic experts to work exploring how best to set rates, but by May 1918, he had thrown up his hands at the complexity of the problem and announced an across-the-board increase of about 28 percent. Before government officials returned railroads to private control, they raised rates another 32 percent.[76] And one historian notes that even with this rate increase, the railroads ended up in the red.[77]

In retrospect, the ICC's pioneer regulators were better mechanics than visionaries. They resolved thousands of rail-shipper disputes without formal hearings. But as nonexperts, they lacked the economic tools and the imagination to understand, then to see and act on, the big picture. Not a single railroad man or economist, except for Daniels, sat on the ICC, even though Commissioner Lane had conceded it was "not . . . law but economics" with which the ICC dealt.[78]

SPIRIT OF ENTERPRISE LOST

No writer has communicated more passionately the failure of government's attempt to tame the wild railroads than Albro Martin, who argues, "What was lost in the Interstate Commerce Commission regulation era was more than money, it was a spirit of enterprise . . . the sine qua non of economic growth." But, he notes, *profit* was a dirty word to the "archaic progressives." Large profits, he said, "meant someone got something he didn't deserve." Many Progressives could not distinguish between profit poured back into capital and that taken out as personal income. To them, it was all pelf.[79]

Many volumes have been written about the effect the railroads had on America up through the First World War, most often by their detractors and, more recently, by their defenders. Scholars' conclusions have diverged widely, but on this point they agree: the railroads, America's first big business, were the dynamic force that enabled this agrarian nation to become a giant commercial power. Yet by the First World War, the industry was reeling on the ropes.

In the reasons for this remarkable turnaround lies plenty of blame for all the players: those who shipped goods by rail, politicians at all levels, the railroads, their regulators, and the people. But in fact, all were merely pursuing their own narrow self-interest; entrepreneurs were acting like entrepreneurs. What had failed, in fact, was laissez-faire capitalism, and those who had set out to find an alternative had had little time and no road map to guide them. The challenge that arose had called for a sophisticated citizenry, statesmanlike leaders, and enlightened businessmen. None of them had measured up to the task. Indeed, it would have defied logic and human nature had that happened. But business, government, and the public proved that this new republic could learn from mistakes. A new megabusiness, for which government literally paved the way, lay around the corner. And the public response to it would be vastly different.[80]

· 3 ·

THE GOOD ROADS CRUSADE

---

*Freeing us from the compulsions and contacts
of the railway, the bondage to fixed hours and
the beaten track, the approach to each town
through the area of desolation and ugliness
created by the railway itself, it [the automo-
bile] has given us back the wonder, the adventure and the novelty which enlivened the way
of our posting grandparents.*

—Edith Wharton, "A Motor-Flight Through
France"

RAILROADS CHANGED THE WAY PEOPLE THOUGHT ABOUT THE NATURAL order. No longer did life have to be lived in one's hometown. A person could go down to the depot, climb aboard a train, travel fifty miles to visit another city, and still be home for supper. With their horizons lifted, people started to look around for other ways to improve on nature. The telegraph had shortened America's distance from Europe and had awakened interest in the Continent. In 1869, Mark Twain's *Innocents Abroad*, which depicted the experiences of adventuresome Americans in Europe, sold thirty thousand copies within six months of publication.

So when readers of the thousands of popular magazines that proliferated after the Civil War learned that a new product to individualize transportation would be unveiled at the 1867 Paris Exposition, they could not wait to pick up the next issue. Pierre Michaux's new invention was the bicycle. At the time, the internal combustion engine was still a sputtering workshop model, and a generation would pass before it came into commercial use. But early industrialists in America and Europe knew all about gears and wheels, and they soon were manufacturing bicycles in quantity.[1]

Overnight, new magazines sprang up to herald the "era of the velocipede," as bicycles were called. *Harper's Weekly* commissioned Winslow Homer to depict the New Year of 1869 riding in on a bicycle.[2] The public response was phenomenal. Think of it—no longer did people have to agree where to travel; each could go his or her own way. Railroads had emptied roads of people; now the dirt thoroughfares became crowded again. Perhaps for the first time ever, the idea of traveling the road for pleasure was born.[3]

EUROPE'S RICH ROAD TRADITION

European countries benefited from a road-building tradition stretching back to Roman times. France had founded the École des Ponts et Chaussées (School of Bridges and Roads) in 1747 to train engineers, who under Napoleon would build an extensive national highway network that cut travel time in half and that the emperor would turn to his advantage in wartime. Since 1836, French citizens had had to pay taxes to maintain their local streets. Yet in the United States, all byways outside major cities were miserable. So while Americans read avidly about the European bicycle craze, rural citizens spent most of the time on their shiny two-wheelers dodging the ruts and skirting the mud.[4]

Enter Colonel Albert A. Pope of Hartford, Connecticut, one of those rare souls whose flair for marketing matched his talent for manufacturing. Realizing that the bicycle would soon become a white elephant without smooth surfaces to ride on, the factory owner helped found in 1880 the League of American Wheelmen, which dedicated itself to politicizing Americans and to agitating for better roads. People at the time learned nearly everything from the printed word, so Pope helped finance publication of *Good Roads Magazine, Bicycle World, Wheel,* and *Wheelman* magazines, hoping to gain a wide following for his movement.

The groundswell produced by the American Wheelmen would dovetail with the growing power of the Grangers. If the railroads had given the Grangers something to be against, good roads would offer them something to be for. America had carried on a love affair with the railroads, which in turn had treated her badly. Those unhappy memories made her embrace a new lover, the bicycle, with exaggerated ardor. Government had helped canals, turnpikes, and railroads, realized the bicycle proponents; why should it not aid the bicycle industry as well? While local Wheelmen worked the state legislatures, Grangers traveled to Washington in 1893. There they asked Congress to deliver mail to the nation's farms, an undertaking that would require major road improvement.[5]

"A Dreary Spectacle"

In Montezuma, Iowa, the teenaged son of a grain and lumber dealer read the popular magazines of the 1890s describing mobility he could not experience, and he was frustrated. In Tom MacDonald's hometown, wooden wagons laden with flour, lumber, and building materials headed for the farms over earthen roads. On the way, they passed farm wagons carrying grain to the elevators in town. But each spring and fall, mud brought this brisk commerce to an abrupt halt, and those foolhardy enough to traverse the soupy troughs that passed for roads then found their horses mired up to the knees and their wagons up to their hubs. The *Railway Gazette* at the local drugstore said that some farm towns had only four months a year when the roads were good enough to haul produce comfortably.[6]

But the sturdy youngster was too restless to accept this semiannual shutdown with midwestern stoicism, as merely the will of God. "It was a dreary spectacle," an interviewer would write years later. "It depressed him in a way that he never forgot. MacDonald resolved to do something about it."[7] Railroad lines crisscrossed the Hawkeye State at the time, and they doled out favors liberally. Total tax assessments on Iowa railroads exceeded $44 million, and Progressives such as Albert Cummins suggested that they were scandalously low.[8] Many ambitious young men saw railways as the industry of growth. Not MacDonald; he determined to enter Iowa State College, to learn road building. The young man more than reached his goal: he would oversee the greatest highway program in world history (see chapters 6, 9, and 10).

FORGING A ROAD-BUILDING COALITION

The 1893 news item was hardly page-one material: Congress had set aside ten thousand dollars to fund an Office of Road Inquiry (ORI). Behind the modest measure was a man who would do more than any other to crusade for good roads over the years ahead. Roy Stone, whose service in the Civil War had won him the rank of general, was a white-bearded civil engineer with riveting eyes, who had attained some prominence in New York. So when he was asked to come to Washington to head the office he had sponsored, with the modest title of "special agent and engineer for road inquiry," Stone left a secure position for the unknown.[9] His effective campaign for better roads, conducted from a government soapbox and working cooperatively with business and the public, would set a standard very different from the public-centered European model—one that would distinguish the American highway system from any other in the world.

Stone knew his task was straightforward but difficult. The taxpayers would use good roads, so it must be they who would pay for them. But the people had to want them badly enough, Stone knew. So he argued ingeniously to any group that would let him speak that Americans were already paying road levies, which he called "the mud tax." Farmers who cannot get their produce to the market lose sales, he preached, and this costs country farms eighty-eight cents an acre each year. Stone zeroed in on public school classrooms, to condition young Americans' minds. In 1896, he urged a teachers' convention in Buffalo, New York, to "preach the gospel of good roads," using voluminous teaching materials his office would supply for the asking.

Rails Sniff Profits in Good Roads

Early road marketeers even used geometry to convince the haughty railroads that good roads would benefit railways the most. If farmers' horse-and-wagon teams can conveniently travel three miles from the farm to the local depot, the rationale went, then the market for the railroad is within a three-mile radius. But if smoother roads could double that radius, argued a *Good Roads Magazine* writer in 1892, the three outer miles would contain three times the land area of the inner three miles, thus quadrupling the carrier's market.[10] By 1896, some railways eagerly heeded Stone's request to carry materials and machinery to improve roads at reduced rates. In return, the League of American Wheelmen paid them a backhanded compliment: "We should always give the devil his due. . . . As a rule, railroad corporations are not often troubled with big-heartedness. The seeming liberality of the railroad companies is merely a display of good sense and good business. . . . Every wagon road is a feeder to a railroad."[11]

The Age of Page

As Stone was groping for a foothold, a twenty-three-year-old Harvard-trained geologist named Logan Page took a job as a testing engineer for the Massachusetts Highway Commission. France had tested road materials for durability for decades, but the practice was unknown in America. Although the Romans had used multilayered surfaces, drainage ditches, and curbs from nearly the time of Jesus, their practices had lain dormant for centuries before being rediscovered and improved upon in the eighteenth and nineteenth centuries by such men as Pierre Tresaguet in France and Thomas Telford and John Macadam in Great Britain.[12]

Yet Americans had no such tradition to fall back on.[13] In 1877 workmen paved Washington's dusty Pennsylvania Avenue with hot asphalt, and similar efforts in New York, Chicago, San Francisco, and Buffalo soon followed.[14] But this technique was much too expensive for country roads. Where farm roads had been improved at all, counties used stone dust or clay to bind gravel, but neither substance stood up to the increasing traffic. Page's experiments in Massachusetts won notice from the Department of Agriculture in Washington, which invited him in 1900 to set up the first national road materials laboratory.[15]

Only the imagination of the engineer limited those early experiments. Some localities laid wooden planks lengthwise; others mixed stone and slag from blast furnaces. Engineers copied Macadam's technique of hard-packing small stone and earth.[16] The ORI's Stone, with typical intensity, then hit on a method he vowed would at last link all of America's large cities: steel roads. He envisioned a double track, each track five to six feet wide with a carriage road at either side, laid level with the roadway so the wheels might easily pass onto or off of the tracks. In 1898 rapt onlookers at the Trans-Mississippi Exposition in Omaha watched a single horse on a steel track haul an eleven-ton load that would require twenty horses on a dirt road. But the idea was too expensive to apply to America's wide-open spaces and never caught on.[17]

RFD AND THE AUTOMOBILE

If the bicycle craze marked the beginning of the national drive for good roads, two phenomena emerged in the mid-1890s that were far more significant: rural free mail delivery (RFD) and the automobile.

While European governments had been delivering mail to farms for decades, the deplorable American roads had made such a thing unrealistic. Before RFD, a rural citizen had the most limited of horizons. No telephone yet existed, and one often had to travel five miles to town to pick up a newspaper or learn the latest news from the depot's telegraph office. During the muddy seasons of spring and fall, school and church attendance fell off dramatically. Heady with the power of collective action that succeeded in creating the ICC, the Grangers were on a roll. Now they petitioned Congress to deliver mail directly to the farms.[18]

The Mail Order Revolution

Passage of RFD in 1893 created its own momentum. Within a decade, 8,600 carriers were traveling two hundred thousand miles a day, delivering mail to nearly five million farm people. Soon mail pouches were laden with thick catalogs from Sears and Roebuck, offering sewing machines for $13.25, electric washing machines for $3.50, or a double-runner sled for $0.93.[19] Rural residents could sit on the front porch and wait for the latest stories by Rudyard Kipling and O. Henry in *McClure's* to be delivered to their doorsteps.[20]

But the post office allowed carriers to stay home if the roads were not fit to travel. Creating an entitlement, then frustrating its delivery, caused a predictable response. By 1903, Representative Walter P. Brownlow of Tennessee proposed sending states the then-staggering sum of $420 million to build postal roads so the mail could get through. Although his bill failed, it marked the first of road advocates' fourteen annual drives that finally put Washington into the highway business.[21]

The railroad had broadened people's perspectives, the bicycle had let its rider choose his or her course, and RFD had created a reason for rural folk to write their congressmen. But it was the demand in Europe and America for the horseless carriage that pushed the movement to critical mass. George Selden, a Rochester, New York, patent attorney, had developed a three-cylinder internal combustion engine in 1877 yet could not get anyone to back it financially. But soon investors clamored to support others working on the same concept, first manufactured for sale by the brothers Charles and Frank Duryea of Springfield, Massachusetts.[22]

Motorizing the Masses

In 1895, nearly all cars in the world were made by Benz in Germany and P&L and Peugeot in France. In Britain, Sir Herbert Austin vowed to "motorize the masses" with his seven-horsepower lightweight car. But America was a quick study. By 1899, thirty U.S. companies turned out more than 2,500 cars a year. In May of that year, Ray Stannard Baker wrote in *McClure's* that auto companies formed in that year alone in Boston, New York, Chicago, and Philadelphia had amassed an astounding $388 million in capital.[23] A young Franklin Delano Roosevelt said he did not think much of the automobile's future after "a busted tire" interrupted his European honeymoon in 1905. But that did not deter his fellow Americans.[24] By 1912, U.S. companies manufactured as many autos as France, Britain, Germany, and Italy combined.[25]

Automobile driving had started out in Europe as a novelty, a rich man's sport. By 1897, the Auto Club de France had recruited a thousand members, who spent their weekends touring through the countryside. Exhibitions of the new conveyance drew tremendous crowds; one at the Tuileries in Paris in 1898 attracted 140,000 paying visitors. By 1900, fed by newspaper accounts of city-to-city trial runs, American clubs organized, following the European example of socially restrictive membership, high dues, and elaborate facilities. But elitist clubs failed to catch on in the more egalitarian United States.

Driving without Lessons

New automobile buyers, with scarves flying and goggles askew, would often take their new runabouts on the roads without ever before having sat behind the wheel of a car. In Birmingham, England, a woman drove her new Austin from the showroom some twenty-five miles before realizing that no one had told her how to put the car in reverse. She had to recruit passersby to pick up the car and turn it around so she could return home. It would be years before driver training was generally required on both sides of the Atlantic.[26]

But if this alternative to the railroad appealed to a monied elite, the automobile underwhelmed the average citizen. Its relative speed scared animals, stirred up clouds of dust, and damaged primitive roads. Gradually, American states required that cars be registered, drivers licensed, and speeds regulated. States began taxing these new "conveyances of the rich."[27] Some motorists felt themselves frustrated at every turn: "If his car broke down, he was fined for obstructing traffic. If he did not give notice of his approach, he was charged with negligence. . . . A driver crossing a state line—sometimes a county boundary—not only had to buy new license plates; he had to get a new driver's license. If he took his car on a ferry, he had to drain the gas tank."[28] But the times were prosperous, and people of means were buying.

Many horse riders vented their resentment at having to share the road with nonnatural contraptions, to which the U.S. automaker J. Frank Duryea shot back: "The horse is a willful, unreliable brute." Not only do horses cause many accidents, Duryea noted pointedly, "but cars do not defecate on city streets."[29]

MOTORISTS BAND TOGETHER

As a blizzard raged outside the Chicago Coliseum on March 2, 1902, members of several auto clubs attending an auto show huddled to defend attacks on motorists and to crusade for better roads. By 1903, the Automobile Association of America (AAA) they created at 753 Fifth Avenue in Manhattan was bustling with activity. AAA gained some fifty affiliates across the country in its first year, as American drivers bought a record thirty-five thousand cars. Aggressive AAA membership drives would eventually bring in thirty-four million members and make the organization a major political force in American life.

Motoring as a Sport

Addressing the first AAA annual meeting in New York, the organization's president, Winthrop E. Scarritt, referred revealingly to automobiling as a "sport," which indeed it was. Races among the beautiful people of Europe and America boosted public interest. The popular press widely reported events such as the "emancipation run" from London to Brighton and Roy Chapin's trip over wretched roads from Detroit to New York City in a tiny car promoted by the entrepreneur Ramsom Olds. France alone had spawned twenty-five auto publications by 1900. The participants themselves cut dashing figures in their open cars. An early writer described the recommended attire for auto touring: "For men, a single-breasted duster with an Eton collar and three patch pockets . . . together with wind cuffs, visored caps, and leggings for repair work. " Women wore "long linen dusters, tucked their lap robes securely about their legs and tied down their hats with chiffon veils knotted tightly under the chin."[30]

Gradually, motor enthusiasts realized that their potential to spur widespread taxpayer interest in good roads was limited as long as the public perceived motor touring as a pastime of the rich.[31] To convince people that cars required a smooth path, Americans had to be exposed to cars and good roads up close. For those in cities, the late 1890s brought new electric taxicabs in New York, as well as London and Paris. These whetted the interest of people who could not yet afford a car, by at least letting them ride in one.[32] But farmers seldom got to the big cities. So if rural people could not come to the roads, a few visionaries decided, they would bring the roads to the people.

"Object Lesson" Roads

The impetus behind one of the most aggressive sales promotions in American history came not from the auto industry or rich sportsmen but from the federal government. The phenomenon, which took the country by storm, was the "object lesson road train," the brainchild of Roy Stone's tiny ORI. In 1893, the Massachusetts Highway Commission, to increase the bang for limited bucks, had parceled out some three hundred thousand dollars among thirty-seven widely scattered road projects, each about a mile long. Once a cross-section of the public could experience the smoothness of paved roads, the reasoning went, the "object lesson" would lead those people to petition their legislatures for more money.

The idea caught Stone's eye. Long on ambition but short on money, he set the seemingly ludicrous goal of applying it on a national scale with only a ten-thousand-dollar budget to draw on. But persuasion helps a good salesperson as much as money, so Stone and his ally Pope wheedled railroads and road equipment manufacturers into providing free equipment, and local governments and individuals into paying for labor and materials.[33] The 1897 experiment at the New Jersey Agricultural College placed six inches of trap rock macadam eight feet wide on a 660-foot section of the main road to the college. This first "object lesson road"—which cost the government $321—helped set off a century-long feeding frenzy for paved roads, on which Washington has since spent hundreds of billions of dollars.

Rails Sponsor "Good Roads Trains"

As the nineteenth century ended, the enthusiasm of bicyclists, motorists, automakers, and the ORI melded into a loosely formed "good roads movement," with its own magazines to spread its message. Stone had left to further his crusade at the helm of the National League for Good Roads, and an Ohio lawyer, Martin Dodge, had succeeded him. In 1901 aggressive activists of the National Good Roads Association (NGRA) organized a traveling train to take the message to the hinterlands.

Leaders in the railroad industry enthusiastically supported the idea; they had become convinced that anything conducive to better thorough-fares would be to the railways' benefit. Bogged down in the mud of spring and fall, shippers deluged the rails with freight during the dry seasons, causing a crushing demand for railcars. Railroads could not afford to keep surplus cars just for the peak times, so backlogs resulted. Their customers, unable to move goods in a timely fashion, became irate.

Good roads leading to every depot would even out the flow of freight and enable rails to get along with many fewer cars. And not only would good roads increase their market radius, the carriers reasoned, but carrying the road materials needed to build new highways would create new rail business. Railroad owners would continue to espouse this rationale for the next thirty years until they realized too late that the unregulated, largely nonunion trucking industry had replaced railroads as America's biggest freight carrier.[34]

The Illinois Central offered an eleven-car train free of charge, and the NGRA sent out advance men to line up donations of labor and materials for demonstration projects. A steam locomotive, with nine flatcars over-flowing with road experts and journalists, pulled out of Chicago on a spring day in 1901 on a sixteen-city tour of five states. The advance agents whipped up enthusiasm in each town days in advance, to make sure a mass of townspeople were at the depot when the train pulled in. Construction crews then spent a couple of days building sample roads of earth, stone, and gravel, varying from a half mile to a mile and a half in length, before moving on to the next town. When astute observers saw every politician in the county clamber aboard the train to get his picture taken, they knew change was in the wind. Dodge, accompanying the first trip from Chicago to New Orleans, described the venture as "the most successful campaign ever waged for good roads."

"An Itinerant College on Wheels"

As the word spread, momentum built. The Southern Railroad sponsored such a cavalcade in 1901 on its own initiative. Its train, carrying a clutch of mustachioed "road experts" in bowler hats, pulled into Lynchburg, Virginia, as fall leaves were turning. On each car was emblazoned in large letters: "Southern Railway Good Roads Train." U.S. Senator J. W. Daniel, on hand to welcome the Southern's train, described it enthusiastically as "an itinerant college on wheels."

Demonstrating the dramatic difference that road paving could make was one thing; creating a durable surface that poor farm counties could afford was another. The effort required both technology and expertise. Again, the government, not private industry, drove the research and development effort. By 1905, Congress sensed which way the wind was blowing, gave the fledgling agency the more permanent name of "Office of Public Roads" (OPR) and endowed it with fifty thousand dollars. Until then, the best that Logan Page, the new director, had been able to do was to mail farmers who sent in two dollars plans for a King Drag. Built by splitting a timber lengthwise and positioning two halves one ahead of the other, the drag made a rigid platform, which a horse would then drag to smooth out the road.[35] Frank Turner, who headed the 41,000-mile interstate highway system in the 1970s, recalls as a boy in Texas working the "road drags," a task required of every adult male who could not afford to pay the county road tax.[36]

The technology was primitive at best. OPR engineers worked feverishly, experimenting with new ideas while glancing nervously over their shoulders at the tens of thousands of automobiles Detroit produced each year. More efficient American production methods helped account for the Detroit automakers' ability to soar ahead of their European counterparts. British manufacturers, for example, made most of the parts that went into their own cars, thus tying up a great deal of capital and forcing them to produce fewer cars at high prices. By contrast, American automakers typically bought their components from vendors, thus keeping their capital requirements lower and enabling them to build more units.[37]

HENRY FORD TAKES THE STAGE

Then the son of Irish immigrants grew inspired by the way Chicago meatpackers hooked sides of beef for dressing on an overhead conveyer belt. Henry Ford adapted the idea and the automobile assembly line was born.[38] And as the automobile market changed from the province of the rich into a reality for the common citizen, auto financing changed to meet wage earners' needs. Early in the century, a car buyer would typically put 20 percent down and pay the rest in four quarterly installments. Then French banks began to experiment with installment loans, a practice that soon spread to the United States and made cars available to millions. Auto showrooms at Ford dealerships proved so popular that the company boasted seven thousand across the country by 1913.[39]

A Car for the People

Few people have captured the spirit of their times as did Ford. Riding the crest of Progressive sentiment throughout the land, his car for the common person at once symbolized freedom of movement, liberation from dictatorial train schedules, and a way to strike back at the hated railroads. He offered his lightweight Model T in "any color you choose as long as it's black" and vowed it would be "large enough for the family but small enough for the individual to run and care for . . . and so low in price that no man making a good salary [would] be unable to buy one."[40]

The railroads had made it possible for humans to go beyond the horizon linearly, but the automobile's scope was limitless. The historian Page Smith observes, "In a society in which many people suffered from an acute sense of powerlessness, in a jungle of machines and increasingly impersonal agencies, one had one's own 'power source' at hand." Smith argues that producing the automobile may have been a more powerful mission for America than spreading freedom throughout the world. "We clearly did not invent it, but we incorporated it almost instantaneously into our economy and our culture."[41]

A Diaspora of Engineers

As the number of motor vehicles increased sixfold from 1905 to 1910 and interchangeable spark plugs, bulbs, and belts let motorists travel far afield, it quickly became apparent that macadam and gravel would not endure the wear of heavy traffic. So from 1907 to 1916, the OPR built several dozen experimental roads, using such materials as oil mixtures, portland cement, concrete, paving brick, and even a mixture of blast furnace slag with limestone, tar, or asphaltic road oil.[42]

But better methods were worthless without engineers competent enough to build reliable roads. Whereas France's highly respected School of Bridges and Roads had been turning out highway engineers for nearly two centuries, America had no similar institution. As a result, country workmen often flew by the seat of their pants, producing too-steep grades, unnecessary curves, and poor drainage. The OPR's Page tried in vain to found an American institute for highway engineers.

As the next best thing, from 1905 to 1915 he released a diaspora of seventy young OPR-trained engineering graduates into positions with newly formed state highway departments, and with counties and colleges. They would ultimately form the backbone of the greatest road-building program in world history. While Page was reluctant to lobby Congress directly, he was a child of the Progressive era. At a time when Louis Brandeis was chiding the railroads for not using "scientific management" to keep costs under control, Page preached a similar "ideology of expertise." He and his early OPR colleagues pressed for good roads not in the service of an interest group or political program but as simple good government.[43]

BERATING THE RAILS

The pace of change in the first decade of the twentieth century was unprecedented and, to many, bewildering. Electricity, telephones, mail order catalogs, and waves of immigrants from Europe transformed the lives of everyone. Sears and Roebuck had sold the first of a hundred thousand disassembled houses that needed shipment to lots in the hinterlands.[44] Railroads had become the whipping boy for much that Americans found wanting in life, so exaggerated portraits of unshackling the beholden rail traveler were common in the popular press. Many who stood to gain from the success of the auto industry took pains to paint contrasting images of the railroads as archaic and the automobile as embodying the "new freedom." The public, eager to experience progress, was an easy sell.

Driving the "Highway Pullman"

The AAA, predictably in the forefront of the effort, observed that the railroads had "robbed the roads of that picturesque and free means of travel [by stagecoach] and nothing ever took its place until the dawn of the motor car." But magazines and books took up the chant as well. In one of the more colorful denigrations of railroad travel, the writer Julian Street journeyed by train to New York City and described his perceptions: "A passenger train roars by, savagely on one side, is gone, while on the other, a half-mile freight train tugs and squawks and clatters. When the porter calls you in the morning, and you raise your window shade, you see no plains or mountains but the backs of squalid suburban tenements with veri-colored garments, fluttering on their clotheslines." A train's on-time arrival once had been seen as "a sign of American technological mastery over bad weather, personal vagaries and hard terrain." But, as one writer observed, a "highway Pullman" let the driver be "his own station master, engineer and porter, with no one's time to make except his own."[45]

Such renowned writers as Theodore Dreiser and Edith Wharton, as well as the etiquette adviser Emily Post, also ridiculed rail travel and glorified the automobile. "Already the railways are complaining that the automobile is seriously injuring its business," wrote the novelist Dreiser. But, he explained, "this is not difficult to understand. . . . At best the railways have become huge, clumsy, unwieldy affairs little suited to the temperamental needs and moods of the average human being. . . . Actually our huge railways are becoming so freight-logged and train yard and train terminal-infested and four-tracked and cinder-blown, that they are a nuisance."

By contrast, Dreiser rhapsodized about the automobile: "Who wants to see the same old scenes over and over and over? But the prospect of new and varied roads and of that intimate contact with woodland silences, grassy slopes, sudden and sheer vistas at sharp turns, streams not followed by endless lines of cars—of being able to change your mind and go by this route or that according to your mood—what a difference! . . . Man must naturally prefer choice. Only the dull can love sameness."[46]

A Jarring Otherness

Before it became possible to travel great distances in relatively little time, most Americans stayed in their hometowns with people of like background and complexion. Long journeys by train, though, introduced Americans to an otherness they sometimes found jarring. One's seatmate might be of a different social class or ethnic origin, or exhibit strange habits. As a *Literary Digest* writer observed:

Everyone who has traveled even to a minor degree has witnessed the uncleanly and often filthy manner in which the drinking-water receptacles on passenger coaches are filled with ice and water. This work is usually performed by the cheapest ignorant laborer, who handles the ice with dirty and unwashed hands, often reeking with coal dirt and "smear," from off the sides of the cars, which he grasps in order to raise himself to the top; and sometimes his hands are contaminated with disease, which is particularly common among this class of employees.

Railroad coach passengers complained of "malodorous salamis and ripe bananas consumed by those unable to afford eating in the dining car." The positive might have seen the population of the railcar as "diverse and colorful," but the negative painted it as "unscreened and hostile."[47]

Few denied that improvements to trains had made possible a smooth, heated, well-enclosed ride that automobiles, with their meager springs and poorly padded seats, lacked. A guidebook of the times advised auto tourists to pack "a block and tackle for mud, at least two spare tires for rocks, a decent set of tools for carburetor and engine, flares and so on." And it added: "Make sure your automobile is fit to fight a long hard battle." Inconvenience galore? Yes. But what was inconvenience in the age of Teddy Roosevelt? After all, the nation's leader set an example of the "strenuous life," in which physical exertion against the odds was a badge of honor and a harkening back to America's agrarian past, which preceded fin de siècle decadence. By contrast, riding a train was "too soft, too effete, too familiar."[48]

A SPORT BECOMES A BUSINESS

By 1910, nearly a half-million motor vehicles were on American roads, 187,000 of them produced in that year alone. The seeds sown by the Grangers and the auto clubs had borne fruit, as fourteen states had set up highway departments by 1904 alone, and about half the states had inaugurated modest state-aid programs, to absorb the growing demand for new roads. Yet, while the number of cars in America had increased 1,600 percent since 1900, the mileage of paved roads had not even doubled.[49]

In 1900, automobiling was a sport; by 1910, it had become a business. The good roads movement had passed beyond a "good government" lobby. Joining consumer organizations like the AAA in pressing for good roads were those with a financial stake in the outcome. The American

Road Makers (ARM) brought together road contractors, road machinery manufacturers, and state engineers, for example. Scores of groups, often with "good roads" in their names, joined the political agitation. But many grassroots organizations were fronts, with no dues-paying members. Funds for organizations such as the National Automobile Chamber of Commerce (NACC) came from their sponsors—auto manufacturers, road materials producers, and the railroads.[50]

The Highway Lobby is Born

General Motors' president, William Durant, recalled years later the beginnings of the American highway lobby: "The whole network taken for granted in later generations was woven in these years—the highways, the fuel and service stations, the mechanisms of registration, insurance and policing—all simply enlarged upon and refined in the following half-century."[51]

To the industrialists, who were now selling glass, rubber, steel, concrete and their end products in numbers beyond their wildest dreams, whatever needed to be done to sustain the boom and to build pressure for good roads simply had to accomplished. Some in Congress had been reluctant to vote monies for the OPR, fearing that such a move might lead to national control of roads. But the floodtide was straining at the gates now, and major federal involvement seemed inevitable.

By 1912, rural free delivery had spread to 1.2 million miles of mostly dirt road, a tremendous boon to the public as well as to Sears and Roebuck. Because the trekking of the mails over sometimes-impassable roads put the government $28 million in the red, bills championing better roads were passed, in the hopes of cutting that deficit. The proposal that five hundred thousand dollars should go to states and counties that put up a million dollars established the principle of matching funds—an idea that would fuel big government for the balance of the century. Counties backed the plan until some realized it meant giving up control to unseen forces in Washington, which would help set standards for spending the money.[52]

Lessons from the "Advanced Countries of Europe"

Europe had clearly fallen behind the United States in building cars by 1910, but the European roads were in far better shape. Congressional proponents now resurrected Roy Stone's "mud tax" argument, with "the advanced countries of Europe" as exhibit A. U.S. farmers paid twenty-one cents per ton-mile to haul produce over their country dirt roads, whereas French farmers paid only eight cents a ton-mile because of their superior macadam surfaces. The thirteen-cent difference was nature's tax on farmers, costing the United States over $500 million a year. From here it was a short logical jump to argue that spending just part of that money would vastly increase American prosperity.[53]

Politically, congressional reluctance to appropriate a lot of money for road building was understandable: constituents would be taxed to provide a service that most could not yet enjoy. Across the Atlantic, a sagacious British chancellor of the exchequer had a better idea. Lloyd George rose in the House of Commons in 1909 to propose that the British road system be self-financing. Citizens would spend more on roads, George theorized correctly, if they knew that the three-pence-per-gallon tax they paid would be earmarked solely for roads. Many years would pass before American politicians adopted his brainstorm, which would prove to be one of the most effective government financing mechanisms of all time. Ironically, it ultimately failed in Britain, partly because the earmarking rule never gained the force of law but rather was only a political understanding, which Winston Churchill years later would erase with a wave of his hand.

Building from the Ground Up

But while the British were brilliantly insightful about road financing, their execution was from the top down. In America, by contrast, proponents were building a highway coalition from the ground up, brick by brick. Logan Page could see dozens of interest groups seeking the same goal but not communicating. To coalesce and focus them, he formed the American Association for Highway Improvement. Its public showcase was the annual National Road Congress, the first of which in 1911 at Richmond, Virginia, sounded a robust call for federal aid to state highway departments. Meanwhile, state highway commissioners and engineers inaugurated the American Association of State Highway Officials (AASHO), with the benign mandate to discuss legislation, plus economic and technical subjects. From its deceptively modest beginning in 1914, AASHO would steadily grow in influence and ultimately help set the standards governing American highway building for the rest of the twentieth century. Like Logan's association, AASHO added to the drumbeat of pressure on Congress.

As a massive network of disparate road interests began to speak with one voice, the highway issue gained high visibility. From 1910 to 1915, no national issue gained greater coverage in both country and city newspapers. Such mainstream publications as the *Saturday Evening Post* and *Harper's* joined the AAA's *American Motorist* and *Good Roads Magazine* in keeping the heat on. The OPR, whose object lesson roads gave it sophistication in field work, now dispatched twenty-seven lecturers to deliver crusading speeches, which, according to later OPR estimates, over two hundred thousand people heard in thirty-seven states.

The railroad boom of the mid-nineteenth century effectively emasculated waterborne commerce, but the railroads remained complacent in the face of a massive sea change threatened by the auto industry. In 1911, the Pennsylvania Railroad volunteered a "road improvement train," which stopped at 165 Pennsylvania sites in two months. The Southern Railroad and five other carriers joined in as well, and from 1912 to 1916, 163,000 people in 650 towns heard their message. The conventional wisdom of the time was that breakdown-prone motor vehicles and the best roads anyone then could imagine were such that cars and trucks would remain no more than handmaidens to the railroads.[54]

A ROAD ACROSS THE UNITED STATES!

Had the railroads taken seriously the dream of an Indianapolis promoter, they might not have been so content. Shortly after Labor Day in 1912, the charismatic founder of a carbide headlight company threw a dinner party for automakers in that city at the Old Deutsche Haus. Carl G. Fisher, a stylish dresser with wide-set eyes and a strong chin, exuded dynamism. After the plates were cleared, he launched into a diatribe on the need for good roads, striking responsive chords in his fellow industrialists. But then the man who had paved a local raceway in brick the year before and inaugurated the Indianapolis Speedway dropped a bomb. "A road across the United States!" the handsome Fisher exhorted his fellow businessmen. "Let's build it before we're too old to enjoy it!"

As his guests sat up and took notice, Fisher sketched out a plan for a 3,150-mile road—which he would call the Lincoln Highway—from New York City to San Francisco. As they reflected on how such a massive scheme would be financed, it may have occurred to the auto manufacturers that there is no such thing as a free meal. Yes, Fisher said, donations from the auto interests would finance the road. After all, who had the most to gain if long-distance travel caught on?[55]

"Peacock Alleys" for the Rich?

But even so compelling a salesman as Fisher could not sway Henry Ford, who was turning out three-quarters of the nation's cars at the time and whose support Fisher knew would be crucial to the effort. James Couzens, Ford's business manager, signaled their strong opposition in a letter to Fisher. Any major transcontinental route should be financed by the taxpayers, Ford believed. Also unconvinced, midwestern farmers decried Fisher's proposed road as a sophisticated PR campaign to win federal tax dollars to build a few "peacock alleys" for wealthy eastern tourists to enjoy. Cities, on the other hand, felt their fortunes enhanced by travel and called for federal control of any such "national routes."

In the end, the Lincoln Highway contributed more to firing the imagination of Americans than to providing them smooth travel, as sections of newly paved road and rutted dirt roads were patched together across the country. When the etiquette advisor Emily Post took a well-publicized cross-country trip in 1915, she asked a well-traveled colleague which was the best road across the country. Without irony, her friend replied, "The Union Pacific."[56]

A CAR "A LITTLE CHILD CAN SELL"

By the teens, the Chevrolet Motor Company had moved into a head-to-head competition with Ford for the burgeoning mass market. While unable to match Ford's $490 price for the Model T, William Durant's factory still could fill only one-third of the demand for a vehicle whose promotional ads proclaimed: "A Little Child Can Sell It." In 1915, Ford was selling more than three hundred thousand "tin lizzies" a year and had cut the price to $360. While only one-third of the automobile market was for cars under $1,400 in 1907, nine years later, 90 percent of cars sold were in that range.[57]

Yet, although the good roads movement was now a generation old, American roads had little to show for its efforts. Most state legislatures had set up highway commissions, and while a few let them supervise county road operations, most gave their commissions no money to work with. And rail-rich Iowa, for example, indicated the priority it placed on roads by making Thomas MacDonald its highway commissioner right out of college and budgeting a mere five thousand dollars a year for his department. Nearly a decade later, he had made little headway in gaining control of highway funding. After all, road construction had traditionally been the county patronage trough. Seasoned politicians were not about to give up their lifeblood to some head-in-the-clouds engineers.[58]

ENGINEERS' SUPERIORITY COMPLEX

Engineers, by believing in their own intellectual and moral superiority over policy makers (an attitude thoroughly in the mainstream of Progressivism), did not endear themselves to legislators. As one engineer described his role: "It is not sufficient for an engineer, or any other educated man, to know. He must act. A part of the engineer's duty is to help in molding public opinion by educating and guiding the public in those matters in which engineers by virtue of their training and occupation have superior knowledge."[59]

The engineers trained by Page and, later, by MacDonald and dispatched to state capitals across the country were largely men from rural towns—many created by the railroads—where antirailroad sentiment continued to run high. In midcentury, when these farm boys controlled this urban nation's state highway programs, it would go beyond coincidence that the programs still had a strong rural bias. The author Phil Patton caricatures the early highway engineers as "the guys left out of playground and cow pasture games," who often wore "efficient horn and metal glasses" and who took "pride in the dull factuality, jargon and caution of their speeches."[60]

A CLASS STRUGGLE

While politicians and engineers eyed each other warily, a pitched battle now developed in Congress over whether state capitals or Washington should control the roads program. The debate threatened to rend the coalition that the good roads movement had so carefully nurtured, as the same class consciousness that tinged the great railroad debates a decade earlier flared anew.

As the AAA allied itself with big cities in favor of "touring roads," Representative Dorsey W. Shackleford took up the cudgels for rural interests, which merely wanted "cheaper transportation and a lower cost of living." Long-distance roads are not practical, argued the Missouri Democrat: "It is an idle dream to imagine that auto trucks and automobiles will take the place of railways in the long-distance movement of freight or passengers." In the end, the clashing forces fought to a standstill.[61]

Major good roads initiatives had met untimely deaths for thirteen annual sessions. When the Sixty-fourth Congress convened in January 1916, Shackleford determined that this session would be different. He had solidified his control over the process by chairing the new House Committee on Roads. Now the Missourian pushed through a compromise between those who advocated long-distance roads and those who championed local ones. Under his plan, states would divvy up $25 million a year, one-half by population and the remainder by mileage of RFD routes. To build the roads, the Federal Aid Road Act of 1916 would set up state highway departments, wresting control in some cases from county governments. The bill sailed through the Senate, spearheaded by Senator William Bankhead, with the imprimatur of both the AASHO and the OPR. It became law with the signature of President Wilson on July 11, 1916.[62]

A SEED IS SOWN

Today, a photograph attesting to the significance of that signing hangs in the cavernous skylit atrium of the new thirty-nine-acre AAA headquarters outside Orlando, Florida. In it, an austerely erect Wilson sits at a desk signing the modest bill to spend $5 million in the first year after its adoption.[c] Next to it is a photograph of another bill signing: a smiling President Dwight D. Eisenhower in 1956 launches the $27 billion interstate highway system, which is conventionally believed to be the birth of America's modern highway system.

Yet just as a human embryo contains the genetic material that will determine its future adult makeup, so the 1916 bill predetermined the creation of the interstate highway system. As seemingly fragile as the first daffodil shoot poking through the April soil, the highway measure had roots that had taken more than a generation to build, for the American highway coalition was built from the bottom up. The painstaking work of the Grangers and motorists' clubs had created a constituency that state legislatures could not ignore.

AAA, NACC, ARM, and AASHO all viewed cooperation as a greater goal than individual independence. The gestures of Page and Shackleford in uniting AASHO and the federal road establishment in a joint venture and the unity between private manufacturers and government engineers were characteristic of the times. In large part, the spirit of the Progressive era had set the tone for their efforts.

The Page-Shackleford model—in providing matching federal-state funds, supervision, and standard setting from Washington, but control by the states—endures today. While the nearly sacrosanct Highway Trust Fund created by the 1956 Interstate Highway Act is the government equivalent of a perpetual motion machine, it became politically possible only because for forty years the highway movement usually remembered that their best interests lay in speaking with one voice.

RAILS IGNORE THE STORM CLOUDS

A generation earlier, in an era of frontier individualism, fiercely independent railroad moguls fought with all their might against hostile governments, which sought to control their actions. But a new century created a new industry, whose public-private partnership was not only symbiotic but synergistic. Had the railroads been born later, their fate might have been different.

In 1916, new track mileage boosted American railroad miles to 254,000. Trackage would trend downhill from then on. "Soon most railroads would start abandoning branch lines and boarding up depots." Yet, wrote the author of *The Ford Dynasty*, "they gave no sign of awareness that their era had peaked out."[64]

A musty congressional report from 1915 contains a prophetic aside: "We believe that permanent highways will result in very considerable adoption of auto-truck hauling in preference to rail transportation where the distance is within a half day's run."[65] The implications of that little-noticed but insightful statement would transform America.

The automobile made itself felt first in rural America, where farmers bought cheap Model T's to drive to town, once Congress and state legislatures had decided to pull them out of the mud. But America's cities were a world apart. Getting around there had been easy for decades, thanks to the ubiquitous trolleycar.

· 4 ·

THE ELECTRIC SHOOTING
STAR

*To the vast majority of investors in 1902, the
[Michigan] Lake Shore Electric looked infi-
nitely more attractive than the motor company
Henry Ford was trying to promote.*

—George Hilton and John Due, *Electric
Interurban Railways*

FRANK JULIAN SPRAGUE, STANDING BY A RICHMOND, VIRGINIA, RAILROAD
siding in the dead of a summer night in 1888, could be forgiven if he felt
very much alone. A thirty-one-year-old graduate of the U.S. Naval Academy,
Sprague cut a striking figure—square-jawed and handsome, with a full
brown moustache and wide-set eyes. But for all the promise his description suggests, the career break that would set him apart seemed about to
slip through his fingers.[1]

Sprague believed that electricity could transform American urban transportation, and he had staked a decade of his life on that conviction. While
inventors and engineers had tinkered with workshop models of electric
trains since the 1830s, they had not been able to find how to transmit current from a central powerhouse to a moving vehicle miles away and to
develop a streetcar motor that could withstand the shocks of rail travel.[2]

In the 1880s, horsepower was still in harness in most American cities,
as beasts of burden hauled open wooden cars with bench seats along steel

tracks on muddy streets at a mere six miles an hour—not much faster than a person could walk. But streetcars required prodigious numbers of horses, which were expensive, survived only four to five years in their grueling labor, and were prone to maladies. (In 1872, an equine respiratory plague called the Great Epizootic decimated eighteen thousand horses in New York City alone.) City dwellers—who had to contend with thousands of horses fouling the streets in the best of times and their fallen carcasses drawing predators in the worst of times, as well as with reeking stables wedged between crowded, steaming tenements—were nearly desperate for a better way to travel.

SEARCHING FOR SOLUTIONS

In fact, entrepreneurs were working feverishly on new alternatives in the 1880s, when streetcars were still a cottage industry and more than four hundred separate railway companies serviced American cities. Some had tried powering cars with small steam engines, which cast soot on their riders and whose noisy belching scared horses as they passed.[3]

More successful were cable cars, which gripped a moving wire cable that ran underground to a giant winding station. Designed in 1873 to negotiate the towering San Francisco hills, 626 miles of cable car lines had been put into use by the mid-1890s, hauling 400 million passengers a year in two dozen American cities. But cable cars were hugely expensive to build, and when a cable broke, stranded passengers on the entire line had to wait for its repair.[4]

Sprague thought he had a better idea. Following graduation from Annapolis in 1878, the young Virginian lucked into an active duty job that let him spend his next four years experimenting with electricity. He then spent a year in Menlo Park, New Jersey, soaking up knowledge at the elbow of Thomas Edison, who had already demonstrated that electricity was commercially practical. Striking out on his own, he set up the tiny Sprague Electric Railway and Motor Company, to develop and build a streetcar motor, mounted between the car axle and a spring, that could supply five hundred volts direct current in a way that eliminated most shocks.[5]

Sprague tried out his invention in 1888 on a twelve-mile streetcar line in Richmond, Virginia. From the roof of each train to an overhead wire ran a pole, at the end of which was a small wheel called a trolley, to keep running contact with the electrified wire. The lighthearted lilt of the word *trolley* would lead generations to adopt it affectionately as a nickname for the electric streetcars themselves. Sprague's concept worked, but many of his contemporaries were toiling away at similar technologies in garages across America, and Sprague knew the race was to the swift.[6]

Later that year, he learned that the West End Street Railway Company of Boston was about to cashier its stable of eight thousand horses and change over to cable cars. Sprague prevailed on its president, Henry M. Whitney, a steamship operator and real estate speculator, to at least visit the Richmond experiment before sealing his decision. After a demonstration, the young inventor had nearly won Whitney over when the Boston company's general manager protested skeptically that if rush-hour congestion bunched up cars along a small stretch of line, the system lacked the power to start all of them up again. Sprague's vehement assurances to the contrary fell on deaf ears.

As Sprague's guests slumbered in a Richmond hotel before returning home, the young inventor knew his future was on the line. If he could electrify Boston's streetcars, he would have gained a giant head start on his competitors; otherwise, he would remain just another struggling small businessman. Sprague waited until his 40 wooden streetcars returned to their garage at the end of their evening runs, then lined up 22 of them in a row on a section designed for only 4. He commanded his power plant engineer to load the feeder fuses, raise the voltage from the standard 450 to 500 volts, and hold on "no matter what."

Then Sprague and his assistants rushed to the Boston visitors' hotel, rousted them from a sound sleep, and persuaded them to come with him to witness a dramatic demonstration. At the flip of a switch, the trolley-cars' headlamps illuminated the darkness one by one and rolled out of the station, until all twenty-two were out of sight. Convinced, the delegation boarded a Boston-bound train and soon persuaded the city's board of aldermen to let Sprague electrify the West End Street Railway.[7]

Few inventions have ever been embraced more quickly and widely than the electric streetcar. Within two years, Sprague was processing orders to build two hundred streetcar systems throughout the country. And while horses still hauled 70 percent of urban railcars in 1890, electricity would power nearly all streetcars a decade later, as diagonal trolley poles and diamond-shaped pentagraphs linking cartops to electric wires became familiar sights on city streets.

By 1900, electric trolley lines were booming. Ads in financial journals hawked securities in new ventures: "To put one's money into street railway development was to bet on the great American future."[8] By 1902, a federal street railway census would show that investors had poured $2 billion into twenty-two thousand miles of electric railway in the United States, carrying five billion people a year—more than seven times the number who rode the steam trains.[9]

STRETCHING THE CITY

The settlement of American cities has always been limited by how far a family breadwinner is willing to commute to work. Horsecars on steel rails pushed out the limits from the downtown core in the mid-1800s, and cable cars caused land booms in some cities toward the end of the century. "Vast areas of property which were nothing but grazing ground and garden patches," wrote one *St. Louis Post-Dispatch* reporter in 1889, "are now built up with a superior class of dwellings," as land prices grew fifteenfold overnight.[10] Electric streetcars, with their greater speed, pushed the city out even farther; in Boston, they stretched the boundaries of dense settlement from two and a half to six miles from City Hall.[11]

Soon speculators were forming land development companies, some of which even started their own streetcar lines. If one moved fast, he could buy inaccessible land dirt cheap, advertise the coming of a streetcar line, and then sell the land and use the profits to build the line—all with putting down little or no money himself. Secrecy was at a premium. Promoters held their projected routes close to their vests, hoping to gain title to huge tracts before the owners grasped their intentions.[12]

Social stratification patterns that would carry to the present day soon set in. Since a one-mile-thick donut-shaped slice three miles from downtown has much less land than one six miles out, near-in land prices soared. Builders jammed three-family houses together on narrow lots, to house artisans, salespeople, and small shopkeepers buying their first homes, people whose long work hours required a fairly short commute. Farther out, professionals and owners of larger businesses who had the time and money for a longer commute found that lower land costs let them build detached single-family homes. The gentry, seeking to construct lavish estates, bought abundant land on the outskirts.

"Moral Influence" of Streetcars

Progressive reformers saw rapid transit as a vehicle to reshape the city. Accessing open land and encouraging home ownership were seen as a social good, and commentators spoke of the "moral influence" of street-cars.[13] The muckraker Burton Hendrick enthused about the trolleys' "enormous influence...in freeing urban workers from the demoralizing influences of the tenements . . . and in extending general enlightenment by bringing about a closer human intercourse.[14]

While the electric streetcars kept to the urban core, steam railroads largely ignored them; any short-hop passenger service they lost was unprofitable anyway. But once workmen began erecting electric poles beyond the city limits, the railway owners sat up and took note. Streetcars typically ran more frequently and at cheaper fares than the steam trains, without covering their passengers with ashes and soot. If they proposed traveling longer distances, to carry the better-heeled suburban commuter, electric streetcars could be a threat indeed.

Soon railroads were speaking out against the trolleys and refusing them permission to construct grade crossings. In Chicago, Detroit, and Toledo, hostility grew into violence as hundreds of workmen for both the trolleys and the railroads fought over projects that would extend streetcar lines. Several New York, New Haven, and Hartford railroad officials spent months in jail and paid fifteen thousand dollars in damages after a prolonged standoff in North Abington, Massachusetts, grew into a riot.[15]

Rushing to Cash In

Still, the 1890s saw a frenzy of competition by businessmen to make their fortunes hauling the masses on short, narrow wooden cars over city streets as an electric hiss crackled overhead. Those who envied the railroad robber barons now found they could make a bundle in rail transport with a much smaller financial investment.

But many downtown businessmen strongly opposed what they considered dangerous live electrical wires. Protesters in Boston, Philadelphia, and New York warned of impending fires and electrocutions. Yet such public opposition allowed political leaders to exact from the trolley companies blood money and concessions, much of which ended up lining the politicians' pockets. Just as states had awarded multiple railroad franchises to spur competition, so did the cities with trolley companies.

Open bidding for streetcar franchises was common, and the boon to city coffers might be a percentage of farebox receipts, annual flat payments, or an agreement to pave the streets over which the trolleys passed or to shovel a city's snow. Some businessmen, in their eagerness to win

franchises, promised as much as 95 percent of the take to the city—
obviously a hopeless proposition. Some promised a "perpetual" nickel fare,
a commitment they would soon regret. A Philadelphia trolley line ended
up repaving the city's entire downtown area as the price for a franchise.[16]

Yet as the urban population swelled, millions needed a ride to work,
offering a bonanza for those companies that could corner even a modest
chunk of the market. Eager investors sank a total of $4 billion into the
ventures. A chronicler of the early days of trolleys calls them "enormously
profitable."[17]

But one needed only to know grade-school division to forecast the
future of the industry if cities kept granting franchises to all who asked.
With company revenues limited to fares collected and even with the
urban population growing, operators were soon slicing up the pie so
thinly that revenues sank below costs. As late as 1897, Chicago had fifteen
competing streetcar companies. Something had to give. And so a feeding
frenzy began, as the strong lines feasted on the weak.[18]

Manufacturing Money

To the average fair-minded citizen, the exploits of steam railroad titans in
weakening their companies by cooking the books while lining their own
pockets may have spelled corruption. To the unscrupulous in the 1890s,
however, it spelled opportunity. Wall Street operators were only too glad to
merge two $5 million trolley companies by inflating their book value to a
combined $15 million and dividing the extra $5 million among the streetcar
moguls and their brokers. "St. Louis Transit, which had no real reason for
existing at all, besides having no track, no cars and no physical plant, was
capitalized at twenty million dollars."[19]

And in fast-growing Chicago, the financier Charles Tyson Yerkes solidified his hold on the streetcar industry by slipping aldermen a million dollars
to give him cheap use of the city streets, on which he built nearly five hundred miles of track. With the face of an aristocrat and the ethics of a jackal,
Yerkes manipulated streetcar securities to amass a $30 million fortune,
which he spent profligately on women, lavish balls, and fine art. But before
long, Yerkes sold out and fled to London ahead of a threatened indictment
in 1901. Yerkes's fame survived his death when he became the model of an
unscrupulous capitalist in Theodore Dreiser's novel *The Titan*.[20]

In following the historical journey of trolleys through twentieth-century
daily life and eventually into the museums, the burden of debt through

corporate exploitation that was rampant in American streetcar history must be borne in mind. If a typical family were told it would have to pay forever a debt equal to a quarter of its net income and for which it would receive no benefit, demoralization and bankruptcy might well follow. That the streetcars managed to hold off those very outcomes as long as they did is remarkable.

TROLLEYS, TROLLEYS EVERYWHERE

Trolleys, considered quaint artifacts today, pervaded all facets of American life at the turn of the century. Faster than horsecars, many were comparatively luxurious in appointment, featuring such things as birds-eye paneled maple ceilings, solid mahogany door frames, and carved panes at the end of each seat, with window curtains of Russian leather trimmed with silk.[21] Just as the automobile's speed and newness later made it the "in thing," so did the trolley become the conveyance of choice. One writer noted, "Trolley cars travel fast enough to produce a feeling of mental exhilaration, which is absent from or scarcely felt by passengers in horsecars." Indeed, a prominent Louisville, Kentucky, doctor prescribed for his patients a two-hour ride on the front seat of an open trolleycar as "the best possible cure for insomnia."[22]

There were trolleycars for commuting, trolleycars to carry the mail, and trolleycars to hire for parties. The state used trolleycars to transport prisoners, guarding the presumption of innocence by separating the convicted from the merely accused. For twenty dollars, a Baltimore and Northern Electric Railway official in a silk topper would arrive at the street corner nearest the home of one who had died and supervise the loading of his coffin into a zinc-lined vault in a black and silver car, closing its large plate-glass door so passersby could admire the casket's opulence on the way to its final resting place. A partition of carved mahogany and frosted glass separated family members from the rest of the bereaved, and call bells could summon ice water from a built-in cooler.

Commuter trains typically had longitudinal varnished wooden seats, and an exterior often "lavish in the extreme," as workmen hand rubbed as many as fifteen coats of paint to a high-gloss finish before applying gilt lettering and scrollwork. Ceilings might depict an elaborate landscape or seasonal decoration. An 1892 author waxed euphoric on the social uplift that fine art could give to the "lives and hearts" of the lower-class rider.[23]

The 1904 Louisiana Purchase Exhibition in St. Louis showcased a particularly lavish private trolleycar for aspiring captains of industry to salivate over. It came equipped with upper and lower berths so its wealthy owners could "live free of the doubtful accommodations of the small towns they frequently passed through"; an observation room at the end of the car, finished in East Indian vermilion wood with marquetry inlay; a full-sized kitchen range, typewriter, and desk—for the gentleman's secretary, no doubt; a dining room finished in Philippine rosewood; and a fireplace.[24]

For a young man to land a job as a streetcar conductor during the heyday of the trolleys was to make his mother proud. Elaborate hats befitting an army officer and navy blue uniforms with double vertical rows of brass buttons made streetcar men walk a little taller. So prized were the jobs that trolley companies could demand strict adherence to standards of behavior, by banning smoking, drinking, gambling, and swearing. Even walking into a saloon while in uniform was grounds for a conductor to be fired.[25]

The trolleys' ubiquity was deliberate. Their owners had no other source of revenue than the farebox, so maximizing loads was the key to profits and—as debts through consolidation proliferated—to merely breaking even. It was not unusual for a trolley line to set up its own amusement park, skating rink, or resort to build ridership; a 1907 census of electric railways found 467 such parks in existence, visited by over fifty million people a year. Taking city folk out into the country also provided a golden opportunity to interest them in a few suburban building lots the line's land development subsidiary just happened to have available.[26]

As demand grew, so did pressure to expand the size of the thirty-foot streetcar, whose base had been kept short in order to negotiate sharp curves better. Soon, articulated cars—jointed in the middle—emerged, to allow two wheelbases to function as one car. As cars lengthened, the traditional entryways at either end of the car yielded to entrances at the center of the car, with wider doors and low steps to accommodate the long hoop skirts of the era.[27] Steel-sided cars gradually replaced wooden ones, which had been particularly vulnerable to sideswipes and shearing blows, from which some cars actually collapsed.[28]

CZAR INSULL

Americans love progress, and throughout U.S. history, national expositions of technology have had a way of nudging the future. So it was with the 1893 Columbian Exposition in Chicago, a city that built its first coal-burning, steam-powered elevated railway in 1892, partly to transport people and partly to put forth its best face to the country. In 1895, in keeping with the tenor of the times, its owners electrified the "El" and built it out to Logan Square, Garfield Park, and Lake Street.[29] Soon afterward, an Englishman arrived who would cut a wide swath through Chicago's transit history.

Samuel Insull, born into modest circumstances in 1859, became at twenty-two the private secretary to Thomas Edison, apprenticing alongside Frank Sprague with one of the century's true geniuses. Within a decade, Insull found himself entrusted with the management of all of Edison's commercial enterprises.

Short of stature but grand of vision, Insull moved to Chicago in 1892, turning down a vice-presidency in General Electric to become the president of the Chicago Edison Company. Soon electric lights burned in thousands of homes and businesses in Chicago and many other parts of the rapidly expanding Midwest, fed by Insull's company and its subsidiaries. Studying how to maximize the use of the huge generating capacity his new steam-electric turbine was churning out, Insull observed that electric usage dipped markedly during the early morning and late afternoon, when commuters were on their way to and from work. It was a short jump to the conclusion that he could sell this excess capacity in volume to electric streetcar companies at rates low enough to monopolize the market. Insull dubbed his concept "massing production"; his publicists would shorten it to "mass production."[30]

Insull had no interest in the streetcar business itself, but with Yerkes gone from the scene, too many competing owners floated in a sea of red ink, trying to carve up the transit pie. "Unify or die" became the rallying cry, and by 1911, the dour, avuncular Insull reluctantly agreed to manage the unified company and become, in effect, Chicago's transit czar, in part to protect his off-peak market. Spearheading the unsuccessful opposition was a young People's Traction League organizer, Harold Ickes, who two decades later would help fashion America's highway expansion as part of President Franklin Roosevelt's "brain trust."[31] Years later, Insull bought the debt-ridden company, introducing such successful innovations as free transfers among its four lines, a convenience that other cities rushed to copy.

AN AUTOMAKER SAVES THE TROLLEYS

The early trolley companies were nearly all owned by private interests. But as cities came to depend on them, many developed money problems from inept financing or management. Those that survived usually did so by selling out to the cities that needed them. Ironically, an automobile pioneer led Detroit to become one of the first cities to take over a trolley line. And he had a very different reason.

On a summer day in 1918, James Couzens, a photogenic mayoral candidate, who argued that Detroit ought to run its own trolleys, rounded up a herd of press photographers before boarding a city streetcar and staging a deliberate confrontation. The Detroit Urban Railway (DUR) had played into his hands by hiking its traditional fare from five to six cents. Couzens handed the conductor a nickel, dramatically refusing to pay the extra penny. The mayoral hopeful provoked the conductor into physically pushing him off the car as flashbulbs popped and reporters raced to the telephones. Front-page coverage of the event led to several days of rioting in Detroit streets and editorial broadsides against the candidate for grandstanding a volatile issue.

On the surface, Couzens was an unlikely figure to be bucking the motor city's ruling elite. Henry Ford's right-hand man for finance knew that his company's prosperity depended on maximizing sales of motor vehicles in competition with Ford's rivals. But Couzens had also watched the growing traffic congestion in greater Detroit, as car production far outstripped government's ability to build roads to ride on. Automaking as an industry is space intensive, so Ford, GM, Hudson, and Chalmers all had staked out industrial enclaves far outside the city on which to locate their plants, some of which employed a hundred thousand workers or more.

"Little Short of Treason"

While executives and some skilled workers could afford to buy homes not far from their work, lower-paid laborers were economically trapped in older urban tenement districts and were unable to buy even Ford's "people's cars." Commutes of up to two hours each way on an overtaxed trolley system led to turnover and chronic lateness. Ironically, the auto industry depended for its prosperity on the health of a competing mode.

The city establishment was up in arms over Couzens's publicity stunt. Its mouthpiece, the *Detroit Saturday Night,* even invoked the ongoing war in Europe in a bristling editorial: "To bellow about tearing up street railway tracks . . . and disorganizing the entire street railway traffic in times when the boys [are] over there . . . is little short of treason." Yet Couzens prevailed in a four-way race and, as mayor, doggedly pursued the public ownership scheme. By March 1922, the DUR saw the handwriting on the wall and sold out to the city of Detroit for $19.9 million, as Detroit took ownership of 373 miles of track. In so doing, it became only the third major American city, following San Francisco and Seattle, to own its own streetcar system. Over the next decades that number would mushroom until public ownership accounted for more than 90 percent of all mass transit rides.[32]

Before long, Couzens would catapult from the Detroit mayoralty to the U.S. Senate, where the veteran automaker would use his public position to help the motor industry he had fought for so often win the battle to motorize the cities, by beating down the forces that sought to regulate motor transport (see chapter 8).

BIRTH OF THE INTERURBANS

Electricity had, in short order, transformed not only urban transportation but the structure of cities themselves. Trolley conductors laughed as they passed still-primitive gas-powered motorcars stalled on dirt roads, their bent-over, goggled drivers turning cranks at the front of the vehicle with caution so the engine's recoil would not break an arm. Yet for travel between cities, the steam railroads still held sway as the sun set on the nineteenth century. A population explosion would insure that their dominance was short-lived.

Greater and greater waves of European immigrants disembarked at Atlantic ports as the century turned, clutching their German cuckoo clocks and remnants of Irish lace as they sought a better life. America was swelling by 1.3 million people a year—not only as a result of immigration but also because Americans were living longer and having more babies. Farmers, plugged into the world now by telegraph, telephone, and rural free mail delivery, were no longer content to stay down on the farm and sought the attractions beckoning from the scores of new cities that the steam railroads had created. In short, the country was an overflowing cornucopia of people on the move. "Have token, will travel" was music to the ears of streetcar promoters, for whom volume held the key to profit. If electric rail travel had succeeded in the cities and their burgeoning suburbs, they asked themselves, would it not work on longer trips between cities as well?

The Interurban—A Brawnier Trolley

Thus was born a new type of railway, with a name—*interurbans*—popularized by Charles L. Henry, an attorney and an Indiana congressman. Brawnier first cousins of the trolleys, these closed passenger trains were heavier and faster than the rickety, open-sided trolleys that filled city streets. An interurban was formidable on approach, leading with its basketball-sized arc headlamp perched above a cowcatcher, blue flashes sparking from its roof whenever the trolley wheel lost contact with the overhead wire. Crowning the open motorman's platform was a high, rounded roof with rows of miniwindows for ventilation at the clerestory level. In the cities, interurbans ran down the center of the street, while outside the city limits, they typically hugged the curb, operating quietly on their own right of way, without the soot, smoke, or noise of the steam railroads.[33] To the consumer, the idea itself was electric: while interurbans traveled at two-thirds the speed of the hated railroads, they ran four to six times more frequently at half to two-thirds the fare.[34]

Unlike railroads, interurbans were easily and inexpensively built. In the 1890s, a promoter could construct one to run on city streets for as little as ten thousand dollars a mile, opening the field to a wider array of investors than the very rich. Starting in 1897 with a short line between Anderson and Alexandria, Indiana, Henry expanded his own project into one of the country's most important interurbans, the Union Traction Company. In 1902 he sold his holdings and bought the Indianapolis and Cincinnati Traction Company.

The Lure of Debt Financing

Once a promoter could satisfy the state that he had substantial capital and that he had secured a franchise from the towns along his route, he had to beat the bushes for financing. But promoters soon fell into some of the same mistakes that had plunged the railroads into red ink. Rather than selling stock, they often marketed bonds, which became a debt of the company. Stockholders have to be repaid only through profits and growth; bondholders are entitled to their promised return, no matter what.

Not that promoters always had a choice; investors considered interurbans much less attractive investments than railroads. Too often, interurban developers would give away their securities as an inducement to bondholders or spread it among the promoters as a gift, thus watering the stock.[35] And if interurban owners mimicked the financial hijinks of their railroad brethren, they sometimes sought to live like them as well, building palace cars with inlaid wood, rosewood paneling, stained-glass windows, wicker furniture, and lettering in gold leaf.[36]

The railroads could not have been expected to welcome their new competitors with open arms, since lower fares and frequent scheduling led three-quarters of all railroad passengers to bolt to the interurbans. Larger railroads, particularly the Pennsylvania and New York Central, regularly asked courts to stop the interurbans from crossing their tracks. Fistfights and other violence grew common. When interurban construction workers attempted to cross the tracks of the California Northwestern, for instance, one of its engineers scalded them with blasts of live steam.[37]

Interurbans More Popular Than Cars

The automobile and the interurbans developed at about the same time, but the interurbans surged ahead quickly. Until motor vehicles became more reliable, offered good springs and pneumatic tires, and were supported by the availability of paved roads, the boom that ten years later would sweep across America would be delayed. When William C. Durant, the founder of General Motors, predicted to an investment banker in 1908 that the auto industry would eventually produce a half-million cars a year, the banker quickly showed Durant to the door.

And so the frenzied interurban boom continued. Ohio alone chartered 144 electric railway companies from 1898 to 1901. As a writer of the time noted, "It is impossible for anyone who was not living in a rural community where there was no thought or knowledge of automobiles but where the community had the possibility of getting an electric line to realize the vision which such a possibility encouraged."[38]

Henry A. Everett and Edward W. Moore fueled the fires of ambition by building an interurban empire, which by 1900 was capitalized at $47 million and is said to have netted $5.5 million a year. Now everyone wanted in on the act and did not care about the competition. The Kansas City Clay County and St. Joseph was built even though six railroads already operated passenger trains between the termini.[39] Indianapolis had thirteen separate lines radiating from its downtown, Toledo nine, and Dayton eight.[40]

Each new railway that jumped into the swim, of course, diluted the pool of passengers on which they all depended. About 35 percent of interurban mileage represented independent owners, while larger corporate interests, including electric power companies, pyramiding holding companies, and steam railroads controlled the majority. Railroads bought interurbans to develop a unified electric and steam railroad passenger service and to add feeder lines to their operation.[41]

Because one could get involved relatively cheaply, local interests such as the Bamberger lines in Utah were able to prosper, at least in the short term. Carl L. Van Doren, an Urbana, Illinois, physician, built an interurban line and would live to regret it. H. J. Heinz, who made a fortune on pickles and catsup, was a partner in the Winona Traction Company of Indiana, formed for religious reasons—to transport congregations to Winona Lake to hear sermons by the evangelist Billy Sunday.[42]

Overbuilding, together with the roller-coaster economy of the early twentieth century, caused many interurban companies to go under before the first train had run. The Toledo, Ann Arbor and Detroit Railroad had graded forty-six of its fifty miles on its Toledo-to-Ann Arbor run, placed all but one bridge abutment, finished its powerhouse nearly to the roof, and laid seventeen miles of track and seven miles of poles when its financing dried up. In spite of later owners' attempts to resuscitate the project, electric trains were never to ride its lines.[43]

Henry's Indianapolis and Cincinnati Traction Company eventually went into receivership and never could raise funds to build further. For the next quarter century, as automobiles cast an increasingly large shadow, Henry would battle against steepening odds to make interurbans work. He was among many at the time who believed automobiles to be only a passing fancy. In a 1916 speech, he predicted: "The fad feature of automobile riding will gradually wear off and the time will soon be here when a very large part of the people will cease to think of automobile rides and the interurbans will carry their old time allotment of passengers." One might forgive Henry for not crediting the fact that in the same year, Congress had embarked on a national road-building campaign. But by 1927, when Detroit produced nearly 2.3 million cars a year and a nationwide network of two hundred thousand miles of paved roads was more than half built, Henry (who would die later that year) was still trying gamely to extend his northern interurban line to Cincinnati.[44]

AN "AIR LINE" FROM CHICAGO TO NEW YORK

Perhaps the grandest example of a failed promise was the visionary 1906 project of the Chicago–New York Electric Air Line Railroad, which planned to double-track a seventy-five-mile-an-hour interurban between the two cities of its name. The Air Line employed wooden cars lettered "New York" on the front and "Chicago" on the back. Its owners published the "Air Line News" to garner interest in the project, the marketing marvel of its time. Its Air Line Stockholders' Association formed fifty vacation camps throughout the United States to rally support for the scheme.

The Air Line planned numerous shuttles from smaller towns to feed the main line to insure high volume. But whereas interurbans of the day kept costs low by running fairly level routes between cities, the Air Line planned to fight topography head on—in one case, by building a fill 1,800 feet wide at the base and two miles long—to avoid a grade. Such an undertaking threw off cost projections wildly. Yet in spite of looming deficits, the Air Line's stockholders stuck by the project.

Even with the advantage of no bonded debt, the company's outlandish construction costs finally forced it into bankruptcy in 1915. Whereas some interurbans were building for as little as $20,000 a mile, the Air Line management in 1909 reported average per-mile construction costs of $334,310 for its Indiana lines.[45]

Los Angeles—City of Rails?

Interurban competition made and destroyed men of its era, yet it typically involved comparatively small financial stakes. But a West Coast player was about to jump into the fray, bankrolled with a staggering $100 million in 1900 dollars. The big money battle that would rage over the next decade in California would transform life in that state and, for the next century, make its transportation network unlike any other.

As Henry Huntington turned fifty, it was becoming clear that he would never realize his one burning ambition in life. His uncle Collis Huntington, who was married to a woman thirty-three years his junior but still childless, had taken Henry under his wing and taught him the railroad business. It was taken for granted that when Collis died, Henry would take the helm of the prosperous Southern Pacific Railroad—taken for granted, that is, by all but that railway's financial backers.

Major bondholders and stockholders of the Southern Pacific just did not like Henry. They prevailed on Collis to "sacrifice" his nephew for the good of the company, by removing him as first vice-president. In an era when investors were increasingly calling the shots, they forced Collis to accede. But Collis gradually solidified his control over the giant railway, and when he felt secure enough, he again named his protégé a vice president. But then, with the birth of a new century, the elder Huntington died. He left his stock holdings to his widow, Arabella, and nephew Henry, whose balding head, full white moustache, and austere mien would have fit well into a portrait gallery of railroad presidents. But such was not to be. When the financiers once more blocked Henry's passage to the president's chair, he decided in frustration to sell out completely.

Huntington Meets Harriman

Southern Pacific stock had sold for thirty-two dollars a share when Collis died in 1900. So when an unimpressive-looking easterner appeared, offering Henry Huntington fifty dollars a share, it was truly a reversal of fortune. In other circumstances, the two men might have become fast friends. E. H. Harriman and Henry Huntington were nearly the same age, both had grown up in central New York State, and both were highly intelligent, forceful, and fiercely ambitious. And Harriman, in one stroke, had enriched Huntington by $50 million. Yet within a few short years, they would become blood enemies.

Arabella Huntington, the widow of Collis Huntington's May-October marriage, was only three years younger than Henry Huntington, and had sold out to Harriman for a similar price. Soon Henry had divorced his wife, married Arabella, and set out to build his own empire. If he could not run the fast-growing Southern Pacific, so be it. He had an even better idea—to create a land development company that would buy up land on the Los Angeles outskirts, increase its value by building interurban lines out to it, and then resell the enhanced land at huge profits.[46]

Huntington moved quickly to buy out Los Angeles County's streetcar operators. Before long, Harriman came to realize that the man he had paid so generously for his Southern Pacific interests was gearing up to compete against his steam trains. Not content to stay within Los Angeles County, Huntington planned to extend electric railways from San Diego north to San Francisco via coastal and inland routes, much of which would duplicate the old Southern Pacific routes. Even more threatening, Huntington abandoned the use of conventional narrow-gauge streetcar track in favor of the four-foot, eight-and-a-half-inch standard-gauge track the railroads used and had the money to buy his own right of way, rather than having to use existing streets. If Harriman guessed that this would let Huntington use freight trains to compete for the lucrative Southern Pacific business, he had read Huntington's mind.[47]

"I am a foresighted man," Huntington observed. "And I believe Los Angeles is destined to become the most important city in this country if not in the world. It can extend in any direction as far as you like. . . . We will join this whole region into one big family."[48] Huntington hired Southern Pacific's former executive vice-president Epes Randolph to head his electric railway system. In the fall of 1901, he incorporated the Pacific Electric Railway Company and soon thereafter built his first line, to Long Beach twenty miles away, then improved the rail line from Los Angeles to Pasadena.

In a day when rural farmers were glad to donate land to streetcar companies who promised to stop near their farm, Huntington paid fifty thousand dollars for a right of way through some walnut orchards to extend a line into Whittier. An indication of the local reception was an editorial by the *Whittier Register*: "Whittier in its matchless location on a hillside now feels the pulsing life of the commercial world in being united to the metropolis of Southern California by the completion of the electric railway." Much less expensive to build than the steam trains, the interurbans could thus run much more frequently than trains and soon proved wildly popular. Pacific Electric hired as one of its conductors young Frank Nixon, a Whittier boy whose son, Richard, would become better known than his father.[49]

A Battle Royal

As trade burgeoned during the prosperity of the century's early years, coastal California boomed, and cargo from abroad steamed into its ports. Part of Harriman's plans for hegemony of the western steam railroad lines included control of the harbor of San Pedro, even though it was being built as a port open to all. Getting wind of Harriman's plans, Huntington drove his crews relentlessly right through one long weekend and crossed Southern Pacific's right of way, stretching its tracks into San Pedro before the company could obtain a court injunction.[50]

Soon, readers of Los Angeles dailies were following the thrusts and parries of the two antagonists as they traded commercial blows. First, Harriman's Southern Pacific in 1903 bought large blocks of Pacific Electric stock, to obstruct Huntington's plans. Later that year, he outbid Huntington for street railway franchises that Huntington sought, paying an outlandish $110,000 for rights worth $10,000.

The next day, to stop the bloodletting, Harriman and Huntington met to work out an uneasy alliance: Harriman's Los Angeles Traction Company and interurban properties would be merged into Pacific Electric. Harriman would receive 40.3 percent of Pacific Electric's stock, making the two bitter antagonists equal partners and letting Southern Pacific control the system's growth. The compromise actually met both men's needs: Huntington's to support his real estate development activities and Harriman's to develop a short-line feeder network for the Southern Pacific.

But then, to avoid Harriman's influence, Huntington set up and then split off the Los Angeles Inter-Urban Railway Company and the Pacific Electric Land Company, controlling all the stock in the new corporations himself. Gradually Huntington snaked his electric railway lines out from Los Angeles to numerous settlements—Glendale, Riverside, San Bernardino—which soon grew populous, and he bought established lines to expand his influence. Huntington and Harriman continued to compete until 1908. But Huntington's devotion to art and other enterprises led him ultimately to sell out—ironically, to the Southern Pacific in 1910.

Other parties were to complete Huntington's interurban lines, but he had laid in place an unprecedented thousand-mile spiderweb of tracks, some extending as much as sixty miles from central Los Angeles. Decades later, when Southern California built its first freeways, most of their routes would parallel the "big red car" lines, where weeds soon would shade rusting tracks and rotting ties.

In most large twentieth-century cities, the need for business to concentrate created vertical cities, even as they expanded at the edges. So powerful an influence on Los Angeles was Huntington that the essential need of his business to disperse created a horizontal city. And his awesome resources made Huntington's empire a caricature of what was happening—though more modestly—throughout America.[51]

THE AUTOMOBILE SPELLS DOOM

How such an efficient mode of transport was born, pervaded American society, and died—all barely within a half century—is more than the story of progress on the move. Trolleys and interurbans copied the financial legerdemain of the freight railroads. Yet they lacked the profits to absorb the huge debt they took on through such devices as watering stock, for passengers and package trade bring in less money than freight. Indeed, competition and overbuilding required that they cut fares to the bone—often suicidally. As unions gained a foothold, their demands for higher wages and job protection added to the debit side of trolley ledgers.

And an industry that took relatively little to get into drew some unsophisticated managers, who simply did a poor job of running their companies.

In addition, by the teens streetcars were competing with motorized transport, which traveled on roads built and paid for by all the taxpayers, while streetcar owners had constructed and paid taxes for their own lines. Railroads, accurately sensing interurbans as a threat, did everything possible to stand in their way. Once the motor industry realized that in the cities lay the last masses of people yet unconverted to the auto culture, it would do its best to deliver the coup de grace.[52]

And if cutthroat competition prevailed in the passenger trade, it was even more intense in the carriage of the nation's freight, where there was vastly more money to be made. When the first farmer removed the rear seat from his new car to haul produce to the market, the die was cast. The age of trucking had begun.

·5·

MOTORING FOR PROFIT: THE BIRTH OF TRUCKING

The highway will never be a competitor of the railway. . . . Far from being a danger to the railroads, the highways we are building will be their faithful allies.

—Thomas H. MacDonald, 1923

The problem arising out of the sudden increase of motor vehicles presents extraordinary difficulties. As yet nobody knows what should be done.

—Justice James C. McReynolds, U.S. Supreme Court, 1925

THE GATHERING DUSK SIGNALED TO HARRY WOODS THAT HIS WORK-day was about to begin, so the stocky young redhead climbed into the cab of his truck. He had just haggled with a local freight broker, who finally agreed to pay Harry eight dollars a ton to haul eight tons of dry goods from Chicago to New York. Now his thoughts turned to the route he would take. He knew he could head east to Pittsburgh, take Route 22 to Philadelphia, through New Jersey into New York. But if he went by the northerly route instead, with any luck he could avoid the state police.

Woods, a gypsy trucker, "flew by night." Like 150,000 other one-man wildcat truckers in the 1920s and 1930s, Harry Woods lived by his wits. Several times he had gone to jail—overloaded trucks, improper license, insufficient waybills. He had learned to keep his eyes open. Eighty-five miles outside Chicago, he stopped by a café in Walkerton, Indiana, for a cup of coffee. There he compared notes with fellow wildcatters. Are any roads out? Where are the troopers hiding? Do you know anybody in New York who can give me a backhaul? Just inside the Ohio border, Woods took a brief rest at Bob and Hazel's truck stop in Bryan, then stopped for gas at Ted's in Sandusky, near Lake Erie. His odometer told him he had gone 310 miles, which let him know he was getting about five miles a gallon.

A gypsy trucker since high school, Harry had learned which truck stop operators could be trusted and which would rat on him to the police. He could trust Ted, for instance; word had it that he used to be a bootlegger. Everybody, it seemed, was getting into trucking, and truck stops had sprung up to meet their needs: hot meals, companionship, bulletin boards to pass messages among truckers, showers, even bunks at some.

Woods, now bone tired after two full days of travel, sustained only by catnaps and coffee, had managed five hundred miles. His bruised body ached from bouncing over rough roads on a hard leather seat. His chest was sore; he had to operate the double stick-shift with his sternum and right hand while steering with his left. The New York police were more casual than the tough Pennsylvania troopers, so Harry relaxed now, visiting a while at Little Em's and Little Mike's Truck Stop in Little Falls, New York, then reaching New York City by the morning of the fifth day of his trip. His cargo unloaded, Woods drove to a phone booth on Tenth Avenue, gave a man two dollars, and received in return the location of a company that needed a load hauled back to the Midwest. Of his pay for the haul to New York, Harry had about thirty dollars left, and much of that would go for gasoline, food, and truck expenses on the way home.[1]

To Be One's Own Boss

If the railroads were tailor-made for the rich and the Horatio Algers, trucks held out an elusive brass ring to the common man. The average

Joe might become a wage slave for a railroad, but for just a few hundred dollars down payment, he could buy a truck for $2,000 to $5,000, take eighteen months to pay, and become the captain of his fate. By the late 1920s—the heyday of the independent trucker—two-thirds of the three million trucks on American roads were operator-owned. Those who owned most of the rest had five trucks or fewer. For millions, it was the American dream come true.

But most people entering this atomistic new industry were unschooled in the ways of business, so they often failed. Many under-priced their service, figuring out only what they would need to have left after paying for gas, oil, and food. Forgetting or not knowing how to amortize their truck loans and insurance and to set aside a reserve for repairs put many truckers quickly on the skids. But for every trucker who went under, another hopeful young man emerged to buy his rig and take his chances.[2]

Why Trucking Grew

In the late 1910s and early 1920s, trucking grew like a field of weeds, for several reasons: entry into the industry took little money or skill, the heavy hand of government had not yet set up standards to keep people out, trucking offered an inherent flexibility of movement railroads could not match, railways had more business than they could handle, Americans were enjoying a technology-driven consumer revolution, and the profile of American cities was changing.

As America prepared to enter the First World War in 1917, the Wilson administration had focused on how to mobilize the railroads for wartime. Already 325,000 trucks dotted the rutted paths that passed for roads, but they were prone to breakdowns; and the new federal road-building pro-gram had not had time to construct many. Europe, at war since 1914, had tooled its factories to mass-produce motorized vehicles for the war effort. By the end of hostilities, the British alone had contributed 56,000 trucks, 23,000 automobiles, and 34,000 motorcycles and motorbikes.[3] But if American truckmakers were eager to meet the need, the near paralysis of the clogged rail lines meant that thousands of new trucks had to creep to the East Coast under their own power, over nearly impassable roads. By the time 50,000 American trucks finally reached France in 1918, hostili-ties had virtually ended.[4]

l taken over the railroads com-
s. Those who made domestic
ons on raw materials, down to
trucking factories were encour-
be saying to the hundreds of
re really not much help to the
the domestic load off the rail-
and materiel to Europe.
es. The national truck popula-
one. To urban businesses using
obvious and revolutionary. No
and wagon to the depot to pick
ery was door to door. Breakage
d been eliminated. And unlike
ers could undercut rail rates at
s their lines back in 1920, they
ed to truck transport for good.[5]
ustomers turned out to be the
for hauling produce from the
years marked new highs for
rriers welcomed anything that
oading docks and railyards, as
y too glad to oblige.

Os lounged on front porches of
eir Sears catalogs, as Pierce-
then streets, sending up clouds
idless—sewing machines, cof-
n makers, washing machines.
ding to what a shipment was
truckers won from them con-
is, they were taking away the

cream of the crop.[6]

In the early years of the century, large businesses dependent on rail freight typically located near a rail siding or the depot itself. But as cities grew in population, they expanded from the core. New businesses set up on the outskirts; downtown manufacturers needing space for expansion moved to the urban fringe, where land was cheaper. To those manufacturers, no longer a stone's throw from the railroad station, transport of incoming shipments took on new importance. Railroads generally considered truckers helpful in carting the goods from the depot to their final destination. It occurred to few rail carriers that for many truckers, this was the foot in the door. When the rails brought goods from Gary, Indiana, to Chicago, motorized rigs at first carted them the few miles to their buyer in the Windy City. Very soon, though, that buyer was accepting the truckers' offer to drive to Gary and carry the shipment the whole way.

INDEPENDENT TRUCKERS ABOUND

Jack Keeshin was among thousands of young men competing with the railroads for their less-than-carload freight. Invited not to return to high school after a corridor slugfest, Keeshin rode the rails for a while, then accepted an offer of a team of dappled-gray mares he could use to haul produce to Southside Chicago for his father's vegetable business. Expanding his operation to four teams while still a teenager, he traded them in for a Grabowski motor truck and founded the Keeshin Southwest Motor Company in 1918.

In his memoirs, Keeshin describes the life of an early trucker whose rig held a two-cylindered, chain-driven engine with carriage lamps and isinglass windshields: "When I would drive those trucks over cobbled streets, and over mud roads as well, after five or six miles I'd have to get off the seat and rub my back for fear my kidneys would fall out." In an age before service stations, drivers did not dare travel without an extra set of chains, additional jack shafts, plenty of wire, and a can of ether to loosen oil, which commonly congealed in the crankcase when the truck was not in use. Keeshin recalled:

How many times I had to build a bonfire under the crankcase, and when I had done so, and lit that match, I had to make sure that the ether was already in the petcocks, and that I was ready to crank the motor and jump right in. Otherwise, if one didn't start right away and get the truck off the fire it meant only one thing—being blown to Kingdom Come!

"In those days, when a trucker had a bill of lading in his pocket and he was sent out on delivery," Keeshin said, "nothing stopped him." Hauling eighteen thousand pounds of Fig Newtons on a six-day trip from Chicago to South Bend, Indiana, a distance of only ninety miles, he found himself mired in sand near a cemetery just beyond Michigan City. He reported:

> I was determined to get my load through, so I saw no alternative to going into the cemetery in the wee hours of the night so as to pull up about twenty-five small headstones which I put beneath the wheels of the truck in order to pull out of the mud or sand. . . . The police kindly let me get my truck to the plant for unloading, and, eventually, the people found it in their heart to forgive the impetuous spirit of Jack Keeshin, who never violated a cemetery again![7]

The competitive pressures on independents such as Jack Keeshin's company were enormous. Not only did they have to learn business methods by the seat of their pants and compete against many others for the same business, but the lack of predictable backhauls could wipe out temporary profits overnight. Arriving in Chicago after a ten-day trip from New York to find no load available to truck back East was disheartening, if not disastrous.

So, many one-truck operators sought shelter by affiliating with larger trucking companies such as United Motor Lines or Allied Trucking, which commonly insured their shipments, guaranteed return loads, tutored unsophisticated truckers in business methods, and hired local agents to follow through on damage claims. By the late 1920s United, for example, had a network of 110 trucks and ten warehouses spread over a 1,200-mile area. Consolidated truckers, through efficiency and stable rates, hoped to be able to compete with price-slashing gypsies, who may have priced themselves out of business but also drained patronage from those trying to live within the law.

A Field Day for Lone Rangers

Yet for those lone rangers who chose to fly solo, the opportunities were as abundant as the challenges were daunting. While some fell by the wayside, others prospered. Relatively few independents, in fact, lived outside the law—perhaps only 5 percent. Yet because they usually charged below-market rates, they exerted an effect on the market out of proportion to their numbers. At one time, itinerant truck peddlers hauled 60 percent of America's fruits and vegetables. In eastern-central states, wildcatters often drove directly to coalfields, loaded trailers with ungraded coal, and trucked it directly to private homes in the cities, sometimes driving retail coal dealers out of business.

Others, such as Keeshin, operated legitimately and developed sound business practices that allowed them to stay afloat as others were going under. Keeshin developed a reputation for handling shipments efficiently and paying damage claims promptly. Awakened in the middle of the night to learn that one of his trucks had crashed and burned, Keeshin pressed his crews into action, duplicating the fourteen lost shipments immediately at his own expense and loading them onto another trailer. Keeshin later boasted that they arrived only six hours behind schedule.[8] Keeshin, whose men in 1920 hauled twenty-five trailers, a decade later had a hundred plying newly paved highways throughout the Midwest and grossed a half-million dollars a year.[9]

The experiences of independent truckers on the frontier of this new industry are as varied as the individuals themselves. John F. Ernsthausen of Norwalk, Ohio, adapted the back of his 1909 Overland in 1913 to deliver eggs, made enough money to buy out several other independent truckers, then lost everything in the high-rolling days of the stockmarket of the 1920s. Carl Ozee left the railways in 1911 to work his way up in his father-in-law's cartage firm in Mattoon, Illinois. By offering faster service than the railroads, Ozee managed to land Procter and Gamble as a customer, and by the mid-1930s his 2,200 trucks and trailers were on the road in six states. Lillie and Willard Drennan of Hempstead, Texas, were supporting themselves quite nicely in 1929 hauling for the oil fields, when Willard died suddenly, leaving his wife to support the family. Undeterred, Lillie strapped on a six-shooter for protection, climbed into the cab, and carried on the business, becoming the first licensed woman truck driver.[10]

Trucks existed basically to serve the railroads, said the conventional wisdom of the day. They posed little threat to their rail brethren in hauling goods twenty miles or more, both because the trucks of the time broke down so often and because American roads were still largely unimproved. Thus, railroads welcomed the early truckers, since short hauls were unprofitable for the railroads. Yet at the same time, entrepreneurs such as Jack Keeshin and Harry Woods were quietly, determinedly extending their range to hundreds of miles. Unlike the railroad owners, who had to seek permission every time they changed a rate, these truckers were beholden to no one and could undercut rail rates at will. Perhaps the rail analysts of the day had failed to factor in the sheer tenacity of working people who have that rare chance to make it as their own bosses.[11]

WASHINGTON, STATES LINK ARMS

Just as ominous to railways should have been the popularity of the federal roads program, which in 1921 led Congress to declare as national policy that smooth-surfaced roads would link every county seat in the nation—that era's equivalent of pledging to land a man on the moon (see chapter 3). And moving to the forefront of the lobbying effort were some unlikely power brokers—the engineers from the American Association of State Highway Officials (AASHO). Their quiet marshaling of facts had convinced Washington to split the cost of a system of national routes, yet to let the states themselves choose where it would go. This device calmed the fears of those who worried that the federal government wanted to create and control its own national highway system, as some European nations had done. Only 7 percent of all state roads would qualify, eventually creating a two-hundred-thousand-mile federal-state system. In the 1950s, its major roads would be folded into the interstate highway system.[12]

Now, instead of enduring narrow earthen pathways whose bumps made the driver's teeth rattle, Keeshin and Woods and their ilk could move farther, faster on graded roads with drainage and curbs. The new highways were yet a far cry from the interstates; America's vast expanse made concrete and asphalt surfaces prohibitively expensive at the outset except for heavily trafficked roads. But truckers could comfortably haul a load of watermelons 200 miles, competing with the rails far beyond the 20-mile short haul some considered the limit of their capacity. And as they proliferated, truck stops and gasoline stations—in rural areas sometimes located right outside their owners' homes—sprang up to service the new trade.

The Myth of Truckers as Short Haulers

As early as 1917, the Beam Fletcher Corporation operated 22 five-ton White trucks between Philadelphia and New York, carrying 400 tons a day. In 1918, the Liberty Highway Company set up a motor express route between Toledo and Detroit, with a four-wheel-drive Walter truck hauling 3 five-ton trailers. In 1917 and 1918, the Goodyear Tire and Rubber Company ran its trucks around the clock from Akron to as far as Boston.[13] By the mid-1920s, trucking had become America's largest wholesale producing industry, ranking ahead of such giants as gasoline, rubber, and meatpacking. By then, the blossoming industry handed paychecks to five million and attracted $2 billion in Wall Street money.[14]

Yet the curious myth persisted into the mid-1920s that trucks were destined to be simply adjuncts to the railroads. While Detroit was working double shifts and new road graders and rollers were trundling along the byways of every state, those railroaders without imagination looked about them and saw that only a small number of roads had been improved and that most trucks were still primitive conveyances, with solid rubber tires and cushions with few springs. "There was a constant tendency to believe that conditions had stabilized, a failure to see the basic nature of the secular trend downward."[15]

Good Roads Energize Automakers

Nothing energized Detroit like the federal commitment to good roads embodied in the 1916 and 1921 highway acts (see chapter 6), ensuring that trucks would not remain unreliable and uncomfortable for long. Advancements in refrigeration, beginning with such rudimentary forms as grass and sawdust insulation and barrels of water and ice, extended the distances that trucks could carry perishables. Electric headlights and tail lamps replaced oil and acetylene lamps, making it safe to drive at night. The pneumatic tire, together with smoother roads, vastly increased the comfort and thus the scope of truck travel.[16]

As early as 1918, some highway builders sensed the profound implications of the trucking industry. Charles Upham, Delaware's chief highway engineer, spoke for most state highway department heads when he warned that heavy use of trucks was more than a wartime phenomenon: "The heavy truck will be utilized for transporting freight and express within expanding limits. Therefore, we must build and maintain in such a way that our roads will withstand as permanently as possible, the demands of future heavy truck traffic."[17] Then, just as the trucking industry picked up speed, a former automaker raced to the aid of the truckers' competitors, the railroads.

A PROGRESSIVE REPENTS

The First World War had been a boon to the railroads. Washington had not only assured them a generous profit while under government control, but running the railroads had taught the federal government much about railroad economics. Never again would the industry have to face a united populist movement whose leaders simply did not understand the business they were railing against. The wartime experience taught Congress, first, how vital the steel arteries of rail transportation were and, second, that they would atrophy without the ability to attract private capital.

Senator Albert Cummins had lost little of his antirailroad fervor during wartime (see the prologue and chapter 2). He was determined, as leader of the Interstate Commerce Commission (ICC), not to see the rails returned to private hands once the troops returned home. He was concerned, he said, about the "great army of widows and orphans" who owned railroad securities, but he felt that "they had no more right to excessive profits than millionaires." His committee debated scenarios ranging from the status quo to a return to private ownership to consolidation into one giant private rail system—everything, in fact, but loosening Washington's regulatory hold on the companies. Three decades after Congress created the ICC, its continued pervasive effect on the industry was taken as a given.

But Cummins lacked the votes to nationalize the rails. And becoming the chairman of the commission in 1918 made Cummins focus on the importance to the nation of keeping the railroads going. And that would take capital. "In the situation as it is today," a financial editor wrote, "the roads could not borrow in the private market, any more than the nominal government of Russia could borrow."[18] Cummins wanted to maintain the weak roads without giving excessive returns to the strong. "Declaring that it was too late to punish anyone for the mistakes of the past," Cummins said all railroads should be consolidated into sixteen systems that would compete with one another and would be guaranteed a rate of return. Senator Robert LaFollette, Cummins's ally through the years, was apoplectic (see the prologue and chapter 2). The bill would "let loose an orgy of railroad manipulations," the Wisconsin legislator said. "Jay Gould would turn green with envy if he could see how his successors . . . are about to exploit the people."

History would credit Cummins with passage of the 1920 Transportation Act, since he chaired the committee that wrote it. Ironically, little in it was to Cummins's liking: the idea of linking rail lines into systems with a transportation board overseeing them had died. The act sanctioned theretofore-invidious pooling, exempted railroads from the antitrust laws, and instructed the ICC to consolidate the nation's railroads into a limited number of systems, a step the ICC would never get around to. Most importantly, Washington assured the industry and Wall Street of a 5.5 percent to 6 percent profit margin, with any surplus being used to offset the deficits of weaker, less productive railroads. And to avoid crippling rate wars, the 1920 act let Congress set minimum freight rates.[19]

Detroit Spoils Rails' Revival

But no sooner had the railroad received what it considered long-overdue relief and recognition from the nation, than a new threat emerged, far more potent than the allied opposition of all the angry Progressive senators in Congress had been. "The auto and trucking industries, and not shippers or radical state legislatures, were to nullify the benefits to the railroads of the Transportation Act."[20]

It was the railroads' bad fortune to return to grace precisely at the time when the nation's population profile and lifestyles were undergoing a sea change that played directly into the hands of their chief competitor, the truckers. As the only carrier that could ship long distances into inland cities, the railroads now faced new logistical challenges created by consumerism and dispersed cities.

How easy it had been in the old days to roll up a railcar to the spout of a grain elevator, fill up the car, and deliver it to one destination. Rail managers now seemed equally concerned with less-than-carload (LCL) freight. Shipments of consumer goods in one car might be destined for six different buyers. And since the purchasers themselves might be in several different cities along the line, sorters had to be hired to make sure the first shipment off was the last one loaded. Expanding urban centers meant a shipment could not simply be rolled up to a rail siding, but a way had to be found to get it from the depot to its destination, often many blocks or a few miles away. In the linear world of the opening frontier, the railroad had been king. But dispersal demanded flexibility, and as ever, technology rose to the occasion, as inventors created in the truck a mode that met the market.

THE CRISIS OF CRUMBLING ROADS

Logan Page's near two decades of tireless promotion of better roads had paid off by 1918 (see chapter 3). Legislation was at last in place to create hard-surfaced roads. Drawing on the trailblazing work of such road engineers as Pierre Tresaguet of France and John McAdam and Thomas Telford of Great Britain, the Bureau of Public Roads (BPR) was designing roads suited to the modest wear and tear that local cars would cause. But then disturbing news began filtering into Page's Pennsylvania Avenue offices: the newly constructed roads were already falling apart. Page quickly dispatched BPR engineers across the country to assess the problem. The reports that filtered back were distressing.

Prevost Hubbard, a BPR expert on bituminous pavements, wrote to his boss: "Hundreds of miles of roads failed under the heavy [wartime] motor-truck traffic within a comparatively few weeks or months." The surface, whether bituminous, macadam, or concrete, did not seem to matter—disintegration was everywhere, Hubbard found. "These failures," he said, "were not only sudden but complete and almost overnight an excellent surface might become impassable."

It was becoming clear that the roads had not been designed for the heavy loads they were now carrying, largely because no one had expected the truck traffic that the war and the resultant trucking boom would produce. Democracies predictably react slowly to the need for change, and most states had not set realistic limits on the weight a truck could carry and mechanisms to enforce limits, where they did exist. Trucks could not increase their earnings by trailing many cars behind them, as could locomotives, but they could maximize their profit by overloading their trailers. By the late teens, cries arose that trucks were not paying their "fair share" of taxes, since all taxpayers paid to build roads whose existence had led to major profits for the truckers. It soon became clear that states must cap weights trucks could carry but also require tires that would cause less wear and tear. In response, rubber manufacturers rushed the pneumatic tire into production in the late teens.[21]

Page had been under a grueling pace for years, and as postwar pressures arose for Washington to step up its road building, highway interests looked to him to quarterback the effort through Congress. He had developed good rapport with the states through AASHO, and on December 9, 1918, he carried with him a newly drafted road-building bill supported by the Wilson administration to present to an AASHO executive board meeting in New York. But before he could address the meeting, he died of a sudden heart attack, and his death plunged the national road-building drive into confusion. A sign of how influential these road engineers had become was that Congress quickly accepted AASHO's nominee, Thomas Harris MacDonald, as Page's successor (see chapter 3).

MR. MACDONALD GOES TO WASHINGTON

Although MacDonald was only thirty-eight, he had headed Iowa's road-building program for fourteen years and had already served as AASHO's president. Short and built like a fireplug, MacDonald's hair had already begun to thin, lengthening his forehead. His eyes fixed intensely on whomever he directed his gaze at, and his lip line rarely wavered from the horizontal. MacDonald knew that Page, after his many years of federal service, received only $4,500 a year. Although eager for the challenge, MacDonald demanded $6,000 to move his family to Washington, D.C., no doubt sensing the magnitude of the task on which he was about to embark. Agriculture Secretary Henry Wallace (see chapter 3), who knew MacDonald from his Iowa days, met his demand. If one could characterize Page's relationship with AASHO as harmonious, the ties MacDonald would develop with the organization over the next thirty-four years could be better described as synergistic.[22]

When MacDonald came to Washington, he kept one foot in Iowa, by remaining an AASHO board member. Page had been their friend, but MacDonald was one of them. The move was quintessential MacDonald and a key to the success he would have in the nation's capital over the next thirty-four years. For not only would the young highway engineer link hands with his brethren in state capitals; he would serve as well on boards of private and public interest groups that lobbied for action by Congress and his own Bureau of Public Roads (see chapters 6, 9, and 10). To MacDonald, no "we" and "they" dichotomy existed between those seeking roads and those building them. "We" became the state and federal governments working hand in glove with the auto, cement, steel, and rubber industries, to vastly expand America's road network. "They" meant everyone else. MacDonald also helped create and nurture umbrella groups such as the Highway Education Board and the Highway Research Board, which would openly unite the public and private sectors to lobby and propagandize (the word is his) for better roads.

Two Industries in Sharp Contrast

The contrast between the interdependent, mutually supportive road community and the railroad industry—whose wagons had pulled into a circle to defend themselves against the outside world—could not have been greater. Could one imagine J. P. Morgan from the railroads, John D. Rockefeller from their shippers, and Albert Cummins from Congress marching hand in hand toward a common goal? It would have been unthinkable. And any formal link between the rails and government would have been immediately decried as socialism, or as that enemy of the day—bolshevism.

Taking pains not to ruffle the feathers of the railroads, MacDonald spoke and wrote widely on the theme that the railroads had nothing to fear from the road interests he was assembling into a potent lobby. "The highway," MacDonald flatly declared, "will never be a competitor of the railway. . . . Far from being a danger to the railroads, the highways we are building will be their faithful allies." Truck competition with the rails, MacDonald said, was limited to trips of forty miles or less, and the railroads should be glad that trucks were willing to take such unprofitable business from them.[23]

Enterprising truckers, however, were already driving hundreds of miles on terrible roads that would only get better as time went on. Moreover, much of the business lost represented manufactured merchandise—transported by custom at higher rates than bulk transport—so the rate for a console radio would be a good deal higher than for a bushel of corn. The short-haul tonnage that trucks siphoned off would be much less dramatic than the percentage of rail revenues lost.[24]

Margaret Oberlin, MacDonald's only surviving child, recalls the Washington that her family moved to from Iowa in 1919 as "on the order of a small town, where the streets were filled with horses and wagons" and where Congress worked part-time. MacDonald, his wife, and his daughter and son moved to a large, rambling house in Edgemoor, Maryland. Years later, the family homestead would be razed to accommodate a high-rise building, a logical result of the revolutionary road-building program that MacDonald pursued, a project that would eventually suburbanize America.[25]

STORM CLOUDS AHEAD

Any well-informed railroad person in 1921 should have perceived the storm clouds that lay ahead. Geometric increases in truck production, enthusiastic congressional support for building national routes to carry trucks long distances, and business consumers' embrace of trucking as the mode of the future—the facts were open for all to see. Why, then, did the railroad industry not react more strongly against the unregulated growth of a competing industry? Ironically, while the birth of the trucking industry carried the seeds within it of the railroads' long-term demise, both truck production and road building offered the railways abundant short-term revenues. At a time when the overbuilt industry needed new business to survive, it welcomed the chance to haul steel, glass, rubber, and vehicle components to Detroit; new cars to the fledgling dealers across America; and concrete and asphalt to new road sites. Short-term gratification anesthetized the railroads against the pain of a long-term steady decline in freight revenues.[26]

The railroads could have formed their own trucking terminals, thus beating the truckers at their own game and offering seamless point-to-point transport to customers. They may have refrained from doing so partly out of fear that such a move would have raised the antitrust enforcers' hackles. The railroads were working for the first time in harmony with the ICC and Congress, and their memories of the kind of bloodbath that had marked their earlier history were all too fresh.[27]

Gradually, however, the railroads began to feel the competitive effect of an industry to which government supplied a free right of way, while the railroads purchased, maintained, and paid taxes on their own and even paid taxes on the roads built to support their competitor. Some railroads began to mount a publicity campaign, to complain that Washington was subsidizing their competitors unfairly. Their voices reached the White House, where President Warren Harding sent a message to Congress that only its subsidy made motor haulage profitable; that if burdened with its proper share of the cost of the highways, motor transport would prove its inherent wastefulness.[28]

RAILS AND TRUCKERS LOCK HORNS

By the 1920s, Congress was becoming aware that the anticipated strain on roads during the next several decades would be intolerable without new taxes and restrictions on growth of the trucking industry. Well ahead of Washington, states had begun to impose fuel taxes and registration fees and use restrictions on trucks. It would be more than a decade before Congress itself adopted a gasoline tax and even longer before it threw a harness around the trucking industry, which by then held the railroads in a death grip.

By the mid-1920s, the competition between truckers and the railroads had grown so intense that the protagonists were bankrolling lawsuits all the way to the U.S. Supreme Court. Initially, the issue seemed to be whether and to what extent state government could regulate the truckers. The Court had visited the question in a railroad context nearly four decades earlier. The Court in the Wabash case (see chapter 2) held that states could not interfere with the operation of railroads whose journey took them from one state into another. This 1886 decision energized Congress to pass the Interstate Commerce Act the next year. Yet a 1925 case, which applied the same result to the truckers, failed for a full decade to generate legislation to rein in the truckers.

Just as hundreds of years of commercial relations in Great Britain had set the stage for court decisions in the 1870s and 1880s affecting the railroads, so they informed court deliberations about whether and in what manner trucks might be regulated The common law inherited from England provided that government had no cause to interfere with a business that carried its products to market in its own vehicles, which were considered private carriers and thus exempt. Common carriers, by contrast, hired themselves out to anyone This, courts had held, gave the public a stake in whether they operated fairly. A third type of carrier was one that worked exclusively for only a few shippers. Carriers that could prove they were "contract carriers" for ju t a few businesses were considered exempt. Predictably, some common carriers sought to portray themselves as contract carriers to avoid being regulated.

So when on a trip across Michigan to a Toledo automaker the Duke Cartage Company's forty-seven trailers hauled car bodies for three separate Detroit plants, Michigan police pulled them over. Michigan law says you are a common carrier and need a state permit to operate, the officers told Duke's drivers. The outraged company owner dispatched his attorneys to attack the law as unconstitutional, and the Supreme Court sided with Duke. "The state," the Court held, "has no power to fetter the right to carry on interstate commerce within its borders" by unnecessary regulations.[29]

The next year, the Court underscored its holding in a California case involving a trucker named Frost. But the Supreme Court justices understood that the cases now coming before them centered on whether a state could promote one economic group or industry over another. While allowing the California trucker to ply his trade, the Court hinted that if a state legislature chose to favor a particular industry as public policy, it would not interfere with that choice.[30]

The Duke and Frost decisions were a blow to the railroads but advanced the truckers' cause. The National Association of Railroad and Utilities Commissions (NARUC) now sprang into action, demanding that Congress shackle the truckers. But Congress, for then at least, turned a deaf ear.[31]

MacDonald—Friend of Railroads?

MacDonald, in speech after speech (his collected addresses fill fourteen volumes) and in article after article, stressed the limited nature of road travel. But even as he was contending that road travel would always be subservient to the railroads, empirical evidence was building that such was not the case. As late as 1925—several months after the watershed Duke case had cleared the way for truckers to compete unrestricted in interstate commerce—MacDonald insisted to railroads that they had nothing to fear.[32]

But a growing trend of railway activity directly challenged MacDonald's assumptions, as railroads in growing numbers petitioned the ICC to let them abandon lines. In 1921, the Boston and Maine cited "the growth of automobile travel" as the reason for its having an average of only three passengers on its summer resort line to Jefferson, New Hampshire.[33] The same year, "increasing competition by motor vehicles" led the Ocean Shore Railroad Company to abandon two lines in northern California.[34] "Automobile and light-truck competition has deprived the railroad of its passenger, mail, express and local-freight traffic," said the Silverton Railway in 1922 in seeking permission to discontinue a line to a mining site in Colorado.[35] The "improvement of the highways and the resultant competition by autotrucks" led the Marietta and Vincent Railroad to abandon an Ohio line to a stone quarry in 1922.[36]

So the applications mushroomed during the 1920s. Yet MacDonald, remarkably, waved aside abandonments in general as simply marking the exhaustion of mining operations.[37] The ICC was not as sanguine. In 1926, several months after a MacDonald speech regarding the mining situation, it considered trucking growth serious enough to launch a nationwide inquiry into the magnitude of the problem. Holding hearings in thirteen cities from Portland, Oregon, to Asheville, North Carolina, the ICC staff listened to hundreds of farmers, railway executives, state legislators, and highway commissioners. By that time, members of Congress, sensitive to a growing concern back home, had introduced legislation to regulate interstate trucking.[38] When the ICC issued its findings in 1928, its decision was pragmatic but myopic. Undoubtedly, the commission found, truckers had sharply curtailed rail freight tonnage. However, the rails gained business in shipping truck tires, bodies, and truck and auto parts. No harm, no foul. The long-term implications of its decision—that the railroads' new business consisted of carrying the coffin to their own funerals—seemed lost on the commissioners.[39]

Road and Rail Each Evolve in a Vacuum

The ICC's micromanagers, in a rare global commentary, opined in 1928 that the new motor and air modes created a new commercial playing field and called for "a definite coordination of all existing transportation agencies on land, water and air."[40] The ICC was not alone in calling for the several modes to work together. During the 1920s, Canadian and British trucking and rail industries were responding to the motor revolution by the simple principle of comparative advantage—that it made sense for the railroads to haul long distances and for the truckers to haul short distances and handle delivery from the station to the customer; in short, to work together rather than at cross purposes.

Nothing since then has set American transportation apart from that in other industrialized democracies as much as the degree to which road and rail each developed in a vacuum. Each mode, seeking capitalistic ends, viewed the other as a competitor. Seeking common ground, even when such was mutually beneficial, was somehow trading with the enemy. Coordination could have come from government, but private enterprise has traditionally fought interference from the public sector, even while seeking its subsidies. Politically, legislators have been rewarded at the polls for respecting the demands of their constituents for short-term advantage. Voters have seldom, if ever, clamored for long-range, coordinated planning.

And so, the highway industry continued to grow, its varied elements melding into a mighty orchestra, with Thomas MacDonald conducting. Out of the limelight but silently pulling the strings, the nation's chief road builder laid the groundwork for the greatest public works project in world history. To accomplish it, he first had to create the greatest political lobby in world history, and MacDonald was about to prove that he was up to the task.

·6·

THE TROJAN HORSELESS
CARRIAGE

*Here is an opportunity to do a big, basic work,
such as comes to few in the course of a lifetime. . . . There is no work more worthwhile.
The individual who fails to vision the importance of the task has no moral right to hold a
position of authority in its performance.*

—Thomas Harris MacDonald, first memo to his
staff as director of the Bureau of Public Roads,
1919

THE MAN CHECKING INTO THE BLACKWELL, OKLAHOMA, HOTEL IN 1920 introduced himself as Thomas MacDonald, of the federal Bureau of Public Roads (BPR). Word spread fast in the small town that something important was about to happen. In a day before *McDonald's* meant hamburgers, *MacDonald* meant roads, and roads meant business, and business meant prosperity. Soon the visitor was luxuriating in the best hotel accommodations Blackwell could provide. He found that his money was no good there, as town fathers wined and dined him, even cashed his checks gladly and guided him around to visit their county road improvement projects. Returning the next day to tie down some money from their powerful visitor, "MacDonald's" generous hosts found the imposter gone and his checks turned to rubber.[1]

Thomas Harris MacDonald, while still in his thirties, had indeed become

"Mr. Highways" (see chapter 5). In Woodrow Wilson's Washington, service in Congress was a part-time job in a city of horsecarts and trolleys. Senators and congressmen left their constituencies in the winter by steam train, spent several months in Washington tending to the nation's business, then returned home to resume their law practices or tend their farms. While in Washington, they few largely by the seat of their pants. Staff specialists to help members evaluate and counter executive branch proposals were rare.[2]

Yet the Progressive era had demanded that what you know rather than whom you know should govern public decision making, so Congress was newly respectful of information. Where data are the coin of the realm, knowledge is power, and MacDonald had an extraordinary mind for information. Within two years of arriving in Washington in 1919, the balding, beefy Scotsman had come to dominate the fledgling highway community simply by gathering, using, and manipulating the largest database in town.[3] Short, solid, and sober as a bulldog, MacDonald exuded the quiet determination of a man bent on getting his way.

MacDonald: Roads Would Have Prevented Civil War

MacDonald's commitment to extending asphalt tentacles from coast to coast was single-minded. National highways, he said, would foster a "broad Americanism," born of citizens' learning about other parts of the country as their Model T's chugged from state to state. MacDonald went even further: If modern highways and automobiles had existed in 1860, he declared, America never would have had the Civil War: "The intersectional misunderstanding which gave rise to it could not have reached the critical stage of war had it been possible as it is now for the Southern planter to spend his summer in Maine and the New England businessman to journey southward in his own car for golf at Pinehurst and a winter vacation in Florida."[4]

The young man from America's farmbelt brought a nearly messianic zeal to the job. In a day when road travel was not much better than when Jesus walked the roads of Nazareth, MacDonald understood that roads smooth as tabletops could transform every facet of American life. People take highways for granted today because they are seemingly as plentiful as water, but at the beginning of the century their scarcity gave paved roads a magical quality.

No sooner had MacDonald taken the helm of the infant government enterprise than a challenge confronted him that would call for every ounce of his considerable skill.

GOVERNMENT STRUGGLES TO STAY AHEAD OF THE CARS

Shining new roadsters and wooden-sided trucks were taking to the nation's roads in staggering numbers in 1919, production having doubled in only four years, and Congress had committed itself in 1916 to help states build enough roads to keep pace with the demand. The fact that cars and trucks would fundamentally change the way Americans lived, worked, and played was now becoming clear. Popular magazines had shown dramatic photographs of the awesome Panama Canal, completed in 1914, and those in the know said the cost of a nationwide network of roads would dwarf the $352 million spent on the canal.

Government's role in America's life was still small, but politicians could not fail to sniff the opportunities for political gain in the spending of so much money.[5] Who would build this network of national roads— Washington or the states? If states constructed their own roads, how would they agree where to link up at their borders? And if Washington decided where to build them, what role would be left for the states? European capitals had taken control of road and rail building throughout their countries (see chapter 3), but centralized control did not sit well with many rugged individualists.

Congress had said that the states could choose where to build roads, while Washington would pay half the cost and oversee the projects. But wartime shortages stopped the program dead in its tracks. By the end of the war in 1918, less than a half-million dollars had been paid out to the states, and only twelve and a half miles had been built.[6] State legislatures together had authorized more than $400 million to build roads, but the states had few trained engineers. Counties had built most roads until then, but their road commissions were often cesspools of corruption, and professionally run state highway departments to replace them had not gotten off the ground. Yet people and businesses, caught up in the fever of owning a conveyance that could travel anywhere, clamored for good roads.

CITIZENS GROW RESTLESS

Impatient Americans complained that the job just was not getting done. And even where roads did exist, Sunday drivers often ran into a field of weeds at the state border, where no link with the neighboring state had yet been planned.[7] Increasingly, citizens felt that if the states could not provide adequate roadways, then the federal government should build and control a national road system. The idea made sense as well to the auto, rubber, cement, and steel industries, which realized the ease of petitioning one national government rather than dozens of smaller ones. Soon they had merged into the Highway Industries Association and called for a fifty-thousand-mile national highway system.[8]

Gradually sentiment for a national road system grew into a groundswell. But MacDonald, who would have been a shoo-in to head the program, had misgivings. As Iowa's state highway chief, he had traveled across the state by railroad, on foot and on horseback, deciding from personal experience what kind of a road should be built in Keokuk or whether that bridge over in Ames needed replacing or just shoring up. While he believed in a guiding hand from Washington, MacDonald realized shrewdly that letting the states decide where roads should go would give the program stronger political legs than it could have as a national program. And distanced as it would be from the actual road projects, a national program could be a convenient scapegoat for the states when things went wrong.

Then too, the farmboy in MacDonald was worried about the growing brain drain from the nation's farms. The 1920 census showed for the first time that most Americans lived in cities, and the trend was continuing. MacDonald worried that a national roads commission would be tempted to build long-distance through routes for tourists who sought the big cities, thus diverting money away from efforts to get the rural folk out of the mud. Farmers, who rarely left the county of their birth, commonly saw such interstate highways as thoroughfares for the rich.[9] But MacDonald found himself more and more outnumbered.

MACDONALD RACES TO RECLAIM ADVANTAGE

From his Washington, D.C., offices a half-block from Pennsylvania Avenue, where three hundred engineers and clerks sifted through proposals from communities such as Kansas City, Harrisburg, and Tallahassee, MacDonald watched with alarm as the national commission movement gathered steam. By 1919, not only had 775 civic organizations signed onto the crusade but so had most of his former colleagues in state highway departments, as well as tire manufacturers, automakers, the National Grange, Rotary International, the Highway Industries Association, the American Automobile Association (AAA), and the Portland Cement Association.

The national crusade may have had the money and the numbers, but MacDonald had a singular advantage: his office controlled the only existing national roads program, which still had two years to run. The way to defuse the opposition, he realized, was to flog his federal-state partnership to produce roads on such a scale that the national commission backers would simply have to fold their tents.[10]

MacDonald set out to turn the state engineers around. Soon states found their projects approved within four days of application. Across America, children walking home from school now stood transfixed, watching revolving cement mixers disgorge thick gray soup and heavy steel rollers tamp down sticky, hot tar on nearly fifteen thousand miles of new roads, with a similar volume approved and ready to go. Barely a year after arriving in Washington, MacDonald boasted that his collective projects were broader in scope than the vaunted Panama Canal endeavor. Now the newly engaged American Association of State Highway Officials (AASHO) engineers began to listen to MacDonald's argument that the national commission idea threatened their autonomy, and gradually fell in line to oppose it.

Next MacDonald turned to the manufacturing interests themselves, the executives whose fortunes might depend on which plan Congress adopted. Time was short—the five-year 1916 highway act would expire the next year—and he needed to land a fish big enough to cause lesser ones to jump into his boat. The automaker MacDonald succeeded in reeling in was none other than the leader of the opposition—friendly, charismatic Roy Chapin. Not yet forty, he was already a legend in automaking.

In His Merry Oldsmobile

The young tatterdemalion approaching the Manhattan hotel one November day in 1901 was eager and friendly, but caked with mud from head to toe. The doorman firmly turned him away. His hotel was hosting the New York Automobile Show, and he'd catch the dickens from his boss if he let some tramp in to wander among the well-heeled visitors coming to look at the contraptions that people were saying would change America. Apparently, no one had told the doorman that disheveled Roy Chapin had just pulled off the greatest feat in the short history of automobiling—driving a low-priced car all the way from Detroit to New York City.

Chapin's boss was Ransom Olds, the Michigan automaker, who had decided to say nothing to the New York exhibitors in case his man did not make it. Olds had tapped his twenty-one-year-old mechanic to drive an Oldsmobile runabout 860 miles over a thin ribbon of dirt road, to demonstrate dramatically that a $650 people's car could be roadworthy. Until then the farmers' jibe that the automobile was a rich man's toy had been on target. Olds sought to prove them wrong.

Chapin left Detroit in late October seated behind the curved dash of his tiny open car, holding the steering roc between his legs and bracing for the chill that sets in after the leaves have fallen. Cylinder gaskets blew repeatedly on uphill climbs, and Chapin had to dismount every few miles to reinflate the tires with a bicycle pump. But nine days after he had started, Roy Chapin's primitive conveyance chugged down Broadway to the hotel. Olds's gamble had paid off: one New York dealer was so impressed with a car that cost well under an average worker's annual salary that he snapped up a thousand Olds runabouts on the spot.

Unlike many other auto mechanics of the day, Chapin was equally at home in the corporate suite. Leaving Olds to pursue his own venture, the urbane, outgoing Chapin—already a millionaire at age thirty—became the president of the Hudson Motor Company. Aggressively promoting his burgeoning industry, Chapin three years later helped Carl Fisher develop the Lincoln Highway (see chapter 3). During the First World War, Wilson prevailed on Chapin to help move wartime supplies by rail and to plan alternative road routes, should America enter the European war.[11]

By 1919, Chapin headed the National Automobile Chamber of Commerce (NACC), which like so many other industry groups favored the national commission plan. But after meeting with MacDonald, Chapin praised his "very cooperative attitude." Before long, MacDonald's command of an impressive array of facts had won over the young automaker, who marveled at MacDonald's "dispassionate engineering opinion."[12] Chapin abandoned the helm of the national roads commission crusade and joined the massive propaganda machine MacDonald had begun to set up. He would become a long-time ally and supporter of "The Chief," as staffers in the Department of Transportation even today reverentially refer to him.

Turning the Tide

Chapin's conversion helped turn the heads of other national commission backers, but MacDonald's task still seemed Sisyphean. The tiremaker Harvey Firestone had launched a formidable transcontinental "Ship by Truck" caravan, carrying with it speakers, films, ads, and handbooks, designed to create a firestorm for the national commission. Motorists now found themselves deluged with professionally crafted AAA booklets. Auto dealers pasted on their showroom walls two hundred thousand posters arguing the wisdom of having the federal government build and operate the nation's roadways.

But, unexpectedly, things began to break MacDonald's way. For in the two years since the debate began, a reaction had set in against the Progressive credo that federal, rather than state, legislation was the best way to cure all manner of social ills. This visceral fear of the evils of big government worked against the national commission idea. Sam Rayburn, a young Texas Congressman who would go on to become the Speaker of the House, noted that he was "sick and tired of the federal government's everlasting sticking its hand into the affairs of [his] state."[13]

With the national commission suddenly in trouble and the federal-state partnership cranking out roads at a record pace, MacDonald's program became highly popular. In 1921, Congress voted to let each state choose which 7 percent of its roads Washington would link into a national highway system. The *Engineering News Record* described the 1921 passage as an "overwhelming vote of confidence for the U.S. Bureau of Public Roads."[14] The primary roads this act created would thirty-five years later become the skeleton of the interstate highway system.

SELLING ROADS LIKE HAWKING DETERGENT

Several elements had helped MacDonald win his first Washington challenge and would make him uncannily effective over the next three decades. He stuck to rational, ostensibly apolitical arguments; projected an image of unassailable integrity; let others take credit for his successes; enlisted supposed neutrals to make his own arguments; and avoided ad hominem attacks, no matter what the stakes. The trust that these qualities engendered became apparent in 1922 when Congress let his bureau approve binding state highway contracts even before it had earmarked money for them.

But MacDonald accepted as well that information could be used to manipulate, to obfuscate, and to mislead if his greater purpose justified such means. His credibility with Congress was enormous. Typically, MacDonald spewed forth a barrage of charts, graphs, and tables to accompany his customary blizzard of facts, far beyond the capacity of any member to absorb but which nevertheless left the subtle, subliminal message: "This man knows what he's talking about." When confronted by an accuser, which was rare in MacDonald's Washington, he would assail the person with a plethora of facts. Those like Chapin, who labeled MacDonald apolitical, failed to grasp that cultivated apoliticism can sometimes be the best politics.[15]

MacDonald's Trade with Congress

In effect, MacDonald had made a trace with Congress: if they would let him base highway construction on mer t, he would let them take the political kudos for new highways, which proved to be the mother's milk of their reelection campaigns. As straightforward and sensible as this may seem, members of Congress, who had risen through the ranks of blatantly corrupt county governments, viewed MacDonald's approach as new.

Perhaps what set MacDonald apart from his fellow engineers and certainly his railroad competitors was his early recognition that to sell roads, Washington would have to market them like a detergent. He knew consumers had a free-market choice to travel by road, rail, or water, or lately, by air. If he expected Americans to buy roads and pay for them, he had to give them a good reason and make them feel that they were paying a fair price for the product. So MacDonald named himself the point man for the highway-motor complex in the unprecedented marketing crusade that lay ahead.

CRANKING UP THE PROPAGANDA MACHINE

MacDonald adopted a mantra for his campaign: use of public roads is an inalienable human right, as opposed to use of the private rails, which is a privilege based on a fare. The principle that access to public roads ought to be open was old, but not universally accepted. Since the Middle Ages in Britain, for example, town fathers had maintained the roads that ran through their towns. American county governments continued the practice. But this largely involved filling in ruts in dirt roads and keeping them free of debris. When governments began building sophisticated turnpikes with hard-packed surfaces and drainage, they commonly charged tolls to their users.[16] Yet throughout his career, MacDonald steadfastly opposed charging tolls, even when in the 1930s it would mean going head to head with the president of the United States.

In 1923, when radio broadcasting was in its infancy, MacDonald took to the airwaves to address the nation on the similarity of roads and radio. Listening through the crackling reception of radio's early days, Americans heard MacDonald intone: "Radio is free as air; and the open road is symbolic of freedom." At a time when countless Americans felt used and abused by the private railroads and trolleys, MacDonald did not hesitate to note that "no corporation controls them [roads] and the only restrictions on their use are those imposed for the public good."[17]

With millions of new cars spilling onto the roads each year, government revenues from fuel, excise taxes, and registration fees were growing even faster than the unprecedented spending on roads. The BPR, which paid out a paltry $4 million in 1919, spent $88 million only five years later. Yet in Britain, the reality that highways had become a cash cow prompted Chancellor of the Exchequer Winston Churchill to abolish the earmarking of the petrol tax agreed on in Parliament in 1909 and let the torrent of road revenues overflow into the public coffers for other uses as well. In 1926, he rose in Parliament to answer with élan the pleas of motorists that the Road Fund was sacrosanct:

> Entertainments may be taxed; public houses may be taxed; racehorses may be taxed; the possession of armorial bearings and manservants may be taxed—and the yield devoted to the general revenue. But motorists are to be privileged for all time to have the whole yield of the tax on motors devoted to roads. Obviously this is all nonsense. . . . Such contentions are absurd, and constitute at once an outrage upon the sovereignty of Parliament and upon common sense.[18]

MacDonald made the growing highway movement seem larger than it was by setting up new, seemingly independent groups to crusade for good roads. The Highway Education Board (HEB) generated prohighway "propaganda," before the word gained its invidious cold war connotation. Though the HEB was ostensibly independent from the Bureau of Public Roads (BPR), HEB offices sat hard by those of the BPR in the Willard Building, and MacDonald sat on the HEB's board of directors.

In 1920, realizing that the mushrooming population of cars and trucks would soon destroy new roads unless Washington could build them stronger, MacDonald helped create the Highway Research Board, locating it within the National Academy of Science, where it gained an aura of impartiality. For MacDonald, however, the HEB served as an information factory that allowed him to feed information selectively from Washington to the states through AASHO and from AASHO back to Congress. The rectitude of this proud corps of engineers trained by MacDonald and Logan Page (see chapters 3 and 5) gave their congressional testimony a special credibility and helped mask the fact that AASHO was essentially just another lobby.[19]

During the 1920s, surveyors sighting with sextants, construction workers dragging rollers, and legislators calling for more road money became commonplace across America. The new public-private highway coalition was rolling out ten thousand miles of road a year by 1922. Fast on their heels were Detroit's production lines, which, before Black Tuesday brought the boom to an end in 1929, would turn out 26.7 million cars.

LOVE FEST OF THE HIGHWAYMEN

The regal Grand Ballroom of Washington's Willard Hotel on Pennsylvania Avenue was decorated to the hilt. Long, narrow flags of the original thirteen states hung vertically between massive arched windows, above which were draped semicircles of red, white, and blue crepe bunting. The two hundred people gathered at the black-tie-optional dinner on this crisp October evening in 1922 radiated prosperity, self-confidence, and enthusiasm. Had it been a presidential election year, one might have taken the affair for a gathering of Republican fat cats, each plunking down a worker's biweekly wage to hear a major policy address up close from their party's nominee.[20]

In fact, this gathering *was* intensely political, and the attendees would roundly applaud a series of tub-thumping speeches; it just didn't happen to be electoral in nature. The innocuous-sounding HEB had convened a rally for its massive propaganda campaign, to sell the American people on building literally a never-ending stream of highways.

While better roads helped speed shipments to rail depots and gave railroads short-term business in hauling concrete and steel, some railroaders began to smell a rat as early as 1916. For the seeds sown for good roads, when carried to harvest, they realized, could make the motor truck a potent competitor with the railroads. Already, some were calling for raising highway taxes or—more unthinkable—putting motor trucks under the control of the rabid Interstate Commerce Commission. The highwaymen decided the time had come to lay some fertilizer of their own.[21]

MacDonald's Guiding Hand

Now, in surveying the assemblage from the ballroom's raised dais, the moon-faced MacDonald could congratulate himself. The HEB had come a long way indeed in the short time he had been in Washington. President Warren Harding had sent a greeting, exhorting the highwaymen to integrate rail, road, and sea into one interdependent system, rather than planning for roads alone in a vacuum. His remarks would meet polite applause, but this gathering was single-minded in its dedication to a solitary mode of travel.

MacDonald had brought together the elements necessary to "awaken the public" and make it so enthusiastic about highways that citizens would zealously lobby their own representatives. His was not a short-term goal; the HEB was looking decades, indeed generations, ahead. It would have its greatest impact, MacDonald knew, in focusing on the very young. If the HEB were successful, these youngsters would be so conditioned by adulthood that as voters and consumers, they would vote for and use the nation's ever-expanding road system more than rail, sea, and air. The railway leaders could have made a similar sales pitch to the young if they had wished to, but they did nothing.

Indoctrinating the Young

Already, in three short years, the Highway Education Board had involved five million children and adults in contests and awarded full college scholarships. The HEB forecast that having young Americans think and write about such topics as "How good roads help the religious life of my community" would be "a mighty influence at the ballot box when road bond issues and highway programs [were] up for rejection or approval."[22] Tens of thousands of teachers competed in a safety lesson contest, with the winner feted at the White House. A half-million schoolchildren listened to classroom talks by members of the HEB speakers bureau. The HEB made movies and handed out booklets telling how improved highways enhanced domestic life.

While the HEB promoted itself as a quasi-governmental agency, its friends in private enterprise were only too glad to pick up the tab—not only for this lavish evening but for HEB's operating budget as well. Kicking in their share were NACC, the Rubber Association of America, and individual manufacturers and their suppliers.[23]

As if it were necessary, successive speakers seemed bent on convincing one another that the movement in which they were engaged was a noble one. Because of the auto industry, declared C. C. Hanch of the NACC in a tub-thumping speech, 2,430,000 people were working in 1922. And, he contended, 83 percent of all the world's cars at that time drove on American roads. Hanch opined: "Each day the social and economic influence of the car extends into some new field and throughout the world, the instinctive desire for individual transportation asserts itself in the demand which we see reflected in a constantly growing use."[24]

Built from the Ground Up

MacDonald had built his coalition painstakingly. While surveying the crowd on this proud evening, he could pick out friends—such as H. H. Rice, the newly named president of GM's Cadillac division, and John J. Tigert, the U.S. commissioner of education—as well as allies from the Granite Block Manufacturers Association, the National Paving Brick Manufacturers' Association, the Portland Cement Association. All in attendance were laboring for the same mighty purpose, from which they hoped to benefit. And to make sure the word would get out, MacDonald had arranged for S. S. McClure of the popular magazine *McClure's* to speak. "You can today judge a civilization by the condition of its roads. . . . We know that the English-speaking people made the fundamental inventions that annihilated space," he said, jingoistically.[25]

Those who had never heard George Graham of NACC had to hold onto their hats. A master of overblown phraseology, Graham exhorted his audience that transportation's boon in lowering "the cost of necessities and enjoyments of life is the reply to the malcontent or Bolshevist who raises his voice against our institutions." Graham asked his audience to use his message in proselytizing the unconverted, and he warned darkly that recent ill-considered calls for taxes on cars had endangered the success of their crusade. Since revenue laws, then as now, often tax luxuries more heavily, he argued that cars had become a necessity of life and called on government to abolish excise taxes on them. Further, Graham declared to appreciative applause that "all money levied on the automobile industry should be applied to the highways"—a theme the highwaymen would sound for decades until in 1956, Congress achieved this hard-won goal.[26]

His evangelistic style contrasted utterly with MacDonald's coaxing manner, which tended to make friends of former enemies. Harvey Firestone, for example, who had fought MacDonald's state-federal highway partnership only two years before, had now like Chapin become his ally. The tiremaker donated the college scholarships that the HEB gave to high school students. Now in his midfifties, Firestone had benefited mightily from the good roads movement. In 1900 he had started the Firestone Tire and Rubber Company and watched it grow in lockstep with the auto industry. By 1935, his company would boast forty thousand employees.[27]

GOVERNMENT AND BUSINESS TIE THE KNOT

The public-private partnership MacDonald had nurtured had created a national policy to further the ends of one industry over another. Railroads—the nation's first big business—had become the archenemy of the federal and state governments three decades earlier. And now, they could only watch in awe as Washington and Detroit developed a symbiosis so strong that where one left off and the other began had blurred. Rail leaders did not protest the partnership because they did not yet perceive the highwaymen as a threat, and the railways were making money hauling road materials and new cars. Their great awakening would happen in the 1930s, when they would be up in arms.

HEB board meetings put government engineers and bureaucrats in touch regularly with auto and rubber executives and engineering professors. And the network that the highway-motor complex was creating soon would include congressmen as well. The close communication fostered by MacDonald insured that the industries would be involved with policy decisions, in stark contrast to their railroad brethren.[28]

Not only did the policies of government and business aid and abet one another, but their personnel moved between goverment and industry in a seamless continuum. Auto executives with stockholdings in their company moved into government, openly helped legislate profits for themselves, then returned to their industry, to harvest those rewards, in a day before Congress outlawed such dealings.

The need to mobilize the United States for the war in Europe first drew automakers into the public realm. In 1915, President Wilson named Howard E. Coffin, the vice-president of the Hudson Motor Company, to head the Council for National Defense. Coffin tapped Roy Chapin, his boss at Hudson, and Alfred E. Reeves, the NACC chairman, to help as well. And while one could portray the wartime government service as patriotic duty, in fact the automobile industry benefited greatly from wartime mobilization, expanding its plant capacity to manufacture wartime vehicles. By being in the vortex of decision making about wartime needs, auto executives gained from inside information. And when the war had ended, Washington and the motor industry locked themselves in an ardent embrace that has continued to the present day.

Automaker Protects Industry in Senate

In 1922, Michigan voters sent James Couzens, Henry Ford's former right-hand man (see chapter 4), to the United States Senate. Within a decade, Ford's former finance chief would chair the Senate Interstate Commerce Committee, where he would effectively block legislation to regulate the motor industry (see chapter 8).

When railroads complained that car and truck competition was killing them, a blue-ribbon committee emerged in 1923 to study whether corrective action was needed. It would prove the government equivalent of the fox guarding the chicken coop. For the "students" of the problem included insurance companies, which were reaping a bonanza from automobile insurance, and savings banks, whose car loans enabled the middle class to buy automobiles on time. To lend gravitas to its recommendations, the National Transportation Committee named President Calvin Coolidge as its chairman. Predictably, the committee concluded, first, that the motor industry helped, not hurt, the railroads and, second, that regulation should continue for the rails but not for motor vehicles.[29]

In 1932, President Herbert Hoover named Chapin his secretary of commerce, the chief proponent of policies to aid the country's business community. There Chapin would help craft policies to aid the motor industry, before returning to it after Hoover lost his bid for reelection.

Francis duPont did not merely switch hats; he wore two at once: while his family's stock controlled the General Motors Corporation (GM), the wealthy duPont served on the Delaware Highway Commission from 1922 to 1949. In 1953 he would succeed MacDonald as the BPR director, and a year later he would become one of the key players in convincing President

Eisenhower to propose the "Interstate Defense Highway System"[30] (see chapter 11).

Charles Wilson in 1953 would leave the helm of GM to become President Eisenhower's secretary of defense. At his confirmation hearing, Wilson summed up the highwayman's credo, in the oft-quoted line: "What's good for our country is good for General Motors and vice versa."[31] And former auto dealers headed the federal post office and the Interior Department as well.[32]

ROADS AT ANY COST

MacDonald, now in his early forties, stood securely at the helm of the largest public works undertaking in world history. He had developed a reputation in and out of government as an icon of integrity. But on closer examination, some of MacDonald's statements were not only self-serving and propagandistic but downright false. Time and again throughout the 1920s and 1930s, MacDonald sought to ease the qualms of those who feared that the growing highway-motor complex would threaten the railroads. President Warren Harding had noted in 1921 that highways already carried more than half of the country's commerce.[33]

Others charged that motor competition had caused nearly 3,800 miles of track to be abandoned since 1916. Deflecting this thrust, MacDonald alleged in 1925 that barely 4 percent of track abandoned since 1920 could be written off to highway competition. And 58 percent of abandonments, he maintained, represented mileage that led to played-out mines. He invited doubters to confirm his figures by using ICC files.[34] In fact, such an examination of ICC published reports from 1921 to 1925 shows that quite the contrary was true: aside from rail lines that shut down for unrelated business reasons, the majority of abandonments *were* the direct result of automobile competition, a far greater figure than that for the abandonment of mines.[35]

The discrepancy is of more than academic interest. The assessment of a reason for the railroads' decline was important because Americans had invested billions of dollars in railways. Those within the railroad community and without had foreseen since 1916 that increasingly sophisticated motor vehicles driving on smooth roads could become a potent competitor of the railroads.[36] Millions of voters—indeed many members of Congress—owned railroad stock, the value of which would plummet if automobiles and trucks proved to have caused the railroads' demise. Therefore, the word had to go out that highways and motor vehicles helped, rather than hurt, railroads; and that stance had to be promoted long after the partial fiction had for many been unmasked. Perpetuating the illusion not only maintained the popularity of motor travel but ensured solid prohighway support in Congress.

DEFENDING THE TRUCKERS

Since the highway community and the motor industry worked hand in glove during the 1920s, one can understand MacDonald's promotion of Detroit's interests, which in turn advanced his own highway agenda. But MacDonald continued to defend truckers, even in the face of proof that unregulated interstate rigs were tearing up the roads. Federal courts, hearing detailed testimony from those who maintained that trucks were destroying the new highways agreed that such was the case.[37] Yet MacDonald, in numerous speeches and writings through the 1920s and 1930s, steadfastly maintained that any damage was negligible. Writing in Scientific American in 1932, MacDonald declared: "The roads we are now building are not destroyed by trucks. Be sure that every statement you see or hear to the contrary comes more or less directly from a narrow-visioned defender of the railroads as they have been; and not from one who has any conception of the needs of the future or the actualities of the present."[38]

By the early 1930s, when the clamor to regulate motor vehicles was rising, MacDonald would testify before the Interstate Commerce Commission in 1931 that interstate motor-freight traffic carried "a small part of one per cent" of all freight. Even railroads and truck manufacturers agreed that the amount of interstate motor freight was at least between 2 percent and 3 percent.[39] While the difference seems minuscule in retrospect, MacDonald's dismissive attitude diverged sharply even from that of the trucking companies, which opposed regulation. The truckers conceded that the future of long-distance trucking was bright. By the end of the decade, trucks would haul 10 percent of all interstate freight, and the percentage moved rapidly up through the double digits in the decade following.[40] Yet MacDonald continued to downplay the effect that motor vehicles were having on the railroads.

What Were His Motives?

While MacDonald's role in building a national highway system was in theory totally independent of the industry that made vehicles to drive on those roads, the reality was far different. What his personal motives were in misrepresenting facts, in apologizing for truckers, and in going to the mat repeatedly to defend the motor industry against all attackers are lost in the mists of history. His public statements appear to have been accepted practically without criticism. Yet an examination of the records now shows that MacDonald dissembled and misrepresented his movement on more than a few occasions.

MacDonald probably did not receive any personal gain from the motor industry or its affiliates, but he could not have been a more effective spokesman for the industry had he been on full-time retainer to it. Repeatedly putting his considerable prestige on the line for the industry no doubt helped swell its coffers. And yet, at a time when payoffs to public officials were commonplace, the evidence fails to suggest that MacDonald benefited directly from his zealous cheerleading. Probate records, for instance, show that his estate at death barely exceeded twenty-five thousand dollars.[41]

Apparently, MacDonald was impelled by a need to become the greatest highway builder ever. In the late 1920s, he observed grandiosely that only three great programs of highway building had taken place in recorded history: that of the Roman Empire from Caesar to Constantine, France under Napoleon, and the United States during the 1920s.

THE PUBLIC BEWARE

The kind of symbiosis that resulted from the highway-motor nexus would be seen later in the relationship between America's military and its defense contractors. On the eve of leaving office in 1961, President Dwight D. Eisenhower warned of the dangers of the military-industrial complex: "The total influence—economic, political, even spiritual—is felt in every city, every statehouse, every office of the federal government. . . . In the councils of government, we must guard against the acquisition of unwarranted influence, whether sought or unsought, by the military-industrial complex." Had the father of the Interstate Defense Highway System substituted "highway-motor" for "military-industrial," his warning would have been just as apt.[42]

To the highwaymen in the 1920s, there seemed no limit to the cars they could produce or the roads they could build. But as the decade neared its close, they came to realize that they were not making much of a dent in urban areas. There, trolleys moved the masses quickly and efficiently, in spite of their growing financial problems (see chapter 4). Yet more people lived in cities than on the farm, and if they could not be persuaded to buy automobiles, a massive market would be left untapped. Urban America, some within the highway-motor complex decided, was the last frontier.

·7·

DERAILING THE TROLLEYS

I seen my opportunities and I took 'em.

—George Washington Plunkitt

THE URBAN TROLLEY INDUSTRY RADIATED GOOD HEALTH IN THE MID-1920s, if ridership is any guide. In 1923, more straphangers rode the urban rails than ever before and—more ominously—than ever after. In a day when city workers were used to living cheek by jowl in urban tenements, the electric streetcar was for most a meeting place as well as a conveyance. Chatting and enjoying the scenery with fellow travelers (in the years before that term gained a sinister tone) was the order of the day. In the early 1920s, the Los Angeles Young Men's Christian Association (YMCA) founded the Commuters' School of Southern California, to help people improve their minds by studying during daily trips. The idea was a flop, but when the line installed bridge tables on several longer routes, commuters loved that.[1]

Yet for others, the trolley—often owned by a large, nonlocal railroad or utility company—was the only commuting option and had become a "symbol of coercion and the power of big business," no matter how efficient or convenient its service might be.[2] The automobile had taken America by storm.[3] Henry Ford's Model T reduced car prices across the industry dramatically. Some better-paid trolley commuters succumbed to the lure of magazines' full-page color ads, which beckoned them to join "the new order of things" and buy cars.[4]

To say that automobiles stood in the way of the trolleys as the First World War approached is doubly true: not only had individual motorized transportation captured the imagination of the common citizen, but Fords and Chevys now shared the road with the trolleys, whose iron rails had dominated the middle of the street for several decades. The automobile was the new kid in town, who knew that everyone had heard about his prowess and flexed his muscles with impunity. A Buick touring car could pass a trolleycar stopped for passengers, but if a line of automobiles blocked a trolley's passage, all it could do was wait. For the streetcar industry, which prided itself on forging the quickest route from point A to point B, the frustration was palpable.

THE TROLLEY DECLINE BEGINS

Those who first perceived how the motor industry would jeopardize streetcars were not the rail owners or the general public but the investors. As early as 1920, a Canadian financing expert testified to an Ontario commission that "the idea of any one suggesting financing of an electric interurban road would not be given very serious consideration."[5] The capital markets understood that the streetcar industry suffered from multiple ailments: a top-heavy debt, government regulation that did not apply to streetcars' competitors, rising labor and materials costs, union rules, obsolescence, and a popular perception that driving a car cost less than riding a trolley.

Streetcar lines owned by railroads often groaned under their parents' heavy debt from overbuilding, stock watering, and huge prices paid to gain monopoly control. One-third of interurban lines were independently owned, and even they followed in the railroads' high-rolling footsteps and now strained under the same load. Further, those interurbans that competed with railroads had to undercut rail fares set unrealistically low by hostile regulators, and thus they found themselves starved for income.

Interurbans, as rail companies, fell under the burden of state and local regulators, which did not encumber motor transit until 1935. So while regulators told streetcar operators where they could travel and how often and what they could charge, bus lines were free to roam and charge at will, often skimming the cream of the business and ignoring unprofitable routes. The nearly universal nickel trolley fare had become sacrosanct, keeping revenues fixed. Yet labor unions were winning raises for workers that doubled the hourly wage for common labor between 1915 and 1920. Inflation raised living costs, and after 1914, wartime material shortages inflated the purchase price of streetcars. Yet no amount of explanation seemed persuasive enough to convince regulators to grant a politically damaging fare increase.[6]

Organized labor, which had long since unionized streetcars, commonly required that a motorman and a conductor be used on each trolley car. But labor had not yet organized the fledgling bus lines, which were free to use one man as a motorman-conductor, thus cutting costs.[7]

Swimming Against the Tide

And if those handicaps were not enough, the down-at-the-heels streetcars found it difficult to compete against "the latest thing." As millions of Americans followed the course of coast-to-coast auto races and magazine articles about celebrities and their automobiles, cars came to be seen as the fresh new plaything; to be seen riding the trolleys was terribly déclassé.[8] Magazine ads played on breadwinners' guilt, showing on one page a smiling family riding in a gleaming, new open-touring car, while on a facing page, downcast parents and their children boarded a drab, crowded streetcar. Riding the trolleys is "wrong," one hard-sell ad argued. "It's not fair to your children—your wife—or yourself."[9]

The jitney, a private motorcar that stopped at trolley stations to lure passengers off the rails, was so named because *jitney* was slang for a nickel, the customary charge for a trolley ride. And while city and state governments quickly outlawed the thousands of unregulated jitneys that suddenly appeared to harvest the prime interurban trade, the vulnerability of streetcars to motor competition had now been exposed.[10]

Decisively to some, operating a car seemed to cost less than the average two to two and a half cents per mile the trolleys charged. Riding the spanking-new roads was practically free at a time before most states levied gasoline taxes. In fact, taxpayers paid for those roads out of general government revenues, but few people had access to those figures or the inclination to factor them in to the actual cost of driving.

Car owners probably did not go beyond the surface costs of fuel, taxes, insurance, repairs, and loan amortization to calculate such hidden charges as the opportunity cost of government land lost to highways, the governmental expense of operating traffic courts and police patrols, and the human toll of highway deaths and injuries. Such factors as air pollution and dependence on foreign oil were merely lurking in the wings. So to the extent that urban car owners ever calculated relative costs, they would likely reach the simple but flawed conclusion that it was cheaper to ride a car than a trolley.[11]

Money for Roads, None for Trolleys

For city policymakers, public transit as a political issue loomed much larger then than it does today because so many more people rode the commuter rails. So if the financial burdens on streetcar lines led to shabbier cars and slower service, constituents could ring up their representatives to demand that something be done.

Yet in the vast majority of cities, "doing something" didn't extend to subsidizing the private trolley companies. Even though state and federal governments were massively subsidizing car and truck owners by building a nationwide system of paved roads, there was a "popular conception of transit as a private business and the automobile as a public good."[12]

The Boston, New York, and Philadelphia city governments were exceptions in subsidizing the trolleys, and a few cities decided that the best way to improve transit service was for them to buy the lines outright, in the European tradition of public transit ownership. Most other cities that took over transit lines did so only decades later as owners of last resort for the cadaverous remains of the once-proud people-movers. While the trolley industry was already on life-support by the 1930s, the highwaymen deserve the credit for pulling the plug.[13] An unlikely alliance between a school dropout and one of America's biggest corporations would speed the trolleys' demise.

Dropout Leaves Rails for Roads

No one wrote "most likely to succeed" beside Roy Fitzgerald's name when he quit school in the seventh grade to work as a laborer at a Minnesota railroad construction camp. But young Fitzgerald's ambition—to make lots of money—was as big as his resources were small, and he soon realized that his future lay not in railroads but in motor vehicles.

In 1916 and newly married, Fitzgerald took a night job in an Eveleth, Minnesota garage, where he washed cars, sold gas and oil, took care of the office, replaced spark plugs, and learned auto mechanics by the seat of his pants. Fitzgerald enjoyed driving his boss's bus, carrying miners two miles from town to the mines on the Mesabi Range. So when his employer decided to leave the bus business in 1919, his young employee's big break was at hand. Scrounging loans from two of his brothers, Fitzgerald bought out his boss, picked up another used bus, and worked daily from 5:00 A.M. to 9:30 P.M., hauling miners and schoolchildren. In a day when motor vehicles were fragile and balky, bad roads took their toll, and Fitzgerald spent his down time making repairs.

Soon his Range Rapid Transit Company was buying up old Packard seven-passenger cars, converting them to fifteen-passenger buses, and offering runs as far as Duluth, sixty miles away. His success made his brothers sit up and take notice. Soon, Ralph left the mines and Ed quit his job as a cook, and they joined their brothers John and Kent in Roy's burgeoning venture. By 1925, the company ran twenty-five buses over a network of routes.[14]

Fitzgeralds Pave Their Future

As the 1920s progressed, the Fitzgerald brothers watched as steam railroads disgorged carload after carload of asphalt, cement, and steel along rutted country roads, to build the thousands of miles of paved highways that Congress had approved in 1921. Until then, the interurban streetcars had been quickest at moving riders between cities. Their builders had logically chosen the most direct route between cities, so often the new roads paralleled the interurban lines. The advent of pneumatic tires and paved roads let fledgling bus companies boast of a ride that equaled the interurbans' in comfort. Now, if they could compete for price and speed, the Fitzgeralds knew, buses could give the interurbans a run for their money.

An astute observer would have seen quickly that the interurbans entered this fight with one arm strapped behind their backs. The private owners of interurbans had to buy, maintain, and pay taxes on the roadbed their trains used. However, the federal and state governments supplied the right of way for the buses, which paid minimal vehicle registration fees and, in the states where a gasoline tax was charged, only one or two cents per gallon in taxes. To add insult to injury, the interurbans also had to pay taxes on the roads their competitors used.

The Fitzgerald brothers were no fools. Soon they had set up bus lines running between cities in the Rocky Mountains and the Midwest, leaving intracity transit to the trolley companies. Gradually, they increased their circuits until 1933, when their buses started trekking from Chicago to Paducah, Kentucky, four hundred miles away. Farmers found the bus light years ahead of a horse and wagon, but buses did not make as large a hit in the cities, where spiderwebs of electric trolley lines had offered frequent and cheap service for decades.[15]

The bare-bones Fitzgerald family business was at the far end of the corporate spectrum from General Motors (GM), the nation's largest automaker. Yet while neither knew it in the late 1920s, in a few years they would conspire to transplant the heart of American urban life.

AUTOMAKERS LEAVE NO MARKET UNTAPPED

Was there no limit to the number of cars, buses, and trucks that GM, Ford, Chrysler, and the rest could sell to the American public? Any corporate executive who could boast doubled sales in four years would find his stockholders jubilant, and Detroit had done just that between 1919 and 1923.[16] But then sales began to level off as consumers came to realize that they could buy a serviceable used car for a much lower price than a new one.

The automaker Charles Nash claimed that Detroit had reached the saturation point for new car sales as early as 1923. Others, including the bullish trade magazines, disagreed. As late as January, 1930, the magazine *Motor* berated the faint of heart: "People will continue to buy [new] automobiles. . . . They don't like old cars." But Walter Chrysler recalled later that he had felt the "winds of disaster blowing" by early 1929.[17]

In their imposing four-tower Detroit headquarters, General Motors executives nervously sensed trouble ahead. They had invested mightily in plant, to compete with the millions of Model T's rolling off Ford's production lines, and their profit projections depended on steeply rising motor vehicle sales. To GM's president, Alfred P. Sloan, Jr., the leveling demand for new cars "meant a change from easy selling to hard selling."[18]

GM: We Must "Reorder Society"

The 1920 census showed that, for the first time, a majority of Americans lived in cities, and American cities obviously held a largely untapped market for motor transportation. While the urban gentry had vied with one another to buy the most stylish new runabout, the aging, turn-of-the-century electric trolleys still moved the masses. So Sloan and his fellow automakers decided to do nothing less than "reorder society...to alter the environment in which automobiles were sold."[19]

One way to do that "was by getting intercity rail passengers out of trains and into cars."[20] So in the early 1930s, GM approached railroads and electric utility companies, which owned most urban trolley lines, and offered to buy their electric streetcar lines, which GM would then replace with buses. But as GM's bus division president, Irving Babcock, later recalled, "We were having great difficulty in convincing the power companies to motorize and give up their streetcars."[21]

AN UNLIKELY ALLIANCE

The Fitzgerald brothers' business was also growing, but when a Yellow Coach Bus Company salesman tried to interest him in buying and converting a streetcar franchise in Galesburg, Illinois, Roy was skeptical about investing in "broken down or worn out street car railway systems."[22] Besides, motorization took big capital, and the Fitzgeralds were just a small operation. But the Yellow Coach salesman persuaded Roy that his lack of money did not matter. GM, it turned out, controlled Yellow Coach.

Although a grade school education handicapped Roy Fitzgerald's discourse, he was an astute businessman. He soon was scrutinizing financial records of failing urban trolley lines, dismissing some investments as hopeless and jumping into other cities with both feet. A trolley-dependent commuter would find a bus in its place the day after Roy came to town. Asked how he tried to wean people in Joliet, Illinois, away from streetcars, Roy said, "We never done anything about the streetcars. They discontinued operating ... in the city one night, and we starting operating modern busses...the next day." Typically, Fitzgerald cut back on fares immediately, then stood on the streets to see how many people were still walking to work. If need be, he would trim fares some more.[23]

With GM as his backer, this small fry was soon hobnobbing with top executives from such corporate giants as Standard Oil and Firestone Tire and Rubber Company. Together, they schemed to create a motor monopoly in nearly four dozen cities across the country, taking over more than one hundred electric transit systems in the process.[24] Despite knowledge of the law forbidding such a monopoly, GM embarked on the plan; eventually, GM and Fitzgerald would stand trial for criminal conspiracy in a Chicago federal court.[25]

In 1932, frustrated with having to wait for failing streetcars to go on the market, GM decided to bankroll a conversion operation itself. Its first objective was to replace city streetcars with motorized buses. Creating a market for automobiles would follow.[26] One of its first successes was in New York City, where it converted the world's largest streetcar network to GM buses over eighteen months.[27]

In 1955, GM General Counsel Henry Hogan testified before the Senate's antitrust subcommittee that he had persuaded GM to front three hundred thousand dollars and create its own holding company—United Cities Motor Transit—which performed successful transplants in Kalamazoo and Saginaw, Michigan, and Springfield, Ohio. "In each case," Hogan said, "[GM] successfully motorized the city, turned the management over to other interests and liquidated its investments."[28]

GM had not been prepared for the public outcry these conversions caused. The high-visibility carmaker had taken pains to build a positive corporate image, to better sell its Chevrolets and Buicks to millions of eager consumers. GM knew that urban trolley riders were a rich lode, but how would these straphangers react if they associated GM with the destruction of their cities' decades-old streetcar system? As luck would have it, GM never had to face such a conundrum. Roy Fitzgerald saved them the trouble.

Fitzgerald jumped at the GM offer to help him buy up and scrap city streetcar lines. With the collapse of the financial market during the Great Depression, Fitzgerald knew that financing for a fledgling operator like himself was difficult at best. GM had bought Yellow Coach—which had brought Roy into the tent—from John Hertz, who had decided that his fortune lay in renting vehicles, not selling them. And all it required from Fitzgerald was an agreement to buy only Yellow Coach buses for his new lines.[29]

The Money Was Right

Announcing to city residents who had relied on electric streetcars for two generations that those systems would be replaced overnight by a yet-untested conveyance was an unpleasant task. But Fitzgerald didn't seem to mind, as long as the money was right, and GM thereby avoided unfavorable publicity. With GM's backing, Fitzgerald moved from Galesburg and Joliet to Tulsa and Jackson, Michigan; and Montgomery, Alabama.

So cooperative was GM that it even provided engineering and marketing surveys; detailed in each city the number of streetcars operating, bus routes, present and projected revenues, and routing and passenger makeup; and walked Fitzgerald's personnel step by step through the conversion process.[30] So neatly did Fitzgerald's operations meet GM's objectives that it soon stopped its own program of converting city streetcars.[31]

Fitzgerald, heeding his agreement with GM, told the transit systems he would buy only "if a deal could be made with the city for complete bus operations—that we [he and GM] were not interested in operating streetcars."[32] But with or without General Motors, the number of trolley companies he could convince to sell out set the limit on his operations. It looked like a long haul ahead for GM and Fitzgerald. But before long, an unexpected development greased the wheels of fate.

UNINTENDED CONSEQUENCES JEOPARDIZE STREETCARS

Corporate bigness, the sin for which American government has made many an enterprise pay, prompted the U.S. Senate in 1928 to investigate the burgeoning public utility industry. The fortunes of electric power companies and streetcar lines had been joined at the hip since the 1890s. In those days—before people cooked, lit their homes, and warmed themselves with electricity—utilities typically sold most of their power to the trolleys. So natural was the combination, in fact, that electric companies commonly bought and operated trolley lines themselves.

But while streetcars had provided the margin of profit in the early days of the century, utilities watched their trolley earnings dwindle by the 1920s, while revenues from household electricity soared. By the Great Depression, massive unemployment had cut trolley commuting drastically, and many trolley companies were running in the red. Fortunately, their corporate parents had deep pockets and typically subsidized their weakening children, hoping for better days.

Yet sustaining urban transportation in the darkest days of the depression brought no goodwill to utility companies. Like the railroads before them, the unregulated companies had mushroomed, often monopolizing a territory, then raising prices. By the 1930s, three giant holding companies, representing the empires of Samuel Insull, General Electric, and the Morgan banking interests, held a lock on half of America's electric power.[33] But sparsely settled farming areas—still without electricity—had watched the country advance without them. Now they asked Washington to buy up or at least regulate the huge holding companies, behind which they saw the conniving hand of the Wall Street establishment.

They found a friend in Franklin Delano Roosevelt, the newly elected president, who championed a bill to make utilities break up their conglomerates and get rid of businesses that did not supply electric service. One of the enterprises falling under this directive was the urban streetcar.[34] The Wheeler-Rayburn Act, which Congress embraced in the summer of 1935, reflected the strong public sentiment for sweeping changes but actualized the worst nightmares of Wall Street.[35] The legislative victory filled reformers with the warm glow of a noble mission accomplished. Once again, the evils flowing from megabusiness had been eradicated.

Trolleys Glut the Market

But another edict—the law of unintended consequences—would soon provide an ironic twist that might cause those same reformers to rue the day they had imploded the holding companies. For suddenly, scores of trolley companies, which carried millions of Americans to work and had been held above water by their wealthier owners, now glutted the market. Balance sheets swimming in red ink made them vulnerable to takeover on the cheap. And waiting in the wings were Fitzgerald and GM.

In 1936, Illinois Power and Light Company, one of many companies forced to divest, dumped on the market streetcar lines in Bloomington, Quincy, Champaign-Urbana, Decatur, Danville, Kewanee, and LaSalle-Peru. Fitzgerald and GM realized that if they moved quickly, they could motorize American cities within a matter of years, not decades. Soon Fitzgerald was huddling with Babcock, Yellow Coach's president, in Detroit. Less than six months after the Holding Companies Act passed, they had formed National City Lines (NCL)—itself ironically a holding company—for their own booming ventures.[36] Studding NCL's board of directors were executives of GM and its Yellow Coach and Greyhound affiliates. In their own conversion attempts, GM and Fitzgerald had publicly called motorization the wave of the future. Yet when Fitzgerald set out to interest investors, he found few who thought that replacing urban trolleys with buses was a financially sound move.[37]

Self-Interest Generates Coalition

Fitzgerald concluded that those benefiting from conversion—suppliers of buses, tires, and petroleum products—would have to help finance the operation if it were to succeed. GM approached Greyhound and Firestone for financial help, and both jumped at the chance to join in, although Greyhound was already a captive of GM, which had assumed $1 million of its debts to keep this volume bus consumer healthy.[38] When Fitzgerald moved into Joliet, Illinois, and East St. Louis, Missouri, Greyhound staked him to a hundred thousand dollars, and GM sold him buses on credit.[39]

The sudden glut of streetcar lines had created a buyer's market, and Fitzgerald kicked a lot of tires, offering distress prices and finding some takers. Two generations earlier, municipalities had wrung concessions from prospective trolley owners. But times had changed. When Fitzgerald converted Montgomery, Alabama's "very bad" streetcar system in 1936, the city was only too glad to repave the streets to accommodate Fitzgerald's new buses. East St. Louis's trolley company, losing ten thousand dollars a month, quickly acceded to Fitzgerald's ultimatum that he would not be responsible for its now-useless streetcars or tracks.[40]

In Cedar Rapids, Iowa, as in cities across America, road building and mushrooming car ownership in the 1920s had dispersed the city's population, diluting the density essential to public transit. Buses, Fitzgerald found, could cover sparsely settled routes more cheaply than streetcars.[41] Baltimore's transit company, before Fitzgerald's intervention, had adjusted by using streetcars on the heaviest routes, trolley buses on medium routes, and buses on feeder lines. This required suburban commuters to transfer from bus to trolley both entering and exiting the city, an inconvenience that convinced thousands to buy more convenient automobiles.[42]

ROY FITZGERALD HEADS WEST

In 1937, GM-controlled Greyhound tried to interest Fitzgerald in the fast-motorizing Pacific Coast. But again, Fitzgerald found investors unwilling to stake any operation that could not show an earnings record to back up its projections. Recognizing shrewdly the self-interest that GM and Standard Oil of California would have in motorization, Fitzgerald "suggested to them that the only way that the company could be started on the West Coast was through some private financing by people who understood the business." By early 1938, GM and Standard Oil had helped him form Pacific City Lines (PCL) and had kicked in most of its million dollars in capital.[43]

In city after city, Fitzgerald insisted on monopoly control, refusing to compete with other trolley companies.[44] Of course, city streetcar authorities had to approve Fitzgerald's takeovers. So it helped to have private consultants with GM connections make seemingly impartial recommendations to city fathers, based on data fed them by GM and NCL.[45]

Bus Rides for a Nickel

The nickel fares that trolleys had almost universally charged at the turn of the century had by now gone the way of the dodo. But Fitzgerald had received such a favorable deal from his oil and motor backers that he was able to roll back the clock in city after city, slashing fares in Montgomery from a dime to a nickel and in Kalamazoo, Michigan, from seven to five cents.[46]

Soon the Minnesota farmboy was meeting with GM top brass at Chicago's fashionable Drake Hotel overlooking Lake Michigan, as GM and Standard Oil of California poured what would amount to $9 million into the effort during the 1930s. GM proved only too glad to supply Fitzgerald buses; Standard Oil of California and Phillips Petroleum, to supply fuel; and Firestone, to sell tires. But in each case, the suppliers insisted that NCL agree in writing to buy their products exclusively, cutting out any competitors. As part of the bargain, NCL had to require anyone buying a converted line never to "return to electric vehicles."[47] As a Standard Oil of California executive testified later:

> We could see . . . from our standpoint, it was going to create a market for our product—gasoline, lubricating oil and greases. . . . If the Fitzgeralds were able to accomplish anything along this line on the Pacific coast, then other people would do it, and this would open up even more markets for us."[48]

MOTORIZING CITIES IS JOB ONE

As the crusade progressed, a curious thing happened, which suggests that the motor interests cared less about short-term profit than the long-term motorization of cities. GM welcomed into the deal the Mack Truck Corporation, a direct competitor now that it had branched into manufacturing buses. Agreeing that Mack could have nearly half of all bus sales to NCL, Irving Babcock, the president of GM's Yellow Coach subsidary, said "the more the better."[49] For its part, a Mack internal memo projected a "probable loss" for the NCL investment but observed that would be "more than justified" by future bus and truck sales.[50]

The journalist Jonathan Kwitny suggests "that the real profits were going to be made from sales of cars [trucks, in Mack's case] after the destruction of mass transit opened the way for a huge public network of streets and highways. That this is what happened offers some justification for the explanation that it was intended."[51] By this theory, Mack did not take profits from GM but rather aided a fundamental industry sea change, allowing both companies a quantum leap in profits in the years ahead.[52]

Skirting the Law

The Sherman Antitrust Act forbids companies from ganging up to restrain a competitor—in this case, the trolley industry and its suppliers. GM almost certainly understood this. Babcock and GM's treasurer, H. C. Grossman— both key players in the conspiracy—were attorneys. And a Phillips Petroleum officer acknowledged in a letter to Grossman problems with the "propriety and perhaps legality" of the investor-supplier agreement.[53]

Corporate Giants Hide Identity

In the summer of 1939, R. F. Leonard, a Firestone assistant treasurer , wrote to a GM representative:

> I have been in New York this week hobnobbing with Roy Fitzgerald and some of the others who are interested in our proposition. I also understand . . . General Motors and Mack Truck were in, also that Standard Oil of New Jersey and Standard Oil of California were in. . . . Everything seems to be going along very nicely and I do think we will probably all benefit by the arrangement.

Noting Firestone's desire to remain anonymous in the transaction, however, Leonard explained, "We put our stock in the name of two of our employees who are acting as nominees."[54]

Standard Oil of California used as fronts the names of two other companies, wishing to shield its identity from the California Railroad Commission.[55] Standard Oil's treasurer, Henry Judd, recalled, "We didn't want to have people in the community feel that if the service was not what they wanted ... the complaints would rest with Standard Oil of California." Yet as Kwitny observes, "This seems strange behavior from companies that defended themselves [at a federal conspiracy trial] on the grounds they had performed a noble public service by hastening the advent of the bus."[56]

By the late 1930s, NCL controlled twenty-nine local trolley companies in twenty-seven cities in ten states. Suppliers had begun funneling into its tank the first of $37 million invested over the next decade.[57] At the time, more than twice as many people rode streetcars as buses; in less than a decade, bus riders would outnumber trolley riders five to four.

Gridlock, 1940s Style

By the early 1940s, America's auto-centered policies had created an ironic twist. In cities such as St. Louis, Baltimore, Los Angeles, and Oakland, Fitzgerald found "a lot of large [auto] traffic lines," which hampered efficient bus operation and required NCL to keep open some of the streetcar lines it had hoped to convert.[58] The beginnings of urban gridlock may have alarmed urban planners, but such bureaucrats clearly did not control the process of American urban development.

In 1943, the expanding ranks of NCL conspirators added General American Aerocoach to its ranks and formed the American City Lines, which soon bought up the massive Los Angeles Railway for $13 million. Then it began converting nineteen of LAR's twenty-five lines, ripping down its transmission lines, tearing up its track, and scrapping its electric trains in favor of buses.

Conversions Served GM's Purposes

Shuttling by train between New York and Chicago in the early 1940s, officials of GM, Firestone, Standard Oil of California, Mack, and Phillips Petroleum negotiated deal after deal. But after the Second World War, GM would leave the business entirely, its sales manager explaining, "It was the policy of GM to get out of all these investments. . . . They were temporary financing plans. . . . They have served their purpose."[59]

But while the NCL conversions served a larger purpose for the big players, they also abetted Roy Fitzgerald's more parochial desire for personal wealth. Once the NCL-acquired properties could no longer pay their way, the company sold eighteen systems to municipal transit districts at high profits. It netted $6.5 million in Los Angeles and $5.1 million from San Francisco's Key System alone.[60]

BROUGHT TO JUSTICE?

Another world war had come and gone before the conspirators were held accountable. By then, more cities' trolleys were in museums than on the streets. In the late 1940s, federal prosecutors in Chicago charged the conspirators with colluding to monopolize the sale of buses, petroleum products, tires, and tubes used by those transport companies. The indictment alleged that their agreements required the NCL to buy all its supplies from the defendants, use their capital to buy up local systems, and require subsequent buyers never again to use electric-powered transit.

The trial limned the stark contrast between the motives of Fitzgerald and his more sophisticated corporate bedfellows. The prosecutor pressed him to admit that he had known his contracts with Phillips and Firestone would exclude their competitors from competing for the NCL's business. Fitzgerald readily admitted he had known that but said no one had ever told him the NCL scheme was illegal and that his only motivation had been to make a buck. By contrast, the prosecutor made much of the fact that kingpins Grossman and Babcock were both lawyers and must have known they were breaking the law.

The prosecutor, Jesse O'Malley, then probed how corporate collusion let Fitzgerald undercut market rates:

O'MALLEY: In these smaller cities, you had certain advantages; you had shorter runs, isn't that correct?

FITZGERALD: Yes, sir.

O'MALLEY: And I think in most of those cases you did not have to pay much if anything for the franchise, isn't that correct?

FITZGERALD: That is right.

O'MALLEY: Now did I understand your testimony to be that your contracts with these supplier defendants were one of the factors which enabled you to charge the five cent fare?

FITZGERALD: Yes, I think so. I think it had a lot to do with it . . . because we were getting reasonable financing.

More sophisticated was the defense of the indicted corporate giants, who had hired legions of attorneys to defend them in the 1949 trial. Among them was twenty-nine-year-old John Paul Stevens, then a junior counsel for Phillips Petroleum, who would work his way up to become a U.S. Supreme Court justice.[61] GM vigorously defended its funding of the NCL scheme as simply helping out a smaller affiliate during tough depression times. The Court was not convinced. It convicted NCL, PCL, Firestone, GM, Phillips Petroleum, Mack Trucks, and Standard Oil, among others. Individuals found guilty included Roy Fitzgerald and H. C. Grossman.

Yet for their roles in concocting and perpetrating a criminal conspiracy—which helped change the dominant urban energy from electricity to less-efficient petroleum and to alter American urban life forever—the Court fined the corporations five thousand dollars each and the individuals one dollar.[62] One authority estimates that the conspiracy had already yielded its participants $30 million to $50 million in profits. The Court's restraining effect on their future activity was predictable.[63]

If criminal statutes are designed to deter illegal activity, the 1949 conviction—upheld on appeal to the U.S. Circuit Court of Appeals for the Seventh Circuit—is an example of failed justice. By 1955, GM had realized its goal of motorizing American cities. Not only had most trolley systems died, but all other modes of public transit—buses as well as trolley coaches—were in decline as well. Of every seven people who rode streetcars in 1947, only one still patronized them a mere eight years later.[64]

THE DEATH RATTLE

Buses had helped toll the death of the trolleys, yet they proved largely a transition to automobiles. For several decades, trolley cars the length of four automobiles had each carried fifty people to work. By the 1960s, the drivers of 70 percent of their successor vehicles—the automobile—would enter the city alone.

As interurbans were starved of capital and beset by draining competition on unfavorable terms, their death rattle became nearly audible. The railroad historian George Hilton describes a ride on an interurban line in its last days:

Particularly on the wooden cars the bodies jerked back and forth and threatened to fly off the tracks every time the cars started or stopped quickly. Windows rattled in their rotting sashes and interior doors that would no longer close banged against their frames. The gentle rolling motion of earlier years gave way to a violent rocking that made it impossible to keep parcels in the luggage racks, and the rocking in turn was intensified by twisting lurches as one set of wheels passed over a dip in the rails where the ties had rotted. . . . Sometimes it was possible to get up a hill only if the car shot down the previous hill and over a quivering trestle at top speed. . . . Some cars developed permanent lists to one side as springs weakened.[65]

The corporate names of individual interurbans belied, in some cases, very human stories of striving and failure, hope and betrayal. Poignancy attended the death of some of the lines. Whereas many promoters leveraged the financing to maximize their profit while minimizing their risks, other independents staked their own money, backed by local businessmen who were forced daily to look into the eyes of devastated investors whose retirement savings had sometimes been wiped out by investing in their risky ventures. The historian Carl Van Doren writes of his physician father's anguish as his Kankakee and Urbana line spiraled downward:

My father at that time was deeply troubled. The last of his enterprises, an electric railroad that would run north and south through Urbana, was still in its earliest stage; yet even then he may have had more qualms about it than he was ever to confess. The line would compete not only with the Illinois Central railroad, which it paralleled, but with automobiles and trucks—more numerous every year, and destined in the end to bankrupt this little Kankakee and Urbana Traction Company of which he was president. People put money into it because he asked them to; they believed in him and he believed in it, for his initial faith in it was very strong; and thoughts of these people were to rob him of much sleep before he died.[66]

AND IN RURAL AMERICA . . .

While city arteries were undergoing major surgery, literally millions of trucks roamed the hinterlands, siphoning off longer-haul business from the railroads and carrying it over the hundreds of thousands of American paved roads. Competing with the rails was like shooting fish in a barrel, since the handcuffed railroads needed to check with their boss in Washington before making each move, while unregulated truckers could undercut rail fares at will. The U.S Supreme Court had held in 1925 that Congress could rein in the truckers, but by the early 1930s, they still had the run of the road. Yet a move was building to throw a harness over what would prove to be a bucking bronco.

·8·

APPLYING THE BRAKES

*Our railroads . . . fulfilled a great purpose, but
if we had no railroads today, we never would
think it necessary to build them.*

—Senator James Couzens, from his statement to
a Senate hearing, 1932

IN FEBRUARY 1932, UNEMPLOYED PEOPLE STOOD HUDDLED ON THE ICY
streets of Washington, selling apples and pencils for spare change. A
young government investigator, Leo Flynn, also felt the bitter wind as he
pulled open the massive door to the Senate Office Building, a stone's
throw from the U.S. Capitol. But coming indoors brought scant comfort
to the young investigator, who knew another icy bluster awaited him four
floors up.

As he strode along cavernous, marble corridors the length of football
fields, Flynn carried a report labeled "Interstate Commerce Commission
Investigation No. 23400"—the kind of pallid government publication that
usually gathers dust among thousands of others. Yet its content had caused
railroad and motor industry spokesmen to rush to Washington, to put
their own spin on its findings. Their forum would be a U.S. Senate committee hearing more aptly described as a free-for-all.[1]

Flynn opened the tall, varnished wooden door to Room 412, where the
Senate's Interstate Commerce Committee was about to convene. Small for

a Senate hearing room, the high-ceilinged chamber bespoke a comfortable elegance, with its center line of three pendulous crystal and silver chandeliers punctuating an ornately paneled ceiling and with a massive white-marble fireplace anchoring the room at its far end.

The hearings had drawn unusual interest. The pretense that truckers could never seriously compete for railroad business had been shattered, and the frenzied competition between the two modes was reaching fever pitch. Rail bulk freight was in free-fall—down by half in the last six years alone, in part because of the Depression. But accusatory fingers also pointed at Detroit, which had caused motor registrations to triple during the 1920s.[2] Yet while the Interstate Commerce Commission's (ICC) iron hand set minimum railroad charges, three and a half million trucks and one hundred thousand buses drove between states as they pleased, undercutting fixed rail rates at will. Railroad fortunes had been wiped out in a few short years: an investor who spent $256 for a share of New York Central stock in 1929 found it worth $9 three years later.[3] Things were so bad that the morning *New York Times* had reported zealous railroad unions reluctantly conceding to a 10 percent pay cut, to trim growing rail losses.[4]

FLYNN FACES FORMIDABLE FOE

Seated in the chairman's place directly in front of the huge fireplace was a square-jawed senator who carried himself in the confident manner of men who have made a fortune from a good idea and hard work, as indeed James Couzens had. Ford employees had called him the "driving force" behind the company's most successful period; after he left, "the company was never so successful again."[5] So well had this self-made man prospered as the number-two man of Henry Ford's monumental enterprise (see chapter 4) that when he quit at age forty-three in a huff with Ford—over a political, not a business dispute—he was worth a reported $40 million to $60 million.[6]

But unlike the independent entrepreneur who has no use for the give-and-take of politics, a fire to seek public office had burned in Couzens's belly since childhood. Born in Canada in 1872, Couzens, as a child, reproached his mother for not giving birth to him in America. "I can never become King of England," he told his mother seriously. "But if I had been born in the United States, I could be President."[7]

Couzens did the next best thing: he ran successfully for Senator from Michigan in 1922, after converting Detroit's streetcar system to municipal control during his stint as mayor (see chapter 4). To Couzens, motor transport had simply supplanted railroading as part of an inevitable historical evolution. The fact that the motor industry's competitive edge stemmed as much from government subsidy as public popularity seemed lost on this energetic bull of a man. In the decade since his election, he had worked his way up to chair the Senate's Interstate Commerce Committee, which held the future of the railroad and motor industries in its hands. The railroads would find him to be "about the worst Chairman" possible.[8]

A career as a regulatory lion tamer for the ICC had molded Leo Flynn's well-defined worldview just as surely as James Couzens's role as a free-enterprise master builder had shaped his. In 1926, Flynn's bosses had dispatched him on an unheralded but bold mission to the hinterlands. Commissioners and staff alike had come to realize that the motor revolution, which had held out such promise to revitalize the railroads, was now seriously bleeding them, a trend masked by the general prosperity of the era.

Railroads, of course, had joined the early chorus for better roads. But the 1921 Highway Act, by linking every county seat in the nation, had cut the umbilical cord between the road and rail forever and freed the motor truck from its dependence on railroads.[9] Still, the ominous implications were lost on the ICC, which encouraged railroads to pour $5.72 billion into expansion during the 1920s.[10] But by mid-decade, the rails, saddled with debt and declining business, beseeched the ICC to let them abandon thousands of miles of line whose trade they had already lost to unregulated trucks. Rail leaders and shippers began to complain to the ICC that trucks were not only competing with them but competing unfairly and illegally.

The ICC tapped Flynn to hold hearings in thirteen cities from San Francisco to Boston to Dallas, to determine just how bad things were. (Decades later, a motor-dependent society would call this "going outside the Beltway.") Hearing from four hundred witnesses, Flynn returned to Washington convinced that the time had come to bring interstate trucking into the ICC tent.[11]

But the ICC commissioners had cold feet. The rationale in their 1928 report was curious: the rails had lost tonnage to short-haul trucks, but they had gained freight by carrying the rubber, steel, and glass needed to make motor vehicles and the finished roadsters, trucks, and buses from Detroit to the showrooms. Therefore, no action was needed. That this was akin to the railroads carrying the coffin to their own funeral was an irony that didn't seem to concern the ICC.[12]

The reason for the ICC's stance is unclear. Perhaps it was the overwhelming workload under which the ICC already labored, with each beleaguered commissioner hearing and deciding an average of seven hundred cases a year. The ICC may have proved reluctant to take on an industry nearly as large as the railroads and far more complex, because it did not see how it could cope with the work. As the ICC chairman, Joseph Eastman, complained frequently, the crushing workload simply left commissioners no time to reflect on the big picture.[13]

But the trends the ICC had first spotted in 1926 had only intensified by 1932, by which time the country had fallen into the worst depression in its history. In the intervening six years, lucrative less-than-carload rail freight had fallen 60 percent, while motor-vehicle registrations rose to 26.5 million in 1929.[14]

Self-starters, pneumatic tires, and improved brakes and transmissions made motor vehicles increasingly road-worthy at a time when the federal government had completed nearly two hundred thousand miles for them to drive on.[15] And while railroads had predictably whined about motor competition in 1926, now the complaints broadened, even including some from truckers. For most trucking concerns were still small outfits, and ruinous competition from wildcatters was poisoning what should have been a very abundant well.

HOW TO DOVETAIL ROAD AND RAIL

A century old, the nation's railroads had still not learned to get along, and decades of regulation by hostile forces had frozen them into a defensive posture, as their creative young minds fled to industries with a future. The ICC made light of the railroads' plight in 1931 in rejecting their "desperate" plea for a 15 percent fare hike, assuring them they would remain "the backbone and most of the other vital bones of [America's] transportation system" for the foreseeable future.[16]

Rather than focusing on how to attract customers to the rails, railroads had responded to the motor onslaught by fighting highway appropriations, demanding that Washington regulate truckers, and diversifying into trucking themselves. From 1925 to 1930, railroads increased their truck fleets eightfold, to seven thousand trucks. They absorbed independent bus companies, buying up Greyhound stock, and operating buses on the new highways that often paralleled their rail lines.[17] Once the motor companies saw railroads competing with them truck for truck, some suddenly found motor regulation more palatable.[18]

So in 1930, the ICC again sent Flynn into the field for another round of hearings. Testimony of hundreds of witnesses made it obvious to Flynn that rail and road were working at cross purposes. If trucks could collect less-than-carload lots and consolidate them at railroad stations, railcars could more frequently be filled to capacity. And running buses and trucks on less-used rail routes could justify the ICC abandoning those lines, he concluded.[19] The dovetailing of road and rail would save money and eventually reduce the prices Americans would pay for washing machines and console radios.

In his report—which echoed the opinions of visionaries before and since—Flynn argued that rail, motor, water, and air modes ought to be orchestrated through regulation, each to do the job it does best and cheapest. Otherwise, each mode operating in a vacuum would inevitably overbuild, and consumers would pay for the resultant waste in higher fares. It was the kind of insightful overview that the ICC had not proved able or willing to contemplate. Flynn's evenhanded report had won him praise even from some truckers.[20] But most motor lobbyists, fearing the unknown, strenuously opposed Flynn's thinking.[21]

Standing Up to the "Manhandler"

A less determined bureaucrat might have cowered before the imposing, dogmatic Senator Couzens, a hot-tempered man whom a frightened Ford employee once referred to as "a manhandler" who kept subordinates in awe.[22] But Flynn was certain that his country's growth depended on road and rail working together—just as certain as the Michigan Senator was that the railroads' time had come and gone. As Couzens called the hearing to order, his mane of white hair rose above his high forehead, blending into the white-marble fireplace behind him, his flinty eyes framed by dark, round horn rims as he fixed his gaze on the first witness.

Flynn took his seat at the witness table and prepared to challenge the laissez-faire milieu under which Couzens had made his millions. He had barely finished describing how scores of hearing witnesses across America had called for curbs on motor vehicles when Couzens waved a newspaper clipping at Flynn and began quoting from a 1931 *New York Times* column by his old colleague, Henry Ford:

Some sections of the country have developed almost without railroads and others will develop that way. Whole sections of the globe will skip the railroad age, such as Russia and China. There the future transportation will flow along the highways and in the air, exactly as it will with us.

"Do you agree with that?" the testy Couzens asked, pressing his witness. "No, sir," Flynn replied simply and continued reading his testimony.

Couzens Outnumbered

Couzens, with his strident views, would prove to be distinctly in the minority on the committee. As Flynn read on, committee members chimed in to buttress his testimony that tens of thousands of unregulated trucks and buses were overrunning the regulated railroads, like ants at a picnic.

The buoyed young investigator now launched back into his testimony, but the irascible chairman was growing warm. "You need not read any further," he said, cutting off the witness. "I think we have the trend of it." Boldly, Flynn ignored the chairman and proceeded to testify that America's largest railroads had lost some $280 million in passenger revenues between 1921 and 1929. And while America's population had grown by leaps and bounds, railroads' lucrative less-than-carload freight was down 14 percent.

Couzens, who felt that the railroads' misfortune simply confirmed their obsolescence, jumped in: "Is there any hope for those railroads in that condition, any future for them, if they are losing their traffic to that extent?" He had played into the hands of Flynn, who countered that railroad-motor competition was hardly free and open: "No matter how much they lose, under the law they are required to keep on operating."

The Question of Regulating Trucks

The chairman stalked his quarry, pressing Flynn to concede that shippers' trucking charges would rise if Washington regulated trucks. Senator Hamilton Kean, a New Jersey Republican, broke in:

KEAN: Well, of course, for they get the use of the highways which the people pay for free.

COUZENS: Let us not let that stand in the record. That is not a fact.

KEAN: Why not?

COUZENS: We will have plenty of testimony later on to determine that.

In fact, the only testimony that would support the premise would be that of "Chief" Thomas MacDonald of the Bureau of Public Roads.

Truckers Hauling 1,500 Miles

Flynn went on to echo rail officials' concerns about the new ability of trucks to travel long distances: "Some years ago, no one thought ... that they would never [sic] go beyond the short-haul limit. Now they are hauling automobiles and other commodities 1,500 miles."

If things were so bad, asked Couzens, why did few shippers or members of the public complain about things as they were?

"It seems to me," said Flynn, "that it is not so much a question of public demand as a question of the public need, or whether it is in the public interest. I think it is a matter of experience that it is very rare that the public rises up and demands a thing until something has happened. . . . Then everyone wants it." Flynn concluded, ceding to other witnesses: truckers, who opposed any restrictions whatsoever; utility commissioners, who wanted stronger medicine than the further study Couzens had prescribed; and railroads, which wanted all truckers to be regulated.

But when Larue Brown, the general counsel for the National Automobile Chamber of Commerce (NACC), objected to even gathering information about trucking patterns, let alone regulating motor vehicles, Kentucky's crusty Senator Alben Barkley (later, Harry Truman's vice-president) angrily retorted: "The giving of one business an advantage over another and thereby allowing interstate commerce and the instruments of interstate commerce to be used so as to make one man prosperous and another unprosperous. Now that can not be done."

Just to make sure everyone understood his viewpoint as the hearings closed, Chairman Couzens observed that not only was the highway-motor community blameless but, in fact, "the railroads would have destroyed the trucking industry if they could have."[23]

Couzens Holds Back the Tide

Couzens managed to keep the lid on the bubbling cauldron of sentiment for trucking reform among his committee members. For senators were also reluctant to burden further thousands of unemployed people who had bought rattletrap delivery trucks to keep food on their tables. And while New York governor Franklin D. Roosevelt would campaign across the country for reform during 1932, the Hoover administration—looking for recovery "right around the corner"—resisted any major changes.[24]

As tales abounded that truckers treated shippers unfairly, small manufacturers in a Depression economy had little money for expensive court battles. The Grangers had mobilized the grassroots workers and carried the torch for shippers in their grievances against the railroads (see chapter 2). But the average American family—focused, sometimes desperately, on food, clothing, and shelter—found it hard to get excited about regulatory reform.

THE PUBLIC LOVES MOTOR TRAVEL

Perhaps most importantly, Americans were madly in love with motor travel and their newfound freedom of movement. When railroads hiked their rates, riders could focus on the fare and compare it unfavorably to the cost of gas at the pump. Yet the true costs of motor travel were increasingly diffuse. To the per-mile cost of gasoline, an informed consumer should have added the costs for purchase and financing, insurance, and maintenance; car and road taxes, including road damage by trucks; and the costs for added police patrols, traffic courts, and land that the government bought for highways. Because such costs were never lumped together, motor travel gave the illusion of being not only more convenient but cheaper. But the collective protestations of the railroads to that effect were "a voice in the wilderness."[25]

Couzens's committee kept one eye on the ICC too. Two months after Flynn had testified, it declawed his recommendations by supporting regulation of buses but opposing it for trucks. This effectively removed any remaining pressure on Congress to sponsor serious legislation.[26] While the breeze of political change whistled through the trees on Capitol Hill, the Babel of voices had immobilized the committee, which would not even report out a reform bill in 1932. Seven years had passed since the Supreme Court had ruled that Congress alone could solve the problem, yet three

more years would go by before Congress acted. By that time the highwaymen would have a hammerlock on American transportation that they
would never relinquish.[27]

THE MARKETPLACE HOLDS SWAY

Later in 1932, the U.S. Supreme Court turned up the heat. Ruling in a
Texas case that "excessive loads on trucks are damaging the highways,"
the Court held that if Congress would not regulate interstate motor commerce, the states could do so themselves. Truckers had argued that the
railroad-rich state of Texas was merely trying to protect rail fortunes by
trying to keep trucks off the road. The Court okayed that, holding that
promoting "a fair distribution of traffic" between road and rail is a proper
state function.[28]

Yet in most states, the marketplace continued to hold sway. Free to do
as they pleased, the nation's Depression truckers acted in ways as diverse
as their population. Thousands of gypsies flourished, shining like fireflies
and then abruptly disappearing in the night, often leaving their customers in the lurch. Hustlers lured newly unemployed, often unschooled
men with low down-payments to buy trucks they could not afford. Once
the monthly payment came due, the new truckers would scramble desperately to undercut their rivals, to bring in any cash they could to pay the
bank.[29]

Unregulated contract truckers hired themselves out as common carriers
and crossed state lines deliberately to avoid regulators. More responsible
haulers like Jack Keeshin (see chapter 5), who had a hundred trucks on
the road by age thirty, feared that the truckers' varied interests would prevent their ever working together for a common goal. But unlike the railroads, who let themselves be dragged in shackles into the regulatory
arena, Keeshin decided to get out front, hoping to help steer the vehicle of
inevitable regulation.[30]

A Railroad Double Agent

The railroads could have improved their lot by aggressively marketing
their own product. Instead, they poured millions into erecting dikes to
hold back the motor tide, including even employing a double agent. In
early 1932, as truckers and railmen clashed in a Washington Senate hear-

ing room, Joseph Hays, a prominent American trucking lawyer-executive quietly entered the employ of six midwestern railroads. His job: to pressure the states to clamp down on truckers. By telling his trucking colleagues that he was merely trying to help road and rail cooperate, Hays was able "to conduct [his] activities without question."[31] He traveled unobtrusively from town to town, setting up taxpayers' committees to lobby for ordinances that would burden truckers and keeping his identity as a railroad employee hidden. Traveling with Hays was a salesman for Black and Decker, who would sell truck scales to towns and tutor policemen on how to enforce weight laws against truckers. By pushing the salesman into the forefront, Hays assured his bosses, "Railroads cannot in any way be criticized for [my] activities."

In his final report to railroad employers, Hays said, "My original objective was to substantially eliminate the long-haul movement of automobiles, tires, and butter by motor truck. . . . I am pleased to say that . . . the gross of the trucking industry in Iowa was materially retarded."[32] Meanwhile, the Iowa lawyer maintained the trust of some of the same truckers he had betrayed. Keeshin describes in his memoirs the assistance received from "my good friend, Joseph Hays." Together, for different motives, they would seek to tame the wild world of trucking.[33]

The Specter of the Railroads' Demise

The railroads had laid off 750,000 men—one-third of their work force—since 1929; meanwhile, sales of new cars were in free-fall, having dropped 75 percent since the stock-market crash of October 1929. Glamorous names such as Pierce-Arrow and Stutz, which massive magazine advertising had made household words, would soon fade from the scene. Heraldic figures such as William Durant, the former GM president (see chapter 4), had filed for bankruptcy.[34] Washington's primary task was to help preserve motor and rail jobs, but the federal government's schizophrenic response was to *loan* money to the rails to upgrade their rights of way while building *free* rights of way for their competitors. For the nation's road-building effort was no longer a means to an end but had become an end in itself.

The postwar ICC knew its iron hand had helped cripple the rails, and now its pendulum had swung the opposite way to passivity, as it urged the lines during the 1920s to borrow more money and allow generous dividends instead of forcing the painful cost cutting and stock wringing that the situation demanded.[35] Now saddled with nearly $6 billion in additional debt, railroads struggled desperately to keep afloat, by nearly halving their operating expenses and trimming dividends.[36]

So enmeshed in the nation's life had railroads become that when they sneezed, America caught a cold. Whereas automakers owned much of their own stock, railroads had borrowed heavily from insurance companies, universities, and thousands of small investors, who depended on quarterly dividend checks for their daily bread. Some investors bemoaned "the ruinous effect which the rampant automobile was having on American community life."[37] A blue-ribbon panel of academic and insurance interests with rail-heavy portfolios, chaired by former President Calvin Coolidge, concluded that Congress must now stop subsidizing the motor industry and start regulating it.[38] Clearly, if the rail industry were allowed to fail, many businesses would suffer further, and untold thousands of Americans would soon be on the dole.

QUANTITY PRODUCTION REIGNS

For its part, the motor industry had overproduced massively during the late 1920s, anticipating a new-car market that simply was not there. The cutthroat competition that resulted killed off such smaller companies as Chalmers, Maxwell, Pullman, Locomobile, and Stevens-Duryea.[39] As early as 1929, Clarence E. Eldridge, one of the industry's own leaders, blamed his fellow automakers: "It is they who by their insatiable ambition, their blind worship at the shrine of the goddess 'quantity production' have created this situation." Eldridge, the sales manager of the REO Motor Car Company, went on to castigate manufacturers who not only set arbitrary quotas for dealers, then shrank their sales territory, to make them scramble to sell cars, but also made fairly new cars obsolete through model changes.[40]

By the 1930s Americans had become so enamored with motor travel that even the Great Depression did not keep the jobless out of their aging cars. When one transit company offered the unemployed free buses to ride to a Works Progress Administration job site, more than half the applicants arrived by automobile. Dust-bowl nomads piled their belongings atop their beat-up cars, leading Russians viewing the film version of *The Grapes of Wrath* later to ask, "How can these people be poor when they own a car?" Will Rogers quipped that Depression-era Americans would be the first ever to ride to the poorhouse in an automobile.[41]

Yet while motor and rail companies went out of business, reorganized in bankruptcy, or otherwise struggled to survive, the American highway industry—thanks to government pump priming—boomed. During the 1930s, paved-road mileage nearly doubled, to 1.367 million. The American Automobile Association added now-familiar routes, such as U.S. 1 along the East Coast and Route 66 from Chicago to Los Angeles, to its proliferating maps.[42] While opposed to handouts, President Hoover had justified massive highway spending as a jobs program and pumped a record $175 million into the highway pipeline. By mid-1932, more than a half-million men were at work shoveling dirt and rolling asphalt.[43] But many desperate social needs now competed with road building. As an Illinois highway engineer lamented, "The day of highway hysteria is over. The bubbling good roads booster, with his sentimental appeal, must be replaced by the highway economist armed with sound plans."[44]

INSIDE THE LION'S MOUTH

On September 17, 1932, six weeks before election day, Franklin Delano Roosevelt placed his head inside the lion's mouth. He chose a speech in Salt Lake City—the conservative bastion of the Mormon church—to pledge that, if elected, he would shake America's two biggest industries to their roots. Utah had voted for only one Democrat for president in the twentieth century, but 1932 was an uncommon year. Many voters felt captive to eastern financiers, whose depredations had helped strip paychecks from thirteen million breadwinners, among them one-third of the country's railroad workers.[45]

The son of a railroad executive, Roosevelt had "never lost his boyhood zest for traveling slowly around the country in a private Pullman car." Yet if railroads exerted a nostalgic pull on him, the governor had also studied transportation economics at Harvard with William Z. Ripley, perhaps the foremost expert of his day. He understood the practical and political need for government to keep a hand on the railroad brake.[46]

With characteristic panache, Governor Roosevelt selected the Mormon Tabernacle for his promise to integrate road and rail into the nation's first-ever transportation policy. Both national radio networks considered this address so important that they carried it live.

As the famed Mormon Tabernacle Choir's rendition of the "Star Spangled Banner" reverberated through the tabernacle, a throng of eight thousand rose in a "remarkably enthusiastic" tribute to the Democratic candidate.[47] Speaking from the pulpit, the charismatic nominee pledged that Washington would support the railroads but warned that they must first trim down their "topheavy" debt and agree to integrate their operations with motor, water, and air transport, in the national interest. And no longer is it fair, he said, to expect railroads to compete with subsidized, unregulated truckers, who "naturally . . . can often haul passenger and freight at a lower rate than the railroads."[48]

"The cause of many of our problems," Roosevelt declared, is "the entire absence of any national planning." He vowed to reverse that by beefing up the ICC and putting truckers under its thumb for the first time.[49] Roosevelt had preached a gospel that would put Utah in the Democratic column for years to come. It was, in the parlance of the time, a boffo performance.[50] Now all he had to do was live up to his promises.

Remarkably, both the motor industry and the railroads approved the speech beforehand, at least in principle, reported the *New York Times* correspondent Jim Hagerty, who twenty years later would become the press secretary to Dwight D. Eisenhower, the president who would deliver the coup de grace to the railroads by championing the Interstate Defense Highway System (see chapter 11).

·9·

HARD TIMES

We must give Fuehrer Hitler credit for build-
ing a system of superhighways in his country
[that would provide the German people with]
innumerable peacetime commercial, indus-
trial, social and cultural benefits.
—House Roads Committee Chairman Wilburn
Cartwright, 1938

IN THE 1930S, AS NOW, THE GAP BETWEEN HIGH-MINDED CAMPAIGNING
and on-the-ground governing proved very great. In early 1933, scores of
reform plans swirled around Franklin Delano Roosevelt, the new president. He might have expected schemes to nationalize truckers and railroads to go nowhere. Yet FDR would soon discover that, even though the
motor and rail industries were both in dire straits in early 1933, forces
would oppose even modest plans for them to work together so they might
survive.[1] Bowing to the free-enterprise system, Roosevelt would first try to
cajole road and rail into competing fairly with one another voluntarily.
When that failed, he would try for stronger measures and find the
entrenched road and rail interests lurking in the bushes to thwart them.

Americans had watched their "can-do" society crumble around their
shoulders, in a mélange of corruption, ineptitude, and wiped-out savings.
The day's best-sellers reflected the aura of disillusionment: John O'Hara's
Appointment in Samarra, Thomas Wolfe's *You Can't Go Home Again,* John
Steinbeck's *Grapes of Wrath.*[2] While radios blared the hit song "Brother
Can You Spare a Dime?" New York department stores took advantage of
the vast pool of unemployed people by requiring a bachelor's degree for a

job applicant to become an elevator operator. One family went to court to change the name of their four-year-old son from "Herbert Hoover Jones" to "Franklin D. Roosevelt Jones," to "relieve the young man from the chagrin and mortification which he is suffering and will suffer."[3]

SAVING BUSINESS FROM ITSELF

Congress, knowing it had to move quickly to mop up from the excesses of laissez-faire capitalism, quickly adopted two measures. The National Recovery Act (NRA) was designed to "save American business from itself" by urging that industries regulate themselves through codes of "fair competition." The Emergency Railroad Transportation Act created a federal coordinator of transportation to knock railroaders' heads together; ironically, its biggest achievement would be to finally rein in part of the motor industry. The era of diesel trains had arrived, but cars and roads preoccupied the nation and led FDR to cast an eye toward Germany, as he envisioned a coast-to-coast superhighway.

As draining as the road-rail battles had become, America's truckers skirmished with equal fervor among themselves and with the labor unions that had begun to organize the industry. Labor demanded that any voluntary industry code should safeguard good wages and a forty-hour work week. But what about seasonal drivers, who work round the clock at harvest time and build a nest egg for the lull after the harvest? Southern business leaders argued that higher wages would keep out black truckers. Some felt uniform rates could stabilize the industry and prevent wildcatters from having a field day, while consumer advocates charged that higher costs would inevitably follow.[4]

TRUCKERS RESIST

The Code of Fair Competition would have a turbulent eight-month life, which would end up doing little for the nation but which would coalesce the truckers as no mere congressional act could ever have done. It charged state authorities with signing up truckers in each state. For a three-dollar fee, truckers would receive a Blue Eagle emblem to display on their trucks. Suspicious of government meddling and skeptical that government could really make things better or effectively enforce the code's provisions, many truckers resisted the call to sign up voluntarily. A dialogue between an enforcement agent and a Georgia trucker typifies the dilemma:

AGENT: Do you want to register?

TRUCKER: Go away, boss. You know us niggers can't register and vote.

AGENT: You are not registering to vote. You are registering your vehicle with the Government under the Code of Fair Practice for the Trucking Industry.

TRUCKER: Cap'n, ah ain't got no truck

AGENT: Well, the Code applies also to horse-drawn vehicles.

TRUCKER: Boss, anybody kin tell you I'se always practiced fair. Do this heah thing cost any money?

AGENT: Yes, the authorities have fixed a $3.00 assessment as the proper charge for the cost of registering the vehicles under the Code.

TRUCKER: *(Heading toward the door)* Boss, I am sho' sorry, but I ain't seen $3.00 since Buck was a calf. Tell Uncle Sam I sho' hates it, but if I had $3.00 I wouldn't even speak to him.[5]

Undaunted, state authorities pressed on, eventually registering three hundred thousand trucks, 80 percent of them one-truck firms. Yet the system was basically toothless, cumbersome, and bureaucratic, and it eventually fell of its own weight. By 1935, it was clear that truckers could not clean house by themselves.[6] But in the process, they had gained an "industrial consciousness."[7]

A Socialist to Rule Reactionaries

To harmonize the reactionary conservatives of the railroad industry, FDR chose as his transportation czar Joseph Eastman, a man who was philosophically a socialist. While America's business revered the "invisible hand" of the free market, this fallen-away minister's son worshipped "the guiding hand of government control."[8] Eastman had been a protégé of Justice Louis Brandeis since their days fighting corruption on the Boston Elevated Railway. At age twenty-three, Eastman told an Amherst classmate that he saw socialism not as a moral question but as a matter of practical wisdom and accepted that "we have not reached the stage of human development and altruism which permits such an organization of society."[9]

The railroads' overbuilding and withering rate wars had made Eastman doubt that if left alone, the rails would see that it was in their own best interests to produce efficiently.[10] Yet he also recoiled from the "wasteful duplication" he had seen regulators impose on business. Any business so integral to the national economy, he concluded, simply ought to be government owned. The success of the Boston Elevated Railway under municipal ownership and the increased efficiency of the nation's railroads under First World War government control only strengthened his belief.[11]

In 1919, Woodrow Wilson named Eastman, then thirty-seven, to the ICC, upon the recommendation of Brandeis, who labeled him "hard-headed—honest, courageous."[12] Remarkably, Eastman met scant opposition from conservative railway magnates. The calm, portly, and slightly rumpled mien of this lifelong bachelor made him less than threatening to the industrialists it would be his job to corral.[13] The most attractive feature in Eastman's long, fleshy face was his hazel eyes, which held the gaze of his listeners.[14] A model of Progressivism in full flower, Eastman had proved himself to be "the professional public servant dedicated to finding the common good."[15] Eastman would soon prove himself the ICC's most distinguished, hardest-working, and most effective commissioner.[16]

Eastman's first few months as transportation czar brought home to him the unbridled advances of the motor industry. Although trucks now carried only 10 percent of all intercity freight, most was lucrative short-haul trade.[17] And 90 percent of shippers, railroads, chambers of commerce, and truckers surveyed told him that they favored regulating motor transport.[18] In response, Eastman called for combining road and rail into one system, "without cross purposes and all manner of lost motion," under the ICC umbrella.[19]

Eastman's fortunes would get a boost in 1935. Early that year, having watched NRA's experiment in self-regulation crumble, he asked Congress to take the truckers in tow. He readily admitted that this would cause rates to rise and would increase the size of trucking companies. But Eastman, like some Progressives, believed economies of scale could make big businesses more efficient, and that was in the public interest. Challenging him, ironically, was a senator who had forged one of America's largest corporations. James Couzens, as a corporate wizard who ought to have known, argued that "the mere size of an institution is no assurance of efficient or competent management." But the tide had turned, and most interested parties had jumped on the reform bandwagon.[20] When the U.S. Supreme Court ruled the self-regulating NRA unconstitutional, the die was cast.

But the Motor Carriers Act, passed in 1935, was a pale reflection of Eastman's dreams. It regulated only the rates of that one-fifth of truckers deemed to be common carriers.[21] Passage of the Motor Carrier Act was a tribute to Eastman's evenhanded consultative style. But his major goal—to integrate road and rail into an interdependent transportation system—had eluded him. Political compromise had diluted the act, rendering it largely ineffective, and the rails continued to face many of the same competitive hurdles as before. By the late 1930s, nearly one-third of total rail mileage of the largest carriers lay in receivership as the recovering economy relapsed.[22]

In 1938, FDR once again asked Congress to reorganize the ICC and to meld all transport modes into one transportation department.[23] While the railroads would have been the intended beneficiaries of such a scheme, it was railroad labor and management that scuttled the plan. Even playing cards with a stacked deck was more palatable to them than contending with further government involvement. Organized labor feared, correctly, that coordination would involve consolidating rail lines with a resultant loss of two hundred thousand jobs. But while the railways temporized, their motor competitors were looking ahead and pulling into the passing lane.[24]

HANDS OFF OUR TAXES!

Amazingly, people drove even more during the Great Depression. Revenues from state fuel taxes had soared from 1929 to 1932, even while the nation's other tax revenues plummeted, as one quarter of the country's workforce was jobless. Watching general revenues dry up, Washington had imposed a penny-a-gallon gas tax for the first time in 1932, an ominous portent.[25] In the highwayman's ideal world, climbing tax revenues meant more roads to hold more cars to generate more taxes to build more roads. But in the depths of the Depression, the road advocates were understandably concerned, for they felt the covetous eyes of cash-starved states upon them. With every state collecting a fuel tax of from two to six cents a gallon, twenty-one states had been able to stop using property taxes to build main roads.[26] Next, they feared, people would demand that government siphon off fuel taxes for schools or other needs, as European countries had been doing for decades. One commentator warned, "The motor tax has become a big red apple within easy reach, viewed with slavering lips by every agency of government." Indeed, by 1932, sixteen states began to divert fuel revenues to other uses.[27]

Diversion became a word that the highway community spat out sneeringly. When FDR—tinkering under the hood to jump-start America's economy—created the National Industrial Recovery Act, one might have expected road advocates to be pleased, since it meant $400 million in new money that the states did not even have to match.[28] But the development worried MacDonald because the added Washington money made it easier to justify diverting state gas taxes. And if state highway taxes became separated from highway spending, roads might eventually have to compete for appropriations with welfare and prisons and become just another government program.[29]

So the highwaymen put out the word that Americans must oppose diversion at all costs because it gave state legislators a license to spend. The *Washington Post* called it the "exploitation of motorists for the benefit of the state."[30] By 1934, the highway lobby got its way: the Hayden-Cartwright Act agreed that using motor vehicle taxes for something other than building or maintaining highways was "unfair and unjust." It would end federal road aid to any states that continued to do so.[31]

BUILDING ROADS WITHOUT A PLAN

The depression recovery had become a national quest. Everywhere, one saw Blue Eagle insignias, displayed on front doors and car windshields with the motto, "We Do Our Part," making it nearly unpatriotic to oppose job-creating road construction. Yet even while more and more highways were under construction, the leveling off of car registrations convinced some that the market for automobiles had reached the saturation point. In Los Angeles, of all places, the California Railroad Commission suggested in 1935 that "the competitive impact of the automobile has reached its peak."

It may have been a national duty to favor road building, but transit officials reminded motorists that the decline of mass transportation would contribute to unemployment as well. In 1937, a transit publication alleged that "well organized groups" deliberately tried to "unpopularize" streetcars and replace them with the automobile. In 1933, a Corning, New York, bus company warned that bus drivers would soon lose their jobs if motorists kept giving rides to hitchhikers.[32] Few paid heed.

So in the darkest days of America's economic history, the golden age of road building continued. The federal-aid highway system, linking all county seats in the nation, accounted for only 7 percent of total road mileage. Villages, truckers, farmers, urban planners, highway engineers, shippers—all had their own agendas, and no mechanism existed for them to agree where to build the other 95 percent. City dwellers wanted to end bumper-to-bumper traffic, farmers wanted to get from the farm to the market fast, planners sought to promote social cohesion, and engineers wanted roads that could hold more cars.

Those lobbying their councilman or state legislator most effectively got their favored strip of road paved, usually without regard to how it tied in with others. "Political disputes, not budgets and designs, proved decisive." The result was a series of "complex, ambivalent and inconsistent road programs."[33] But few had the will or the patience to step back from the process to tie the loose ends together. For road building per se was the success story of the demoralized 1930s.

THE DIESEL AGE DAWNS

Recognizing the futility of waiting for help from Washington, the railroads began innovating, to stimulate business. By the mid-1930s, gleaming new passenger locomotives roared into the station, minus smokestacks and boasting sleek aerodynamic curves that led people to call them "streamliners." Gone were the firebox and sooty embers; the day of the diesel had arrived. To underscore the dramatic change, the stark black of the steam locomotive yielded to brilliant reds and oranges. Magazine ads announced "A New Era Dawns in Transportation." Rudolph Diesel, who first noted diesel's superiority over steam in 1894, had sold his locomotives in Europe for years, but his technology now had vaulted the Atlantic.

Designed for luxury passenger travel, diesel trains boasted such features as club cars and ice bunkers at the bottoms of Pullman cars for air conditioning. As Europeans had discovered, passengers love luxury, and the new trains surprisingly made money. In a historic irony, the greatest beneficiary of the diesel craze happened to be General Motors, which jumped into diesel production with both feet when "our competitors thought we were crazy."[34] Gamely, some railroads put freight trains on frequent passenger-train schedules, to compete with the flexibility of truckers, and offered overnight delivery. Yet the preoccupation of the nation was new jobs, so the White House was thinking roads, not rails.

A SUPERHIGHWAY ACROSS AMERICA

Scanning the December 13, 1934, *Washington Post* over breakfast, a local reader could have learned that night baseball was coming to the National League and that

Carole Lombard was playing in downtown Washington in *The Gay Bride*. Page one showed President Roosevelt enlisting Bernard Baruch and Calvin Coolidge to help plan how to take the profit out of war and staging a presidential photo-op with the doctor who delivered the Dionne quintuplets. Nowhere did the newspaper announce an afternoon meeting that would resonate farther than any story that made that edition: FDR's secret plan to build a transcontinental superhighway.[35]

As millions of drivers now swarmed like ants across a national network of roads, rising highway fatalities and injuries demonstrated the hazards of letting motorists on or off heavily traveled streets at will. So in the late 1920s, the BPR began to experiment with highways that only let people on or off every few miles. Its first limited-access highway opened in 1928 and ran from Arlington, Virginia, to George Washington's home at Mount Vernon. The same year, the BPR helped build the Skyline Drive. In the 1930s, it helped build the Blue Ridge Parkway, and in 1934, the Natchez Trace Parkway in Tennessee and Mississippi.[36] And as early as 1923, New York's Bronx River Parkway had demonstrated the safety of using a median to separate opposing lines of traffic.[37]

FDR DISCOVERS HITLER'S AUTOBAHNS

The most sophisticated superhighway in the world was being built by a young, ambitious German politician. Adolf Hitler accelerated a plan begun in 1929 to build forty-five hundred miles of limited-access roadway with two 30-foot lines of traffic separated by a grassy strip. Hitler's roads chief had declared that such a system "can exist only in a country in which the people and the State, under strong leadership, devote themselves to the constructive tasks of peace."[38] The project, known as the *Reichsautobahnen*, or "National Auto Road," had caught FDR's notice.[39]

But innovative highway design was not what caused FDR to summon Thomas MacDonald to the White House this brisk December day; it was finding jobs for the one out of every four workers on the streets.[40] The National Industrial Recovery Act had put a half-million men to work building roads, but voters commonly saw these efforts as state projects, since the money was channeled through forty-eight highway departments. Politically, the president knew the perception had not sunk in across the country that Washington was doing all it could to relieve unemployment.[41] FDR at midterm felt the need to bring the focus back to Washington. So the president had conceived a radical idea to put hundreds of thousands back to work building the biggest roads project in world history and to get American business to pay for it.

So legendary had MacDonald become as a can-do bureaucrat that FDR tapped him as the man for the job. Roosevelt and MacDonald were both in their early fifties, but the similarities seemed to end there. The jaunty, breezy president and Treasury Secretary Henry Morgenthau, both patrician Ivy Leaguers, on this day greeted the laconic BPR chief as sunlight streamed through the Oval Office windows. They were taking the measure of this farm-belt native, who had won stunning credibility on Capitol Hill while serving five presidents.

A Self-Financing Superhighway

FDR sketched out his visionary plan on a map of the United States. He drew a thick black line running west and south from Worcester, Massachusetts, to the Delaware Water Gap, then branching south toward Florida and west toward San Francisco. Professor William Z. Ripley at Harvard (see chapter 8) had taught Roosevelt in 1903 that land increases dramatically in value when a road is built next to it.[42] Carrying this a step further, Roosevelt proposed that Washington buy a two-mile strip of land coast to coast, snake a highway through the middle of it, and sell the newly valuable adjacent land to developers attracted by the highway's proximity.[43]

Britain, which had used the procedure successfully, called it "excess taking." But America, unlike Britain, had a constitution, as a brake against arbitrary authority. Unlike taking land for a public use such as a school, the practice of condemning land, enhancing its value, then reselling it to generate money so ran against the grain of America's concept of private property that states had outlawed it in the 1920s. When FDR made his plan public, critics would brand it a "socialistic scheme."[44]

MacDonald kept his own counsel after hearing the president's grandiose plan. But megahighways had been on the BPR's drawing boards for years; the problem had been how to pay for them. Even had FDR's excess-taking scheme proved workable, the president knew that the road would have to charge tolls to help pay for itself. And tolls were an idea against which the BPR chief dug in his heels harder than an Iowa mule. Consumers would not only have to pay at the gas pump and the tollbooth, he said, but also would have to pay the tax collector, because not enough people would use toll roads to pay their costs. No bigger roads booster than MacDonald existed in America, but even he had vastly underestimated the lure of the open road.

Roosevelt delayed announcing such a controversial program until after the 1936 election.[45] Yet in spite of that historic landslide, the popular president found that the highway bureaucracy had a lock on the nation's roads program so powerful that he seemed unable to break it. FDR envisioned a cornucopia of political benefits if he could regain control of federal highway spending. In 1937 he would make his move, but the victorious, charismatic president had underestimated a colorless bureaucrat from Iowa.

ARM WRESTLING WITH THE PRESIDENT

The politician in Franklin Roosevelt stood in awe of the immense power of the Bureau of Public Roads and its resourceful leader. Government leaders in Europe, Central America, and South America were beseeching MacDonald to teach them how to build roads. He traveled widely now, hoping thereby to open new markets for American rubber, steel, and cement. While in Holland during a European tour, an awestruck aide cabled home, "To walk through these hotels with [MacDonald] reminds one of the attention Joe Louis gets in Grand Central."[46]

Congress let the BPR guarantee roads to states before the legislators had even appropriated the money, so the agency had an independence that rankled the president. Seeking to seize the highway pursestrings, FDR pressured Senate Democrats to rescind the law. In a "bitter attack," Roosevelt complained that the BPR's contract authority tied his hands. That, the diminutive Representative Carl Hayden of Arizona replied tartly, was "exactly what the Congress intended to do."[47]

If he was to make his mark as a road builder, FDR knew that he would have to adopt another tack, so he returned to his vision of transcontinental highways. Setting the pace in superhighways, Adolf Hitler's autobahns—which MacDonald called a "wonderful example of the best modern road building"—were already speeding domestic traffic throughout the German countryside. FDR asked MacDonald to prepare three east-west and three north-south routes.[48]

An Expensive Hobby Horse

FDR's transcontinental toll road had become his $2 billion hobby horse, and he nurtured the project assiduously on Capitol Hill. The president revived the concept of "excess taking" and proposed that Washington rent the surplus land to highway concessions and sell off the remainder to home builders.[49] Just as determinedly, MacDonald denounced the scheme to Congress. The Senate Roads Committee, some of whose members owed their 1936 election to FDR's coattails, nevertheless immediately and unanimously rejected the president's position.[50]

In 1939, MacDonald sought to bury the toll-highway idea in a report the size of a small book, arguing that tolls would cover only 40 percent of the total cost. Only a quarter of FDR's proposed fourteen-thousand-mile system would need more than two lanes, MacDonald said, making the cost of toll booths unrealistic. He drew his projections from state-of-the-art mechanical traffic counters, developed with the help of IBM. Yet what the BPR measured was the volume and nature of trips cars and trucks made *on existing roads*. Significantly, what BPR's surveys did not calculate was how people's habits would change if they had a high-speed, limited-access toll road to drive on.[51]

A less skillful politician than FDR might have sulked or lashed out when defeated so soundly on a policy issue. Instead, the president chose to race ahead and lead the parade for the concept that had defeated him. Transmitting MacDonald's report to Congress, FDR threw in the towel, conceding that superhighways were needed only in metropolitan areas with congested roads.[52] Transcontinental federal toll roads had died aborning.

THE FIRST SUPERHIGHWAY

Yet to Americans mired in hard times for nearly a decade, broad high-speed highways were the promise of a brighter future. The concept had sparked imaginations at the state level, such as in Pennsylvania and Connecticut, where a more bullish outlook prevailed than in Washington.

In a monumental irony, railroads would help make possible the grandiose experiment that would create a working model for America's interstate highway system, the building of which nearly drove the final nail into the railways' coffin. In the early 1880s, the rail titan William Vanderbilt and steelmaker Andrew Carnegie conspired to take on the mighty Pennsylvania Railroad, against which both had grievances. The Allegheny Mountains had historically impeded trade from moving between the Atlantic and the Ohio Valley. Vanderbilt planned boldly to blast nine massive mile-long tunnels through the mountains, creating a gateway from east to west for his South Pennsylvania Railroad, thus challenging the Pennsy's supremacy.

In the preregulatory era, such rail skirmishes had often led to withering rate wars, convulsing the financial markets. Twenty-six men had already lost their lives in constructing the project on which Vanderbilt had spent $10 million dollars when J. P. Morgan's heavy hand intervened. The New York financier possessed such clout that he stopped Vanderbilt's dream dead in its tracks and got both protagonists to hoist a white flag. Twenty-five hundred workers walked away from the partially completed tunnels, a two-hundred-mile gash through Pennsylvania's heartland, which lay eerily dormant for a half-century.

In the 1930s, entrepreneurs suggested finishing the railroad tunnels and creating a thoroughfare for automobiles, not trains. But financiers refused to back the endeavor. They agreed with MacDonald that such a super-highway, with two 12-foot lanes in each direction, a 10-foot median, and a maximum grade of 3 percent (borrowed from the German autobahns), simply would not generate heavy traffic. In the nick of time, federal money saved the $61 million project—not because of any faith that the turnpike would succeed but only that it would create thousands of jobs in the still-sagging economy.[53]

Riding the Yellow Brick Road

The fact that truckers could cut their time from Pittsburgh to Philadelphia nearly in half would more than justify their paying the $1.50 toll, and would insure the Pennsylvania Turnpike's success. Soon 118 contractors and ten thousand construction workers labored day and night for twenty months to complete the monumental effort. During its first year, an average of sixty-five hundred people a day used the turnpike, nine times the figure MacDonald had projected. The age of the American superhighway had arrived.

The Pennsylvania Turnpike, though by far the grandest, was not the first American four-lane limited-access road. California's Arroyo Seco Parkway, also opened in 1940, was a forerunner of the Los Angeles freeways. Connecticut's Merritt Parkway, conceived to fight congestion on the Boston Post Road—a historic stagecoach route—carried 18,800 passenger cars a day within a year of its 1938 opening. In Washington, MacDonald watched as motorists and truckers disproved his theory that masses of people would not pay tolls where they could ride lesser parallel roads free.[54]

The turnpike was not merely a route to tourist attractions; it *was* a tourist attraction. Tourists could enjoy a roadside picnic while watching convertibles whiz by, and then devour an ice cream cone in one of Howard Johnson's twenty-eight flavors while cruising at seventy miles an hour (there was no speed limit in the early days). For truckers, service plazas offered dormitory bunks, lounges with radios, pinball machines, and lunch counters. S. W. Marshall the Pennsylvania Turnpike's chief engineer, driving along his creation for the first time, said, "I felt that I had just entered a different world, like Dorothy in the Wizard of Oz, and I was on the Yellow Brick Road."[55]

By 1940, it was clear that superhighways were here to stay. Speaking for the American Road Builders Association, Charles M. Upham, an engineer, sketched his vision of the American future: "This rich and productive nation will be like the 'promised land of honey and gold' when the belligerents abroad tentatively settle their differences. . . . America has wealth, culture, power! Our coastlines are the frontiers of a civilization. We are the custodians of Shangri-La "[56]

A continent away, a tyrant stormed westward through Europe, on a cataclysmic mission that would draw America outside itself for the second time in a generation. Shangri-La would have to wait.

·10·

A WAR ABROAD, A CONFLICT AT HOME

If we are to have the full use of automobiles, cities must be remade.

—Paul Hoffman, the president of the Studebaker Corporation, 1939

By the late 1930s, Adolf Hitler's capacious autobahns had sparked Americans' imaginations. The ability to drive long distances at high speeds without a stoplight intoxicated people, just as the notion of owning one's own motorized conveyance had at the turn of the century. In 1939, far and away the most popular exhibit at the New York World's Fair was General Motors's Futurama. As six hundred people at a time rode through GM's mockup of America's future, recordings synchronized for each rider's chair told how someday soon everyone would be able to speed at 100 miles an hour on fourteen-lane superhighways and how expressways would be routed strategically through cities, to bulldoze ugly slums and outmoded business districts.[1]

Ironically, the German fuehrer, an "auto freak" himself, was about to give American railroads their finest hour. For the second time in a generation, the United States went to war, a conflict whose similarities and dissimilarities from the First World War both played into the hands of the railways.[2]

As America approached midcentury, railroads had reaped a bitter harvest of ruinous overregulation, uninspired management, and public hostility. The highwaymen's carefully orchestrated plan to win passengers and freight away from the rails had borne abundant fruit. The idea that railroads represented America's past, and cars and trucks its future, had by 1940 become deeply entrenched in the American psyche.[3] During the Second World War, a shaft of sunlight would break through the clouds that railroads had lived under for several decades, while discord broke the highwaymen's ranks for the first time. But the rails would face their biggest challenge when postwar prosperity led to car fever.

RAILROADS TO THE RESCUE

The railway titans knew that the only thing they hated more than being forced to cooperate with their competitors was losing control of their businesses, as had happened during the First World War. Now, facing another wartime mobilization, they vowed not to repeat their mistakes of a generation earlier. Fortunately, President Roosevelt was a friend of the railroads, both by personal inclination and by growing up in a railroad family. Railroads had proven his mode of choice as president, and he logged twenty thousand miles a year aboard his heavily armored private car, the "Ferdinand Magellan."[4]

So when Ralph Budd, the respected president of the Burlington Northern, beseeched FDR to let the rails mobilize privately for war, the president agreed and put Budd in charge. Unassuming, democratic, and willing to listen, Budd stood in stark contrast to the autocratic moguls of an earlier era and proved just the right person to convince his industry cohorts that their best interests lay in pulling together for the war effort.[5]

The plight of the railroads at the advent of the First World War had been too little capacity and too much business; a generation later the reverse was true. Urged by the Interstate Commerce Commission (ICC) to overinvest, the lines had added 15,000 steam locomotives and 850,000 freight cars in the 1920s and 1930s, but motor competition had left many lying idle on rail sidings.[6] The Depression and competition had forced the industry to cut costs and boost efficiency, leaving it lean but with excess capacity to absorb large numbers of soldiers, tanks, and supplies.

Setback for Detroit

The wretched condition of most American roads had hampered the usefulness of primitive trucks and buses to First World War mobilization. But with millions of trucks driving on a new network of coast-to-coast highways, the highway-motor interests prepared for a major wartime role. William S. Knudsen, GM's president, whom FDR drafted to aid the mobilization drive, advised the president to "bury the auto manufacturers under defense orders—three times as much stuff as they can make with their present facilities."[7] The motor industry awaited eagerly the chance to do well by doing good.

Then, quite unpredictably, these prospects plummeted. In the early days of the Second World War, Japan seized Southeast Asian rubber plantations, and in the Atlantic, German U-boats sank coastal oil tankers bound for American shores. Before long, Washington was strictly rationing rubber and gasoline, and imposing a thirty-five-mile-an-hour speed limit to conserve both commodities.[8] The shortages caused automobile and trucking production to screech to a halt, as Detroit retooled its production lines to produce planes, tanks, and ships.[9] At the same time, coal-fired steam railroads surged to the fore. By the war's end, they would move 97 percent of wartime passengers and 90 percent of its freight, posting profit margins they had not seen since early in the century.[10] For the first time in decades, the highwaymen felt unappreciated. Thomas MacDonald bemoaned privately in 1943 the administration's failure to see "the highway system as being a critical war-time resource."[11]

Technology and geography smiled on the railroads as well. Advances in traffic-control systems, larger railcars, and more powerful locomotives allowed the rails to move half again as much freight as in the First World War, with nearly a third fewer locomotives and a quarter fewer freight cars.[12] And a war fought on two fronts added to efficiency. In the First World War, railcars had shipped passengers and materiel across the country to East Coast ports and returned home unprofitably empty. Now their westbound backhauls sped toward California ports, where Far East shipments padded their earnings.

Rails Seize the Advantage

No longer could rail executives afford to sneer, "The public be damned," chastened as they had been by decades of public reproach. Aware that an efficient wartime effort would improve their image, railroads seized the public relations advantage, placing full-page color ads in such popular magazines as *Collier's* and the *Saturday Evening Post*. The Pennsylvania Railroad, "Serving the Nation," touted its twenty-three thousand women working as section hands, dispatchers, and train crews while their men battled for freedom overseas. The New Haven Railroad tugged at mothers' heartstrings by picturing "The Kid in the Convoy" and pledging "to provide whatever he needs . . . without hesitation . . . without a word."[13] The rail terminal was again the focus of the community, as magazines pictured civilian workers at rail terminals selling departing soldiers cigarettes at cost and giving them baskets of books and jigsaw puzzles.[14] Detroit was reduced to running billboards reading, "There's a Ford in your future, but the Ford from your past is the Ford you've got now, so you'd better make it last."[15]

Wartime rationing made the rails thrive not only in military carriage. Domestically, railways carried nearly three-quarters of the nation's goods and commuters during the war, as truck traffic fell 30 percent.[16] Thinking ahead, the rails wisely used their unprecedented profits to whittle down their debts, as companies in receivership during the 1930s regained solvency. Before the end of the Second World War, the U.S. government felt compelled to take over the lines only once—during a three-week union strike.[17] For the first time in decades, Americans smiled on the rails as a friend of the public. But mighty lines such as the New York Central and Southern Pacific would soon find that their oasis of prosperity was only a mirage, built as it was on a temporary crisis.

THE CONSENSUS FRAYS

Unity among competitors had helped the motor interests overtake the squabbling railroads. Yet now, as millions of American men fought overseas, troubling discord began to invade the highway community. And for the first time, the railroads harmonized while the highwaymen sang off key. At the heart of the problem lay the fact that America was growing up. From 1916 on, Washington had built roads largely to get the farmer out of the mud, while well-heeled cities took care of their own needs. But now such a simple formula no longer worked, as urban interests, organized labor, and planners fought for seats at the table, and members of the fast-growing highway-motor lobby began to quarrel among themselves.

America's population had been fleeing the farms for larger towns and cities since 1920.[18] But if the votes were now moving toward the city, the urban tax base was beginning to erode, as aging nineteenth-century commercial and housing stocks deteriorated and more affluent citizens used their new motorized mobility to move beyond the city limits. The federal-aid highway program had been geared to rural areas and relied on cities to pay for the cost of their own roads. Yet urban motorists for years had kicked in more motor-related taxes than they received back.[19] Now, for the first time, cities began to demand a piece of the pie.

Labor Presses Its Agenda

Labor, hardly a force to reckon with when Washington started building highways, had organized millions of Depression-weary workers aggressively and now fought for its own agenda of higher wages and benefits for highway workers. And planners, among President Roosevelt's favorite people, were drawn to highways as a way to reshape the neighborhood and commercial life of the postwar American city. Yet when the highway engineers who had knit America together with asphalt thought about cities, they focused simply on building more roads to relieve crippling congestion.

Besieged by would-be new players, the highway coalition found that even the interests of its traditional members began to veer off one from another. The old consensus that had left railroads in awe was now fraying around the edges. Since 1916, Washington had doled out highway money based on a state's area and road mileage as well as population, favoring large but sparsely settled states. But as hordes left the farm for the city, urban states began to resent paying more than their share of gas taxes to subsidize states with few residents. City leaders now asked for a formula based on population, while those in wide-open spaces predictably resisted.[20]

The state highway engineers had long been the farmer's friends, but the essence of their job was to manage traffic, and traffic was clearly in Chicago, Los Angeles, and New York, not Butte, Biloxi, and Kennebunk. While the Grange (see chapter 2) and the Farm Bureau Federation begged Congress to "get [the] rural people out of the mud," the American Association of State Highway Officials (AASHO) urged Congress to choose between six hundred thousand miles of road carrying 83 percent of traffic or two million miles carrying 17 percent. The U.S. Chamber of Commerce jumped on the urban bandwagon, calling money spent for lightly trafficked roads "just plain national socialism."

When the American Automobile Association (AAA) and other burgeoning auto clubs had lobbied for federal highway money in the early 1900s (see chapter 3), people had scoffed at the idea that roads could be long-distance servants of commerce. But now that thirty thousand truckers had come to depend on good roads for their daily bread, their agenda diverged sharply from that of the auto clubs, and even truckers could not agree among themselves what they wanted. The AAA and long-distance truckers, seeking wide commercial avenues, resented cities' cries for something to be done about traffic jams. But urban haulers predictably wanted better trunk roads into cities. And small truck outfits called for states to build the roads, while nationwide truckers wanted national standards, to make their lives easier as they chugged along from state to state.[21]

Roosevelt Sees an Opening

Watching while the highway coalition developed gridlock of its own was President Roosevelt, who had long been frustrated in trying to seize the reins of the politically potent federal highway program. Congress had soundly rebuffed his plan for national toll superhighways in the late 1930s (see chapter 9), but now that traffic congestion was plaguing Americans like a worsening toothache, FDR saw a chance to gain the initiative. Well aware of the inexorable drift to the cities, he was charting a new philosophy of road building that would replace Adam Smith's invisible hand with his own. The traditional highway interests would react to his doctrines as to the squeak of chalk on a blackboard.

As far back as 1939, the president had created the National Resources Planning Board (NRPB), to plan for America's future. He named as its consultant the economist Wilfred Owen, whose newfangled ideas curled the hair of the highway-engineering community. Appalled by the scattershot overbuilding of highways during the Depression, Owen had the startling idea that localities needed first to decide how their land should be used most rationally, to harmonize neighborhoods, businesses, and public uses. Only then should they fit highways into that blueprint. Otherwise, he warned, the work of single-minded highway engineers would "dictate what the plan shall be." His commentary turned out to be a prophecy.

Highway builders, like the railroad titans, hated such social tinkering. The raw power of both created new cities and towns, as housing and businesses clustered by the new rails and roads. The highwaymen would say this was simply letting market forces work, even though where government decided to place the roads determined where people would live and work. Owen, on the other hand, felt that one overarching federal agency ought to synchronize road building with housing, recreation, and agriculture. His colleagues went so far as to suggest that government might need to buy or lease all railways and roadways to insure fairness among rail, water, air, and road users.[22]

CITIES: THE LAST FRONTIER

Automakers sitting at Detroit's drawing boards had learned to keep one eye on Washington, and they welcomed the new urban-friendly policies, as they envisioned new dealerships in cities—the one place where they had not yet saturated the market. Studebaker's president, Paul Hoffman, spoke to a broad audience in 1939 when he wrote in the *Saturday Evening Post*: "Many of our cities are almost as antiquated, trafficwise, as if they had medieval walls, moats, drawbridges." He called cities "the greatest untapped field of potential customers."[23]

Seeking to advance these watershed ideas, yet wary of the power of the highway coalition, FDR set up the urban-oriented Interregional Highway Committee (IHC) in 1941. He brought traditional engineers and visionaries together and named his sometime-nemesis MacDonald its chair.[24] Its mix of disciplines led the IHC to the pregnant conclusion that highway building was not merely an end in itself but a way to mold the declining American city while reviving it. At the core of the concept was a twofer: by cutting a selective swath through "cramped, crowded and depreciated" cities and routing downtown highways along river valleys, Washington could eradicate "a long-standing eyesore and blight" while easing gridlock.[25] The autobahns may have inspired the interregional highways, but on one element they differed fundamentally: the German roads sought to serve the cities, while the American roads aimed to change them. The variance would become startlingly apparent a generation later.

To the highwaymen, the Roosevelt administration's visionary proposals were anathema. Michigan Representative Jesse P. Wolcott warned that a "small coterie of individuals who would socialize America" were taking control of American highway policy.[26] A member of the House Roads Committee decried the NRPB's "cradle to the grave" recommendations, under which Americans' lives were "mapped out, and planned and controlled and regimented."[27]

The "Road Gang" Digs In

To counter the perceived drift toward White House control, the highway coalition went underground in 1942 to seek common ground. Meeting for lunch each Thursday behind closed doors in Washington, 240 oil, rubber, and auto bigwigs, top highway bureaucrats, trade association executives, and public relations specialists debated how to maintain hegemony in the highway field. No press releases issued from this secret society, referred to by Washington insiders as simply the "Road Gang."[28]

Wartime delayed the IHC's report until 1944, when it unveiled its blueprint for a thirty-two-thousand-mile interregional highway system. MacDonald praised it as "the key to the functional rebuilding of our cities."[29] After a decade of trying, Roosevelt now had his best chance to gain the upper hand in road building from the fractured highway interests. But the timing for launching a presidential crusade could not have been worse. Having served longer as president than any other man, the war-weary FDR faced a fourth election campaign in the fall, and progressive heart disease was already sapping his strength. After years of developing and nurturing his philosophy to counter the Road Gang, FDR apparently lacked the energy or the will to do anything more once he transmitted the IHC's report to Congress.[30]

The president's plan faced an uphill fight even with FDR at the helm; without him, it had no chance at all against the entrenched interests. So when Congress took up the matter in 1944, the highway-motor lobby was free to work its will. "In the face of men organized and committed to agency and business independence and local autonomy in general, planners and their comprehensive plans were no match," as 110 witnesses paraded before the House Roads Committee to protect the equipoise the highwaymen had so carefully built up over three decades. Rural-oriented road advocates succeeded in scaling back the urban elements of the bill.[31]

Now, interstate boosters began to speak loftily of how superhighways "turned space into time." Engineers spoke of extending the "isochrones," lines describing the distance one could travel in a given time. No longer was the measure of travel how far you had to go, but rather how long it would take you.[32]

The Good Life at Last

The end of the Second World War would find America and Europe in drastically different conditions. Those varying conditions and the respective responses to postwar challenges would make road and rail in Europe and America vastly different, a reality that would carry implications into the twenty-first century.

Living surrounded by hostile neighbors had led European countries to nationalize their railroads even before the war, which had rendered road and rail travel impossible. Nine out of ten French trucks were out of commission. Berlin was "a city of the dead."[33] The massive need to rebuild created for Europe a tabula rasa, which allowed it to correct mistakes of the past. While electrifying existing coal- and oil-based railroads might have been an intolerably expensive political option, it became a smart choice when starting over. It did not hurt, incidentally, to have the American resources from the Marshall Plan to help pay the costs.[34] With nationalized railroads, European governments had a built-in incentive not to allow their countries' highway-motor complexes to gain dominance and thus sap business away from the railroads. And the absence of a motor lobby such as existed in the United States made Europeans' continued support of railroads much easier.

American economists and pundits, fearing millions would be out of work after the war's end, found their anxieties misplaced, as 1945 saw history's greatest spending binge begin. Americans, working long hours in the defense effort and able to buy only essentials, had developed cabin fever. They had vacationed at home, bought bootlegged tires when their bald ones blew, and traveled by rail only on what government labeled "slack days."[35] In the process, they had saved up $44 billion. Now they unleashed their pent-up demand with a fury, as American business rushed in to slake consumers' thirst for the good life. The home builder William Levitt offered Long Island houses to veterans for $6,990 each. And for a payment of $250, they could put a Crosley convertible in their carport.[36]

Automakers Reject Homely Volkswagen

Detroit tooled up to crank out 2.1 million cars in 1946 alone. One option it examined during the postwar occupation was manufacturing a tiny car already popular among Germans. But car companies rejected it, leaving it in German hands. The automakers felt that the homely Volkswagen would be "unappetizing for the consumer market."[37] By 1948, auto production would double again. The floodgates of highway building strained too, as the BPR, with $624 million in unspent money, just waited for the word to lay asphalt. The coffers of state government bulged as well, with nearly a half-billion unspent dollars.[38]

But those expecting concrete fingers to begin snaking across America immediately would be disappointed. President Harry Truman, who had taken office in 1945 upon FDR's death, gave first priority to housing for returning veterans, diverting steel and cement from road building. And the infusion of consumer spending had sent road material prices and labor costs soaring. Paying fair market value for urban rights of way was vastly more expensive than expected, and postwar engineers built roads to higher standards, with thicker pavements—all of which added to the tab.

Yet in spite of the staggering expense, states grew impatient waiting for Washington and began building major roadways themselves: limited-access roads such as New York's Cross-Bronx Expressway and Brooklyn-Queens Expressway, Detroit's Edsel Ford Expressway (costing more than $6 million a mile), and Chicago's Congress Street Expressway let commuters race toward their split-level homes in the new suburbs, usually unimpeded by stoplights. Yet hikes in state gas and excise taxes barely kept pace with inflation.[39] Soon states would discover a way to make the roads pay for themselves and generate a handsome profit as well. And as the auto age exploded around them, the newly popular railroads joined the quest for the consumer's dollar.

RAILROADS SWIM UPSTREAM

America's railroads had never been in better shape than at the end of the Second World War. Their bankrolls full and their debt whittled down, the rails had won a grateful public's newfound respect through their wartime efforts. Government still subsidized their competitors and Americans lusted beyond all reason for new cars, but the railways determined that this time, the highway-motor industry would be in for a fight.

Rail passenger traffic had been a loss-leader for decades. Yet the trickle of red ink from passenger service quickly became a river, in the face of inflation, motor competition, and onerous union settlements. Gone were the days when a Chicago and Northwestern train to Omaha could offer travelers thirteen entrees, six kinds of game, and twenty-five desserts.

Conductors now watched Kaisers and Studebakers speed by on parallel highways, burning gas at twenty-six cents a gallon and driven by the millions of long-time rail commuters seduced away from the rails. Lower revenues meant that the railroads had to cut costs or die, yet escalating union wages for engineers, conductors, and brakemen were wiping out the diminishing profits. When the Budd Company introduced revolutionary self-propelled railcars for short passenger routes that required only two people to operate, rail brotherhoods scuttled the savings by insisting that unnecessary brakemen, firemen, and flagmen be added to the crews.

Revamped Services Briefly Spark Interest

At that point, Robert R. Young, the five-foot, six-inch, 135-pound chairman of the Chesapeake and Ohio rolled up his sleeves for a fight. Young, who had quit as GM's assistant treasurer to speculate in railroad ventures, would become a colorful and dominant railroad figure during the 1940s and 1950s. This bantam rooster took on all comers, both outside and inside his industry. The service-oriented rail chief arrested public attention with popular full-page magazine ads calling his own industry's Pullman sleepers "rolling tenements." He decried the mandate that passengers switch trains in Chicago in an ad captioned: "A Hog Can Cross the Country Without Changing Trains—But YOU Can't!"[40] Yet Young's fighting spirit was infectious. His industry colleagues enlisted the designer Raymond Loewy, whose modernistic packaging helped sell Pepsodent toothpaste and Frigidaire refrigerators, to design the trains of the future. More than two million people flocked to the Chicago Railroad Fair in 1948 to board the latest in streamlined diesel trains. But would the people pay to ride?

They would indeed. Despite their fondness for cars, consumers knew they couldn't sleep overnight and dine in style in a Chevrolet. So the millions of dollars spent on streamliners such as the "California Zephyr" and the "Oriental Limited" proved money well spent, as luxury passenger trains set ridership records for their railroads in the late 1940s.[41] Passengers on Young's "Chessie" streaked from Cincinatti to Washington while dancing to live music and enjoying movies, aquariums, and children's playrooms.[42] Such people-pleasers as "vista dome" cars and private roomette-with-bath "Slumbercoaches" prospered throughout the 1950s.[43]

Yet in spite of aggressive railroad marketing, the inexorable drift to automobiles continued, cutting down the volume on which all railroads depended. Rail-passenger operating losses quintupled from 1946 to 1953. Unable to do more, railroads petitioned the ICC to let them shut down lines so often that 30 percent of passenger rail trackage was abandoned from 1947 to 1957. The 112,000 miles left were scarcely half of the industry's peak trackage in 1916.[44]

Rail Freight Slips Away

American railroads knew that if they were to survive outside a museum, they would have to rely on freight, which historically had more than made up for passenger losses. Therein lay a dilemma: if Farmer Brown wanted the best rate to ship his tomatoes to market, truckers could haggle and reach an agreement with him on the spot. But a railroad had to write to Washington for permission, which might not come for several months. Not surprisingly, truckers regularly won the contracts. To stay competitive in service, several dozen rail lines began overnight service of up to 450 miles for lucrative less-than-carload cargo.[45] But the handwriting was on the wall. For every five railcars carrying less-than-carload freight in 1940, only one was left in 1960.[46] Handcuffed by smothering regulation, freight lines ended up by default with long-distance, low-profit bulk shipments such as coal and grain.

And when truckers introduced highway rack trucks to carry shining new Frazers and Pontiacs from the factories to the dealers, railroads watched a major customer slip away. Carrying motor products over the years had helped anesthetize the railroads to the pain of steadily losing ground to trucking competition. But now truckers could drive five or six new cars onto a trailer, compared to the three or four cars that yardmen could wedge laboriously into a more constricted railroad car. By 1958, less than 10 percent of new cars would travel by rail.[47]

STATES PICK UP THE BALL ON HIGHWAY FUNDING

As the Korean War loomed in 1950, the dam that had held back the massive demand for new highways burst. Suddenly advanced road-paving machines began laying asphalt ribbons through two-hundred-foot swaths of land in Pennsylvania, Ohio, New Hampshire, and Maine. And every few miles a new artifact large enough to fit one person straddled each new lane. Builders called them tollbooths, and they would do for state governments what lotteries would accomplish decades later—earn bundles of

money. Given inaction in Washington and worsening rush-hour bottlenecks at home, states had decided to take matters into their own hands.

Before the war, the Pennsylvania Turnpike and the Merritt Parkway
had shown they could not only pay for themselves but turn a profit as well.
In 1947, Maine tested the waters first, opening a 47-mile stretch of toll
road. Then the Pennsylvania Turnpike doubled its 160-mile span to cover
nearly the entire state and threw off a cash surplus of $5.6 million by
1948.[48] Yet New Hampshire's new 15-mile toll link proved "enormously
profitable from the outset." By 1954, nineteen states would create toll-road
authorities.[49]

Revival of state toll roads sent a collective shudder up the spines of the
highwaymen, who had cultivated relations with Congress that guaranteed
they would continue to get their way. For toll-road authorities were laws
unto themselves, usually raising capital from bond sales and spending it in
ways harder for the lobby to influence. *Engineering News* lamented the
independence of toll-road authorities and feared they could "become just
as pernicious an evil as the privately owned toll road of a century or more
ago." Ominously, a BPR study found that the trend was likely to continue—that another seven thousand miles of road had enough traffic to
justify tolls.

The Toll-Road Bonanza

So great had the financial rewards proven that states went to unusual ends
to build toll roads. Even a hundred-foot-deep marshland near Secaucus
failed to deter New Jersey road builders and their corporate investors. Into
the swampland they drilled forests of twenty-inch sand-filled pipes, which
acted as wicks, absorbing the water and causing the silt and muck to settle
into a solid foundation on which to complete the 118-mile, $255 million
New Jersey Turnpike. Drivers proved only too glad to pay $1.75 in tolls, to
cut driving time from New York City to Wilmington from five to two
hours. Traffic exceeded expectations by half, and an $18 million a year net
profit flowed into state coffers.

No sooner had Ohio sold $326 million in bonds to build its own turn-
pike than Indiana announced it would build another to link with Ohio's.
Before motorists knew it, they could drive from New England to Chicago
with nary a stoplight. MacDonald's notion that it made no sense to pay
tolls when one could ride a parallel road free exploded, as the average toll-
road user in 1953 paid four times the cost of driving on a free road.[50]

The highway coalition had never been so frustrated. While states removed thousands of miles from the purview of state engineers, scores of narrow and competing interests gridlocked in Congress. And the Scrooge-like federal government collected $2 billion a year in gas taxes and excises while doling out to states only a half-billion.[51] Congress had prohibited such a diversion by states in 1934, AASHO argued as it demanded that the federal gasoline tax be repealed.[52] If the highway revenue bucket sprang a hole, New York auto dealers knew their businesses would suffer too. Their association declared urgently that Congress must "seal every leak."[53]

Everyone Should Pay for "Freeways"

Then in the summer of 1947, four hundred shippers, auto associations, truckers, and oil distributors under the banner of the National Highway User's Conference (NHUC) demanded an end to the "special, class taxation" the federal gasoline tax represented. Since the tax penalized those with a longer commute to work, it was unfair. Instead, they demanded that everyone—drivers or not—should pay for "freeways."[54]

For three decades, the power generated by the highway-motor lobby speaking as one voice had been self-evident. But now each interest focused more on defending its own turf and less on promoting the overall goal of building highways. So splintered was the highway community that for the first time in a quarter-century, even AASHO could not unite to support a bill before Congress in 1948.[55]

The paralysis within the highway community would continue during the next two years. In 1950 an NHUC president pushed a familiar alarm button in warning that unless road users could agree on a unified strategy, railroaders would take advantage of the situation to "promote their own selfish objectives."[56]

MacDonald Calls It a Day

MacDonald had controlled American road building during the 1920s and 1930s with an iron hand concealed inside a velvet glove. But as the highway-motor complex splintered in the late 1930s and the 1940s, the sober engineer from Iowa no longer held sway, though no one else did either. But while state highway chiefs in Austin, Dover, and Tallahassee predictably brought parochial concerns to policy making, MacDonald had developed the outlook of one who has traveled the globe.

This "man of few intimates" was nearing seventy in 1950. Although most of his state and federal career had focused on building rural roads, his national perspective had broadened him, and his twilight years exposed MacDonald to the new phenomenon of urban thruways. His appreciation of the policy challenges they created was unusually insightful and far-sighted among his contemporaries. As early as 1945, he had urged state highway officials to consider "economic and social values" in planning the interstate routes.[57] And he worried that "before dwellings are razed, new housing facilities should be provided for the dispossessed occupants."[58]

Unlike most of his fellow engineers, MacDonald saw the single-minded focus on urban roads over rails to be disastrous. Speaking before AASHO in the fall of 1947, MacDonald called for an end to "the preferential use of private automobiles" in cities and said the association should "promote the patronage of mass transit. . . . Unless this reversal can be accomplished, indeed, the traffic problems of the larger cities may become well nigh insoluble."[59] His skills might have enlightened the self-serving factions which, in a few years, would wage war in the halls of Congress over the interstate system. But in 1953, Dwight Eisenhower—the seventh president he had served—asked for MacDonald's resignation. When he was needed most, MacDonald would be gone.

· I I ·

INTERSTATE SOCIALISM

America lives on wheels, and we have to pro-
vide the highways to keep America living on
wheels and keep the kind and form of life that
we want.

—Treasury Secretary George Humphrey, May
2, 1955, quoted by Mark Rose in *Interstate*
Highway Politics

ON NOVEMBER 1, 1951, AS THE LAST DRY LEAVES FELL FROM WASH-
ington's trees, hundreds of businessmen massed at the opulent Mayflower
Hotel to witness a revival of support for the distressed highwaymen. GM's
president, Alfred P. Sloan, Jr., had formed the National Highway Users'
Conference (NHUC) in 1932 (see chapter 10), in part to counter "railroad
efforts to hamstring competitive forces."[1] Sloan nurtured its growth
through the 1940s into a three-thousand-member political behemoth,
whose hulking presence in Washington had served notice on Congress
that the highway community spoke with one voice. Seeking mass public
support for the "freedom" of the American road and for opposition to
"threats to automobility," NHUC had shown films lauding truckers and
the joys of driving to nearly fifty million people and handed out nineteen
million copies of Emily Post's "Motor Manners."[2]

Arthur C. Butler, NHUC's energetic director, called the organization's latest crusade "Project Adequate Roads" (PAR), a modest and seemingly innocuous title that belied the project's ambitious goals and organization. When the Grangers had mobilized to fight the railroads nearly a century earlier, they had gained their strength by organizing at the grassroots level (see chapter 2). Now NHUC took a page from the Grangers' book by envisioning a network of state and local PAR chapters that would push for a ten-year federal road-building blitz.[3] William Randolph Hearst, the powerful newspaper publisher, jumped on the bandwagon, flogging his editors to produce three million lines of prohighway propaganda over the next five years.[4]

With the gulf between farm and city interests widening beyond reconciliation, NHUC realized that part of the lobby must be thrown overboard if the highway steamer was to stay afloat. So it stacked the deck against the farmers. The urban bloc that controlled NHUC had conceived an ingenious pseudo-scientific system to build roads where they were most "needed." Using traffic counters, PAR's engineers intended to rate roads by their sufficiency for the traffic that rode over them. Obviously, congested and decaying urban roads would get attention before less-used rural ones. But by using a systematic, rational approach to prove the obvious, NHUC hoped to devise an unassailable plan.[5]

NHUC's subterfuge was transparent, and farmers manned the barricades against PAR. Soon the fabric of the coalition's massive patchwork quilt began to fray, then to unravel rapidly. First, highway engineers gradually peeled away, deciding that they could better spend their efforts countering the threat of state toll roads. Then the massive American Automobile Association (AAA), irked that truckers were not willing to pay more for the roads their heavy loads were scarring, split off. By 1953, Project Adequate Roads had become inadequate, having dwindled to truckers and truck manufacturers, who even argued among themselves.[6] Unknown to them, a frustrated president was pawing the ground and about to take matters into his own hands.

GRIDLOCK IN THE WHITE HOUSE

Wartime had demanded that people do for others; now, after the war, with households reunited, they were only too glad to turn inward: grilling steaks on the new barbecue in the new back yard, watching *Dragnet, My Friend Irma,* and *Ozzie and Harriet* on the new console TV, listening to the new transistor radio play "Shake, Rattle and Roll," or just playing Scrabble on the new recreation-room floor. Issues such as race, which would soon preoccupy the country, lay dormant, as suggested by the title of Ralph Ellison's 1952 book, *Invisible Man*, about a young black man's sojourn in American society. Factories strained to meet the overwhelming demand for products. In 1954, General Motors (GM) celebrated the production of its fifty-millionth car by paying more than $6 million to sponsor Jackie Gleason's television comedy hour.[7]

America in 1952 had elected Dwight Eisenhower, a popular wartime hero, as president. Few people knew about his strong belief that America should invest mightily in superhighways. Eisenhower, separating himself from Harry Truman's indifference toward roads and Franklin D. Roosevelt's use of highways for social tinkering, saw road building as a way to "flatten out the peaks and valleys in employment" and to promote social order.[8]

IKE'S EARLY LESSONS

As a young lieutenant in 1919, Eisenhower accompanied a transcontinental army convoy of sixty trucks beset by breakdowns, mud, sand drifts, and impassable bridges. The experience demonstrated dramatically to him how not being able to get from point A to point B thwarts progress. Then as the Supreme Commander of the Allied Forces in Europe during the Second World War, Eisenhower had witnessed the diametric opposite: smooth autobahns speeding German soldiers and materiel efficiently on their deadly mission.[9]

A year into his term as president, Eisenhower had begun to complain about the congressional gridlock over highway legislation. In April 1954 he enlisted several trusted aides to produce a massive plan for breaking the logjam in Congress.[10] Before long, they had split into two equally deadlocked factions, straining to take the country in opposite directions.

Leading one of the factions was one of the president's West Point classmates and a retired army general, John H. Bragdon, who had overseen military construction during the Second World War before Eisenhower called him to the White House to join the Council of Economic Advisers. Understanding from his recent European war experience how important broad roadways were to national defense, Bragdon thought it folly to let states decide how and where to build major highways. Instead, he said, a National Highway Authority should be a command central, dictating where and how expressways would be built and financing them with tolls.[11]

Coming from a different tradition was key aide Sherman Adams, as close to a chief of staff as Eisenhower had. Formerly governor of New Hampshire, Adams had been on the other side of the federal-state high-way relationship, and he understood the wrenching effect Bragdon's pro-posals would have at the state level. He agreed that Washington should finance the new roads but said that states should continue to control where and how those would be built. To add stature to his arguments, Adams sought the input of a high-profile heavyweight road official from New York—Robert Moses, the autocratic public works director for New York City.[12]

Moses: Hacking at Cities with a Meat Axe

The colorful, outspoken Moses in 1953 called upon Congress to spend the outlandish sum of $50 billion on superhighways through the traditional BPR-driven methods used since 1916.[13] The autocratic superbureaucrat, more powerful than any New York politician, held no elective office but headed a dozen state and city agencies, which built toll roads and cleared slums. He controlled the Triborough Bridge and Tunnel Authority, which collected millions of dollars daily in tolls from commuters entering Manhattan and routinely ran roughshod over community protests over his bulldozing of slums that lay in his way. "You can draw any kind of picture you like on a clean slate," Moses once said, "but when you're operating in an overbuilt metropolis you have to hack your way with a meat axe."[14] Predictably, Moses weighed in with Adams's goals.[15]

Instead of countering the congressional logjam with a unified plan, Eisenhower's aides had only deepened the clash of ideologies already war-ring on Capitol Hill. So the president turned to the BPR itself. MacDonald's successor was the jut-jawed Francis duPont, for a generation Delaware's chief highway builder. To say that this scion of a chemical empire had grown up around highways and automobiles would be a vast understatement.

Highways in His Blood

Francis was the son of T. Coleman duPont, who in 1912 had built on family-owned land America's first superhighway, a generation ahead of the first modern turnpikes. He designed the ninety-seven-mile, $4 million project from Wilmington to Dover, with all-weather pavement, slow lanes for trucks, and a trolleyway, partly as a publicity tool to help him win election to the U.S. Senate and partly as "an idealistic mission." Two years later, a friend persuaded duPont to buy two thousand shares of a company that would later become General Motors, sparking his interest in automaking so much that by 1922, duPont had taken over the rapidly growing automaker.[16]

The younger duPont, a civil engineer, had chaired the Delaware Highway Commission for twenty-three years. Fresh from state service, he understood the depths of dissatisfaction in American state capitals. He advised Eisenhower that the time was right for the White House to launch a major initiative.[17] Now, with midterm elections approaching, Eisenhower had to factor politics into the equation as well. He knew that distressed economies can mow down incumbent presidents. His Council of Economic Advisers had urged him to smooth out the upturns and downturns of economic cycles by injecting public works money into the economy at strategic times. In the spring of 1954, Congress had tried to quell restless natives in the state capitals by hiking highway spending more than half, to a record $875 million; earmarking $175 million of it for the interstate system; and sweetening the federal share to 60 percent. As big a jump as that was, Eisenhower had something far bigger in mind.[18] He knew that in July the nation's governors would head to upstate New York for their annual conference and a break from the heat. Ike decided it was time to make his move.[19]

EISENHOWER'S "GRAND PLAN":

As he neared the midway point in his first term, the president's stewardship had been temperate, cautious, and pinchpenny. As the nation's governors looked forward to a presidential address during their "serene and clubby" working holiday on Lake George, the notion that their penurious president was about to propose the greatest public works project in world history was beyond their wildest imaginings.[20] Frustrated and angry that Washington took in far more at the pump than it gave back for roads, the governors the year before had demanded an end to the two-cent-a-gallon federal gas tax. When Ike had failed to agree, the states had decided to give up on Washington and build the roads they needed themselves. Some dismissed Congress's infusion of road money as—in the words of one governor—only "an act of appeasement."[21] Indeed, the forty-year federal-state marriage that had built a two-hundred-thousand-mile network of "good roads" across the country—the largest highway system in the world—seemed to be veering toward the rocks.

Because his brother's wife had died over the weekend before the governors' conference, Ike substituted his young vice-president, Richard Nixon, to unveil the most radical plan ever proposed by an American chief executive. In passionate prose taken from Eisenhower's own notes, Nixon sketched out a "Grand Plan" over ten years to end "an annual death toll comparable to the casualties of a bloody war," wastage of billions of hours in traffic jams, and the plethora of lawsuits clogging the nation's civil courts.[22] The $50 billion scheme would build forty thousand miles of superhighway across the land, at a time when diners at fine Manhattan restaurants paid three dollars for steak and all the fixings.[23] The scope of the plan was stunning: America's entire federal budget was only $71 billion; the Marshall Plan to rebuild Europe entirely had cost a mere $17 billion. The necessary concrete could have built six sidewalks to the moon.[24] And the theretofore conservative president called the plan merely "a good start."[25] Conceived as a capitalistic milestone, the project would be transmuted by congressional alchemy into a quasi-socialistic program that would transform America forever.

And yet the governors' initial reaction to the president's plan was hostile. "We want the federal government to get out of the gas and fuel oil fields once and for all," demanded one governor after hearing the speech.[26] But the more they talked and let their imaginations work, the governors began to realize that the president was inviting them to help fill out the skeleton of a transforming plan. The next day, the *New York Times* reported a "marked lessening" of opposition, and by the end of the conference, the governors had dropped their demand to end the federal gas tax entirely and had agreed to fall in line behind the president.[27]

Eisenhower: An Echo of the New Deal?

The *Times* carried the president's plan and the governors' reaction as front-page news for three days. The columnist Doris Fleeson called it an echo of the excesses of the New Deal.[28] But *Life* magazine—failing even to mention Eisenhower's grandiose scheme—ran a lavish pictorial spread by Margaret Bourke-White about the state toll-road movement, as it churned out concrete along the roadsides from Augusta, Maine, to Rock Island,

Illinois. For politicians in state capitals, the question would be whether they could keep more control over their state's highway program by jumping on Ike's bandwagon or by building toll roads in their states.[29]

How the once-symbiotic federal-state partnership had come to such a pass, how the popular president recouped and nearly captured control of the highway program from the bureaucrats, and how the highwaymen thwarted his plan for two years is a story of exploitation, myopia, greed, inattention, and cowardice.

Franklin Delano Roosevelt, a much more activist president than Eisenhower, had been thwarted repeatedly in trying to seize the steering wheel of the nation's road-building machine. But MacDonald, who had often stood in Roosevelt's way, was gone now, and his successor had a very different philosophy of engineers' role in government. DuPont's view— that engineers should be the policy makers' loyal foot soldiers—paved the way for Eisenhower to shift the highway community's fulcrum of power to the White House for the first time.[30] In 1955, Ike moved duPont to the Commerce Department as a special assistant, bringing the federal highway program under the administration's umbrella.[31] And yet, while willing to take orders in a way that MacDonald had been unaccustomed to doing, the eloquent, persuasive duPont deserves major credit for working behind the scenes to shape the outlines of the interstate highways.

VIEWING THE FUTURE THROUGH A WRAPAROUND WINDSHIELD

By September 1954, the internecine warfare over how to pay for the interstates had erupted again within the White House. But in America's towns and cities, a development even more important in shaping the interstate highway system arose—the unveiling of Detroit's new models for 1955. Most of the postwar styles introduced before 1955 had been boxy and functional, but rumors flew during 1954 that styling and mechanical alterations to the 1955 models were about to create a fundamental change in the new-car market. GM, Ford, and Chrysler had let it be known that a big move was afoot, so in late 1954, millions flocked to their glassy new neighborhood showrooms to gaze at the Chevrolet Bel Air and the Pontiac Star Chief, with Strato-Streak V-8 engine, painted in two-toned "Avalon yellow" and "raven black." Detroit introduced wraparound windshields, and Cadillac sparked a coming craze with a strange-looking back end resembling the fins of a fish. The golden era of automobiles had arrived. Sales would rise an astounding 37 percent from 1954 to 1955. And all those car buyers would want the fastest roads money could buy, to try out their high-horsepower engines.[32]

To formulate a plan that Congress would buy and to steer it through rocky shoals, Eisenhower would need a firm hand on the tiller. He turned to General Lucius Clay, who had been his trusted aide-de-camp in Europe, and a military engineer who had supervised the Berlin Airlift.[33] Austere, with bushy eyebrows and a hawkish nose, Clay was inured by his military and business background to chain-of-command decision making. After the war, he had become the president of Continental Can Company and had served on GM's board of directors—a position he would continue to hold even while crusading within government to build superhighways that would help his company sell more cars.[34] But he would prove a naïf amid the influence peddling and log rolling on Capitol Hill.

Clay, accustomed like his colleague Bragdon to broad national efforts, proposed that a Federal Highway Corporation should finance and direct the operation the way a commanding general would wage a war. But his approach threatened the power base that the American Association of State Highway Officials (AASHO) had built up over nearly forty years. DuPont's persuasive jawboning convinced the powerful engineers to come around, but with the proviso that states continue to design and build the actual roads.[35] By January 1955, Clay had recommended to Eisenhower that the national authority finance the interstates through $27 billion in bonds—scaled back from the original $50 billion estimate—to be paid back through gas and tire taxes.

THE ROAD-FINANCING DILEMMA—TO BORROW OR TO PAY

Before the bill could travel up Pennsylvania Avenue to Capitol Hill, the White House had to decide whether American drivers should pay for the mammoth project at the gas pump or the toll booth, or whether all Americans would share the cost through bond issues. The decision would speak volumes to American consumers about whether their government believed in borrowing or in pay-as-you-go financing, and about whether business or consumers would end up paying the bill for the new commercial freightways. Eisenhower, like Bragdon, thought the interstates should be toll roads. However, AAA, the governors, and highway officials—particularly in western states—were already coming out against the idea.

Clay told the president that tolls imposed on previously free roads would lead to a "revolution" in several western states. His argument won over Adams, who had supported Ike's toll philosophy, and the key aides soon decided on thirty-year borrowing, which motorists would repay at the pump and in license fees. And in another massive departure from tradition, truckers for the first time would have to pay their way through higher taxes.[36]

As popular a president as Eisenhower was, his bold scheme created a firestorm in Congress, where Democrats ousted from control of both houses in the 1952 landslide had regained power. For the next sixteen months, pitched battles would rage over financing, control, and distribution, with no side able to amass a majority in both houses. The final outcome would affect the lives of 150 million Americans dramatically, by deciding where they would live and work, whether they or their children would pay for all that concrete, how greatly the American voter could influence the process in years ahead, and whether in the American march of progress, road would finally vanquish rail.

Newspaper readers could glimpse the future by reading the daily headlines. In 1955, a clutch of "mourners" rode New York's Third Avenue Elevated Railway one last time before it fell to the wrecking ball, while Los Angelenos battled a siege of auto emissions they nicknamed "smog." Yet most citizens mourned instead the death of film idol James Dean and drooled over Ford's new two-seat Thunderbird.[37]

The bonding notion gave Democrats a readymade issue, as they telegraphed alarm that borrowing would cost the nation billions in interest, to be repaid by future generations. And even the president's own party had misgivings. Adams warned Eisenhower that old-guard Republicans—"continually trying to stop . . . radical ideas"—took a dim view of bonding.[38] Virginia's Senator Harry Byrd called the concept of borrowing outside the federal budget "the end of honest bookkeeping."[39] New Mexico's Senator Dennis Chavez labeled it a "banker's bill."[40] And the powerful truckers insured an impasse by refusing to spend more than the two cents a gallon they were already paying at the pump.

When America's highway program was largely a rural affair, few had quibbled with the formula that made land area and road mileage count as much as population in deciding how much each state should get. But widely varying state demographics threatened the unity necessary to build an interstate system, as urban states demanded that the formula put a greater emphasis on population.[41]

EISENHOWER UNDERESTIMATES OPPONENTS

Highway users, contractors, and engineers had fallen in behind Eisenhower's line of march, but apopleptic farmers complained that the bill favored cities. The Senate Roads Subcommittee chairman, Albert Gore, Sr., denounced the plan's $11 billion in interest, which he said "should be spent on roads."[42] Clearly, the president needed to compromise to retain control of the process. Yet Eisenhower's instincts, honed in military bunkers, told him to stay the course. In so doing, he had underestimated his opposition.[43]

Truckers won a warm reception and rail advocates a cold shoulder from Gore's subcommittee during 1955 hearings in the same ornate room in which the highwaymen had successfully resisted regulation a generation earlier. Transit leaders warned that to struggling urban transit, the interstate highways would be "the straw that breaks the camel's back." An economist from the Association of American Railroads called the interstates subsidized "commercial freightways," which would "seriously impair the capacity of the railroads as instruments of defense."[44]

Indisputably, using trucks on interstates required the extra cost of wider roads, thicker pavement, and higher overpasses. Denying that truckers should pay for the added expense, the American Trucking Association (ATA) argued that the prospect of some future national emergency dictated the need for the interstates to be built for use by heavy military vehicles—a potent argument in the "duck-and-cover" cold-war era.[45] And since the nation's defense benefits car and truck owners alike, the rationale went, they should pay equally.

A "Show of Political Incompetence"

By the spring of 1955, Senate Republicans deserted their president to hand him a nearly two-to-one repudiation, in favor of Gore's traditional formula, a bill that "studiously avoided the question of where the needed additional revenue would be found."[46] The House, trying to push through the president's initiative, met a Babel of opponents. Truckers and petroleum refiners decried the bill's call for higher gas taxes. The rubber industry was upset over the proposed tenfold hike in tire levies. Teamsters yelled that the bill taxed large trucks too heavily, while the AAA bellowed that it did not tax trucks enough.[47] The railroads assailed the truckers' resistance to any new taxes, citing ATA's own admission that the interstate system would save heavy trucks over $1 billion a year, and called for tire taxes to rise from five to fifty cents a pound.[48]

Hearings on the House bill, which ultimately went down to defeat, offered insight into the highwaymen's objectives. At one point, Texas highway booster Representative Brady Gentry asked duPont: "But is it not true that the highway system needs of the United States of America are almost without limit, and will they not be almost without limit on and on?" DuPont—the Delaware highway builder, GM's director, and a holder of millions of dollars' worth of GM stock—replied, without irony: "I hope so."[49]

Yet even having his ears pinned back by the Senate failed to convince the president to compromise. Better no bill at all than a bad bill, he felt. The 1955 session would end without an interstate highway program. *Life* called Congress's deadlock "as scandalous a show of political incompetence as our democracy has seen in years."[50]

As tempers cooled between the 1955 and 1956 congressional sessions, the splintered highway coalition came to realize that the one thing they hated more than one another's positions was the specter of centralized control by Washington. Gradually, truckers, road contractors, and engineers now allied themselves with governors and congressmen, deciding not to kill the goose that had laid the golden egg.[51] Protecting the market for more than nine million cars, trucks, and buses each year—only 5,200 of which were imports—was paramount.[52]

The president, it turned out, had overplayed his hand. As the 1956 session would demonstrate, Eisenhower's intransigence and later inattention let the interstate program slip through his fingers and transmute into a far different form than what the president had envisioned.

SELLING THE CITIES

During the winter recess, headlines from the hinterlands proclaimed that cities had given up on Washington and would build superhighways themselves. In 1955 alone, urban governments sold $310 million in highway bonds for local projects. Chicago planned 33.5 miles of expressways costing $350 million, Detroit was ready to build expressways with a pricetag of $363 million, and New York City poised to construct $600 million worth of roads and bridges.[53]

But cities themselves reflected the congressional split over whose ends superhighways should serve, so cities approached the job in markedly different ways. Trailblazing mayors such as Richard Lee of New Haven, Connecticut, harnessed roadways to the renewal of fully one-quarter of his city, using them to buffer residential from commercial uses and to protect neighborhoods. Other cities, such as St. Paul, Minnesota, ignored such concerns and planned highways purely according to where the traffic was.[54]

As 1956 dawned, Eisenhower had grown restless with quibbling over methods of financing: "I wanted the job done." The president passed the word that he was ready to compromise on national control and bonding.[55] He sent the message that he would no longer insist on a national highway authority, and he assured states that they would continue to work with the BPR as they had done for four decades.[56] Congress would match his determination for closure.

A DEAF EAR TO THE RAILROADS

The nation's railroad leaders watched the highway battle rage around them as if their industry did not exist. In 1956, the Association of American Railroads (AAR) submitted a book-length tome to the House Ways and Means Committee—by far the most detailed evidence any witness had presented to the committee—analyzing, among other things, the gasoline-tax burden on cars and trucks. A railroad economist riled truckers by arguing that car owners paid five times more than truckers in weight per gallon of gas and thus heavily subsidized the trucking industry. No doubt hoping to arouse popular anger against heavy trucks, the rail representative called for large increases in diesel-fuel taxes to compensate.[57] Committee members praised AAR's meticulous testimony effusively, then proceeded during their deliberations to ignore it.

The reenergized highway-motor lobby now made an all-out effort, hauling in witnesses from such diverse groups as the National Association of Off-the-Road Tire Retreaders, the International Association of Ice Cream Manufacturers, the American Bakers' Association, and the National Rural Letter Carriers' Association.[58] The diversity of interest groups underscored the telling point made by Studebaker's president, James Nance, that one in every six workers was involved "in the manufacturing, selling, servicing and commercial use of motor vehicles."[59] Profits generated from that collective enterprise paid for massive lobbying efforts on Capitol Hill, designed to shift the tax burden from commercial users to automobile owners.

And the only group to speak for the car users, who would pay several times their share for the interstate system, was the 4.6 million–member AAA, which in 1955 had campaigned for a fifty-cent per-pound tax on truck tires, tubes, and camelback (rubber used for retreads).[60] Yet in ten months, the only defender of car owners had pulled back to request a tepid five-cent hike.[61] One student of the debate feels that the sheer power of the truckers' lobby cowed the AAA into submission.[62]

THE SEARCH FOR A MAJORITY

Legislative strategists knew that breaking the congressional bottleneck would depend on several things: winning the urban vote, spoonfeeding the highway-motor lobby a palatable financing plan, reassuring states that had built toll roads that they would be reimbursed, neutralizing the antidiversion forces, and doling out money in a way that would mollify both urban and rural states. The 1955 House bill had failed by a 292-to-123 margin.[63] And many congressmen who had voted against it came from cities, which would clearly benefit from the interstate system. Obviously, communication had broken down somewhere.

Racing to the rescue came the BPR engineers, who over the years had proven remarkably adept at politics, their disclaimers to the contrary. On the theory that a picture is worth a thousand words, the BPR made available to congressmen its "Yellow Book" in 1955, showing a map of each major urban area in the country, setting forth the proposed interstate routes. Overnight, hometown newspapers depicted the new interstate routes on their front pages, gaining voters' attention and attracting the keen interest of land speculators.[64]

The American Municipal Association (AMA) climbed on the urban bandwagon as well and sought to present a united front to Congress. When Philadelphia's Mayor Richardson Dilworth urged the AMA to insist that each urban interstate include a rail transit line, the AMA turned him down, fearing its united ranks might splinter over the public transit feature.[65] For attacking gridlock effectively had now taken a back seat to slum clearance at city halls, which "exulted" that Washington would pick up 90 percent of the tab for highways that bulldozed through unsightly slums at the same time.[66] Fueled by intense lobbying and newfound citizen support, urban votes for the interstate system would soar from sparse in 1955 to nearly unanimous in 1956.[67]

Financing would not be such an easy sell. The House Roads Committee chairman, George Fallon, knew that interstates built to accommodate tractor-trailers would cost much more than if only cars drove on them. Unless truckers paid a premium for the privilege, said the *Baltimore Democrat*, car owners would end up subsidizing the nation's truckers.[68] Charging that Fallon's committee just did not "understand" the tax issues, the powerful ATA persuaded the House leadership to shift the tax portion of the bill to the more business-oriented Ways and Means Committee.[69] With the ATA shouting and the AAA only whispering, it was clear which special interest Congress would heed.

By now, even truckers had begun to blush when insisting on no tax increases and had conceded that they would be willing to pay $1.50 per thousand pounds of weight, a modest hike that would allow members of Congress to tell their constituents that they had not let those truckers get away with murder. But in the Senate, the young majority leader, Lyndon B. Johnson, was ramming through an exemption that would let the first thirteen tons of truck weight travel tax free.[70] But these proposals were small change compared to a brilliant stratagem being quietly developed in the House—one that would clinch the deal.

THE PERPETUAL MOTION MACHINE

Diversion of highway revenues to other government uses had been a hot-button issue for a generation. Now a creative solution emerged that greased the skids for interstate legislation to pass the 1956 session as resoundingly as the 1955 bills had failed. The vehicle was the Highway Trust Fund—the political version of a perpetual motion machine. Designed to assuage those angry that Washington was spending less on highways than it was taking in, the fund was a diversion-proof vessel into which receipts from the Esso and Texaco oil companies poured and funneled out again, directly into concrete mixers and right-of-way purchases.

The fund's attractiveness lay in its limiting of political accountability. The interstate program's directors could spend money as it came in, without going back to Congress for authorization. For the highwaymen, it meant "assured continuous financing of roads without the need to justify them to politicians outside the coalition."[71] With one stroke, it satisfied those who wanted spending linked to revenues, those opposed to diversion, and congressmen, who would now have one less vote to justify at election time.[72] It would become a sacred cow to which Congress would pay homage, even to the present day.

The final bill, passed in June 1956, asked no "extraordinary sacrifices of

Forced to mobilize for war in 1917, President Woodrow Wilson found the overworked, overregulated, and dispirited railroads unable to carry all the men and materiel bound for Europe. He turned to Detroit's nascent motor industry, which organized convoys of trucks with such labels as "Packards for [Gen.] Pershing." But their slow progress over the rutted dirt roads that snaked from Detroit to the Atlantic coast provided an object lesson on the need for Washington to help the states build smooth highways. *(Photo courtesy of the Federal Highway Administration.)*

Before the automobile, railroads doomed stagecoach travel over America's turnpike roads. Success of the "Best Friend of Charleston" over the six-mile route it began in 1830 in Charleston, South Carolina, led to a fever of expansion and investment in the railroad industry, which created such mighty giants as the New York Central, the Baltimore and Ohio, and the Pennsylvania railroads. *(Photo courtesy of the National Archives.)*

EMIGRATION

TO

IOWA and NEBRASKA, U.S.

The next Colony will leave Rochdale for Lincoln Nebraska, on Wednesday, June 28th, 1871.

The Burlington and Missouri River Railroad Company will provide the Colony with Through Tickets from Liverpool to Lincoln, at the following Rates :

				£	s.	d.
Steerage on Steamer and 3rd class Railway	....			11	11	0
Ditto	Ditto	1st	Ditto	....	15	2	5
Intermediate Ditto		1st	Ditto	....	18	5	5
Cabin	Ditto	1st	Ditto	....	24	11	5

A Guide will be furnished to accompany the Party from the Landing Port to their Destination, and every arrangement will be made for the care and comfort of the Colony, until they are finally settled in their New Home.

HOMES FOR ALL!

More Farms than Farmers! More Landlords than Tenants!

WORK FOR ALL WORKERS!

2,000,000 Acres of LAND for SALE

At from Four to Fifteen Dollars per Acre, on Ten Years' Credit, and only charged Six per Cent. Interest.

Those intending to join the Colony, should apply to the undersigned at once for full information and Copy of the Guide to Iowa and Nebraska.

ASHWORTH & PARKER,

2, River-Street, Rochdale ; and 4, Corporation-Street, Manchester,

Agents to the Burlington & Missouri River Railroad Company.

JOHN TURNER, PRINTER, DRAKE-STREET, ROCHDALE.

In the 1860s and 1870s, Congress, eager to tame the western wilderness and fearful lest European powers beat them to it, gave land collectively as large as Texas to the railroads. The land grants and rail access to this new land soon attracted both investors and settlers from the East and abroad. *(Poster courtesy of the American Association of Railroads.)*

Railroads did not merely help towns grow; they created settlements that would have no other reason to exist. Cities such as Omaha, Tulsa, and Wichita sprang up overnight. But the railroad was the only practical way to reach them, and the robber barons' monopoly pricing devastated farmers who depended on the railroads to transport their crops to market. In response, government soon put a century-long hammerlock on the railroads. *(Photo courtesy of the Association of American Railroads.)*

Once the Duryea brothers of Springfield, Massachusetts, unveiled a commercially produced motor vehicle in 1893, the "good roads" movement hit its stride. Experimentation became rampant as engineers built plank roads, brick roads, and "corduroy" roads. Here, exponents of a steel road, similar to wide railroad tracks, demonstrate their concept at the 1896 Trans-Mississippi Exposition in Omaha. *(Photo courtesy of the Federal Highway Administration.)*

Railroads could travel long distances, but the newfangled automobile could go anywhere—in theory, at least. As young men named Buick, Nash, and Chrysler sought their fortunes in Detroit, the American Automobile Association was among the first organizations to promote auto touring. Here, spring mud challenges a roadster in 1907. Teddy Roosevelt touted "the strenuous life" from the White House, and many saw the rigors of auto travel as an adventure. *(Photo courtesy of the Federal Highway Administration.)*

Early motorists were largely unpopular and looked upon as a nuisance. In this *Harper's New Monthly Magazine* cartoon from 1914, a foolhardy driver steers into the path of a locomotive. Many saw automobiles as toys for the rich and proposed highways as "peacock alleys." *(Illustration courtesy of the National Archives.)*

In America's cities, the horse yielded to electric-powered trolleys in the 1890s. Trolleys were inexpensive to buy, and manufacturers and operators soon overbuilt, piling on crushing debt that, with the aid of a conspiracy led by General Motors, helped ensure their eventual demise. In this photo of the corner of Chicago's Dearborn and Randolph streets, horse, motor, and trolley traffic strangle one another as commerce strains to move to its destination. *(Photo courtesy of the Federal Highway Administration.)*

By the 1920s, American planners had learned the basic lesson that building more roads worsens congestion, not lessens it. Here, before the term "gridlock" entered the lexicon, drivers in downtown Washington, D.C., experience it in 1927. *(Photo courtesy of the National Archives.)*

Thomas Harris MacDonald, who headed the federal Bureau of Public Roads from 1919 to 1953, was a force as powerful as his counterpart at the FBI, J. Edgar Hoover, yet was virtually unknown to most Americans. It was MacDonald who united highwaymen—that band of engineers, automakers, roadbuilders, tire and cement producers, and steelmakers—and thus set into motion a process that would transform America. Here, MacDonald *(right)* prepares to greet President Herbert Hoover in 1932, as they inspect the Mount Vernon Memorial Highway. *(Photo courtesy of the National Archives.)*

By the early 1930s, the regulated railroads and the unregulated truckers had become blocked in a struggle to haul the nation's commerce. Each sought to harness technology to gain a market advantage. In this photo, a railroad worker in Lake Charm, Florida, feeds an ice chipper as it fills a new refrigerator car loaded with sweet corn. *(Photo courtesy of the National Archives.)*

Will Rogers joked during the Great Depression that America would be the first nation ever to go to the poorhouse in an automobile. Here, a convoy of early auto trailers from Flint, Michigan, hauls new cars to showrooms across the land in the 1930s. The trailers soon stole auto haulage away from trains, which would recapture the business in the 1980s. *(Photo courtesy of the Federal Highway Administration.)*

REICHSAUTOBAHNEN
in DEUTSCHLAND

Adolf Hitler's autobahns inspired Americans, who soon planned limited access turnpikes divided by medians. This poster for the 1936 Olympics in Berlin was part of a media campaign to demonstrate the peaceful use of highways. In a few years, however, the fuehrer would appropriate German superhighways to carry out his deadly mission. The tower in the foreground displays a Nazi swastika. *(Poster courtesy of the National Archives.)*

As the railroads fought back to compete against subsidized highways in the 1940s, they poured money into such innovations as the luxurious California Zephyr and domed passenger cars for long-distance travelers, like this Chesapeake and Ohio lounge car pictured in 1948. *(Photo courtesy of the National Archives.)*

As America entered the 1950s, many American railroads upgraded to more efficient diesel engines as Congress prepared to legislate the Interstate Defense Highway System. Steam locomotives, such as this Northern Pacific freight train chugging through Montana in 1956, prepared to belch their last. *(Photo courtesy of Barclay Robinson, Jr.)*

Ever-worsening auto congestion, air pollution, and dependence on foreign oil have led transportation planners to look with new favor upon the railroads. Trains such as this X-2000 from Sweden have been tested on American routes. An American-built model is likely to offer regular 150-mile-per-hour passenger service before the end of this century. Magnetic levitation technology promises hope for 300-mile-per-hour travel in locations, such as Texas, where new track can be built. *(Photo courtesy of Master Communications Group.)*

principle, practice or cash from any group."[73] A conference committee agreed that the rural-based status quo would prevail for the first three years, after which population would take precedence. Cars and trucks would pay an added one cent at the pump, and truckers would pay some modest levies. A much-relieved Eisenhower, suffering from a bout of ileitis, signed the bill from a hospital bed on June 29.[74]

Truckers benefited most from the interstate bill, holding proposed fifty-cents-a-pound tire-tax increases to three cents. And yet they grumbled. One freight executive groused that, were it not for the urgent need for highways, "every red-blooded trucker" ought to wage an "out-right, last ditch battle against the entire program." However, he said, "that is what the railroads want the truckers to do so the truckers would be blamed for killing the highway measure, which the scheming railroads had set out to do by 'hook or crook.'"[75]

LOBBY GAINS URBAN COMPLEXION

The complexion of the highway-motor lobby had changed during the four decades that Washington had been building roads. Urban interests eclipsed rural ones, as truckers' did car owners', and industries such as touristry signed on. But through it all, Detroit, the AASHO, and the BPR steered a steady course. It was they who insured that highways would drive urban planning, and not the other way around. "Roads, whether in 1938 or in 1956, were going to be built for commerce," says the highway historian Mark Rose. "Proponents of industry practices, of business autonomy, of local initiatives, and of governance by established routines in trucking and engineering circles had managed to block those who were driven by an urge to plan American transport and American society in detail."[76]

The highwaymen had learned the hot buttons that would sell the public on their program: "talk of privacy, of private property, of individualism."[77] But little effort was made in the increasingly pluralistic American society to seek umbrella values and from that, to chart a course of action. And so each interest looked to its own particular needs apart from the whole, just as each transport mode had been doing for generations. Independent individuals all, following the American way.

Ironically, the burgeoning ecomony that the interstates helped to create in the world's leading capitalist country carried inescapable overtones of socialism. Any mode of transport requires both a vehicle and a pathway Railroads, the quintessential free-enterprisers, owned both their trains and their tracks. But Congress built, owned, and maintained the interstate pathways it supplied free to commercial motor vehicles.

Congress insured that a war-conditioned generation would embrace the interstate program by naming it "the National System of Interstate and Defense Highways." Yet as an indication of the true role defense played, one critic reports that the interstate builders never consulted the Pentagon about what specifications military transport would require. By the time the Defense Department advised the highwaymen in 1960 that such equipment as Atlas missiles called for a sixteen-foot underpass clearance, 2,200 bridges and other roadway structures had already been built to a fourteen-foot standard.[78]

After the interstate-building program was well under way, the president also awoke to unexpected realities of the plan he had pushed. On a summer day in 1959, Eisenhower's limousine was on its way to Camp David, Maryland, when the president noticed a huge earthen gash extending through the northwest section of the city. Asking the reason for this massive intrusion of bulldozers, he learned from an aide that this was his interstate highway system. Eisenhower recoiled in horror. His interstate concept, borrowed from the German model, had been to go around cities, not through them. Amazingly, he had been unaware during the lengthy congressional donnybrook that the only way the interstates could become a reality in this increasingly urban nation was to promise cities enough money to eviscerate themselves.

The president immediately enlisted Bragdon and his staff to figure out how to stop the paving over of large sections of American cities. But the BPR dug in its heels at every turn. Nearing the end of his term, Eisenhower concluded that his hands were "virtually tied," and he reluctantly gave up, but not without reflecting on the wastefulness of thousands of motorists "driving into the central area and taking all the space required to park the cars."[79] In a few years, his comments would prove prophetic.

·12·

A NEW AMERICA

THE CLEAR WINNERS OF THE CRUSADE FOR SUPERHIGHWAYS WERE THE
highwaymen, who had labored toward this goal for a half-century. Built
to accommodate the heaviest trucks, the freeways would boast at least four
12-foot lanes, divided by a 22-foot median, and 10-foot shoulders within
rights-of-way as wide as 300 feet.[1] Contractors computed that for every
million dollars spent on the $27 billion system they would use 16,800 bar-
rels of cement; 694 tons of bituminous material; 485 tons of concrete and

clay pipe; 76,000 tons of sand, gravel, and crushed stone; 24,000 pounds of explosives; 121,000 gallons of petroleum products; 99,000 board feet of lumber; 600 tons of steel; and 57 new bulldozers and other pieces of machinery. Multiplied by 44,000 miles of megahighway, it spelled a bonanza for the highway-motor complex.[2]

The clear loser was the American public, although it would be years before that would be commonly understood. Road and rail, had they competed on a level playing field, might each have thrived without substantial public subsidies. But when a country needs both modes and decides to feed one and starve the other, it ends up shouldering the loser's dying carcass as well.

Congress's decision to invest in forty-one thousand miles of broad "freeways" doomed any chance the railroads had to recapture a solid share of passenger traffic. Some railway executives publicly bewailed the move, but many secretly heaved a sigh of relief. Since most railway passenger traffic had been a loss-leader for decades, the executives hoped that new competition from the interstates might justify their pleas that the Interstate Commerce Commission (ICC) let them abandon it altogether. Then they could concentrate on freight, where technology and a landmark ICC ruling gave them a fighting chance to survive.

BOOM TIME FOR HIGHWAY SUPPORTERS

The advent of the Highway Trust Fund made clear that the long courtship of people and cars was only foreplay. In signing the 1956 Interstate Highway Act, President Eisenhower slipped a golden wedding band on Americans' fingers, as a nation of motorists vowed to buy more and more automobiles and gasoline, while the Highway Trust Fund established by the act promised in return a stream of concrete ribbons across the land, a literally never-ending stream of roadways (see chapter 11). Whole new industries now joined the highwaymen to protect their hard-won gains by bankrolling the campaigns of highway-friendly congressmen. The American Automobile Association, the Auto Manufacturers Association, the American Petroleum Institute, and the American Road Builders Association (ARBA) were old hands at the game.[3] But the interstate highways' pervasiveness would bring new beneficiaries into the fold: hotel and motel operators, housing and restaurant developers, real estate agencies, and Wall Street bankers—literally anyone who contributed to or benefited from superhighways.[4] When ARBA broke ground for a new building next door to the Federal Highway Administration, Senator Jennings Randolph and Representative George Fallon smilingly turned shovels of dirt for a project that would draw America's forty-year-old public-private partnership even closer together.[5]

ARBA was sitting pretty. Not only did it have God's blessing and an unlimited bankroll from the Highway Trust Fund, but its key friends had found their way into influential posts in both houses of Congress. Senator Randolph, a West Virginia contractor, had been the ARBA treasurer for a decade prior to winning election in 1958. The same year, ARBA member Robert "Fats" Everett of Tennessee won election and a coveted assignment on the House Roads Subcommittee. And the seamless link between government and business that had served so well for four decades worked both ways. When the Bureau of Public Roads (BPR) commissioner, C. D. Curtiss, retired in 1957, ARBA was only too glad to put him on its Washington payroll.[6]

INTERSTATES: CATHEDRALS OF THE CAR CULTURE

The interstates were the cathedrals of the car culture, and their social implications were staggering. Within a decade, they would alter beyond recognition where and how Americans lived, worked, played, shopped, and even loved. Watershed changes loomed in politics, agriculture, and land economics. Rushing to meet the demand for new cars was not only Detroit but Europe, as Volvos, Austins, Fiats, and Volkswagens appeared on American roads. The debut of major league baseball in Los Angeles and San Francisco in 1958 signaled a new westward migration, caused in part by California's pioneering freeways of the 1940s and the bedroom communities that quickly sprang up around them.[7]

Engineers as Political Operatives

A current observer might conclude that the interstate highways' engineering designers were simply unimaginative. Compared to the soaring grace of the Brooklyn Bridge or the uniqueness of each art deco bridge on Connecticut's Merritt Parkway, every standardized span over the interstates is an unembellished horizontal line. But the system's designers only followed the "form follows function" architecture of the 1950s. Their mentors included Albert Kahn, who designed the General Motors Building in

Detroit and various factories; Ludwig Mies van der Rohe, whose spare, clean lines inspired countless urban office towers; and the modernist French architect Le Corbusier (Charles-Edouard Jeanneret). The influential sculptor and writer Horatio Greenough argued that "any design that expressed function efficiently and simply was necessarily beautiful."[8]

So detail and verticality yielded to the horizontal line, which the architect Frank Lloyd Wright referred to as "the line of freedom"—an ideal image for those planning to enhance the independence of the American road.[9] Once the uniform, straight interstates replaced scenic, winding two-lanes, forbidden would be such distractions as signs hawking Mail Pouch tobacco or the sequential messages spaced along the road from Burma Shave, a company selling a brushless shaving cream, such as: "Henry the Eighth...Sure Had Trouble...Short-Term Wives...Long-Term Stubble."[10] A motorist dropped on any stretch of expansive asphalt would be hard pressed to know where he or she was. The sameness of the interstates would prove a metaphor for a generation of people who welcomed consistency and quality control in their hotels, restaurants, and service stations, as improved roads beckoned them to venture farther from home.

Yet the unelected engineers who set out hellbent to redesign America had spent their college years studying not sociology, economics, or history but subsoil content, pavement durability, and infrared spectroscopy.[11] Successors to Thomas MacDonald in Washington and the nation's capitals—many trained by him—carried on his legacy of diligence and rectitude. But to keep Americans satisfied, they would need the vision of Einstein and the wisdom of Solomon.

Congress mandated in 1956 that highway planners forecast the level of traffic in 1975 and build the interstates accordingly. But the planners simply could not extrapolate accurately from the then-current traffic conditions, because conditions change; they might have asked elected and appointed officials what they'd like their cities to look like in 1975 and let highways serve that path of development. But a noble mission burned in the breasts of this cadre of technocrats: instead, development should serve the highways. The interstates would lure retail service businesses to access points like moths to a flame, they reasoned. This aggregation would itself generate new traffic, which would in turn require even more capacious highways.[12]

Predictably, real estate surrounding the exits skyrocketed in value, as speculators scurried to cash in on America's historic land rush. To diffuse the tremendous political pressures on them and to protect the program from scandal, Congress had assigned the squeaky-clean BPR to help state highway officials determine the exact routes and access points. And here, the engineers—largely fastidious men with slide rules in their pockets— developed an impact far beyond their numbers and political clout. For moving an exit a mile to the west or east could make one landowner a fortune and ruin another. Frank Turner, who later served as federal highway administrator, recalled refusing a motel chain's plea for him to divulge the location of a particular ramp—information that could have made Turner a millionaire.[13] None of the highwaymen cared about actual locations the way engineers did; contractors and automakers would make money wherever the roads ran. But the engineers cared single-mindedly about traffic, which had everything to do with location.

A NEW WAY OF LIVING

On the local roads that the interstates replaced, small grocers, florists, and druggists had grown up over the years, their low land costs reflecting their relatively modest profits. Now they could only wave forlornly at their former customers streaking by on the new superhighways. While such merchants' profits plummeted, few could afford to move near interstate exits, where land prices had increased sometimes twenty-five fold.[14] But for nationwide chains like Sears and Howard Johnson's, whose corporate parents could afford the stiff new land prices, the interstate exit sites would concentrate their customers wonderfully. Large retail outlets clustered at the foot of ramps in strips of connected stores with collective parking lots. Developers would build twenty thousand of these shopping centers over the next generation. Offering an ideal climate in which nationwide chains could thrive, the shopping centers by the 1960s grew into malls, with names like Northgate and Shoppers' World, and drew even more traffic.[15] Teenagers with DA haircuts and bouffant hairdos flocked to these commercial cornucopias overflowing with Barbie dolls, Buddy Holly albums, and best-selling novels such as Jack Kerouac's *On the Road*.[16]

So in fact the highway engineers *did* have a plan for America, one in which roadway locations and market forces rearranged homes and businesses at will, often without substantive input from elected leaders.[17] And as the engineers worked away, the project ballooned as their grandiose plans required more money. Less than 2 years into the program, the $27 billion, 13-year project had grown into a $41 billion, 16-year one.[18]

TRADING MONEY FOR FREEDOM

The interstate highways immeasurably transformed American life, for the furrowing of a 250- to 300-foot gash forty-one thousand miles from Maine to California couldn't be done without stepping on some toes. Much of the mileage followed existing roadways but widened them markedly. Governments throughout history have seized private lands, but a democracy instead substitutes money for freedom by paying fair market value to the eager and outraged alike, as condemnation lawyers prospered. Farmers retired to Florida clutching their profits from selling the centuries-old family homesteads or tobacco fields, which soon yielded to J. C. Penney's stores or cloverleaf interchanges. Small grocers, who had become fixtures of neighborhood life and who were too old to move, were lucky to land jobs stacking cabbages at the new A&Ps near the freeway exits.

But to many other city residents, the interstates spelled hope. On paper at least, they allowed a breadwinner to commute double the distance in the same time. Thanks to low-interest Federal Housing Administration mortgages with twenty-five- or thirty-year terms, legions of cityfolk realized their dream of having a single-family home with its own yard—all for ten thousand dollars. Long Island's Levittown, a bedroom community that drew largely blue-collar urban apartment dwellers, spawned thousands of similar settlements across the country.[19] The FHA encouraged the trend, encouraging banks to lend on millions of new low-risk suburban homes while openly refusing to stake money on older city properties. One FHA manual cautioned: "Crowded neighborhoods lessen desirability" and "older properties in a neighborhood have a tendency to accelerate the transition to lower class occupancy."[20]

Sleepy farming villages at the outskirts of cities doubled their population within a decade as their cornfields gave way to row upon row of tract houses. In thousands of bedroom communuities, "the surveyors seemed barely to be done before the moving trucks started arriving." And following the exodus from the cities were the auto dealers, eager to be the people to know in their new communities. Ford's president, Robert McNamara, tapped a brash marketing wizard in his thirties to flog the suburban market. "If there are people in a subdivision and if there are businesses," Lee Iacocca exhorted his dealers, "there will one day be a Rotary or Kiwanis Club there as well" to let a car salesman make contacts.[21]

THE BIRTH OF THE TWO-CAR FAMILY

Car ownership meant not having to depend on anyone else—unless, of course, the car broke down. For no longer could the car owner catch the trolley instead, and buses depended on volume for their profit, so service proved spotty in sprawling suburbia. Then too, if Dad needed the car for business, Mom was stuck at home all day. But the Lee Iacoccas of the world were not about to be daunted by such a trivial problem. The answer was simple: buy a second car.

Out on the expansive interstates, truckers became American cowboys on wheels and insured the immortality of that image when country-and-western disk jockeys began playing odes such as "Tombstone Every Mile" and "Looking at the World through a Windshield." The advent of the CB radio allowed truckers to form vigilant cross-country convoys and defy speed limits—and thereby to cultivate a renegade image.[22] Interstate truck stops grew into villages, offering the long-hauler motel rooms, laundromats, TV and game lounges, truck washes, restaurants, and even specialized newspapers published by groups ranging from the American Trucking Association (ATA) to the Association of Christian Truckers.[23]

LIFE REVOLVES AROUND THE CAR

Driving on the freeway was the next thing to flying. Automakers, with a straight face, promoted sweeping rear fins as a way to keep a driver's Chevrolet Impala or Chrysler Imperial from leaving the road at high speeds. The car as simply a conveyance was now obsolete; life now revolved around it. People deposited their paychecks at drive-in banks, grabbed a bite at the drive-in burger stop, then entertained themselves at drive-in movies, where not infrequently they conceived their young. According to one survey in the late 1960s, nearly 40 percent of marriage proposals took place in the front—or back—seat of an automobile.[24]

Adaptable Americans often accommodated the interstates' volcanic changes quite well. The owner of Sanders Court in Corbin, Kentucky, found his booming fried-chicken business wiped out when an interstate routed traffic seven miles to the west in the mid-1950s. So sixty-six-year-old Harland Sanders reinvented himself, cruised through the South and Midwest—a pensioner sleeping in his car while marketing his secret recipe to new franchisees, who would locate at the foot of interstate exit ramps. By 1963, "Colonel" Sanders had six hundred franchises for

Kentucky Fried Chicken.[25] A Multimixer milkshake salesman named Ray Kroc so admired the volume business done by early drive-in restaurants that he convinced the brothers McDonald to sell him franchising rights to their fast-food business. A key to Kroc's success was his buying up land along the new highways, then leasing it back to the franchises. By the mid-1960s, his chain of McDonald's hamburger restaurants earned more from rents than from Big Macs, fries, and milkshakes.[26]

Preinterstate motels had gained a reputation as illicit lovenests and, in the words of FBI Director J. Edgar Hoover, "dens of vice and corruption."[27] Even those on the up and up varied widely in quality. With millions now vacationing hundreds of miles from home along the open road, a market developed for clean, functional rooms that looked the same in Omaha, Nebraska, as in New Haven, Connecticut. "Buster" Johnson, who had parlayed a single Massachusetts drugstore fountain into hundreds of roadside eateries, decided to branch into attached lodgings, imparting a bit more dignity by using his given first name, Howard.[28] The Holiday Inns and Ramadas, with their sanitized toilet seats and packaged minibars of soap for the weary—and wary—traveler, were not far behind.

The advancing interstate system attracted even archaeologists, who arranged with highway builders to complete digs just ahead of bulldozers, to prevent irreplaceable relics from being destroyed or buried forever under several feet of paving material. Among their finds were a thousand-year-old American Indian skeleton in New Hampshire, complete with the bone arrowpoint that had sent the brave to his grave; a Chinese labor settlement discovered as Interstate 80 prepared to roar through Lovelock, Nevada; and Oregon artifacts of the Calapooia Indians dating to 3,000 B.C.[29]

PASSENGER RAILS SLIP FARTHER BEHIND

By 1958, the car culture, together with the ICC's smothering policies and the railroads' malignant neglect of all but luxury trains, had shrunken rail passenger travel to less than half of what it had been during the 1920s. Western carriers in sparsely settled areas easily convinced the ICC that they should cut loose unprofitable passenger lines; but because of the strong demand for rush-hour service in eastern cities, the commission forced railways to keep providing commuter services, even at a loss. Thus, expensive diesel passenger trains and their featherbedding crews spewed red ink onto rail ledgers, as they sat idle except for the five commuting hours each weekday.[30]

Rail riders complained increasingly of passenger cars strewn with debris, chronically late, too hot in the summer and too cold in the winter, and of abuse from surly conductors. The writer Peter Lyon tells of a trip on the New York Central's Wolverine in which "the bread in the dining car was moldy, and the litter of beer cans and bottles in one of the coaches 'looked as if there had been a party and nobody had cleaned up afterwards.'"[31] Bustling depots gave way to stark, dimly lit stations with peeling paint and boarded-up lunch counters. The fabled porters, whose signature headgear won them the name "Red Caps," gradually faded away.[32] Less than a month after Congress ushered in the interstate era, the *New York Times* ran the headline "2 Railways Plan Fare Rise to Deter Pullman Travel," accompanying an article unmasking a Pennsylvania Railroad and New York Central scheme, the motives of which were already all too clear to their passengers.[33]

Freight Offers Hope

Freight was another matter. Truckers, who thought the interstates would give them a permanent edge on the railroads, now found their beleaguered competitors fighting back, with a boost from technology. Soon some truck drivers would moan to Congress that the railroads were wiping them out. Western lines such as the Union Pacific and the Norfolk and Western still competed favorably with truckers in their long hauls of bituminous coal. But giant eastern carriers such as the Pennsylvania and the New York Central hauled freight only half as far and to downtown destinations, where trucks had the edge on flexibility.[34] As if that were not enough, truckers witnessed hundreds of factories flee high-wage northern states for the nonunionized South.

"Big John" Helps Save the Railroads

To raise volume dramatically in competition with gypsy truckers, the Southern Railway spent $13 million to buy five hundred state-of-the-art aluminum hopper cars, each carrying a hundred tons of grain. The railway called them "Big Johns," a nickname that soon spread through the industry. Truckers and even other railroads were up in arms and howled to the ICC about what they considered ruinous competition. Ultimately, the ICC let the rails cut their rates by 60 percent. The gamble on Big John had paid off; the Southern tripled its grain shipments.[35]

In the Northeast, a glimmer of hope for the railroads emerged when in 1954, the ICC ruled—over truckers' "doleful howls"—that they could haul rubber-wheeled trailers on flatcars, a technology called piggyback-ing.[36] This let a railroad haul its own trucks on flatcars and drive them from the depot directly to their customers' doors. And by renting out flat-car space to trucking companies, they could enhance their revenues even more.[37] By 1960, more than half a million flatcars would be filled with high-value, less-than-carload freight.[38]

Piggybacking was a lifeline thrown to a dying industry. The rails would clearly need it; by 1957, they were carrying less than half of all freight hauled between cities.[39] Yet apoplectic truckers beseeched the ICC to ban this "unfair" competition. Starving railroads found the new business too tempting to play by the rules, and soon their trucking rivals helped unmask rebates by rails to the shippers—harking back to the oil paybacks to John D. Rockefeller, outlawed since 1903.[40]

TRUCKERS AND RAIL OWNERS CLASH

Congress, in a rare moment of introspection in 1958, wondered whether the interstates' effect on railroads was deepening the nation's recession. But when Florida's Senator George Smathers called an inquiry before his Interstate Commerce Committee, angry truckers elbowed by the twenty-five railroad witnesses to complain that it was they, not the railroads, who faced extinction. "They are asking you to hold our arms behind us while they annihilate us," wailed one Michigan carrier.[41] An ATA spokesman warned that any public subsidy Congress gave to passenger trains would only enable their freight operations "to inflict heavy and perhaps fatal damage" on truckers.[42]

Tiptoeing carefully between interest groups, Smathers's committee amended the Interstate Commerce Act to encourage competition, but in wording sufficiently ambiguous to invite court challenges by both rail-roads and truckers. As the federal judge Henry J. Friendly noted wryly, "The legislators had tackled a tough problem, had looked long and hard at it, and then, caught between conflicting pressures, had come up with a whimper."[43] When railroads contended that the new law let them charge below cost when competition demanded, the Supreme Court in 1963 upheld their argument, over the wails of the trucking industry.[44]

Big Johns and piggyback cars could slow, but not reverse by themselves, the steady decline in rail profits. But in the late 1950s, a Santa Fe Railroad executive traveling abroad came upon a European railcar hauling a dozen new automobiles on one flatcar. American railroads had shipped new cars from Detroit in the 1920s, wedged in three or four to a boxcar. But rubber-wheeled road trailers, developed in the 1930s, could hold double the cars and drive them directly into the showroom. The railroads had found themselves out in the cold. At last, by the mid-1950s the rails had their revenge by quickly adopting the car-hauler overnight and watching their market share soar.

The innovative spirit, so long absent from America's railroads, seemed to have returned—and not a moment too soon. But the policy of one industry was up against the one-sided transportation policy of a nation; try as they might, the railroads still swam upstream against a raging current. While their profits had nearly doubled from 1961 to 1965 alone, railroads' tepid 3.69 percent rate of return lit no fires on Wall Street, where the lines desperately hoped to attract investors.[45]

The Struggle Deepens

Stoking the competitive embers, rail carriers vowed to use means fair and foul to win back their share of the market. Historically, fixed trackage meant railroads had to lure industries to locate along their right of way, since they could not usually deliver to the companies' doors. Railways advertised in *Fortune* and *Business Week* for companies seeking to relocate. The Southern Railroad carried its "Look Ahead—Look South" theme in four hundred newspapers. Now the competition from the commercial freightways hastened the efforts; steel mills and breweries began locating adjacent to rail trackage. Between 1954 and 1969, for example, the Union Pacific convinced nearly four thousand companies to locate on its lines.[46]

But motor competition made it no longer enough to boost rail fortunes; "development men were expected to do all they could to insure that it [freight] did not move by truck.' Railroads in the late 1950s methodically warned farmers that a flood of itinerant truckers was depressing the prices of their corn and tomatoes. The rails, which had willingly played the pitiful martyr when it served their purposes, also had learned brass-knuckle brawling and tactics worthy of CIA agents.[47] While they made high-minded appeals to Congress and the ICC, they were engaging in back-alley, bare-fisted scraps.

As early as 1949, Pennsylvania Railroad executives created bogus motorists' clubs to lobby for taxes on trucks so heavy that their profits would evaporate and to push for weight limits, while rail executives lurked in the background.[48] But that was only the beginning. Eastern railroads paid over four hundred thousand dollars a year in fees and expenses to a slick public relations firm, which created phony auto associations and tax leagues, recruited university professors as hired guns, and fed their propaganda to syndicated columnists. State by state, its network pressed successfully to raise truckers' license fees.[49]

Truckers retaliated in kind, taking to the radio and the new medium of television in Pennsylvania to win passage of a "big trucks bill," allowing each truck to carry five additional tons. After Governor John Fine vetoed the bill, outraged truckers sued two dozen railroads, alleging that they had conspired illegally. While the U.S. district court agreed that the railroads' "purpose and intent" was "to hurt the truckers in every way possible," the U.S. Supreme Court reversed that decision.[50] Superhighway competition or not, the nation's railroads had signaled they might be down but they weren't yet out.

WHINING GROWS INTO A MIGHTY ROAR

Superhighways, routed through cities by political compromise, had fundamentally changed American culture and the way the nation would be viewed around the world. Complaints from a few carping ivory-tower academics or a few "negroes" uprooted from their shanties was a small price to pay, in the view of many, to gain a new American prosperity. But as the acrid aroma of hot asphalt hung in the air across the land in the 1960s, two unexpected things happened: the frustrations of the dispossessed erupted in widespread urban violence, and the disaffection with the interstate program spilled over into the general urban populace. Ineffectual whining by a relative few evolved and coalesced into a mighty roar, as Congress came to realize that it had a massive political problem on its hands.

· 13 ·

TROUBLE IN PARADISE

*The most serious obstacles in our roadbuilding
program are not money, nor engineering problems, nor cruel terrain—but PEOPLE.*

—James J. Morton, special assistant to the U.S.
secretary of commerce, 1964

ASIDE FROM THE SOUR-GRAPES GRUMBLING OF RAILROADS, NARY A VOICE
had risen in Congress against the interstate highways when they were
created. Americans seemed to revel in the suburban way of life that faster
roads made possible. You couldn't walk to the soda shop, to mass at St.
Mary's, or to a movie at the Bijou as you could in the city. Dad took the
car now to work downtown, and the family had to buy a second car for
mom's carpool and shopping. But driving in the new aerodynamic Chevrolet
Impala was lots of fun, and the interstates were sure to end the terrible traffic
congestion plaguing the routes downtown.

Such euphoria was to be short-lived, for the 1960s brought news of corruption, fraud, displacement of hundreds of thousands of people, and cost
overruns in the world's grandest public works program ever. And those
directly disaffected, especially those in the cities, found their voice at city
hall, in the state capitols, and in Congress. Soon muckrakers were writing
polemics reminiscent of ones by Upton Sinclair and Ida Tarbell (see chap-

ter 2), with such self-revelatory titles as *Superhighways—Superhoax*, *The Pavers and the Paved*, and *Road to Ruin*. As Congress scrambled to hold the national consensus together, state highway engineers roared on, undeterred by the "nature lovers and bird watchers" lobbing grenades at them.[1] Inevitably, a highway-centered national policy made passenger railroads and some freight lines wards of the state. But disillusionment with interstates and a deus ex machina from the Arabian desert combined to produce a new railroad renaissance—this time in the cities.

SEEDS OF REBELLION

The first stirrings of what, a decade later, would become a full-blown freeway revolt began in a Hartford, Connecticut, suburb in September 1957. Connecticut General Life Insurance Company, an old-line establishment on the city's graceful Bushnell Park, had taken great heat for its decision to abandon Hartford and build an ultramodern, low-slung home office on a rolling greensward in neighboring Bloomfield. Aware of the questions raised about the interstates' effect on cities, Connecticut General sought atonement in the court of public opinion by hosting a high-profile conference on the megahighways' effect on America's cities. Few basking in the national superhighway euphoria were prepared for the critical outcry of what came to be called the Hartford Conference.

On September 9, 1957, the same day that black students clashed with school segregationists in Little Rock, Arkansas, a battle waged inside Connecticut General's headquarters over another issue that would haunt America for the balance of the twentieth century—whether America should think through the likely impact of the interstates *before* constructing them. As the nation's top highway officials fended off attack after attack, a variety of speakers called for less building and more thinking. One federal housing official predicted that the interstates would generate "a planless scattering of homes, factories, stores and what have you . . . in clusters of suburbs . . . that will lie like a pall over the landscape." The homebuilder and future congressman James Scheuer of New York asked whether America would want "to see cities which are inhabited by low income white and colored people, while around the city lives a ring of middle and higher income whites." And the criticism sharpened.

Mumford Throws Down the Gauntlet

Congress and President Eisenhower had justified building the interstates, in part, for national defense. But the author and gadfly Lewis Mumford rose to brand this rationale "flagrantly dishonest." He predicted: "Their highway program will, eventually, wipe out the very area of freedom that the private motorcar promised to retain for them."[2] Then Mumford threw down the gauntlet. He demanded that bulldozers be shut off until metropolitan areas could figure out how to work megaroads into the lifestyle of the affected region. Cities had evolved by slow accretions of development, sometimes over hundreds of years. To allow outside forces to slash a 250-foot concrete swath through miles of downtown, displacing homes and businesses, was not a trifling decision. The conference enthusiastically joined Mumford's demand for a two-year halt on interstate construction.[3]

The call to stop the interstates sped across the nation's teletypes, and the highway builders' reaction was swift and sure. "The economic penalties . . . would be tremendous," thundered William Bugge, the president of the American Association of State Highway Officials (AASHO). How could city bureaucrats have the gall to halt concrete mixers just so some pie-in-the-sky schemes could be devised?[4] The imperious state engineers had their blueprints at the ready; they had already designed the signature red, white, and blue emblem that would brand each interstate road.[5] Bertram Tallamy, the interstates' quarterback at the Bureau of Public Roads (BPR), said that moving ahead would not be a problem; state highway engineers would just impose their own plans on any cities that had not gotten around to developing them.[6]

"Bypassing" the People

For many decades, grocers, restaurateurs, and haberdashers had settled along trafficked roads, offering their wares to people who settled in neighborhoods behind the business strips and to travelers, who could pull off the road at the merchants' front doors. But moving traffic speedily meant drivers could get on or off an interstate only every mile or two. So words like *bypass* and *limited access* became curses to dry cleaners and drugstores who lost their traffic and their savings in the name of progress. Engineers in the field reported, "Try as we might, we have not been able to halt the loud outcry of the motel, restaurant and service station people."[7]

The problems mounted. By 1959, the interstates' price tag rose by more than 50 percent (see chapter 12). Remarkably, Congress had sold to the public America's biggest federally funded project ever without detailed estimates. And buying up expensive city land cost much more than interstate designers had expected.[8] The 1958 recession forced Congress to speed up highway spending before gas revenues could catch up, so by 1959 the legislators had to hike the two-cent gas tax another penny.[9] All this was not good news to the folks back home. Highway-friendly Senator Albert Gore, Sr., warned that the superhighways he had championed (see chapter 11) were now in "grave danger."[10]

JUSTICE FOR ALL?

In 1956, Congress decreed that road builders had to consult with their critics before laying concrete, since the interstates would disturb millions of Americans' lives. However, state highway officials won their demand that state capitols control how the interstates got built. This assured that hearings would be held when—and if—state officials wanted them.[11] So when engineers in 1957 planned a public hearing in Nashville, Tennessee, on a scheme to level 750 homes and businesses, they placed no notices in newspapers and instead put placards advertising the wrong date next to "Wanted" posters at eight post offices outside the area affected. Those public officials who had been clued into the correct date showed up to praise the plan, so the hearing record predictably indicated unanimous support for the project.

But black owners of small businesses displaced by the Nashville project defied pre–civil rights strictures and bravely marched into court. They testified that when the interstate razed their modest commercial district in the name of "urban renewal," relocation was impossible. The swath demolished for the interstate had taken nearly all of the commercially zoned land in their ghetto. Neither federal nor state law gave them money to move, and in those Jim Crow days, local law forbade their relocation to white areas.[12] Their claims of discrimination fell on deaf ears. It was not enough to be discriminated against, the judge told them; they had to prove that highway officials *intended* to discriminate against them.[13] An appeals court sympathized with the plaintiffs but offered what would become a common court rationale for ruling against such protestors: "Too much time and money had been spent to alter the proposal."[14]

Not only in cities did Americans chafe under the seismic shock of the interstates. For example, near Springfield, Illinois, Interstate 55 bisected Carl Kolpack's 163-acre farm, creating problems that could not be addressed by the fair-market-value payment he had received. "My buildings are here," said Kolpack, "[yet] my pastures are across the road. But it's four miles around by the nearest overpass. Every spring I'm forced to haul 2,500 bales of hay all the way around here to store it to the barn. Then I've got to haul it back for winter feed."[15] But it was the disaffection of those in the cities that would escalate protests to the boiling point.

A DEAL FOR URBAN VOTES

By 1959 two investigations were under way, one by President Eisenhower, who was furious that his aides had let the interstates plow through American cities rather than around them: he realized that high urban land prices would cut back on the mileage the nation could afford. In 1959 Ike assigned his trusted associate General John H. Bragdon, a member of the Council of Economic Advisers, to find out why his staff had misled him about the true shape of the interstates. (See chapter 11.)

It turned out that his Bureau of Public Roads had cut a deal with Congress, apparently behind Ike's back. In return for the votes of urban congressmen, the BPR had agreed to route the highways to accomplish "urban renewal," often a euphemism for removal of the poverty-stricken.[16] Apparently, city politicians failed to see that those displaced would end up in even more desperate straits, in other sections of the affected cities.

"A Monstrous Spider Called Corruption"

In 1962, millions of Sunday newspaper readers read a *Parade* magazine article whose authors warned: "A monstrous spider called corruption is devouring tax dollars by the millions." The interstates, they charged, were "paved with waste, inefficiency and boondoggling."[17] The House Public Works Committee, sensing the firm ground beneath them starting to shift, tapped Representative John Blatnik to conduct a "hard-hitting" investigation.[18]

While critics lined up to testify at Blatnik's hearings, Eisenhower's inquiry died, as the 1960 elections altered the national and state political

landscape. John F. Kennedy fell into lockstep with his Republican predecessor in urging rapid completion of the interstates to allow "quick motor
transportation of men and material" in time of war.[19] In a sentence, JFK
had let the highway-motor complex know it had little to fear from this
Democrat, who had campaigned as the candidate of change. Echoing
presidents of the previous four decades, Kennedy called for the "properly
balanced use of private vehicles and modern mass transport to help shape
as well as serve urban growth." "Balance," a goal parroted by most presidents since Warren Harding, had become little more than a shopworn
shibboleth.[20]

Beaten Down in Beantown

In Massachusetts, a Republican road contractor won election in 1960 as
governor and began to test the will of urbanites, who were to bear much
of the dislocation caused by the interstates. John A. Volpe had served not
only as the Massachusetts public works director but had headed a national
umbrella group of nearly thirty-five hundred highway contractors. The
Massachusetts Turnpike had snaked east across the state, stopping before
Boston to curve into northern and southern belts.

Volpe announced that his administration would pierce an extension
twelve miles into the heart of Beantown. Three citizen lawsuits failed to
block it, and the extension reached Boston's historic harbor in 1965. But
the experience educated and energized critics. They would be ready when
public officials attempted to tread on their turf in the late 1960s.[21]

THE HONEYMOON IS OVER

The highwaymen now knew their honeymoon with the American public
was over. In 1956, truckers had bitterly denounced allegations that they
might not be contributing their fair share of road costs, a land mine that
Congress had defused by ordering an inquiry.[22] In 1961, the study showed
that indeed trucks fell far short of paying their way in most states.
Truckers, perhaps sensing the shortening public tolerance, quietly agreed
to let their weight tax be doubled.[23]

In 1962—with more than a third of the interstate system open to traffic—uprooted constituents finally persuaded Congress to help pay them
to move to new apartments and storefronts.[24] Yet state engineers grum-

bled and warned that any bill to aid displaced families would introduce "controversy, delay and political pressures into the program."[25] Their myopic intransigence gradually isolated state engineers from their traditional soulmates in the BPR, who quietly withdrew from traditional state-federal committees, which had helped cement their partnership. The state-highway community reacted by drawing its wagons around in a circle and lashing out at its federal partner. The *Engineering News Record* warned darkly that some of the interstates might eventually be nationalized.[26]

Tangling with LBJ

After JFK's assassination in 1963, the highway advocates found Lyndon Johnson much less compliant than his predecessor, particularly when AASHO got off on the wrong foot by attacking his wife's pet program, highway beautification. Lady Bird Johnson had lobbied Congress to provide plantings, wildflowers, and other amenities to ease the harshness of the superhighways' unremitting concrete. But when the state engineers discovered that she wanted to tap the sacrosanct Highway Trust Fund for her good works, they balked. Some saw beautification as "a big plum" waiting to be exploited by those who could make money from it. To the highway engineers, interstate highways were beautiful all by themselves.[27]

Within months, LBJ decided to test the highwaymen's strength. Whether motivated by Lady Bird's honor, mounting public criticism, or the Vietnam War's fiscal drain, the president announced in the fall of 1966 that he planned to freeze a quarter of interstate spending. The lobby's members in Congress denounced Johnson's call as "illegal" and "unwarranted." They called hearings in which the president—berated by strident critics for killing American boys in Vietnam—now was held responsible for highway deaths resulting from his impounding of highway money. By February 1967, LBJ backed down. The *Engineering News Record* chortled that the administration had realized it had a "tiger by the tail" and freed up the money "before the aroused beast mauled them severely."[28]

"Nobody Would Listen"

The state bureaucrats who dispatched bulldozers and cement mixers to construction sites seemed to have learned little from a decade of public questioning about how the interstates were designed and built. The Blatnik hearings continued to yield front-page news into the mid-1960s: some of the freeways had been built as "death corridors," lacking guardrails on their narrow medians, so high-speed Cadillac Eldorados could careen across the grassy strips and into the paths of oncoming Chevrolet Corvairs.[29]

The most riveting testimony came in the spring of 1967 from a zealous Bronx TV repairman, Joe Linko, whose slides showed 150 locations where New Yorkers had died or had been injured "for no reason at all." State engineers, charged Linko, had built city interstates with poorly placed light poles, trees planted too close to roadways, and guardrails that steered a skidding driver into an abutment rather than around it. Linko had spent $3,500 of his own money and four years as a modern Cassandra, "but nobody would listen" in the highway community.[30]

THE CAR CULTURE BLOSSOMS

If anything cemented the highwaymen into American life more than the Highway Trust Fund, it was the American economy's increasing dependence on the automobile culture. By 1968, one in six Americans made, sold, maintained, or drove motor vehicles for a living. Sixty thousand auto showrooms dotting suburbia displayed the latest in fins and in engines with ever more horsepower. Lighted signs erected by Mobil, Texaco, and Sunoco shone, flashed, and revolved above 211,000 service stations. Highway carnage made possible 114,000 auto repair shops, and 40,000 motels greeted weary wayfarers. Automaking consumed 20 percent of all steel and 60 percent of all rubber made in America.[31] The Asphalt Institute ingenuously labeled the highway-motor partnership a "self-perpetuating cycle" of new roads leading to more cars and gas usage, which led in turn to more roads. "Scratch the new roads and the cycle ceases to function," it observed sagely.[32]

With three-quarters of interstate mileage in place or under construction by the late 1960s, more individuals had been displaced than lived in some state capitals. Between 1967 and 1970 alone, 168,519 people—three-quarters of them in cities—would have to pack up and move as excavators raced their motors impatiently outside their doors.[33]

PUBLIC SCORNS DECAYING RAILS

Meanwhile, the burgeoning car culture and wretched rail service had combined to make the American public and its media scornful—if not downright hostile—to passenger railroads. In 1928, twenty thousand passenger trains had whistled through the countryside; four decades later, a mere six hundred were left. Defending a 1967 abandonment petition, the New York Central said its storied "Twentieth Century Limited" sometimes carried more railroad employees than passengers. The famous "Wabash Cannonball," running between St. Louis and Detroit, had shriveled by 1968 to a baggage car, a coach, and a snack bar.[34] But the Interstate Commerce Commission charged that rail managers had deliberately hastened the decline of their own deficit-ridden passenger service.[35] Between 1955 and 1970, front offices handed pink slips to more than 100 railroad workers a day.[36]

America's railroads still fought for their share of freight business, so they could not let public discontent infect the still-solvent side of their operations as it had in the early 1900s. Scrambling for high ground in 1967, the Association of American Railroads launched a massive public relations campaign, ceding passenger traffic to the roadways and pressing the railways' advantage in carrying freight. The association's ad read: "There's more room on the road for the kind of driving you like . . . when highway trailers ride piggyback—the modern way."[37]

One would have been laughed out of the corner bar in 1920 for suggesting that the giant New York Central and its powerful archrival, the Pennsylvania, might one day merge. But by the mid-1960s, the two lines had begun quietly talking about just that. The Central's net operating income had plunged an astonishing 60 percent from 1955 to 1957 alone, caused in part by competition with the new New York Thruway, which paralleled the Central's tracks from Albany to Buffalo.[38] In 1966, these "two senescent giants," in the words of the rail historian John Stover, "tottered into a grim embrace."[39] To add to the merging partners' woes, unions won a concession that workers with more than a decade in service had jobs for life and could not even be transferred to another city—no matter what the needs of the railroad were.[40]

On a Saturday in June 1968, as millions of TV viewers watched a grimy Penn Central train transport Senator Robert Kennedy's casket from New York City to Washington, a CBS reporter, in an aside, called the passenger train as anachronistic as the horse. The poignancy of a dying mode of transport carrying a dead putative president was palpably

ironic. For like Kennedy, the passenger railroads too had been assassi-
nated. A national news magazine called the journey "a rolling catalog of
the physical discomforts that have turned U.S. passenger railroads into
the nation's most unpopular form of mass travel." Thousands of schoolchildren, railyard workers in overalls, and housewives in aprons lined the
route, waving sadly. Were they saying goodbye to a revered politician or
to a way of life?

URBAN POOR ARE LEFT BEHIND

Ubiquitous full-page ads in *Life* and *Look* depicting fun-loving drivers
streaking by in brightly colored convertibles might have persuaded a
newcomer to American shores in the 1960s that every American owned
an automobile. That was not so, and the greatest disparity between illusion and reality lay in the nation's cities, where 60 percent of people still
were carless.[41] In urban hubs with well-developed public subways, such as
New York City, some who could afford a car felt they did not need one.
But the slim pocketbooks of many more—often nonwhite and poor—
cheated them out of the American dream they saw glorified around
them. They traveled by bus or, if their city was lucky enough still to have
one, a public commuter railroad.

The interstate highway program would rob them in other ways as well.
The freeways allowed workers with cars to follow the downtown factories
and corporations as those moved to abundant sites throughout the suburbs.
But ironically, just as the carless watched their employers leave, the trolleys
that could have been their link to suburban jobs died off too. Lacking
money to buy into the new mobility, the urban poor now often lost their
jobs. Those enterprising enough to run a business could count on no help
or money to relocate.[42] Automobiles had become the ticket not only to prosperity but, in some cases, to survival. And to top it off, many people were
about to lose their homes as well.

More money for slum clearance—sanitized under the term "urban
renewal"—had delivered the urban votes necessary in 1956 to clinch the
interstate deal in Congress. Not surprisingly, those largely low-income tenement dwellers and corner grocers whom the superhighways displaced
were upset. Yet when weighed against the nation's progress, such uprooting
seemed a small price to pay—particularly to those who were not paying it.
But the balance would shift, for soon the disfranchised would arise, and the
middle class would feel the effects of America's latest social revolution.

The Cities Burn

New freeways had cordoned off the low-income Watts section of Los Angeles from its more prosperous surroundings, in what became a pattern—whether planned or de facto—in numerous other American cities.[43] The fiery uprising of Watts residents in 1965 foreshadowed problems to come, and in the summer of 1967, flames seared major cities across America—Tampa, Cincinnati, Atlanta, Newark, Detroit. Now Jennings Randolph, the Senate Public Works Committee chairman, was in a quandary. This hulking bear of a man had been a stalwart ally of a "more roads" policy since his days as a West Virginia contractor (see chapter 12). But ghetto residents had told riot investigators that "urban renewal and freeway construction" were among their major frustrations. Randolph appeared shaken by the revelation, for his was a poor state with urban enclaves.

In January 1968, Randolph sounded an alarm to the highwaymen, suggesting that those who criticized the public hearings as shams might have a point. Had Congress really given the dispossessed a chance to be heard, or had it "merely [been] going through the motions of listening to their complaints, comments and criticisms?" he asked.[44] Two months later, the Kerner Commission declared that nonexistent or deplorable public transit had to share the blame for the urban brushfires spreading across the country. The commission called for more mass transit to link city workers with employers that had recently moved to suburbs.[45]

"White Roads through Black Bedrooms"

Randolph called his own hearings later that year.[46] Lining up at the witness table with irate interstate refugees were such respected senators as Kentucky's John Sherman Cooper and Indiana's Birch Bayh, who suggested that America had gone off the deep end for highways. But Senator Randolph's hearings did little to stem the rising tide of discontent in the land. In city after city, critics were coming to see urban renewal as "white roads through black bedrooms."[47] The urban critic Daniel Patrick Moynihan reported receiving an unsigned letter from a disaffected city resident after the Newark riots: "They are tearing down our best schools and churches to build a highway. We are over here in provity and bondage. There are supposed to be justice for all. Where are that justice? Where are justice?"[48]

As critics gnawed on the ankles of road builders from coast to coast, the highwaymen decided that the interstates merely needed improved public relations.[49] In an ostensible attempt to be fair, state engineers commissioned a public survey to measure antihighway sentiment. One loaded question read: "The automobile pollutes air, creates traffic, demolishes property and kills people. Is the contribution the automobile makes to our way of life worth this?" Eighty-five percent of the respondents answered yes. What the survey-takers disingenuously failed to report was that when asked why, nearly half of the respondents had answered, "because it was the only form of transportation available."[50]

ENGINEERS AND POLITICIANS CUT A DEAL

The beleaguered engineers grew increasingly concerned about the future of road building and the Highway Trust Fund. Congress had given this luxury liner to the highwaymen in 1956 as a fortieth anniversary present, but now its recipients feared the fund may have sprung a leak. Over the years, they had fended off calls to pool federal money for airports, railroads, seaports, and highways, so all modes could share it. But in 1966, partially in response to gibes at the high-and-mighty road builders, Congress had created the Department of Transportation (DOT), to oversee all modes of transport. AASHO was apoplectic. Instead of the customary blank check, the group might now receive "some arbitrarily assigned role of highways in relation to total transportation."[51]

The state engineers sought out their still-rabid friends on Capitol Hill for a closed-door meeting to plead for a remarkable commitment—one that would insulate the road builders from the DOT interlopers. They asked assurance that completion of the interstates would be the beginning, not the end, of the megahighway era and that as much or more would be spent on roads in the future.[52] AASHO's rationale: suburbia, whose huge growth the urban interstates had helped spawn, now needed to be served as well.[53] Within a year, the state engineers would call for $54 billion more to finish the system, then already three-quarters complete. The cost to finish the last quarter doubled the initial estimate for the entire system.[54]

The engineers had sniffed that building highways to create jobs or to jump-start the economy, as Franklin Roosevelt and Eisenhower had proposed, was inappropriate social tinkering. Yet their "build them and they will come" philosophy was a much more profound and lasting form of intervention. Arguing for Americans' ability to make free choices, the highwaymen had skewed those choices, because the location of the interstates largely determined where Americans would live, work, and play. Highway engineers reflected happily that expressways increased values of suburban land adjacent to new interstates. What they never seemed to talk about was how urban land values often fell when impacted by highway projects.[55] And every time an acre of apartments or shops fell before an interstate bulldozer, an acre of taxable land fell off the city's tax rolls, shrinking the tax base needed to support an increasingly dependent population.

DISSENT SPREADS TO THE MIDDLE CLASS

The poor have never been popular with the general populace, and as long as the highwaymen could confine protest to the down and out, they could weather the storm. But gradually the media began reporting that the new megaroads were interfering with middle-class Americans' lives as well: bisecting a public park in Memphis, shutting off the Delaware River waterfront from view by Philadelphia's citizens, and cutting through an Audubon bird sanctuary in San Antonio.[56]

In major cities across America, simmering protests now bubbled into antifreeway revolts. Just as the Grangers had discovered strength in numbers in battling the railroads a century earlier (see chapters 2 and 6), so too did the antihighway forces during the interstate era. They raised their fists at barricades in such diverse places as Baltimore; Mt. Vernon, New York; Chicago; and Wilmington, Delaware.

In 1967, busloads of Bostonian picketers descended on Washington's federal highway offices and tried to block plans for an eight-lane inner belt that would displace thirteen hundred households in a historic part of their city. Their burly congressman, Representative Tip O'Neill, called it "a China wall . . . [built] to save someone in New Hampshire twenty minutes on his way to the South Shore."[57] Boston's Save Our Cities Committee battled entrenched highway interests and convinced their governor, Francis Sargent, to oppose the plan and, finally, to bury it.[58]

Similarly, San Franciscans swam heavily against the tide in 1966 by turning down $240 million in federal highway money to block the double-decker Embarcadero Freeway, which would have blocked the view of their picture-postcard waterfront. The locals so adamantly opposed the plans that they dug into their own pockets to fund a mass transit system, the Bay Area Rapid Transit.[59] In Washington, D.C., a battle raged for years over tunneling the south leg of an inner loop under the Lincoln Memorial and along the Mall.[60] And in disparate communities like Detroit, New Orleans, Seattle, and Morristown (New Jersey), residents went to court to block freeway construction. BPR and state highway department lawyers by 1970 raced from courthouse to courthouse, defending dozens of separate lawsuits, as highway trials took on the quality of morality plays, pitting good against evil.[61]

In fairness to the thousands of people who labored in anonymity to build the interstates, it must be said that many thousands of its miles had been completed competently and without scandal. But such a huge undertaking inevitably left massive footprints. The fact remains that the Blatnik Committee ultimately uncovered collusion, nepotism, graft, and fraud in Florida, West Virginia, Oklahoma, Arizona, and Louisiana, which led to the indictment of nearly a score of people.[62]

A SACRED COW BECOMES A BLACK SHEEP

The Highway Trust Fund, regarded in its early years as a sacred cow, by 1970 resembled a black sheep. Urban critics had argued early on that a rail track could carry up to 50,000 people an hour, while a lane of highway traffic would move only 2,200, but they had been shouting into the wind.[63] Yet interstate cost overruns, mounting protests, and worsening gridlock led citizens to ask whether America had been too hasty in abandoning rail transit and whether highway money should be used to bring it back.

It was growing obvious that urban America could not stanch the red ink flowing from its cadaverous commuter transit lines and that the federal government would have to help in transporting carless urban Americans to work. Public transit companies' slim profits had narrowed alarmingly; and by 1963 they had fallen into the red for the first time. By 1972, deficits reached $513 million.[64]

With motor competition thinning their ridership, transit lines rarely could cover even operating expenses—let alone capital expenses—from passengers' tokens.[65] In addition, American postwar prosperity and labor unions' successful postwar efforts in campaigning for the five-day work week meant that workers could stay home on Saturdays, thus diminishing farebox receipts by as much as 17 percent.[66] The trend was inexorable: only one of twenty straphangers in 1945 still commuted by rail in 1958.[67]

To the highwaymen, rail interests promoted rapid transit as a ruse to delay the interstate program.[68] They denounced transit proponents as freeloaders. AASHO had the temerity to declare that the interstates were paying for themselves and that rapid transit "should stand on its own merits and capabilities," instead of looking for a subsidy.[69] Besides, AASHO added, "freeways *are* a mass transit system."[70]

Tapping the Highway Trust Fund

While highway forces barred the front door, transit boosters went around to the back in 1961, securing loans and grants from the 1961 Housing Act.[71] Finally, in 1964, Congress okayed $50 million in capital grants, at a time when the interstate program was spending eighty times that.[72]

It was one thing for Congress to tap general revenues to fund a competitor, but alarm spread through the highway community as its members learned that legislators might tamper with the sacred Highway Trust Fund, which until then had worked like a charm. Money from Texaco gas pumps and Firestone tire stores funneled into Washington and out again to buy steel, gravel, and asphalt for America's landmark thoroughfares in Poughkeepsie, Moline, and Duluth. The fund was a closed, self-perpetuating system and one that shielded Congress from having to vote every year or two on what might be a politically sensitive issue. But some were prepared to divert a part of these hoarded monies to mass transit.

Diversion . . . hated diversion! The highwaymen had killed it in 1934 and thought that they had buried it for good in 1956, but now as the 1970s dawned it was amazingly rising from the grave. They hadn't foreseen that Americans would come to see highway building as a less-than-noble endeavor. The first incursions in 1970 seemed innocuous: money for exclusive bus lanes, passenger shelters, and parking areas.[73] But the highway groups saw such changes as the precedents that in fact they were. Transit advocates, after a decade of trying, had wedged their foot inside the door.

Governor, Your Cadillac Awaits

On a steamy day in August 1970, the sleepy airport outside Lake of the Ozarks, Missouri, looked more like a luxury auto lot. Awaiting the touchdown of planes from dozens of state capitals was a fleet of sleek white

Cadillac Fleetwoods. General Motors (GM) had placed itself once again in the point position in the struggle between road and rail. Its target was the nation's governors, gathering for their annual conference, as they found themselves in a political straitjacket. Constituents were picketing their offices demanding mass transit, but federal law forbade them from side-tracking any highway money for it. Fearing that the governors would ask Congress to tap into the Highway Trust Fund, GM executives thought it prudent to let them know who their friends were.

When their planes swooped down onto the modest runway, GM rolled out a new luxury car for each chief executive to use during his stay. And if he wished, he could buy the Fleetwood at a used-car price when he left. In the growing protransit climate, it would have taken a lot more than a Cadillac to turn governors' heads; in short order, they resolved by voice vote to demand that Congress invade the fund to bring back rail transit. GM, sadder but wiser, returned to Detroit to plot its next move.[74]

THE ROAD GANG UNDER SEIGE

In Washington, the highway advocates had never been under such siege. LBJ had been difficult to deal with, but Richard Nixon—a probusiness Republican but a railroad conductor's son—proved by one appraisal "*totally* antihighway."[75] The days ahead would all be uphill, and the lobby should have seen it coming. LBJ's aides had sensed the gathering storm before leaving office, but when they tried to warn such corporate leaders as Henry Ford II and Harvey Firestone, they found them barely aware of the antihighway movement and unconcerned with its portents.[76]

John Volpe—one of the lobby's own—was in 1970 the secretary of transportation, but he was bidding Congress to invest in subways, rail transit, and buses and to abolish the Highway Trust Fund within five years.[77] Even Senator Randolph had called for money to fund mass transit.[78] There would be no going back. Congress voted a hefty increase for mass transit in 1970 and agreed to pay two-thirds of the cost of tracks and passenger cars for such cities as Baltimore, Miami, and Atlanta.[79]

Pitting Cities against Suburbs

Waves of immigrant votes had helped empower cities to flex their political muscle against rural interests in the 1930s and 1940s. By 1970, rapidly expanding suburbs gained the clout to impose the needs of a scattered population on the American polity. Increasingly, the interstates became the suburbanites' rallying symbol. And mass transit, in turn, was the remaining urbanites' call to arms.[80]

The transit lobby had stuck its foot in the door in 1970; by 1972, its whole leg was through.[81] But the coup de grace that finally opened the floodgates came not from a ploy by one of the protagonists but from actions of Arab potentates thousands of miles away. As the Organization of the Petroleum Exporting Countries (OPEC) came to guard the oil under its member nations' deserts as jealously as the highwaymen had guarded the Highway Trust Fund, the highway supporters had to face the fact that the days of cheap foreign oil were coming to an end.

The Nixon administration, seized by uncertainty and the unthinkable possibility that sheiks might shut off the spigot completely, called on Americans to conserve fuel and to use rail transit where possible. Until 1973, few Americans asked where gasoline came from or pondered who built their highways. But soon, they were leaving jammed streets to sit in gridlocked gas station lines, only to pay 40 percent more for the privilege.[82]

Mass Transit Unlocks Fund

So by 1973, when the interstate system was 98 percent completed or under construction, the dam finally broke.[83] Congress invaded the Highway Trust Fund for the first time, letting states use up to a quarter of its earmarked highway money to buy capital equipment and substitute a mass transit line for a freeway if state and federal road builders approved.[84] The highway advocates, facing a stark choice between sharing the fund with the mass transit "freeloaders" or watching it die altogether, wisely yielded. In recognizing that mass transit was here to stay, the proud state highway engineers swallowed hard and changed their sixty-year-old name to the American Association of Highway and Transportation Officials (AASHTO).[85]

A year later, Washington took a giant step farther, becoming in effect a permanent partner of mass transit authorities countrywide. Not only would Congress kick in four-fifths of the money needed to buy trackage for railcars; it would now share equally in each transit system's operating expenses.[86] By 1975, Washington spent nearly one-third on mass transit what it was shelling out on the interstates.[87] Protransit strategies to block new highways had paid off. In the nation's capital, where antihighway forces had battled against the interstates for two decades, Washingtonians traded $2.5 billion in unused interstate dollars to build a city subway system. Today the Metro, which carries hundreds of thousands of passengers a day, is recognized as one of the world's finest subways.[88]

In 1975, genial Gerald Ford—not a president known for bold policy moves—proposed to gut the foundation of America's highway program completely. Only one cent of the four-cent gas tax would now go to highways, Ford said, with two cents diverted to general revenues and the other cent to states—a formula not far different from that of most European countries. Ford called the Highway Trust Fund "a classic example of a federal program that has expanded over the years into areas of state and local responsibility, distorting the priorities of those governments."[89]

DISPOSABLE HIGHWAYS?

The interstates had become a metaphor for the American society they served. In an age of throwaway diapers and discardable razors, the United States acted as if it were building disposable superhighways, although it did not advertise that fact. For the $100 billion that Washington had spent on freeways, which were built to last twenty years, the legislators had budgeted not a dime on maintenance, trusting that states could assume the burden.[90] But state governments felt hard-pressed themselves. And state politicians found the media more willing to cover a freeway ribbon cutting than a pothole-patching project. Besides, with Washington picking up 90 percent of the tab for new construction, it seemed foolish to spend the state's 10 percent on anything else. And to make matters worse, fuel conservation and higher pump prices led Americans to drive less in the 1970s. This, together with the fuel-efficient cars that emerged in response, meant that governments' gas revenues fell precipitously—just when the superhighways were wearing out.

But Mother Nature and heavy trucks relentlessly eroded the once-proud commuter links. Dealing with washboard surfaces and potholes was not what the interstate generation had bargained for. At first, the commute downtown had been a breeze. But then the immutable truth that highways generate their own traffic made morning gridlock worse than ever before. The highway helicopter became a new fixture of suburban life, a live eye whirring above the interstate, to radio word of the latest traffic tie-up to the bumper-to-bumper commuters below. People in the can-do Eisenhower era, who had defeated fascism and endured a depression, had seemed more accepting of discomfort. Now a sadder but wiser generation—tempered by assassinations, a failed war, and widespread urban unrest—was in no mood to cut its government much slack.

If the states would not fix the crumbling roads, Washington would have to. In 1976, Congress earmarked the first money for such maintenance.[91] Biting their nails over the rising prices of Middle Eastern oil, Congress also agreed that states could trade in unused highway money for mass transit. From then on, the acme of public works projects would give way to the "three Rs" of resurfacing, restoring, and rehabilitating a crumbling network. "The heroic age was over."[92] The cost of deferred maintenance had become so great—state engineers pegged the price tag at $160 billion—that Congress in 1982 had to add a full nickel to the four-cent gas tax and earmarked a penny of it for mass transit.[93]

HISTORY COMES FULL CIRCLE

A resonant symbol of the advent of auto travel had been the laying of concrete over a rail right-of-way in 1940 to construct the Pennsylvania Turnpike. But nearly four decades later, circumstances had changed. In 1978, the Massachusetts Bay Transportation Authority received $607 million—then the largest urban revitalization grant ever made—to relocate its Orange Line. Its new site: a five-mile right-of-way bought originally for the interstate highway system but gathering weeds since antihighway activists had forced its abandonment.[94]

Americans had put all their eggs in one basket, and now the chickens were coming home to roost. No amount of escapism could avoid the conclusion that American road and rail were in crisis. Quick-fix solutions wouldn't do; a basic rethinking of how our people and commerce get around was needed. That would take courage—a commodity in short supply on Capitol Hill.

·14·

THE UNSHACKLING

*I told them [American railroad presidents]
that sooner or later they would have to face
the question of nationalizing American railroads. They all roared with laughter.*

—Louis Armand, director-general of the French
national railways, recalling a mid-1960s speech

BY 1975, MOST OF THE INDUSTRIALIZED WEST HAD LEARNED THAT THE
economic growth generated by thriving road and rail arteries yields in
taxes much more than the subsidies those modes require. The chief
exception was the United States, where the spending of sixty-two dollars
on roads for every dollar on rails had generated unwieldy freeways
afflicted with giantism and a rail system on life support.[1] And the public
demand to preserve competition—that sacred totem of capitalism—led
Congress to encumber railroads and some truckers with unreasonable
regulatory barnacles. For four decades, both industries had begged
Congress to remove the shackles binding them and let the marketplace
work. By the mid-1970s, Congress and the White House began to listen—if only to avoid having to support or own the railroads themselves.

Since most truckers were still unregulated as of the mid-1970s, no one
knew exactly how many trucks plied the road, although most estimates

range from 150,000 to 300,000. The giants, such as Roadway Express, Consolidated Freightways, and Yellow Freight, held sway; the top 100 companies controlled half of all truck freight.[2] But many unemployed people who could put their hands on a few thousand dollars could buy a used pickup and haul beans and corn from the farms into the cities. The roads they drove on were in disrepair, but then the truckers' taxes were not paying fully for the damage trucks caused to the roads either.

But if America's superhighways were fraying around the edges, its railroads had nearly unraveled, the victims of decades of malignant neglect. Yet in the 1970s the country depended on its railways. Millions of commuters rode them to work, and the rails carried nearly twice the ton-miles that the truckers hauled, even though most of that was low-revenue coal and produce.[3] The mountain of accumulated railroad debt was so high that Washington could not expect the passenger and freight railways ever to balance their books unless Congress swallowed their deficits. So, since overweening regulation had not worked and nationalization would make the railroads the public's problem, Congress began to drift toward a strategy of buying the railroads' debt, loosening the Interstate Commerce Commission's (ICC) grip on them, and keeping them in private hands at the least cost to the taxpayers.

An Offer Rails Couldn't Refuse

In 1971—the year that new suburban multiscreen cinemas were showing *The Godfather*—Congress made the passenger rails an offer they couldn't refuse by stitching together the desiccated carcasses of nearly all of America's passenger railroads under the name of the National Railroad Passenger Corporation and nicknaming it "Amtrak." The new twenty-four-thousand-mile system, operating in forty-three states, amounted to a publicly subsidized, privately operated national passenger system. Absorbed were trains with such evocative names as the "Empire Builder," the "California Zephyr," the "Santa Fe Chief," and the "Sunset Limited."[4]

Each railroad got to unload its deficit onto the American taxpayer and then could take its choice: either a tax deduction or Amtrak common stock. Only four railways chose stock over a tax deduction, showing just how bearish rail executives were about the future of passenger rail. During the 1970s, Washington would pour more than $3 billion into the venture.[5]

Rainbow Trains

Early Amtrak trains were not a pretty sight: filthy, debris-strewn, maintenance-starved cars, bearing the variegated faded colors and peeling logos of the parents that had abandoned them, hooked together into what onlookers derisively called "rainbow trains." A demoralized staff, borrowed from the defunct lines, wrote out tickets and reservations by hand when they were not fielding complaints about steam-heated cars that had frozen up.[6] Some sincerely saw Amtrak as a way to revive passenger rail travel, but others regarded it as a cynical move to kill off passenger rail for good, by demonstrating conclusively that a railroad carrying only people could never earn a profit.[7] Even some veteran railroad officials were skeptical. "People like to watch trains but they don't like to ride them," scoffed one rail executive, who dismissed Amtrak as merely "a form of kinetic art."[8] Many assumed that once the rag-tag cars finally wore out, American passenger rail service would pass into history.

Amtrak, in its early operation, was as much a concept as a genuine railroad. Predominantly, it leased equipment from other lines and paid for the privilege of running its passenger cars over their right-of-way. But gradually, as government subsidies increased, its crews began laying welded steel rails on new ties, as it rebuilt portions of track, including the stretch from Boston to New York. Before the 1970s ended, Amtrak had acquired its own modern silver passenger cars with trademark red and blue diesel locomotives and had bought lines from Boston to Washington and Philadelphia to Harrisburg.[9]

But Amtrak was a government-operated passenger system superimposed onto freight lines that had to try to operate at a profit. Manufacturers' "just-in-time" inventory systems allowed Detroit automakers to roll new cars off assembly lines only thirty-six hours after receiving subassemblies, putting a premium on speedy delivery. Amtrak soon found itself side-tracked repeatedly to let express freight trains speed through, causing passengers frequent delays.[10]

MOANS FROM THE RAILROAD GRAVEYARD

Freight engineers had little cause to sneer at their passenger cousins who had become wards of the state. The East had become a veritable "railroad graveyard," as once-mighty lines—the newly merged Penn Central, the Reading, the Boston and Maine, and the Erie Lackawanna—tumbled into bankruptcy in the early 1970s.[11] As steel rails rusted out and ties rotted from deferred maintenance, train wrecks increased. "Slow" orders went out for trains to cut speeds to as low as ten miles per hour for long stretches, while competing tractor-trailers whizzed by on the parallel interstates at seventy miles an hour. So intertwined were the northeastern railroads, which regularly shipped goods over one another's lines, that red ink from one line's balance sheet spilled onto its neighbors' in short order.[12]

Penn Central's bankruptcy trustees abandoned half of that line's trackage, which left jobless not only rail employees but those working for many shippers whom the railroad had originally convinced to locate next to its tracks.[13] Raining down on Congress now came competing complaints by those whom abandonment would dislocate and rail creditors and shareholders, who continued to lose money without any hope that things would get better. And overseeing the process was Department of Transportation (DOT) secretary and former highway contractor John Volpe, who predictably promoted the abandonment of trackage.[14]

THE SPECTER OF NATIONALIZATION

By the early 1970s, both Republicans and Democrats on Capitol Hill were using the word *nationalization* freely, in spite of its socialist evocations. The Nixon administration, pledged to protect capitalism but reading the tea leaves correctly, put its spin doctors to work. State-owned railways, argued a DOT staff paper, had existed in conservative countries such as Tsarist Russia, Austria-Hungary, and Germany before socialism and communism. It wouldn't be the end of the world to have them here; the United States might benefit from them, too.[15] Senator Vance Hartke of Indiana had shocked viewers of CBS's *Sixty Minutes* investigative news program in 1970 by reaching down and pulling out a loose spike from an operating railroad's track. He proposed a bill to nationalize America's rails.[16]

The Coming of Conrail

However, the legislation that would preserve private freight rail service came not from Congress but from a western railroad that was determined to avoid the bugaboo of state control. A quarter of the traffic on the Union Pacific (UP) began or ended in the Northeast, so the UP cared about the health of the eastern systems. It now proposed to cut away the fat from seven bankrupt railroads, stitch them together, and somehow produce a profitable system to be called the Consolidated Rail Corporation, or Conrail.[17] To give the seven failed lines even a hope of operating in the black, Congress agreed in 1976 to absorb the $2 billion they owed their creditors.[18]

Conrail's seven predecessor lines had hauled nearly half the total rail freight in their area on a bloated system of seventeen thousand miles of track sprawled over sixteen states.[19] Yet in the preceding thirty years, northeastern rail tonnage had fallen by a third. Not only had truckers cut into the rail lines' volume but so had a changing world. Tiny transistors now did the job of bulky vacuum tubes, and the fuel crisis forced automakers to slash car weights by a thousand pounds. These were dire developments for railroads, whose revenues depended on weight, and they intensified the scramble between road and rail for what traffic was left.[20]

The new Conrail clearly would need much less trackage to operate. Not only was business down permanently, but computers let operators dispatch and control trains miles away, cutting the number of railcars needed. A network built for turn-of-the-century demands was vastly overbuilt for modern needs. Yet if the ICC held to its rigid rules, Conrail would have to operate and maintain the entire system.[21]

Congress, using piecemeal measures, cobbled together what passed for a solution to a rail freight collapse in America's most populous region. It assured the public unrealistically that Conrail could pay its own way,[22] thus avoiding the socialistic specter of nationalization. And Congress told the ICC to lighten its grip and let Conrail set its own rates within narrow limits.[23] Paradoxically, Washington had to get more involved to insure that government would become less involved in railroad affairs.[24] But few on the inside were surprised when Conrail posted a $340 million operating deficit for the first half of 1977.[25] In Conrail's first five years of operation, Washington would grudgingly spend $4 billion on the venture.[26] But forming Amtrak and Conrail was only half the job—Congress's huge investment would be worthless if the ICC still managed to hog-tie the railroads and those truckers who fell under its umbrella. Some of those affected came to Capitol Hill to tell their story.

REASSESSING GOVERNMENTAL CONTROLS

Virgil Brenneman of Missoula, Montana, a typical trucker testifying before Congress in 1974, hauled lumber and steel across the Northwest in his own rig. If he wanted to carry pine from Butte to Seattle, his lawyers had to apply to the ICC for "operating authority" between those two cities, a costly and time-consuming process that also demanded he show why existing carriers could not handle the traffic themselves.[27] The operating authority hog-tied a trucker to a rigid route, down to such directions as "Turn right on Main Street and left on Maple Avenue." So if a Seattle company asked Virgil to take some steel tubing back to Missoula, he had to decline unless he had a prior ICC okay between those two cities. The prospect of empty backhauls had forced thousands of owner-operators to work for the big outfits cleared to cover all the major routes. Because ICC operating certificates were scarce, they sometimes became multi-million-dollar assets for the large carriers. But the oil crisis of the 1970s made Congress realize that the system was wasteful, gas guzzling and profit draining. If Congress planned to take the shackles off the maverick trucker, Virgil's only question was, "When do we start?"[28]

This Montana lone ranger was among tens of thousands of truckers, railroad employees, and manufacturers vulnerable to congressional edicts to protect or shackle them—not to speak of two hundred million Americans whose prices for oranges, VCRs, and household fixtures fluctuated with the cost of moving the product into the market. If the mid-nineteenth century had taught Americans the predatory effects of unfettered capitalism, the mid-twentieth century offered a sobering lesson on how poorly government had steered the ship of free enterprise. Starving the rails while feeding the roads had made many of the nation's rail lines wards of the state, while the gargantuan highway program had begun to collapse under its own weight. Suddenly, free-enterprise solutions looked good even to a Democratic Congress, which now began to consider liberating the remaining freight lines and common-carrier truckers. The events of 1980 would bring about the biggest revolution in road and rail since the Grangers forced regulation down robber barons' throats in 1887 (see chapter 2).

Loosening Government's Grip

When Congress put trucking under the ICC's thumb in 1935, it actually exempted most of the industry—fleets owned by shippers, truckers working for only a few customers, and for-hire carriers hauling fruits and vegetables. During the 1940s and 1950s, the ICC, fearing withering rate wars that would harm truckers, blocked railways from cutting rates to lure shippers away from trucks.[29] But no one was protecting the railroads, whose profits continued to erode. A trucker hauling fresh produce, for example, could change his rates to reflect a banner crop or a drought by making a phone call. His rail competitor had to apply for a rate change to the ICC, then go through hearings and deliberations over months or years, by which time the market conditions might have changed several times. It was scarcely surprising that by the late 1970s, truckers carried the lion's share of the nation's fresh vegetables and fruit.[30]

In 1976, prodded by Congress, the ICC began to ease its grip on both railroads and truckers.[31] The Commission let truckers take detours up to 20 percent of the length of their trips.[32] This important change meant that owner-operators such as Brenneman could truck lumber from Butte to Seattle, then carry a backhaul to a city near Butte without ICC permission. One-way trips covered costs, but backhauls generated profit. Word spread fast through the truck stops, and the number of independents seeking to join the industry doubled between 1975 and 1980.[33]

President Jimmy Carter campaigned to deregulate transportation across the board. Recognizing the need for public support, the president started with the airlines, feeling that Americans could identify with air travel more easily than freight handling.[34] Carter pushed his deregulation bill through Congress in 1978 and turned his attention to the railroads.[35] But unlike his predecessors, Carter attacked with both barrels, seeking reform legislation while also pledging to "pack the ICC with fervent deregulators."[36]

Carter delivered on his promise, and soon railroads—for the first time in nearly a century—could haul produce in new refrigerated cars, on any terms they wished, and thus compete head-to-head with the truckers. The ICC also let the railways abandon unprofitable lines it had earlier demanded they keep.[37] A Gerald Ford appointee to the ICC went so far as to say that the ICC should stop running the railroads altogether.[38] Clearly, events were building toward an election-year denouement on Capitol Hill.

A SHERIFF TO THE RESCUE

As Carter campaigned for reelection in 1980, the beginnings of deregulation had proved popular with the American public, which looked forward to the lower fares they expected price competition to bring. Senator Ted Kennedy, challenging Carter for his party's nomination, adopted motor deregulation as one of his main campaign themes.[39] Looking over his shoulder, the president flogged Congress to adopt major bills to remove the shackles from both trucking and the railroads in time for the election.

It fell to Representative Harley Staggers, a craggy, white-maned, seventy-three-year-old former sheriff from Mineral County, West Virginia, to close the book on nearly a century of stifling the railroads.[40] Greasing the skids for the watershed he proposed was not only public opinion but the worsening condition of Conrail. In spite of a million dollars a day in operating subsidies, the quasi-public freight line was mired deep in the red. Greater competition, the bill's sponsors hoped, would boost its revenue. Congress knew that the public would not stand for a continual drain on the public purse to support what had been billed as a profit-making business.[41]

The Deregulation Express Runs Fifty Years Late

The ICC had historically been an officious aunt to the road and rail industries, not content to simply drive them to the ball but demanding to dance with them as well. Now Congress told her to simply stay on the sidelines and chaperone. The Staggers bill that Carter signed in October 1980, just before losing the presidential election to Ronald Reagan, let railroads cancel unprofitable services or routes and set their own rates within limits.[42] Congress then evened the rules through a companion measure called the Motor Carrier Act, letting for-hire truckers do the same.[43] Truckers seeking to run between two cities were free to do so, unless existing carriers could prove their competition would be damaging.[44] Despite having existed side-by-side for nearly a century, road and rail had never been allowed to compete within the free marketplace. Clearly, a new day had dawned.

The Grangers had demanded that the ICC control railroad monopolies, but the railways had not had a monopoly in most areas since the 1920s; in that sense, the Staggers bill was fifty years late. Now for the first time in nearly a century, a railroad could set its own terms with a shipper, without ICC interference, as long as others could bid on the publicly posted rate.[45] From that point on, regulators would step in only to stave off cutthroat competition or to prevent monopolies.[46] Piggybacking and Big John hopper cars (see chapter 13) had made railroads more competitive, so the ICC freed piggybacking entirely from regulation.[47]

Unshackling Boosts Profits

Congress had been the truckers' friend during the interstate era. But now that its one-sided policy had hastened railroad bankruptcies, the legislators had little choice in the face of huge deficits but to improve the railroads' competitive position. So while trucking deregulation aided primarily the user and the public, the Staggers Act was largely designed to help the rails and shorten their time as a public charge.[48] The Staggers Act yielded speedy dividends, as the rail industry posted its biggest profits in a quarter-century during 1981. Congress also pushed Conrail into the black by letting it abandon much of its overbuilt system.[49] By 1982, railroads claimed to have regained a "substantial" percentage of the fruit and vegetable trade, which had been lost to motor carriers for decades.[50] But Congress proved unable to undo the railroads' onerous labor contracts, so firemen still crewed on Amtrak diesels, trains needing two people had five to seven, and rail workers were entitled to a full day's pay whenever the train had traveled 100 miles.[51]

Congress, alarmed by the heavy subsidies Conrail had required, served notice that it must show a profit by 1983 or be cannibalized by other carriers. A leaner Conrail—shorn of thousands of miles of unneeded trackage—posted a net operating income of $388 million in 1985.[52] Soon Conrail was a hot property. Wall Street investors, skittish about rail investment for decades, bought the theretofore troubled rail by putting together the largest secondary offering of capital stock in American history.[53]

Presidents and experts had for decades exhorted road and rail to work together rather than on parallel courses. By the mid-1980s, such cooperation had begun, as rail companies crossed over and merged with road haulers. In 1986, Congress paved the way for the Norfolk Southern to buy North American Van Lines and for Union Pacific to purchase Overnite Transport.[54]

A century's epic struggle between road and rail had been waged on an economic playing field largely owned by America. But by the 1980s, Japanese and Korean imports, a strengthening European Economic Community, and Third World economic awakenings let the United States know it was no longer the only game in town. The United States had been through a tumultuous odyssey, amounting to a panoramic exercise that tested both capitalism and democracy. If it is true that we learn more from failure than from success, America should be very wise indeed.

· 15 ·

SAME GAME, NEW RULES

It's not enough to get by any more if the rail-road president knows socially the president of his ten largest shippers. The public is demand-ing higher quality, and everybody's cutting corners to meet the demand.

—Walter Rich, a regional rail president, 1992

AN EARTHQUAKE OR A HURRICANE CAN ALTER FOREVER THE LANDSCAPE around us. Once the cataclysm ends, the land is quiet, and people adapt to its new look, but nothing is ever quite the same. So it was when the Interstate Commerce Commission (ICC) bowed out of its leading role in American transportation and stepped back into the supporting cast. Gone were the stifling restrictions, but also the comforting stability. Trucking firms, which had felt straitjacketed, now could close deals on a handshake, but they also faced the possibility of being swallowed up by a giant com-petitor. Largely gone were the armies of railroad lawyers trying to persuade a recalcitrant ICC that their clients should be able to charge a market rate. In their place were the advertising and marketing experts, aggressively widening their customers' markets. America had yielded grudgingly to its need for a publicly supported passenger rail system; Amtrak would not dis-appoint. And some of the lines that the major railroads had uprooted as weeds now were blooming as smaller but profitable companies.

The playing field in the 1980s had begun to shift as well. While still overwhelmingly favoring road over rail, the federal government muted its support of highways, suggesting that change was in the wind. As a highway system too vast to be maintained properly crumbled and gridlocked, the underused railroads stood ready to offer their excess capacity—a natural consequence of Washington's unbalanced policies. The 1980s would witness hybrid inventions that blurred the distinction between road and rail, and both modes would finally begin to cooperate toward common goals. And the net beneficiary of all the changes—in price and in service— would be the American consumer. For the regulators—whose essential mission was to keep consumer prices down—ironically had held prices artificially high. The ICC-regulated rail and trucking managers had had little incentive to cut costs, scope out the most profitable markets, or learn from success or failure. With the ICC no longer mandating what they could charge and what services they had to offer, the managers faced a new range of decisions.

In the early Reagan era, thousands of nonunion trucking companies flooded the field, pecking away at the railroads' customer lists. While the rails carried most long-haul coal, grain, and chemical traffic and trucks dominated short hauls, a battle royal now ensued over the middle ground—which mode would carry such goods as refrigerators and lawn chairs within a range of several hundred miles. Free roads and lower labor costs gave truckers an early advantage over the rails.

RAILWAY CUTBACKS AND MARKETING STRATEGIES

Hard-pressed, the rail freight lines fought back, taking aim at organized labor. The half-million union members who worked the rails earned an average of forty-two thousand dollars a year, plus another 40 percent for benefits—among the highest union wages in the country. The labor-management rule that 100 miles equaled a day's work dated from the nineteenth century, when freight trains were slower. Collective bargaining in the mid-1980s nudged it up to 108 miles per day,[1] despite the fact that workers covered an average of 175 miles a day, and railroads often had to pay a worker two days' pay for one day's work. Truckers, by contrast, earned an average of thirty thousand dollars a year with 15 percent for benefits.[2]

The threat that deregulation would let railroads abandon lines or sell them off to nonunion short lines was not an idle one. As rail lines trimmed their track mileage from 160,000 to 110,000, labor leaders realized that unless they agreed to a massive overhaul of work rules, they could watch more lines close down, along with jobs. So the union representatives cut a deal with the companies and slashed their workforce 60 percent, to two hundred thousand people. In return, the rails spent $3 billion to buy out members' contracts.[3] Those cuts, coupled with new technology, enabled the freight haulers to carry one-seventh more volume with barely half as many cars and half the employees by the mid-1980s.

A Savvier Generation

The days of monopolies behind them, the railroads set out to convince consumers that "the public be served" had replaced "the public be damned." Timing was key, according to one rail spokesman. If railroads had been deregulated in the 1950s or 1960s, he said, "we would have failed. We simply had no concept of marketing."[4] But a more savvy generation of managers did. Now through high-minded treatises for opinion leaders, skillful magazine advertising, and assiduous lobbying, the industry sought to portray itself as the white knight come to rescue the country from its crumbling, road-dominant transportation system. Soon even truckers conceded that the new philosophy was translating into better customer service. During the 1980s, efficiencies led the rails to haul two-thirds of auto-industry products.[5]

Armed with aggressive marketing and a streamlined payroll, the railroads geared up to do battle. But another major shift in the economy stalled their progress. Railroads, more than truckers, had traditionally been linked to smokestack industries, and a flood of imports from abroad now jeopardized their bread and butter. During the 1980s, railroads watched domestic iron ore, iron, and steel production drop by half, and that of phosphates, industrial sand, pulp, and paper by approximately 40 percent.[6] The rails had wrestled new-car haulage back from the truckers, but as consumers replaced Fords and Chevys with Hondas and Toyotas, that business fell off. Even the remaining domestic cars became smaller and lighter, cutting what the rails could charge to ship them. Playing into the hands of truckers were modern "just-in-time" inventory systems, which required regular shipment of smaller loads rather than occasional huge shipments. So while industrial output during the decade rose by a quarter, 90 percent of total new business the two modes generated went to the truckers.[7]

A Break for the Rails

Then, when things looked bleakest, rails got a break from three unexpected sources: environmentalists, the disrepair of the nation's highways, and technology. New clean-air rules required coal to burn cleaner than that taken from high-sulfur mines of the Midwest. Suddenly, rail trips became longer and more profitable, as industry found itself forced to buy from low-sulfur western fields.[8]

The highway advocates had argued that America's roads were so bad that Congress needed to double the allocation for repairs, for a total of $80 billion to $100 billion a year, and they called for an eighteen-cent-a-gallon tax to finance it. In response, rail leaders argued aggressively that America should save that money and turn to the railroads, which were using only one-third of their hauling capacity, and were safer and three times more fuel efficient than trucks. And the railway leaders noted that they financed their own improvements through Wall Street, not through the public purse.[9] The argument was strong enough to catch policy makers' attention.

The Container Revolution

The real boost came, however, from a revolutionary freight-hauling method that would eventually lead road and rail to work together. Historically, both had to pay workers and risk breakage when transferring a refrigerator, for example, from a boxcar to a truck. But if a load of refrigerators could be placed in twenty-foot and forty-foot metal containers and lifted by crane from train to truck, damage claims and labor costs for loading and unloading could be greatly reduced. Thus, in the 1980s, the intermodal age was born. Containerization—as the process came to be called—soon brought rails more money than any source other than coal.[10] Then in 1984, rails introduced doublestackers—two 48-foot containers, one atop the other—and revamped work rules to let a mile-long train carry two hundred containers with only a two-person crew. Gradually some railroads and truckers—such as the Arkansas trucking giant J. B. Hunt and the Santa Fe Railroad—began road-rail partnerships, loading rubber-wheeled rigs onto freight cars for long hauls and sending the shipper one bill for their joint service.[11]

Yet for all their gains, America's railroads were up against a rival with potent advantages. Lamented one rail spokesman:

Non-union truckers, driving 10 hours, accomplishing their own clerical chores, performing routine maintenance on their equipment, earning half the wages of rail workers and virtually none of the fringe benefits, speed oranges and grapefruits north over government built and maintained highways.[12]

TURMOIL FOR TRUCKERS

The railways could take some comfort, however, in knowing that the trucking industry faced many problems as well. Of the top fifty trucking companies operating in 1978, most—protected by regulation during the 1970s—closed down or merged during the 1980s.[13] Even giant truckers such as Roadway Services, Yellow Freight, and Carolina Freight were hard hit. Yet still the industry revenues equaled 15 percent of the gross national product, as 78 percent of U.S. freight chugged along in trucks.

So tight had the rivalry become, in fact, that road and rail each tried to steal the inherent advantage of the other. Envious of locomotives that trailed endless cars behind them, truckers campaigned in the late 1980s for "longer combination vehicles" (LCVs)—triple twenty-eight-foot or double forty-eight-foot trailers linked to a cab. The railroads retaliated with an alarmist ad campaign showing a woman driver and her children terrified by a tailgating triple trailer. Railroads argued that the LCVs are unsafe (although the evidence was inconclusive) and complained that they would halve gross rail profits.[14]

If deregulation made road and rail happy, it benefited the American consumer as well. In 1980 Congress helped freight railroads get back on their feet by letting them boost rates 6 percent above the rate of inflation for four years. But aware of the influx of new truckers, the rails did not dare—and their rates increased less than 1 percent over that period.[15] Consequently, in spite of record profits in the economy during the 1980s, rails eked out a 0.5 percent profit.[16] Nevertheless, Wall Street investors were bullish—increasing their $35 billion stake in the nation's rails by nearly half in the decade ending in 1992.[17]

Rail and road are very different industries today. There are fewer trucking giants, but 220,000 trucking companies have put an astounding forty-two million trucks on American roads.[18] In the three decades before deregulation, seventy-five new railroads had appeared. But the new rules lured four hundred new companies to take the plunge in the 1980s. The thirteen largest carriers are called class-one lines, of which seven giant ones each earn more than \$2 billion a year: the Santa Fe, the Burlington Northern, Conrail, CSX, the Norfolk Southern, the Union Pacific, and the Southern Pacific. But as the major railways abandoned unprofitable lines, they found willing buyers in the marketplace: 32 regional railroads and 490 locals. And the regionals have amazed many by becoming one of America's new growth industries.

A NEW BREED OF RAILROAD

Norman Rockwell painted towns such as Cooperstown, New York, a bucolic village that seems to have eased only grudgingly from the 1940s into the 1990s. Down the sleepy main drag from the brick Baseball Hall of Fame is the town depot, a peaked-roof frame building wherein a small whirlwind named Walter Rich is running a new kind of railroad.

"The Delaware Otsego wouldn't exist without deregulation—it's as simple as that," declares the forty-eight-year-old president of one of America's thirty-two regional railroads. Rich, a portly lawyer-entrepreneur wearing red suspenders and flashing a ready smile, admits that he got lucky.

One could argue that roadways helped make Rich what he is today. When the state of New York condemned his small line to build a highway in 1971, Rich used his two-hundred-thousand-dollar proceeds to buy a sixteen-mile shortline railroad, then four other lines, among them the bankrupt New York Susquehanna and Western, known in the industry as the "Susie Q." Some might have seen in the NYS&W a chance to expand merely in upper New York State; Rich saw the Atlantic Ocean, for the NYS&W's tracks extended to the New Jersey coast, giving him an entree to incoming water shipments from abroad.

Then came deregulation. The government, shippers, and New York port authorities—all of whom recalled the days of monopoly abuses—were sensitive to the need for competition among carriers. They now leaned on Conrail, whose lines ran from upper New York State south to the Atlantic, to come up with a competitor. Conrail chose Rich's puny thirty- to forty-mile NYS&W as a weak line that would at least satisfy the wolves at the door and sold it a couple of small lines. But as part of the deal, Conrail agreed to haul the NYS&W's freight from Binghamton to New Jersey.

Small-Fry Trumps Conrail

The plot then thickened. Much eastbound West Coast freight runs through Buffalo. If this small-fry Rich could convince the much larger Delaware and Hudson to let him haul its freight from there southeast to Binghamton, he could speed it over Conrail's tracks to the Jersey shore and complete his own transcontinental link. This had not been Conrail's idea of competition. Rich had trumped Conrail once; he soon would again. When negotiations between Conrail and Sea-Land Service, a company that ships containerized freight from the Atlantic ports inland as far as Chicago, broke down, Rich cut a deal with Sea-Land.

Gradually, the NYS&W grew into a 230-mile regional railroad, grossing some $28 million a year. Rich now prints up slick brochures for executives he hosts on inspection tours of his line, and the NYS&W is going head-to-head with giant Conrail in a manner its benefactor never imagined. While train personnel are unionized, most of the NYS&W's staff are not, so Rich's line benefits from lower labor costs and fewer union rules. Regional railroads such as this one account for only 12 percent of the country's trackage and less than 5 percent of freight revenue. But untold in those percentages is the competitive effect the little lines have on the big ones just by being there.[19]

Rich: The Future Is Containers

Chasing the larger railroads, Rich says, "We're getting into intermodal in a big way." In fact, 60 percent of his business is containers. "The future," says Rich, "is rail to truck for delivery." Now that he can move freight coast to coast, Rich says he maintains agents in Hong Kong and Japan to attract import business. And Rich has diversified his operations in other ways. Aware that government must meet pollution standards by 1998, he has contracted with Jersey Transit to run commuter trains over the NYS&W right-of-way. Rich also offers scenic and nostalgic steam train excursions, even though he is losing money on them. In so doing, he is joining a growing rail-nostalgia tourist market, which includes combination riverboat–steam train excursions offered by the Valley Railroad of Essex, Connecticut, and an annual "Glory Days of the Railroad" weekend festival in White River Junction, Vermont.

But deregulation has made the new railroad owners both open and wary. They can approach any shipper and close a deal with a handshake, but they dare not discuss rates with a competitor: such conversations are no longer immune from antitrust lawsuits. "Our attorneys advise us," Rich laughs—but only half in jest—"that if we're ever in a meeting where another railroad starts to talk about rates, you knock over a glass of water and leave, because everyone will recall the guy who knocked over the glass, then left the room."[20]

AMTRAK AND THE CLAYTOR FACTOR

Amtrak did not have a prayer of marketing effectively the bastardized "rainbow trains" it had inherited in 1971 (see chapter 14). But with the purchase of a thousand red, blue, and silver passenger cars and gleaming new locomotives, America's passenger system turned the corner in the 1970s and then steadily increased its ridership.[21] Leading the charge in the 1980s was a retiree who never got to use his easy chair. Graham Claytor, a Harvard-educated lawyer and rail executive, let himself be lured out of a comfortable semiretirement at age seventy to spend the next eleven years at the helm of what appeared to be a thankless mission. The grandfatherly attorney left his comfortable office at a silk-stocking Washington law firm to give Amtrak what it needed—credibility before Congress, in whose hands the troubled railroad would rise or fall.[22]

Amtrak saw a welcoming environment as key to its task. So it bought, rebuilt, and restored historic stations in such cities as Philadelphia, Baltimore, and Chicago, replacing the dreary, debris-strewn stations America had come to hate. Its successful $160 million restoration of Washington's eighty-year-old Union Station—ticket sales rose 25 percent in the six months after completion—created a hub of activity by adding upscale shops and restaurants. By refurbishing these grand dames of railroad travel, Amtrak turned historic grandeur to its marketing advantage and set its sights on reclaiming the cavernous General Post Office Building across from Pennsylvania Station in Manhattan and restoring it to the elegance of the old Penn Station demolished in the 1960s.[23]

New Tactics in Luring Commuters

If the mission of freight trains was to lure customers away from truckers, Amtrak's task was to convince white-knuckled commuters that it offered them a better way to get to work. Amtrak knew that luring executives and secretaries out of their comfortable cars would not be easy. To counter road boosters' claims of flexibility, Amtrak began promoting the notion that on the trains, "Travel time no longer means down time." But to breathe life into that slogan, the line knew it had to offer executives the kind of surroundings they were used to at work. So it bought 125-mile-an-hour Metroliners for its Washington–to–New York run, with telephones and video equipment. Responding to this upgrade, 40 percent of those who travel the 231 miles between the two cities now ride the passenger train.[24] The route breaks even, and 96.5 percent of the trips arrive on time—unlike most of the rest of the Amtrak system.[25] Because of the line's expertise in commuting, state and local authorities, such as the Los Angeles Metrolink and the Virginia Railway Express, at various times have asked Amtrak to operate their commuter trains. For the first time, Amtrak now carries more commuters than rail passengers.

Catchy jingles such as Dinah Shore's "See the U.S.A. in your Chevrolet" had helped lure tourists away from the "California Zephyr" and onto Interstate 95 during the 1950s and 1960s. Undeterred, Amtrak during the 1980s sought to win them back. Evoking an earlier era, Amtrak resurrected the historic routes of its predecessor lines: its "Lake Shore Limited" from Boston to Chicago now covers the same route as the New York Central's luxury "Twentieth Century Limited"; the "Empire Builder" borrows its name from James J. Hill's Great Northern Railroad route from Chicago into the Pacific Northwest.

The Burden of Borrowed Tracks

But passenger rail had it easier in the days of J. P. Morgan. Then the companies owned their tracks; Amtrak leases all but 750 miles of its 25,000-mile system. And the amount of freight on the tracks has mushroomed. In 1902, the "Twentieth Century Limited" made headlines by streaking to Chicago at ninety miles an hour; track conditions now limit all but some western trains to seventy-nine miles an hour. Frequent "slow" orders require Amtrak engineers to decelerate to speeds as low as ten miles an hour in areas of poor track condition or repair. And since Amtrak is passing over another line's tracks, it plays a permanent second fiddle, as freight trains hauling just-in-time inventories sidetrack tourist trains to reach the factory on time. No wonder Amtrak trains arrive on time only three times out of four.

And half of Amtrak's eighteen hundred passenger cars are nearly forty years old and evoke the sturdiness and functional lines of a 1948 Buick. Advertised amenities such as dining cars and viewing cars are spread thin as consumer demand grows, though the line has more on order. The double-decker Superliner cars on its western lines let tourists in swivel chairs view snowcapped mountains and red-clay buttes through glass-domed viewing cars. Soon they will be offered on eastern routes. So popular have the trips become that summer travel is usually booked months in advance. And meals on vacation trains, while not haute cuisine, are prepared on board and easily surpass airline food.

THE LUSTER OF SUPERHIGHWAYS DIMS

Since most trains travel at the same time daily, Amtrak tourists wishing to spend a day sightseeing in a city can hop back aboard the next day. Sleeping accommodations range in several gradations from reclining seats in rail coaches to bedrooms with bath and hot shower enclosed, all in a five-by-seven-foot space. Many travelers spend two or three weeks aboard. "Our family used to see the country on the superhighways," says one Seattle tourist. "But they're not so super anymore, are they?"[26]

Compared to the $18 billion a year that Congress spends on highways, its subsidy to Amtrak is just under $500 million a year.[27] While not breaking even, Amtrak has steadily increased its contribution to operating costs to 80 percent, in part because railway unions have agreed to ease burdensome work rules.

Los Angeles Turns to Rails

As American highway congestion worsened, ridership on America's public transit rose steadily through the 1980s, though not without problems. The center of American rail transit is New York City, through which pass 40 percent of America's transit riders. Every day, 3.5 million straphangers descend on a newly improved system ten times larger than the next biggest ones in Washington and Chicago.[28] In Los Angeles, smoggy round-the-clock congestion necessitated the construction of a multi-billion-dollar subway, which opened in 1992. And where ridership is more modest, cities have adopted postmodern trolleycars labeled "light rail," sometimes reclaiming the weed-infested railbeds that trolleys rode on fifty years ago. Light rail has begun or is anticipated in such places as Portland, Oregon; San Jose, San Diego, and Sacramento, California; and St. Louis, Missouri.

The largest mass transit system built in many years is the Metrolink in Los Angeles, the city whose early embrace of the automobile helped spread its car culture as a model throughout the world. Now crippled with bumper-to-bumper traffic all day—not merely at rush hours—Los Angeles hopes to spread its 114-mile network into a 450-mile spiderweb, using diesel-electric locomotives over existing lines purchased from railroad companies. Ultimately, its nine commuter lines will link five counties and, officials hope, remove up to forty thousand automobiles per rush hour from the roads.[29] Los Angeles in 1992 also opened the first leg of its 21.7-mile subway.[30]

The Road Ahead

The epic struggle continues between road and rail, a saga studded with idealism, avarice, raw ambition, folly, genius, and stupidity. It has occupied nearly half of this young nation's life. America's transportation arteries are so important to the economy that either road or rail industries have stood atop the pinnacle of business production over the past century. But have we learned anything from witnessing and living within this panorama? How will technology change the way the game is played in the twenty-first century? And can we learn anything from our global competitors?

·16·

TAKING STOCK

Thanks largely to motor vehicles, hypermobility has become almost an American birthright.

—World Resources Institute

AMERICA WAS BARELY FORTY YEARS OLD WHEN THE IRON HORSE GAL-loped into national life. Soon it was shaking the very foundations of American life, making some people wildly rich and impoverishing others. Colonists had set up a skeletal government, suited to an economy of farmers and small businesses. But by the late 1800s the railroads' revenues outstripped those of the government itself. So it is easy to understand that the public panicked, out of fear that this overarching industry might swallow up their newfound freedoms.

The world's first big business tested government's ability to bend commercial self-interest toward the common weal. But the nation's three branches of government seemed powerless to harness this new transforming industry. So Congress passed the buck to a new kind of agency, the Interstate Commerce Commission (ICC), and learned a basic weakness of democracy: that in the years it takes to legislate a solution to a problem, the problem itself may have disappeared. For in the three decades it took for the ICC to grow real teeth, the worst depredations of the railroads faded into history. Yet the commission pressed on, animated by reformist flames fanned by demagogues. And while Congress failed to tell the ICC how to do its job and give it the necessary tools, the ICC's micromanagers neglected to develop an industry overview that would have let the commission supervise the railroads systematically.

A DRAINING, DISPIRITING DRAMA

By 1930, a dense network of interconnected paved roads linked every corner of America, and Detroit produced millions of cars and trucks that cut dramatically into railroad business. For Congress and the ICC, competition was the holy grail, and they flogged railroads to engage in it. Yet when motor travel evolved as a competitive counterforce to the rails, both bodies refused to empower the market forces to which they gave such lip service.

And so a draining, dispiriting drama played out over the next half-century, in which the government sapped away the strength of one industry and part of another, by suffocating their operations. Full-throated competition between road and rail might well have led to new abuses, which government could have used its powers to correct. But no one can know what might have happened, because competition was never given a chance. Alternatively, Congress might have decided early on that government should own the avenues of commerce, and thus have nationalized both modes. At least road and rail would then have competed on a level playing field. But freedom-loving Americans would not tolerate such government interference with free enterprise. Conflicting pressures forced politicians toward regulation as a middle ground between a totally free market and government ownership. Yet in practice that choice may have been worse than either extreme.

Congress's failure to lift the oppressive veil of regulation from the railroads and its decision to delay so long in making truckers accountable to the public were direct results of one of the most skillful campaigns for hearts and minds ever orchestrated in this country. Not that Americans would not have embraced the natural advantages of motor travel without congressional help. But highway engineers exist to build roads, and corporations exist to maximize profits. As a corporate plunderer in the motion picture *Other People's Money* observed, "Hey, I'm just doing my job. I'm a capitalist."[1] Such understandable thinking encouraged the highwaymen to create a culture in which only one mode mattered. In selling America on the need for their services, they clearly outshone the railroads.

A public that preferred letting the market work over planning an integrated road-rail network ended up vastly overbuilding, duplicating efforts, and as a result, accepting higher prices because of the wastefulness. Not until the 1980s, after fifty years of lost opportunities, did America witness the two powerful modes competing freely with one another. This new era of road and rail has been a good start. But pure competition is socially blind. Government will undoubtedly face new challenges of protecting the public interest sooner, rather than later.

THE GRUESOME TROLLEY AUTOPSY

A half-century after the demise of the trolley industry, its autopsy continues. Transportation pathologists disagree strongly about why a mode that seems so cost-effective today failed to survive. Little question exists that the industry had serious problems well before General Motors (GM) and the bus-line pioneer Roy Fitzgerald took an interest (see chapter 7). Yet few deny that GM and its affiliates conspired to monopolize the urban market for buses, tires, and petroleum products, if not to monopolize the urban lines themselves. "So what?" ask some experts, who maintain that factors other than the conspiracy did the industry in—that people simply made a free market choice for motor travel.

That argument begs to be examined. The highwaymen worked hard to influence Americans' choice of travel. Early automobile ads chipped away at a breadwinner's psychological freedom to choose by invoking moral terms: that riding the trolleys was "wrong" or "not fair to your children."[2] But more influential were the policy choices that made railways build and pay taxes on their own pathways while sparing rails' competitors from such burdens. Traveling by road seemed cheaper than using the rails, with good reason.

And the "free choice" argument presumes that people would opt for motor over rail travel for *all* their needs—commuting, shopping, business travel, recreation. In fact, people often mix modes, commuting to work by public transit while shopping for groceries and going to the beach by car. Monolithic decisions about using road or rail are likely only when just one practical option exists. By removing electric streetcars from city streets and contracting to forbid their return, those who freely admit they were trying to reshape urban life insured that cityfolk would have only one real alternative.

In a sense, whether the GM conspiracy killed the street railways is beside the point. Society penalizes attempted murder as severely as it does murder itself, to deter the criminal intent that may succeed elsewhere. GM argues that it simply followed the capitalistic impulse. However, its resources and partnerships were such as to subvert the choice implicit in such a free market. Psychologically conditioning buyers through advertising, engaging in massive lobbying to help roads and hurt rails, and regulating one mode while giving free rein to its competitor all have become accepted in American society. But the policies that looked so pacesetting in the 1950s now appear wasteful and counterproductive. Disillusioned American consumers are beginning to recognize their lack of options.

WHEN MEANS BECOME ENDS

These narrowing options relate directly to the interstate highways. By the 1950s the highwaymen had become so influential that America's highway program was no longer a means to a better life but rather an end in itself, now that the highway-motor complex accounted for one of every six jobs in America.[3] Highways had to be built not to meet public needs but to protect private jobs. No one made such an argument when railroads trimmed three hundred thousand workers from their payrolls in the 1980s.

The reality is that America has institutionalized the highway-motor complex as a permanent presence, whether roads are needed or not. The highway advocates are proud of this fact and like to emphasize what a bargain road travel is—that fuel costs have stabilized and that road taxes are a fraction of those charged in Europe. In 1993, Senator Albert Gore, Sr., an architect of the interstate highways (see chapter 11), when asked to reflect on whether he would design the interstates differently today, said simply, "I like them as they are."[4]

Frank Turner, the nation's highway chief during the 1970s, estimated that the interstates, as compared with smaller roadways, save Americans $273 billion in time, vehicle wear and tear, and accident losses.[5] But he mentioned only the surface costs. The true story lies in the costs he did not detail.

Driving's Hidden Costs

Only a political death wish could motivate a member of Congress to vote for a $2.25-a-gallon gasoline tax, yet the auto-centric policies Congress has endorsed over the last several generations have actually imposed a burden of that size on all Americans.[6] So-called highway subsidies are not merely the construction and maintenance costs that road revenues do not cover. Roads also burden taxpayers because of the need for someone to

- patrol highways
- clean polluted air
- insure that foreign oil flows freely to U.S. shores
- subsidize downtown parking for millions of commuters
- dispose of millions of junked cars, tires, and batteries
- cover higher health-care costs associated with the breathing of gasoline fumes
- deal with fuel wastage and time lost in traffic jams
- cope with losses of life and human capacity in traffic accidents
- pay courts and judges to handle personal injury lawsuits
- pay auto insurance premiums.

No longer are such topics only grist for malcontents and utopians. Cassandra today wears a mainstream face: the Department of Transportation, the Brookings Institution, the Federal Reserve system, the World Resources Institute, and a prominent Republican senator, for example. Collectively, they suggest that Americans pay upwards of $300 billion a year—more than the interest on the federal deficit—in charges directly attributable to driving, over and above normal user fees. Since Americans consume an estimated 133 billion gallons of motor vehicle fuel every year, to each gallon purchased for $1.20 today must be added hidden costs of $2.25, if these costs were spread across the population. However, they are not.

Millions who pay the $2.25-per-gallon premium through property, sales, and income taxes and higher consumer prices do not even drive—the elderly, cityfolk who rely on mass transit, and the poor. To have a system in which those who benefit shift the costs to those who do not is not merely unfair; it understates the costs that car users make society pay. And charging motorists less than what their driving costs encourages more driving, which in turn intensifies the problems of overuse.[7]

Roads Don't Pay for Themselves

Drivers who believe their motor vehicle fees and gasoline charges equal the cost of building and maintaining the roads they drive on are misled. Actually, such fees cover only about 60 percent of the $53.3 billion that all levels of government spend each year.[8] The remaining $21.3 billion comes from general tax revenues that state and local governments assess on drivers and nondrivers alike.

In spite of this additional subsidy, American roads wear out faster than legislators earmark taxes to fix them. Congress estimates that 265,000 miles of American roads and 134,000 bridges are in poor condition. Heavy trucks inflict nearly all the damage caused to roads—partially because Americans lay pavement to bargain-basement standards—yet trucks still pay far less than their fair share of the damage they cause. A Brookings Institution study calculates that truck taxes cover as little as 14 percent of the maintenance costs they cause in cities and 29 percent on intercity roads.[9] Washington's own highway builders—hardly enemies of truckers—concluded that a modest thirteen-ton truck causes a thousand times as much structural damage to a road as does a car.[10] No wonder America's $21.3 billion annual road subsidy does not nearly keep pace with even repair needs, let alone new road building.

A Little Help From Our Friends

Highways do not exist in a vacuum; they require a complex support system. Police and fire patrols, traffic controllers, ambulances carrying paramedics, and accident and theft investigators cost billions more. Some examples: government spends $6.1 billion a year on police and safety services, $4.9 billion on administration, and $5.5 billion on interest and debt retirement—the vast majority of these costs at the state and local levels.[11]

The Fallacy of Free Parking

Federal tax laws make it such a good deal for employers to offer free parking to employees that an estimated eighty-five million Americans—90 percent of all commuters—receive this benefit. Yet the market value of a parking space can be two hundred dollars a month in some cities. Employers offer this valuable perk because it is much cheaper than giving a raise for the same amount.

A company, faced with a choice of giving a worker free parking worth $2,000 a year or a raise netting the worker the same amount, will choose free parking nearly every time. For a raise to net a worker $2,000, the company must pay $3,800 just to cover that person's pension contribution; Social Security; and federal, state, and local taxes. Add to this the employer's contribution to pension, Social Security, workers' compensation, and unemployment and life insurance on the raise, and the employer ends up paying more than twice the net value of the raise. The World Resources Institute, using a parking-space value of a modest $1,000 per year, pegs the total cost to employers at $85 billion a year, which they have to pass on to consumers in the prices of their products.

But federal tax law subsidizes free parking, requiring neither employer nor employee to pay taxes on it. Assuming a tax rate of even 25 percent, $21 billion a year is lost to the federal coffers. Yet until 1992, if the employer reimbursed its worker for mass transit tickets, only the first twenty-one dollars of the monthly payment was nontaxable (Congress in 1992 increased the amount to sixty dollars). So Washington's hidden subsidy makes commuting by road rather than rail a very good deal under current law.[12]

Vast parking spaces at shopping malls have become commonplace across America. Yet the acreage they cover represents added costs that the mall owners must pass on to the tenants, who in turn pass them along to consumers through the prices of goods. So people who access a mall by bus or other public conveyance subsidize parking for those who drive.

Thus parking is never free; its true costs are simply hidden from view. But one way or another, the American consumer foots the bill.

Imported Oil Holds Americans Hostage

The United States, with 5 percent of the world's population, consumes 25 percent of global oil, half of which burns in motor vehicles. Since 42 percent of that oil is imported (13 percent of it from the Middle East), America has a huge stake in keeping foreign supplies open and continuous for the benefit of businesses and homeowners alike.[13] It does this not only by maintaining a 600-million-barrel strategic petroleum reserve, to counter oil shortages and even out market prices, but also by tailoring its relations with foreign powers to ensure a steady supply. America would not have participated in the 1991 Persian Gulf war—which cost tens of thousands of lives and an estimated $50 billion in American monies—if Kuwait had not been sitting on one of the world's richest oil supplies.[14]

But wars are episodic. Washington spends an estimated $50 billion each year to maintain a U.S. military presence in the Persian Gulf, in part to keep pipelines open. This includes the costs of supporting the central command, which oversees three navy aircraft-carrier battle groups, one marine and three army land divisions, and the equivalent of nine air wings. It is difficult to sort out political from energy objectives, but if half that presence can be ascribed to oil, the additional subsidy amounts to $25 billion. And half of the $28 billion spent on America's strategic petroleum reserve since 1976 can be allocated to motor vehicles as well.[15]

A Shrinking Tax Base

Today's modern highway system removed sixty-six thousand square miles of land from the tax rolls for roadways, cloverleafs, parking lots, and service areas—a collective mass about the size of Georgia, amounting to 38.4 million acres of land.[16] Undoubtedly, interstate highways greatly enhance the value of land surrounding their access points. But, as noted in earlier chapters, they often diminish the value of land between those points, which once was connected to local roads but is bypassed by the interstates. In addition, countless watersheds, wetlands, parklands, and historical buildings and monuments have been leveled to make superhighways possible.

And in America's cities, the interstates—which once had seemed a plum—have drained off funds. Before construction of the interstates, the worth of urban commercial land vastly exceeded the relatively inaccessible farmland outside. The urban interstates suddenly made the surrounding land accessible, and towns proved only too glad to add to their tax rolls by developing it for shopping malls. So while the inner suburban land shot up in price, the simple law of supply and demand forced urban land values down. For areas with regional tax bases, the net effect may have been to benefit the region as a whole. But in regions such as the Northeast, where each town typically taxes its own citizens, the effect was to impoverish cities while enriching suburbs. Not only did urban land diminish in value, but studies estimate that as much as half of the land in some cities has been given over to roads and related uses, such as parking. Much of the fiscal crisis faced by northeastern cities today leads back to this factor.[17]

Gridlock's True Toll

Gridlock has been the motorist's rush-hour companion since the 1920s, but it has worsened markedly in the last decade or two. In the last decade alone, two dozen newspapers have inaugurated regular columns—with names such as "Dr. Gridlock," "Getting Around," and the "Road Scholar"—to steer commuters around traffic problems.[18] Besides white-knuckled stress and as much as two hours of downtime a day, congestion cuts productivity when employees cannot get to work on time, boosts insurance premiums because the rush-hour crowd is likelier to have accidents, and delays commerce. In a five-year period ending in 1987, traffic slowed by 20 percent or more in Los Angeles, San Francisco, Washington, Atlanta, Seattle, San Diego, Dallas, and Minneapolis.[19] And Los Angeles, America's cultural bellwether for decades, faces freeway congestion dawn to dusk, not just at rush hours.[20]

The Texas Transportation Institute estimates that wasted fuel, lost time, and higher premiums in America's thirty-nine largest metropolitan areas alone totaled $41 billion in 1987.[21] The General Accounting Office believes that the United States loses a total of $100 billion a year in lost productivity from traffic congestion.[22]

The Costs of Dirty Air

The Federal Reserve system, using Environmental Protection Agency data, concludes that six cents from each gallon of gas represents the cost that motor vehicle pollution inflicts on American society, through the annual release of some 350 million tons of carbon into the atmosphere. Typical results include acid rain, lung disease, and forest damages from low-altitude ozone.[23] The American Lung Association (ALA) estimates that Americans' breathing of gas fumes costs forty to fifty cents per gallon in medical expenditures, far more than the estimate in the Federal Reserve study.[24] According to the World Resources Institute, the ALA's figures translate into $9 billion in damages.[25] And this amount does not include what industries pay to comply with the federal Clean Air Act, or the loss of visibility and damage to crops, trees, and vegetation. A related expense, not even quantified here, is how much it costs to dispose of 200 million tires, 8 million junked vehicles, and 138,000 tons of battery lead each year.[26]

Accidents Injure Bodies and Pocketbooks

The generous road standards of interstate highways have undoubtedly helped decrease the number of accident injuries and fatalities. Still, 94 percent of all transportation fatalities involve motor vehicles, even though motor vehicle mileage accounts for only half of the total miles traveled by all modes.[27] Some 1.6 million people are injured and 43,500 people die on American roads each year—about the same number who died in the Vietnam War.[28] But these totals only begin to describe the social costs of the 14.8 million annual traffic accidents.[29]

A federal highway study reports that vehicle accidents in 1988 cost $130 billion in time lost from work; property damage; medical expenses; legal, court, and administrative costs; travel delays; and emergency services.[30] Each year, drivers pay $99.3 billion in insurance premiums to companies, which pay them $80 billion for their losses.[31]

To such a total, one could also add such miscellaneous costs as the psychological effects of noise, the effect that highway vibration has on nearby structures, and the drivers' costs in highway tolls.

An analysis would be grossly unfair, however, not to credit the many benefits of an auto-centered society: the thirteenfold increase in America's gross national product since the birth of the interstates is no coincidence. But while the benefits are clearly visible, the costs are more hidden; both need to be examined in full. To quibble with one or another of the figures just cited is to beg the question, for motoring undeniably generates mammoth social costs while it yields tremendous gains and a better quality of life. So here is the scorecard of annual social costs, which does not even include the numerous nonquantifiable costs detailed earlier:

- General tax subsidies to build roads: $21 billion
- Police and safety services: $6.1 billion
- Highway administration: $4.9 billion
- Interest and debt service: $5.5 billion
- Loss of tax revenues from free parking: $21.2 billion
- Military presence in Persian Gulf: $25 billion
- Annual cost of strategic petroleum reserve: $1.5 billion
- Costs of traffic congestion: $100 billion
- Air pollution and health costs: $9 billion
- Casualty insurance premiums: $99 billion
- TOTAL: *$293.2 billion per year*

American vehicles consume some 133 billion gallons of gasoline each year. If $293.2 billion in ancillary costs are apportioned across the gallonage, they produce an additional $2.25 per gallon, not collected at the pump but collected in other ways nonetheless. Would we as consumers drive as much if we knew that instead of $1.20 a gallon, we were really paying $3.45? And if nondrivers decided to stop subsidizing drivers, how would the figures change?

Perhaps more profound than all of these factors are the costs that no study will ever quantify. A half-century ago, Americans engaged in daily contact with more people than they do now. Rising in the morning, driving to work alone, working in a downtown cubicle, driving home alone, and relaxing in our self-contained entertainment room is a revolutionary change in our daily living patterns. In her seminal work, *The Life and Death of Great American Cities,* the social critic Jane Jacobs concludes, "Lowly, unpurposeful and random as they appear, sidewalk contacts are the small change from which a city's wealth of public life must grow."[32] Can it be that while making us richer, the automobile has made us poorer, too?

·17·

TECHNOLOGY TO THE
RESCUE?

*Red-light running is becoming epidemic
because people are just so frustrated. . . . We
simply must find relief.*

—Thomas D. Larson, former Federal Highway
Administrator

AS POWERFUL AS THE HOUSES OF CONGRESS AND CORPORATE BOARD
rooms have been in shaping the history of American surface transportation, an even more influential chamber has been the laboratory.
Inventions not only made railroads and motor vehicles possible, but at
critical stages in the struggle between road and rail, they boosted the fortunes of one protagonist or the other and often tipped the competitive balance. Air brakes and automatic couplers restored safety to a rail industry
that had angered the public by killing large numbers of people—including its own workers—late in the nineteenth century. Pneumatic tires,
making possible comfortable long-distance travel, laid the foundation for
motor tourism and long-distance trucking. Adaptation of the automobile
carrier enabled the railroads to wrest long-lost business from the truckers.
The ability to carry freight in closed containers cut costs to both road and
rail and, ultimately, to the consumer.

Rails and trucks, still locked in a competitive battle, now wrestle with
issues for the twenty-first century, in which technology promises to transform daily life as fundamentally as the internal combustion engine revo-
lutionized life a century ago. From high-speed trains to remedies for traf-

fic jams, from energy-saving devices to the information revolution, the laboratory has done its job; the open question is whether political and corporate powers have the will to follow. For political cowardice, corporate self-protection, and an American fixation on instant gratification loom as major obstacles to a better life.

CLOGGED ARTERIES

Most Americans' key transportation issue is how to get from home to work and to pleasure and business destinations. Far more than any other industrialized nation, America relies on its highways. As roads fill to congestion, we continue to build more roads, failing again and again to understand that highways generate their own traffic in a never-ending cycle, or perhaps simply ignoring this reality because road building is good for the economy. We cannot abandon our mammoth highway network; nor would we want to. Yet the Department of Transportation itself admits that congestion has reached alarming levels. And since little new construction is forecast, relief becomes more urgent every year.[1]

In fact, scientists have devised new technologies that offer some promising answers. Traffic jams can be eased if we

- motivate drivers to shift rush-hour driving to off-peak hours
- control traffic flow electronically
- divert millions of day-to-day car-bound transactions onto data superhighways, using the home computer as an on-ramp.

But the "freedom of the American road"—the mantra that highway advocates have chanted for generations to sell "freeways" to the public—poses a huge hurdle to changing drivers' daily patterns. Singapore, Southeast Asia's largest commercial port, has long pioneered in fighting highway congestion, by limiting cars allowed on the roads and, more recently, by assessing lower taxes and fees to drivers who agree to travel only at night and on weekends.[2] But calling for limits on driving in "live free or die" America would surely doom any anticongestion plan.

WILL ECONOMIC INCENTIVES CHANGE BEHAVIOR?

More palatable to the American ethos are economic incentives. Chief among these is peak pricing, already used by phone companies to charge more for long-distance calls during the high-volume business day and by restaurants offering early-bird specials. Toll booths installed to exact payment from consumers would only make congestion worse. But electronic technology allows sensors embedded in pavement or in canopies to read bar codes affixed to passing vehicles, record a toll, and bill the car's owner automatically. Nonpayers would not be allowed to reregister their cars. The concept has been tested in New York's Lincoln Tunnel and the Coronado Bay Bridge in San Diego, as well as in Paris, Norway, and Hong Kong.[3]

But new solutions carry in their wake new dilemmas. Do we really want Big Brother knowing where we were last Saturday afternoon? One solution is to use the kind of electronic debit card that some subways use, allowing drivers to prepay their tolls.[4] Toll-road agencies forecast that by the year 2000, a uniform toll-collection system would allow drivers to leave their change at home.[5] First, though, politicians would have to convince the public that it makes sense to pay for what always had been free, in the interests of a smoother commute. Practical politicians concede that peak pricing is politically saleable only when another nontolled alternative is available, so lower-income drivers are not unduly penalized.[6]

Peak, or congestion, pricing has dual advantages: first, if done right, it would spread out the traffic flow so that everybody could get to work more quickly; second, it would generate revenue not only to pay for itself but to help fund the backlog of needed repairs to U.S. roads and bridges. But peak pricing is not as simple as it seems. The notion that "everyone has his price" applies to commuting as well; one person might be willing to pay $1.00, but not $1.50, to avoid a traffic jam. For another person, the tipping point might be higher or lower. Obviously, smooth traffic flow depends on hitting the precise price level that has the desired effect. But toll setting in a democracy is a political exercise, subject to pressures to raise or lower the price level. Washington's highway economists estimate that people would pay sixteen to thirty-three cents a mile more before they would change their commuting habits. But first they would lobby against the increases, which is one reason why current charges on toll highways range between three and ten cents a mile.[7]

SMART CARS, SMART HIGHWAYS

Electronics offers another way to loosen gridlock by creating "smart cars" and "smart highways." Los Angeles and Orlando are among the American cities experimenting with cars that use dashboard computer screens so drivers can plot where they want to go and receive an instant map telling the quickest way to get there. General Motors (GM) is so impressed with the idea that it helped fund the $8 million Orlando "Travtek" project and expects to offer in-car computers soon as an option.

As each car moves, the computer's map moves also, thanks to vehicle-mounted sensors. The map can zoom into a range of one-eighth of a mile or look at the big picture of a thirty-mile range, while a disembodied digital voice directs the driver to "go to the end of Maple Avenue and turn right onto Elm Street." When tourists decide to stop for lunch or a motel, they can touch the screen to see the ever-changing lists of nearby restaurants or lodging, custom-matched to the consumers' preferences for cuisines, prices, or facilities.

Data on traffic densities and crises collected from Orlando's highway-surveillance systems, in-pavement sensors, police cars, traffic helicopters, and construction companies in a five-county area funnel into computers at command central, where staff interprets and relays it by satellite to microcomputers in each vehicle. A tie-up or accident on one highway will lead headquarters to program an alternative.[8] Such intelligent vehicle highway systems (IVHS) are likely to proliferate, as public interest grows and congestion worsens.

"TRAINS" OF CARS

On the horizon are collision-avoidance systems, which automatically steer a driver's car or slam on the brakes or accelerator to avoid an accident, based on data gained from in-pavement sensors. Ultimately, "trains" of cars coupled electronically could be hooked up, traveling under autopilot to maintain safe distances between cars.[9] A GM project near Detroit borrows on military technology by controlling a driver's speed and road position. The system can automatically apply a driver's brakes or accelerator based on clues from obstacles ahead taken in by underground sensors.[10] And in a Washington, D.C., experiment, helicopters video a traffic situation from the air and beam it back to ground controllers, who feed it to on-site police, allowing them to direct traffic more intelligently.[11]

Ideally, smart highways would simply increase the driver's database from which to make informed decisions about how fast traffic is moving and where delays and constructions are. But such intense surveillance creates ethical and political issues as well. Do we want electronic systems to report speeders to a central control system when no police happen to be around? If a governmental agency can program vehicles to feed into traffic lanes and follow closely, is it liable for accidents that happen because drivers took its advice? As systems grow regionwide, will towns have to surrender autonomy over local traffic control?[12] And can drivers be steered toward less congested roads, without merely transplanting congestion?[13]

Another use of smart-roads technology involves personal rapid transit (PRT). Chicago's traffic managers are working to allow commuters on elevated guideways to summon a pod-shaped car holding three to five people in which they choose their destination from a menu.[14] A 3.3-mile PRT system built by Boeing has operated since 1972 at the University of West Virginia at Morgantown, carrying sixteen thousand students, faculty, and staff in cars that each hold fifteen riders.[15] A similar vehicle, the automated people mover (APM), carries 20 to 100 passengers and is used already in sixty-five settings around the world, such as airports, universities, and amusement complexes. Among American users are the Bronx Zoo; the Dallas–Fort Worth Airport; Duke Hospital in Durham, North Carolina; and a mass transit line in Jacksonville, Florida. Using centralized computer controls, the APM systems vary from a cable-drawn shuttle near Tampa to the wheel-on-rail electrified Downtown People Mover in Detroit, which stops at a dozen stations, to the elevated Vancouver Sky Train, which covers some fifteen miles from downtown areas to the inner suburbs. The chief advantage of an APM over conventional rapid transit that is it needs one-seventh as many people to run it as does rapid transit, an important consideration in an era of high labor costs.[16]

DRIVING THE SUPERHIGHWAY FROM AN EASY CHAIR

Perhaps the most promising avenue to relieve congestion is to remove trips by road and rail and shift them onto fiber-optic cable. In 1979, then-Congressman Albert Gore, Jr. first proposed what have been popularly labeled communications superhighways. Ironically his father, Albert Gore, Sr., championed the asphalt variety in the U.S. Senate during the mid-1950s. But as America's flight into cyberspace has proceeded, this new revolution, in terms of public policy, seems more akin to the birth of railroads than the advent of the interstates and poses much the same tug-of-war between the corporate interest and the public interest that took place a century ago.

The skeletal data superhighway has been in place for years. Just as with an interstate highway, the hard part is getting on or off, for the links between the data highway and one's home or business will be crucial. Cable-TV operators and phone companies are converting many of their lines from coaxial cable and copper wiring respectively, to fiber-optic cable, which vastly enhances the amount of information that can pass along a given path.

In the 1970s, the National Science Foundation set up a communications system linking universities, government and research labs, and individual computer users, which has come to be called Internet. Informally Internet has burgeoned into 4,000 local computer networks with about three million users. What Gore and others would do is to build on and off ramps to this megahighway of information, allowing access, at least in theory, by all American homes and businesses.[17]

Data superhighways will blur the lines between television, computers, and information services, allowing on-command access to information of all kinds and rendering TV schedules obsolete. From a road and rail perspective, video transactions will take millions of people off the road. Buying a sweater, paying the electric bill, playing a computer game with someone twenty miles away, having a doctor read your blood pressure, and ordering an infinite variety of movies on demand—all via the home PC—obviously gives the family car a rest. People are, of course, social animals and will want to be out and about, but the opportunities presented by an interactive on-line data superhighway will make unnecessary millions of car-bound transactions.

And pressing on the heels of the data highway proponents are cellular phone companies and others who send information through the air, often via satellite, rather than over wires. May we look forward to data oceans as well as data superhighways?

Access to All or a Few?

Until recently, experts expected government to build the electronic superhighway network, at a cost of $100 billion to $400 billion. But so promising have American communications companies found the economic prospects of the proposed network that they are laying cable as feverishly as nineteenth-century railroaders laid track. And even with a century of antitrust regulatory experience under its belt, America still faces a genuine threat of monopoly control in some segments of the communications industry. Thus, more than a decade after Congress clipped road and rail regulators' wings, it is being asked to impose widespread controls over a new industry.

The century-long struggle between road and rail can guide the forthcoming public debate. When unregulated railroads gained monopolies in the early American West, their "what the traffic will bear" pricing ruined hordes of farmers (see chapter 2). So Congress has a responsibility to protect potential victims of communications monopolies. Telephone and cable companies want government to let them merge, to position themselves for the battles that lie ahead. It is vital that federal and state regulators withhold permission for such mergers until receiving explicit, enforceable guarantees that the mergers serve the public interest.

A key concern is that the system insure access to such users as schools and public libraries, accurately called the "people's universities." If information is to the twenty-first century what mobility is to the twentieth, the gap between rich and poor will surely widen unless sources open to all can access information made available to home computer users.

Conversely, America also must guard against regulation so stringent that it stifles the competitive impulse, as railroads suffered in the early years of this century (see chapter 2). Government must walk a fine line, but it has a hundred years of object lessons to draw on.

The dizzying pace the information revolution is taking also calls to mind the late 1950s, when the highwaymen's rush to build the interstates overwhelmed those calling for a moratorium on construction so that America could plan more carefully how to integrate the superhighways into the nation's life (see chapter 13). Failure to do so contributed to the decline of American cities, air pollution, dependence on foreign oil, and lengthening traffic jams. Congress might have pleaded innocent by reason of inexperience then; it has no such excuse today if it fails to plan for a watershed perhaps as transformative as the printing press.

A Return to Cottage Industries?

A related way to keep drivers off the roads is to let them work from their home PCs or at computerized suboffices nearer their homes. On both sides of the Atlantic, "teleworking" has caught on like wildfire. In the United States, an estimated twenty-seven million people—one in five workers—say they have telecommuted at one time or another. And more liberal tax allowances to employers for teleworkers is aiding the process. Such workers can not only link up with the workplace more easily but also tap into international computer networks.

The "telecottage" idea originated in the early 1980s in Sweden, where workers lived in far-flung communities. Local governments offered worksites in town halls and libraries and gave computer training, to help their residents avoid long commutes in snowy weather.[18] Similarly, Washington is letting thousands of federal workers try out alternative worksites in Hagerstown, Maryland, and Winchester, Virginia. Workers stay in touch with their home offices in the District of Columbia by phones, modems, and fax machines.[19]

TRAINS MORE LIKE PLANES

While gridlock worsens on American roads and airplanes dangerously clog the "friendly skies," the most underutilized mode—one that could take pressure off the other two—is the railroads. Yet while European passenger trains daily travel 160 miles an hour in Germany and 185 in France, and test out at speeds exceeding 300, America's railroads, comparatively, creep along.

Yet the United States now is running furiously to catch up, buying European technology in a serious and credible bid to put trains in daily service by the year 2000 at speeds of 150 miles an hour, with longer-range potential far exceeding that. While American rail technology has languished, most European travelers can already use high-speed rails, and their nations are moving toward a European high-speed railroad network.

Warring Technologies

At issue in Europe is a fierce battle over two competing technologies: first, an updated version of conventional trains, in which a steel wheel still sits on a steel rail; and second, magnetic levitation, in which a vehicle "floats" above the guideway on a cushion of air. Competing Europeans have spent billions for the right to impose their technology on the

European network and to export it around the world, including to the United States.

In Europe, the French government leads competitors in wheel-on-rail technology with its Trains à Grande Vitesse (TGV, "high-speed trains"). First opened in 1981 between Paris and Lyon, the TGV runs on its own dedicated lines not shared with freight, and it uses lightweight cars. Its grades and curves are kept to a minimum, to conserve power and ensure greater speed. Fortune played a part in the French success: the French National Railways (SNCF) built its first line just before a widespread antidevelopment movement in Europe took hold. Its first line has been phenomenally successful at speeds of 168 miles an hour. A second line from Paris to western France operates at speeds of 185 miles an hour. But in fact, engineers have tested the TGV, with passengers aboard, at 306 miles per hour.

High-speed wheel-on-rail approaches actually represent less a bold new technology than a logistical breakthrough and a political commitment. The TGV views its ten-car train as a permanent unit. Therefore, it can use one air-conditioning unit for the entire train and combine wheel units where cars join, thus lowering cost and weight.[20]

By contrast, the technologically more conventional German Inter City Express (ICE) shares existing tracks with freight trains and limits its speed to 160 miles an hour. Its strong suit is luxurious surroundings, featuring such amenities as video consoles in the seat backs to let travelers watch individualized movies.

Sweden's X2000—known as a "tilt train"—is particularly applicable to American rails because it "leans into" curves at speeds of up to 150 miles an hour and offers a smooth ride.[21] So popular was its route from Göteborg to Stockholm, where it is used primarily for business travel, that half of its passengers switched to rail from air.[22] Amtrak tested the ICE and the X-2000 in its northeast corridor service during 1993.

For America, a train such as the TGV exists only in dreams, for the factors that allowed it to be so successful are not possible in the United States. For one thing, the TGV, the ICE, and the X2000 are electrified, while most of Amtrak's passenger rails, except the Washington–to–New Haven run, are not. The stretch from New Haven to Boston is being electrified, but the $800 million that the change will cost makes its extension to many more American localities unlikely. One alternative is to adopt diesel electric locomotives. which travel on either electrified or nonelectrified tracks.[23]

The Outlook for Maglev

Maglev trains, by contrast, rely on linear electric motors built into the guideway, generating a magnetic field that—through the principle of attraction and repulsion—propels the engineless train along the guideway while cars hover above it. As widely as maglev has been reported in the public press, it has never been actually put into commercial service, although thousands of visitors have ridden the Transrapid 07 at a test facility in Emsland, Germany. Because of its motivating principle, the train is extremely quiet (although from the author's subjective experience of one test ride, the TGV seemed to offer a smoother ride).[24]

Maglev trains use two types of electromagnetic principles—repulsive, as the Japanese National Railway employs, and attractive, as the German Transrapid system uses. In the European system, to which this book is limited, the train wraps around the guideway. Magnets underneath help levitate the train about three-eighths of an inch above the guideway surface. To move forward, the train harnesses opposite magnetic polarities, creating a push-pull force that propels the train along. With the development of superconductor technology, which allows a material to carry electricity without electrical resistance, maglev systems can cut down the electrical power needed and also reduce the weight of magnets.[25]

Major manufacturers such as McDonnell Douglas, GM, Grumman, Martin Marietta, and Bechtel have explored maglev for American markets. The first commercially operated maglev train is expected to be a 13.5-mile route from Orlando International Airport to the outskirts of Disney World, and to open in 1998. The $500 million project is being planned by a Japanese combine.[26]

While building new trackage in densely populated areas is virtually out of the question for wheel-on-rail trains, maglev's supporters tout a less invasive method—by building on concrete piers spaced far apart. At its Emsland, Germany, test facility, relatively noiseless trains streak twenty to thirty feet above a pastoral scene of farmers tilling fields, their crops spaced around six-foot-square concrete piers spaced far apart. Maglev proponents say that this allows the builders to buy only the land that the piers occupy.[27]

An advantage heralded by high-speed rail advocates is moving trains directly from downtown to downtown, bypassing the often-gridlocked trip to and from airports. While an airplane can travel twice as fast as a high-speed train on a three-hundred-mile flight, time spent weaving in and out of traffic to and from the airport largely wipes out that advantage. Senator Daniel Patrick Moynihan is maglev's most influential and ardent backer in the United States. He was instrumental in gaining a $7.5 million congressional authorization to build a prototype. To save right-of-way costs, Moynihan would route maglev on concrete piers mounted forty feet above the median on interstate highways. But here maglev's disadvantages become apparent, because stopping in downtown areas will require trains to hook into conventional rail lines as they approach the center unless they can tie into unused trackage. And with interstate highway curves designed for seventy-mile-an-hour traffic, maglevs may have to leave the medians to accomplish a wide enough arc to keep the trains on the tracks.

What is the outlook then? Bad, for steel-wheel or maglev trains to travel major routes at or near 300 miles per hour anytime soon. Good, for steel-wheel trains, with greatly upgraded amenities, to be plying the rails in several densely trafficked corridors before the year 2000 at speeds of 150 miles an hour. Amtrak will design and build in America a hybrid of European trains it has closely monitored to custom-make a train to fit American needs.

CLEANER CARS FOR CLEANER AIR

While the members of Congress tend to be a cautious bunch, they occasionally find themselves ahead of, rather than lagging behind, technology. An example of such forward-thinking action is the 1990 Clean Air Act, which mandates stiff pollution standards that have state governments, automakers, and inventors scrambling to leap into the twenty-first century. The act gave California the right to adopt stricter statewide standards, which it subsequently did, and allowed all forty-nine other states to adopt California's standards if they so wished.[28] Basically the act encourages, and in some cases requires, fuels that burn cleaner than gasoline. The federal government is committed to buying thirty-five thousand alternative-fuel vehicles a year by 1997, a mandate that is both environmentally friendly and provides a market to let auto companies tinker with this new technology.[29]

The leading cleaner-air alternatives seem to be natural gas and electric cars. Natural gas offers lower hydrocarbon and carbon monoxide levels and 70 percent less smog-forming potential than gasoline. And while offering lower miles per gallon, natural gas is somewhat cheaper. But it requires a cumbersome fillup procedure at the pumps, which themselves are few and far between, at least for now.[30] Ford Motor Company has built fifty natural gas–powered cars for starters, and the big-three automakers plan soon to offer it as an option on new cars. Many of the thirty-five thousand natural gas–powered cars on the American roads are in commercial use. Companies such as Entenmann's bakeries have converted whole fleets to natural gas, which reduces fuel costs significantly.[31]

Virtually pollution free and without moving parts, electric cars nevertheless have major drawbacks: their batteries are heavy, the cars are expensive, they cannot go far without a recharge, and recharging stations are scarce to nonexistent. Despite these hurdles, California has mandated that 2 percent of the cars sold there by 1998 be pollution free (which means, in effect, electric), and 10 percent by 2003—which amounts to two hundred thousand vehicles a year. The big-three automakers, drawn by the prospect of this new market and spurred by the restrictions on their old one, are pooling their technology to build an electric car. And while California is in the lead, more than a dozen states are considering similar standards.[32]

To lure the consumer, automakers must drastically cut battery costs, which now mean that electric cars cost twice as much as conventional models, or more. Predictably, surveys show that consumers are happy to help support the environment—if they do not have to pay more to do it. Current lead-and-acid batteries take up 30 times the space and 100 times the weight of conventional gas tanks. But the developer of one battery being developed claims that it will recharge in fifteen minutes and have a lifetime of a hundred thousand miles.[33] Another alternative is fuel-cell batteries, which generate electricity but can replenish their chemicals continuously through a chemical reaction, so that they can run nearly indefinitely.[34] Electric cars are not pollution free; large amounts of coal are consumed in making their batteries. Yet air pollution at one huge power plant is much more controllable than millions of gasoline engines roaming the interstates.

Electric cars present a chicken-and-egg dilemma: few people want to install charging stations for such a (presently) small market, while buyers shun electric cars because there are no places to charge them. Those with an incentive to invest are utilities, such as the Boston Edison Company, for which electric cars represent a new market frontier. Boston Edison and GM plan to install chargers widely at shopping malls and parking lots of major corporations, so visitors may plug in and recharge in as little as fifteen minutes while shopping or working.[35] Others talk of battery chargers buried under highways to charge cars on the move. How to have drivers who use the service pay is an open question.[36] And further out on the horizon are solar and hydrogen fuel technologies. While beyond the scope of this book, they illustrate that the laboratory has no end of surprises in store.

GAINING THE COMMERCIAL EDGE

Technology at once enhances the efficiency of road and rail while intensifying the competition between the two modes. Just-in-time inventory systems require that shippers be able to learn immediately the status of shipments bound for them. Satellites help headquarters spot the locations of any of thousands of trucks, so plants and stores can know when a truck is running late, and dispatchers can find a convenient pickup near a driver about to make a delivery. Such systems allow drivers to punch in extensive messages that will be relayed immediately to headquarters.[37] Aware of these developments, railroads are scurrying to move in the same direction.[38]

Railways hope to co-opt truckers' flexibility by creating an "iron highway" aboard their own trains. At the American Association of Railroads' testing facility in Pueblo, Colorado, scientists have tested a low-slung, easy-on and -off articulated flatcar twelve hundred feet long that holds as many as twenty fifty-three-foot tractor-trailers, speeding to their destination at seventy miles an hour without fear of gridlock ahead. Already in use is the Road Railer, a truck with hydraulically operated steel-flanged wheels, which convert a truck into a railcar that can be attached to a train. At the destination, rubber wheels drop down like airplane landing gear so the trailer can be driven to its delivery point.[39]

FROM GUNS TO BUTTER

Technology not only can help smooth the way for road and rail; it can ease the sting of defense shutdowns. Base closings and defense cuts have cost Texans, for example, thousands of jobs since the late 1980s. Now Texas Instruments, the defense contractor that developed infrared technology to identify moving objects during the 1991 Persian Gulf war, is recycling the principle to help truckers spot objects in the road ahead at night or during winter storms.[40] In Los Angeles, the city's transit authority is encouraging producers of military and aerospace high-tech weapons to retool their production lines, to turn out cars for the city's new subway system.

Aerospace contractors have discovered that the same principles employed to keep rockets and missiles lightweight yet durable can be used toward the same objective for rapid transit vehicles. Electronics expertise helps them develop more fuel-efficient propulsion methods and safer braking. Rockwell International is also using what it has learned about infrared technology to develop smart cars and smart highways, as well as highway-management and railroad-communications systems. Spurring on these defense-starving contractors is the recognition that recent boosts in transit spending—an expected $8.1 billion will be spent by the millennium—justify immediate investing of research-and-development funds.[41]

But all the technological advances in the world will not change America's transportation system to one that can compete effectively in the twenty-first century, unless individuals and businesses are willing to significantly reorder their priorities and trade some short-term gratification for long-term advantage. That challenge looms large as the "American century" draws to a close.

·18·

SINKING OR SWIMMING IN A GLOBAL ECONOMY

Congested highways and crowded airports,
harmful enough now, will be economically
ruinous if not corrected.

—Fred Barnes, *Business Month*, August 1990

NOT WITHOUT REASON HAS THE TWENTIETH CENTURY BEEN LABELED the "American century." In economic growth, in geopolitics, in armed security, and in science, the United States has been preeminent. With resources to spare, the wastefulness, shoddiness, and inefficiency with which Americans built the road and rail network—the nation's economic arteries—were hardly noticed. Europe spent most of the 1900s warring within itself, the Soviet Union slumbered in an economic stupor, and Pacific Rim countries (where "Made in Japan" once signified trash, at least in the West) were inconsequential in the global economy.

All that has changed. While European nations find economic unity easier to dream about than to realize, while Russia and Eastern Europe are still on chapter one of the free-enterprise textbook, and while Japan and Korea suffer economic growing pains, America is not alone among those with a serious claim to world economic power.

The approach of the twenty-first century calls for a focus on those things that will keep America a world leader, and no country can be economically strong abroad if it is weak at home. An economy depends on transactions that move through space, so if its pathways are worn out or clogged, transactions slow or diminish, and economic growth declines. Yet the United States now invests a smaller percentage of its gross domestic product in infrastructure than does any other industrialized nation.[1] And what is spent is showered on profligate, motor-centric delivery systems.

To keep pace, Americans must commit to investing in a new good roads movement, insuring well-built economic pathways—whether of asphalt, steel, or fiber-optic cable. It is time to reverse our fixation on motor vehicles, by offering Americans a choice of travel options within an integrated system that plays to the very different strengths that road and rail possess. This will require a national determination to wean people away from exclusive reliance on the automobile, equalize tax incentives for road and rail commuters, encourage commuter-friendly housing, require the government to teach car owners the full costs of driving, factor social costs into transportation policy, and price travel to reflect those social costs. Americans would do well to take a few lessons from their European neighbors, too.

EXPANDING THE MENU

Given the choice between driving cars or taking trains to commute to work, it is easy to see why over 90 percent of Americans have chosen the automobile: cars are at hand when drivers want them, drivers control their own speeds, cars take them from door to door in relative comfort, cars are private and have their own sound systems, the government subsidizes the roads they drive, and drivers can stow their belongings without having to lug them on a railcar. The only problem arises when everybody else chooses to drive, too.

During the cold war, Western commentators heaped derision on a Soviet system in which people waited for hours to buy the only product available. Can we call the American system saner when millions of white-knuckled commuters crawl to work on gridlocked superhighways that run alongside abandoned railroad tracks covered with weeds?

We can do better than that. The fruit of prosperity ought to be choice, not a smorgasbord of beef tenderloin and nothing else. If a century-long struggle between road and rail has proven anything, it is that each mode has inherent strengths that will always give it a comparative advantage over the other. Locomotives moving along a dedicated steel pathway can move large loads long distances faster and with less energy than can trucks. But only truckers can offer door-to-door service. We need both, and we need them to work together. Most Americans under fifty do not remember the clean, comfortable trains that their grandparents and great-grandparents rode. But the postinterstate generation is about to discover them again.

In 1991, Congress passed the landmark $155 billion Intermodal Surface Transportation Efficiency Act (ISTEA), which for the first time let states and metropolitan areas choose whether they want to spend federal money on roads or rails. The oil, auto, rubber, and contracting industries have weighed in with their predictable demands for road building. But nontraditional interests, such as bicyclists, rail transit advocates, and environmentalists have joined the scramble as well.[2] And the pace-setting legislation has empowered metropolitan planning organizations, composed of local mayors, council members, and administrators. When Europe decentralized road and rail decision making two decades ago, the locals opted decisively for mass transit.[3]

Proponents had hoped ISTEA would cause cities to choose rail transit over highways. But in the act's first 18 months, states and localities invested only about 3 percent of discretionary money in mass transit or nontraditional projects, according to the U.S. General Accounting Office. Such a result frustrates members of the Surface Transportation Policy Project (STPP), a national group including pro transit forces, planners, architects, and environmentalists dedicated to fostering a balance between road and rail. The reasons why America has been slow to change speak volumes about the state of American road and rail in the 1990s: for so overgrown are the nation's crumbling highways that most available money is spent just to keep them passable. And since road and rail have each developed in a vacuum, planning tools to analyze highways focus on moving vehicles while those studying mass transit hone in on moving people. Developing a common language for each will take time. [4]

Highway advocates continue to argue that for every dollar spent building a new road, $2.43 in new consumer buying power is created and that each billion dollars spent generates nearly twenty-five thousand jobs.[5] Yet the Bates College economist David Aschauer has found that spending on public transit doubles those paybacks.[6]

Americans have been raised in the belief that they must go *everywhere* by automobile. Indeed, as the country planned its surface transportation solely around the highway-motor system, that notion became a self-fulfilling prophecy. As millions left the trains, there soon *was* only one way to go. As Amtrak's service steadily improves, that is starting to change. But the

American mindset, caught in a cultural gridlock, needs to change with it. Just as cars have advantages over trains in some situations, the reverse is true as well. While it probably would be foolish for one to take a train, rather than an available car, for grocery shopping, it could well be smarter to avoid the gridlock and parking crush by taking the train to a basketball game in the city. On some days, businesspersons need their cars for daytime appointments. But on others, they could easily leave their cars at home and expand their productive day by getting some work or reading done during a commute. In an ideal twenty-first century, people would have at least two viable choices for every trip they make. They now often only have one.

FROM AUTO-DEPENDENCE TO AUTO-INDEPENDENCE

How then does a free society wean citizens away from an exclusive dependence on the automobile? The answer lies in creating incentives to travel in low-impact ways, requiring commuters to pay the full cost of downtown parking, charging drivers more when driving at peak periods, and using the savings to fund comfortable, frequent public transit.

The American tax system has been used creatively to encourage certain activities and discourage others. While Congress has increased from $21 to $60 the monthly tax-free commuter allowance that employers can give rail transit riders, there is no justification for not equalizing it with the subsidy that motorists receive, which ranges up to $155 per month. The idea is one that employers are finally willing to consider, as they seek to cut costs and reduce the number of gas-powered vehicles commuting to their plants, to satisfy the mandates of the 1990 Clean Air Act.

Consider the example of Hartford, Connecticut. More than three-quarters of those who work in the Insurance City commute—45 percent by solo drives into the city. The typical employer pays half of the average market rate of $130 a month for parking. Now more than a dozen Hartford employers have banded together to begin to charge workers the market rate for parking and encourage them to use mass transit. The move may be a shot in the arm for car and van pooling and may prove the difference between success and failure for a light rail system planned for the region, called the Griffin Line. Until now, its planners had feared that fewer than the ten thousand riders needed to make the project feasible would actually ride. If the employers' plan is implemented, however, it should increase daily ridership to more than fourteen thousand, thus insuring the line's success. This calculus, writ large across the face of urban America, could profoundly change the way people get to work.[7]

Similar incentives can be used to encourage people to live near rail stations or commuter parking lots. The one-acre zoning sprawl that built America's suburbs is inconsistent with efficient travel. Since the age of limits has dawned in America, builders have reduced house and lot sizes, and some people have found that they can buy for less in developments that feature individual units clustered together, with common open space. Given the manifold costs of gridlock, government can benefit by giving tax breaks to developers who build housing near enough to trains that the area's residents can leave their cars at home. Such a move would give light rail the commuting volume it must have to succeed.[8]

Although the kind of peak pricing used for telephone service seems inherently logical, congestion pricing has failed on many roads where it has been tried. The purpose of peak-pricing is defeated if political pressure reduces tolls below the point at which they would change driving habits. And on existing roads, drivers probably would rebel at being called to pay for what had been free. Accordingly, such tolls will likely be most effective on newly constructed roads. And peak pricing will be worthless if it merely diverts congestion to other roads, creating a new set of problems, as has occurred even in Singapore.[9]

The answer may lie in the turn of the screw. As traffic volume increases by 2 percent per year, with road construction falling far behind, each person's tipping point becomes easier to reach. And some feel that the market-driven rationale behind peak pricing will eventually win allies not only among environmentalists and transit advocates, who want drivers off the road, but among real estate developers and employers, who realize that galloping gridlock can lower property values and reduce worker productivity.

GOODBYE TO WASHBOARD ROADS

European countries spend on average four times what America does to build and repair roadways. And as any traveler of European roads can attest, the results show. But America not only lacks the money to keep up its roads; it does not build them properly to begin with. While Washington built the interstates to last twenty years, hoping in vain that the states would find the money to repair them, Europeans built highways to last thirty or forty years. Truckers create the lion's share of

America's highway deterioration, but European axle weights exceed those allowed in the United States, and trucks have not destroyed European roads.[10] In a nutshell, the Europeans build their freeways thicker and with a deeper base than in America. Washington also gives states an incentive to neglect maintenance by paying 90 percent of the cost for new roads, yet nothing for their repair.

Moreover, European governments expect contractors to build roads that last and to guarantee their work for five years. Accordingly, road contractors have their own research-and-development divisions aimed at improving pavement durability.[11] In America, by contrast, the lowest bidder usually wins a highway contract, which removes incentives for innovation. And neither are contractors held responsible. When in 1991 Congress considered a bill requiring contractors to build to performance standards, the measure had the support of Washington's highway establishment, state officials, and advocacy groups; but the Association of General Contractors and the American Road and Transportation Builders Association lobbied successfully for Congress to kill it.[12] Some states, such as Iowa and Michigan, have begun to innovate with new surfaces and construction methods, but progress overall has been very limited.

GOING PRIVATE

Few notions of how to improve government have picked up as much steam as the idea of turning public functions over to the private sector. Congress has earmarked money to study the concept, and California and Virginia, among other states, have turned over more than 100 miles of tolled highway to private interests, including one outfit owned by the redoubtable Ross Perot. But Americans should not bet on private ownership becoming a transportation panacea.

Sources of private capital seek only profitable investments, so they will invest in toll roads only where there are enough commuters to turn a profit. Thus, the interest has so far been limited largely to urban bottlenecks where building an alternative roadway that government cannot afford will relieve congestion. While important, this represents a small percentage of congested road mileage.

Contracted private management of public services holds out more hope. Yet the caricature of government as a bloated bureaucracy and business as a trim and efficient entity is simplistic. First, Americans expect different things of each: government, to raise public money, let all voices be heard, and guarantee due process in achieving a public objective; and business, to move aggressively through opposing views, adapt quickly to changing conditions, and get the job done at the lowest cost. Yet the reason that private management has so often fostered cost containment, innovation, and better technologies is not that it is private per se but that competition keeps companies looking over their shoulders.[13]

Provided with competitive incentives, public employees have proved that they can do various jobs as well as or better than private workers. For example, a New York City repaving experiment in the early 1980s showed that public workers, already familiar with the task, performed for $32,000 a paving job that cost a private crew $57,000 when competing against them on a comparable stretch of road. In other cases, city departments have lost out in competitive bidding to private firms, only to become reenergized by the competitive process and win the contracts back.[14]

Europeans have historically been more comfortable with contracting out transportation services than have Americans, but in both locales subsidies for highways have proved necessary. France has nationalized three of the four private companies that ran its autoroutes.[15] The same has been true of rail privatization. Studies of projects in Boston, northern Virginia, and Orlando show that "none seemingly can cover capital and operating costs on farebox revenues alone."[16]

It appears then that business's role, if any, in delivering public services should be in the realm of managing, not owning, the services contracted. Indeed, California's four private toll-road experiments sell entrepreneurs only the right to collect tolls for a limited number of years on high-speed lanes along freeway medians they build with their own capital, but which the state continues to own. The routes, ranging from ten to eighty-five miles, are in densely populated commuting areas.[17] To the extent that privatization can expand America's total transportation system while protecting access for all citizens, it ought to be encouraged.

A EUROPEAN PERSPECTIVE

Circumstance, culture, and history have led Europe to develop its road and rail systems in ways foreign to American eyes. Nationalizing rail systems early on helped protect some countries from attack and furthered the expansionist dreams of others. Owning countrywide rail systems gave European nations a vested interest in preventing an auto-centered focus.

Obviously their history cannot and need not be replicated on American shores. And while their system is hardly free of problems, certain elements are worthy of examination.

- First, in Europe "collective responsibility has a far firmer tradition" than in the United States.[18] Perhaps where people live in much closer contact than in most of America, attention to how one's actions affect one's neighbors assumes a greater importance. Rugged individualism may come at a price.

- Although many people argue that automobiles simply replaced street-cars as part of a natural American evolution, both cars and trolleys are alive and well in European cities. Germany, for example, loves automobiles—it has given the world the Mercedes-Benz and the autobahns—yet most urban areas of a million people or more have subways, and most cities of two hundred thousand or more enjoy subsidized public streetcar and bus systems. While the vast majority of Americans commute to work by car, a solid majority of Munich's commuters, for example, take its S-bahn fast train in from the suburbs.[19]

- France and Germany have proved that massive investment in passenger rail pays off. The French TGV (see chapter 17) has not only reduced airline congestion between Paris and Lyon by 40 percent, but it generates a 15 percent net profit, which subsidizes the French National Railways' less glamorous lines. The German Inter City Express (ICE) is newer (see chapter 17), but it already has had a similar effect on air travel and has turned the head of Amtrak, which has tested the ICE in America's northeast corridor. Construction of an American TGV is not possible because the system requires a dedicated passenger route with few curves or grades. But the French experiment has shown workers' willingness to change their commuting habits when given a quality alternative to cars.[20]

- Some European countries have reduced highway congestion by limiting truck traffic on weekends, when workers crowd the roads in search of recreation. As an example of how their travel modes work together naturally, German truckers traveling from Mannheim, Germany, to Rotterdam, Holland, typically drive their lorries onto a boat on Friday evening and travel up the Rhine River to Rotterdam. There, the truckers—having spent the weekend with their families—rejoin their cargo on Monday morning.[21]

- In place of downtown business districts packed with smoggy traffic jams, cities such as Amsterdam and Strasbourg are giving their central business districts back to pedestrians. Amsterdam has banned certain travel outright. And driving in Strasbourg is subtly discouraged by a network of one-way streets that soon frustrate the driver, as well as by pedestrians who spill freely into the center of the street to enjoy the beauty of the historic city without being surrounded by the crush and noise of auto traffic. Some forty to fifty cities within the European Economic Community are considering blanketing their downtowns with shuttles or electric cars while banning auto traffic.[22]

- Germany, whose autobahns inspired American interstate highways, has reversed field. For the first time since the superhighway era, it is spending more on rails than on roads, partly because of the strong feeling among environmentalists and the public in general that no further highway development should be allowed. The autobahn from the Swiss border north to Munich, for example, resembles a perforated line, each space representing a stretch where highway opponents have blocked construction in court. And yet, because of the large subsidy poured into its railway, or Deutsche Bundesbahn, Germany is also considering its privatization.

- An example of rival modes working together to exploit the advantages of each exists in Germany. Lufthansa airline charters trains for air passengers who are journeying to its international hub at Dusseldorf, when the distances involved would be too short to make flying practical.

- Some European cities treat public transportation as a positive feature of daily life rather than as a necessary evil. In Britain, for example, the aesthetics of the London Underground—the century-old Grand Dame of world subways—has long been stressed as much as its function. Unlike dingy subway platforms elsewhere, the underground features elaborate multicolored ceramic tiled walls, with each station evoking a different theme. The underground directors commission artists to paint posters, which hang in each station and are sold to the public. Architects compete vigorously to design new underground stations. Short poems by

British writers are sprinkled throughout the subway cars in place of ads for laxatives. While Paris, Munich, and Brussels offer pleasant, efficient people movers as well, the London Underground and its cars, with ancient slatted wooden floors, are a treat for tourists and locals alike.[23]

- In Britain, as in America, the decision to build highways is weighted toward the social benefits they confer and away from the social costs they impose because, in the words of a London transport consultant, "the Department of Transport is operating the investment arm of the motorways." Yet on the Continent, such factors as congestion, pollution, and historic preservation are formally weighted along with speed and traffic control in deciding whether to proceed with a project.[24]

- In Europe, road and rail often dovetail in ways seldom seen in the United States. Multimode passes—enabling a person to travel for one fare on buses, subways, and long-distance trains—are commonplace. One reason the London Underground covers its operating costs—something nearly unheard of in public transport—is that British Rail feeds thousands of commuters to subway stations.[25]

While European surface travel is hardly trouble-free, it clearly offers its citizens a wider choice of travel options than most Americans enjoy.

TRUCKING WITH THE TRUCKERS

An astounding forty-two million trucks ply American roads, hauling 78 percent of surface freight. Yet according to study after study, this $728 billion-a-year industry contributes mightily to air pollution and fails to pay its fair share of highway damage. But the American Trucking Associations' lawyer and writer Robert Pitcher, who is less than sympathetic to the environmental claims, says, "The social costs of pollution must be weighed against the benefits to society of having its goods transported efficiently."[26]

Trucking spokespersons argue that climate-caused pavement changes and poor construction methods inflict the most road damage. Experts tend to dispute the former charge and agree with the latter one. Truckers claim that they have already covered their responsibility, because they absorbed a 150 percent tax hike after a 1982 federal study showed that heavy trucks cause nearly ten thousand times the damage to highways as do automobiles. Predictably, railroads disagree, alleging that trucks continually overload—a contention difficult to monitor thoroughly with the huge number of trucks on the road.[27] Further, truckers argue that they cannot afford to pay more taxes and that their annual profit is a modest 2 percent.[28] If that is so, America should just admit its heavy subsidizing of the trucking industry and then balance the scales by supporting the rails in equal measure. America needs both, and history shows that the economy will benefit in the long run.

CRACKS IN THE HIGHWAY MONOLITH?

Key elements that have separated American and European highway politics have been the former's dedicated fuel tax and its strong highway-motor lobby, which has little trouble convincing Congress to keep fuel taxes low and to draw from general revenues for amounts the motor tax will not fund. After 1956, this lobby managed for nearly two decades to stave off attacks by presidents and powerful congressmen alike to kill the highway fund, as noted in previous chapters.

But the first fissures in the lobby's monolithic control appeared in 1974, when Congress set aside a penny from the federal gasoline tax to go toward mass transit projects. This was less important than it might seem, since Washington still paid states a higher percentage of highway-project costs than transit ones, making a new section of interstate highway politically difficult to vote against. But in 1990, Congress siphoned off 2.5 cents on each gallon of gas for deficit reduction—the program's first diversion for nontransportation uses. And again in 1993, a 4.3 cent gasoline tax passed Congress, once again to be used for deficit reduction. While cutting the deficit is an overarching objective, the precedent for making further incursions into the Highway Trust Fund has nevertheless been set.

Congress's shift of control of road and rail funding from Washington to the states and metropolitan areas has been more subtle but equally significant. Until recently, lobbyists could concentrate their efforts in the halls of Congress, knowing that states took their lead from the Washington highway establishment. With decentralized control, the prospect of lobbying in fifty state capitals and hundreds of urban areas is a daunting challenge to the highway people And to the extent that private interests engage in road building and management, this will also dilute the highway-motor complex's control. For the first time, states and localities could then choose mass transit or highway building on the merits, since Washington would be funding the same percentage of each. And the increased tax subsidies for mass transit riders suggest a significant shift away from roads and toward rail and bus transit.

Just as diverging interests endangered the unity of the highway-motor complex in the 1940s, until the dedicated gas tax brought the lobby's constituents back together, so too are issues of the 1990s threatening to rend the consensus within the highway community. Recent disagreements have shown up over such issues as performance standards that road contractors must meet and, within the trucking industry, the use of triple trailers. And as an increasing number of pressure groups find their voice, keeping the members of the highway-motor complex under one tent will be that much harder.

But the highway advocates need not fear an imminent demise. They will continue to be an important force that needs to be heard. And as power shifts, a new generation of power politics is on the horizon. To the extent that data superhighways become as important to the nation's economy as asphalt ones, Americans can anticipate booms in electric utilities, which would supply power to electric vehicles; regional phone companies, which are eager to expand into the fiber-optic network to create on-ramps for the electronic superhighways; cable companies; and computer companies, which may in the next century be equivalent to the automakers of old. John Sculley, the former chairman of Apple Computer, has estimated that this megaindustry's annual revenues could reach \$3.5 trillion worldwide by the year 2001, more than half of America's present gross national product.[29] Unlikely? How many predicted a generation ago that General Motors would be \$23 billion in the red in 1993?[30]

The last century's struggle between road and rail has been a dizzying ride, one that has affected every American in ways great and small. It has produced not only great prosperity but also great waste and imbalance. Americans, in their fragile two-century-old experiment with democracy, have erred often in the quest for a workable relationship between humankind and capital. As they stand near the threshold of the millennium, a century wiser, do Americans owe themselves a pause to reflect on the lessons they have learned? Or do they press forward on the same path, doomed to let history repeat itself?

NOTES

PROLOGUE: 1917

1. "Inauguration Day Story."
2. Baker, *Woodrow Wilson*, pp. 480–81.
3. "Wilson Sounds a Solemn Note."
4. "Inauguration Day Story."
5. Cable, *Avenue of the Presidents*, p. 185.
6. *Encyclopaedia Britannica*, vol. 19, pp. 837–38.
7. Link, *Woodrow Wilson: Campaigns for Progressivism*, p. 369.
8. "Armed Ship Bill Beaten."
9. Hofstadter, *American Political Tradition*, p. 265.
10. Jensen, *American Heritage History*, p. 284.
11. Hofstadter, p. 264.
12. Cable, p. 185. See also Ford Motor Company, *Freedom of the American Road*, p. 2.
13. Fuessle, "Pulling Main Street," p. 640.
14. Flink, *Automobile Age,* p. 170.
15. Link, *Papers of Woodrow Wilson,* vol. 38, p. 412.
16. "Wilson Sounds a Solemn Note."
17. Ibid., p. 1.
18. Johnson, *Woodrow Wilson,* p. 127.
19. "Wilson Sounds a Solemn Note." See also *Washington Post,* March 6, 1917, p. 3.
20. "Inauguration Day Story."
21. Smith, *America Enters the World,* p. 345.
22. "Wilson Sounds a Solemn Note."
23. Saunders, *The Railroad Mergers and the Coming of Conrail*, p. 36.
24. Jensen, p. 95.
25. Hazard, *Managing National Transportation Policy,* p. 11.

CHAPTER 1: THE FIRST BIG BUSINESS

1. Jensen, *American Heritage History,* p. 16.
2. Itzkoff, *Off the Track,* pp. 7–8.

3. Marx, *Machine in the Garden,* p. 195.
4. Freeman and Aldcroft, *Transport in Victorian Britain.*
5. Marx, pp. 198–99.
6. Stover, *American Railroads.*
7. Marx, p. 194.
8. Ibid., p. 249.
9. Faith, *World the Railways Made,* p. 11.
10. Ward, *Railroads,* p. 30.
11. Ibid., p. 129. Henry Poor was the co-editor of the *American Railroad Journal,* founded in 1832—two years after the country's first railroad began operation.
12. "prior to the war . . . ": Ibid., pp. 129–33; "$23 million": Holbrook, *Story of American Railroads,* p. 84.
13. Burt, *Story of American Railroads,* p. 83.
14. Ward, p. 133.
15. Stover, *Life and Decline,* p. 89.
16. White, *William Allen White,* pp. 184–85.
17. Holbrook, *Story of American Railroads,* pp. 41–43.
18. Faith, p. 317.
19. Mercer, *Land Grant Policy.*
20. Jensen, p. 119.
21. "Of Grants and Greed."
22. Mercer.
23. Stover, *American Railroads,* p. 60.
24. Mercer.
25. Stover, *American Railroads,* pp. 53–55.
26. Burt, pp. 103–7.
27. Sayre, *Albert Baird Cummins,* p. 63.
28. Burt, pp. 76–83.
29. Dunn, *Miles to Go,* p. 30.
30. Stover, *American Railroads,* p. 121.
31. Ibid., pp. 121–22. See also Jensen, p. 152.
32. Ripley, *Finance and Organization,* p. 2.
33. Meyer, *Economics of Competition,* p. 4.
34. White, "Changing Trains."
35. Chandler and Salsbury, *Pierre S. duPont,* pp. 203–9.
36. Itzkoff, p. 7.
37. Holbrook, p. 37.
38. Stover, *American Railroads,* p. 93. See also "U.S. Budget—Historical Statistics of the United States, 1976." The advent of the federal income tax in 1913 and a world war would make federal budgets measured in millions a thing of the past.
39. Ripley.
40. Ibid., p. 5.
41. Holbrook, p. 9; and Jensen, p. 136.
42. Jensen, p. 119.

43. Ibid., p. 136.
44. Stover, *American Railroads*, p. 35.
45. Conant, *Railroad Mergers*, p. 30. See also Ripley, pp. 575–607.
46. Ripley, p. 577.
47. Meyer, p. 6. See also Jensen, p. 144.
48. Ripley, p. 228.
49. Saunders, *Railroad Mergers*, p. 31.
50. Holbrook, p. 92.
51. Stover, *American Railroads*, pp. 10–11.
52. Saunders, p. 31.
53. Faith, *World the Railways Made*, p. 62. See also Martin, *Enterprise Denied*, p. 99; and Josephson, *Robber Barons*, pp. 300–6.
54. Josephson, p. 301.
55. Jensen, p. 147.
56. Josephson, p. 308.
57. Ibid., pp. 308–9.
58. Saunders, p. 33.
59. Josephson, p. 314.
60. Meyer, *Economics of Competition*, p. 4.
61. Tebbel and Zuckerman, *Magazine in America*, pp. 66–67.
62. Martin, p. 11.
63. Ibid., p. 69.
64. Itzkoff, p. 33.
65. Ibid., p. 9.
66. See also Klein, "A Hell of a Way," pp. 22–31.

CHAPTER 2: THE RUNAWAY IRON HORSE

1. Stover, *American Railroads*, p. 121.
2. Saunders, *Railroad Mergers*, pp. 30–31.
3. Stover, p. 127.
4. Chalmers, *Neither Socialism nor Monopoly*, p. 4.
5. Sharfman, *Interstate Commerce Commission*, vol. 1, p. 15.
6. Sandburg, "Chicago."
7. *Munn v Illinois*.
8. Smith, *Wealth of Nations*, book IV, chap. 2.
9. Constitution of the United States, Art. I, Sec. 8.
10. Sharfman, vol. 1, p. 19. See also *Wabash, St. Louis and Pacific Railway Co. v Illinois*.
11. Congress modeled the ICC after some of the weaker state railroad commissions. (Interview with Frank Wilner, April 27, 1993.)
12. "Interstate Commerce Bill Becomes a Law."
13. Chandler and Salsbury, *Pierre S. duPont*, pp. 198–208.
14. *Interstate Commerce Act of 1887*, secs. 1–4, 11.
15. Jensen, *American Heritage History*, p. 145.
16. Chalmers, p. 6.
17. Stover, *American Railroads*, p. 134.

18. Dunn, *Miles to Go*, p. 35.
19. Chalmers, p. 6; Stover, *American Railroads,* p. 133.
20. MacAvoy, *Economic Effects of Regulation*, p. 193.
21. Freeman and Aldcroft, *Transport in Victorian Britain,* p. 250. See also Alderman, *Railway Interest,* p. 224.
22. Saunders, p. 29.
23. Dunn, p. 31.
24. Josephson, *Robber Barons*, p. 443.
25. Ibid., p. 445.
26. Morris, *Rise of Theodore Roosevelt*, p. 733.
27. Martin, *Enterprise Denied*, p. 101.
28. Chalmers, p. 7.
29. Stover, *American Railroads,* p. 137.
30. Sayre, *Albert Baird Cummins*, p. 67.
31. Ibid.
32. Ibid.
33. "so lawyers all . . . ": Hoogenboom and Hoogenboom, *History of the ICC,* pp. 45–46; "Clements": Martin, p. 173.
34. Martin, p. 175.
35. Hoogenboom and Hoogenboom, p. 44.
36. Meyer, p. 7.
37. Chalmers, pp. 7–8.
38. Josephson, *Robber Barons,* pp. 446–47.
39. Stover, p. 138.
40. Martin, p. 102.
41. Stover, p. 138.
42. Carson, *Throttling the Railroads,* p. 72.
43. Chalmers, p. 20.
44. Josephson, p. 450.
45. Jensen, p. 149.
46. Martin, p. 87.
47. Saunders, p. 33.
48. Eckenrode and Edmunds, *E. H. Harriman*, p. 173.
49. Hoogenboom and Hoogenboom, p. 54.
50. Dixon, *Railroads and Government,* p. 3.
51. Chalmers, chap. 3. See also Saunders, p. 38.
52. Sharfman, *Interstate Commerce Commission*, pp. 40–46.
53. Martin, pp. 147–48, 114.
54. "Joint Freight Tariff," July 25, 1904. See also Martin.
55. Kolko, *Railroads and Regulation* p. 169.
56. Martin, p. 101.
57. Hoogenboom and Hoogenboom, p. 56.
58. *City of Spokane v Northern Pacific, Interstate Commerce Commission Reports.*
59. Martin, p. 123.
60. Hoogenboom and Hoogenboom, p. 58.
61. Martin, p. 12.

62. Ibid.
63. Ibid., p. 169.
64. Stover, *American Railroads,* p. 135.
65. Sharfman, vol. 1 , p. 52*n*51.
66. Martin, p. 195.
67. Ibid., p. 225.
68. Hoogenboom and Hoogenboom, pp. 63–64.
69. Martin, pp. 206–24.
70. Ibid., p. 263*n*65.
71. Hoogenboom and Hoogenboom, pp. 69–70.
72. Martin, pp. 272–82; and Kolko, pp. 208–13.
73. Douglas, *All Aboard,* p. vii.
74. Martin, pp. 259–311.
75. Saunders, p. 37.
76. Martin, p. 347.
77. Chalmers, p. 35.
78. Hoogenboom and Hoogenboom, p. 72.
79. Martin, pp. 361–62.
80. Holbrook, p. 10.

CHAPTER 3: THE GOOD ROADS CRUSADE

1. Flink, *Automobile Age,* pp. 2–4.
2. Tebbel and Zuckerman, *Magazine in America,* pp. 57–58, 64.
3. Plowden, *Motorcar in Politics.*
4. Dunn, *Miles to Go,* p. 11. See also Hindley, *History of Roads,* p. 76.
5. *America's Highways,* p. 80.
6. *Railway Gazette,* February 1891.
7. Fuessle, "Pulling Main Street," pp. 640–43.
8. Sayre, *Albert Baird Cummins,* p. 60.
9. *America's Highways,* p. 44.
10. "Railroads and Wagon Roads," pp. 39–42.
11. Ibid., p. 131.
12. National Geographic Society, *Builders,* pp. 16–19.
13. Rowland, *Roman Transport,* p. 11. The fact that Roman engineering prac-
     tices had not come into vogue until most American colonists left for the
     New World may account for the settlers' lack of practical information to
     draw on. The work of Pierre-Marie Jerome Trésaguet in France, and
     Thomas Telford and John Louden McAdam in Great Britain in the eigh-
     teenth and nineteenth centuries showed that using varied stone sizes and
     road pitches, and making surfaces impervious to water could increase road
     durability greatly.
14. National Geographic Society, p. 20.
15. *America's Highways,* p. 47.
16. Ibid., pp. 12–13.
17. Ibid., pp. 66–67.
18. Ibid., p. 80.

19. Keveney, "Solo Drivers May Pay."
20. Tebbel and Zuckerman, p. 109.
21. *America's Highways,* p. 80.
22. Flink, pp. 13, 51–53.
23. "America was a quick study. . . ": Smith, *America Enters the World,* p. 863; "Austin": Richardson, *British Motor Industry,* pp. 73–87.
24. Dulles, *Americans Abroad.*
25. Bardou, *Automobile Revolution,* p. 15.
26. Richardson, p. 182.
27. Bardou, pp. 19–21.
28. American Automobile Association, "The Beginning of the Automobile."
29. Smith, p. 866.
30. Dulles, pp. 144–45. See also Bardou, p. 18.
31. American Automobile Association.
32. Bardou, p. 21.
33. Harrod, "Death Wish."
34. Ibid.
35. *America's Highways,* pp. 45–49.
36. Interview with Frank Turner.
37. Dunn, p. 98.
38. Smith, p. 867.
39. Bardou, p. 20.
40. Smith, p. 868. See also Boardman, *Flappers, Bootleggers,* pp. 8–9.
41. Smith, p. 873.
42. *America's Highways,* pp. 45–49.
43. Ibid., p. 74.
44. *Hartford Courant,* January 26, 1993, p. 1.
45. Belasco, *Autocamp to Motel,* chap. 2.
46. Ibid.
47. *Literary Digest,* October 10, 1914, p. 683.
48. Belasco, chap. 2.
49. Dunn, p. 116.
50. *America's Highways,* p. 76.
51. Weisberger, *Dream Maker,* p. 170.
52. *America's Highways,* pp. 81–82.
53. Ibid., chap. 8.
54. Ibid.
55. Lincoln Highway Association, *Lincoln Highway,* chap. 2.
56. Ibid.
57. Weisberger, p. 169.
58. Fuessle, pp. 640–43.
59. Seely, *Building the American Highway System,* p. 32.
60. Patton, *Open Road,* p. 144.
61. *America's Highways,* p. 86.
62. Ibid., chap. 8.
63. Visit to American Automobile Association headquarters in Heathrow, Fla.,

March 30, 1992. In fact, however, President Eisenhower signed the 1956 bill while he was in the hospital. A federal Highway Administration source says that the Eisenhower picture depicts the signing of an earlier bill.

64. Brough, *Ford Dynasty*.
65. U.S. House, *Federal Aid to Good Roads*, p. 15n12.

CHAPTER 4: THE ELECTRIC SHOOTING STAR

1. Middleton, *Time of the Trolley*, pp. 66, 73.
2. Hilton and Due, *Electric Interurban Railways*, p. 5.
3. Ibid., p. 5. See also Middleton, 'Gems of Symmetry"; and Jensen, *American Heritage History*, p. 252.
4. Flink, *Automobile Age*, p. 3. See also Middleton, "Gems of Symmetry."
5. Hilton and Due, p. 7.
6. Finch, *Highways to Heaven* pp. 44–45. See also Middleton, *Time of the Trolley*, p. 73.
7. Warner, *Streetcar Suburbs*, p. 25. See also Middleton, *Time of the Trolley*, p. 73.
8. Cheape, *Moving the Masses*, p. 7.
9. Flink, p. 3. See also Hilton and Due, p. 7; and Middleton, *Time of the Trolley*, p. 73.
10. Young, *St. Louis Streetcar*, p. 42.
11. Warner, p. 26.
12. Foster, *From Streetcar to Superhighway*, p. 16. See also Middleton, *Time of the Trolley*, p. 77.
13. Warner, pp. 22, 26, 52–55.
14. Cheape, p. 213.
15. Ibid., pp. 83–84.
16. Ibid. p. 173.
17. Middleton, *Time of the Trolley* pp. 78–79.
18. Foster, p. 16. See also Young, pp. 80–81.
19. Young, p. 81.
20. MacDonald, *Insull*, p. 96. See also Nash, *Makers and Breakers*, pp. 193, 236; and Cheape, p. 213.
21. Young and Provenzo, *St. Louis Car Company*, p. 16.
22. Middleton, *Time of the Trolley*, p. 86.
23. Ibid., pp. 86–97.
24. Young and Provenzo, p. 55.
25. Middleton, *Time of the Trolley*, p. 362.
26. Ibid., p. 86.
27. Ibid., p. 111.
28. Young and Provenzo, p. 115.
29. Hoyner, "Metropolitan Chicago Almanac."
30. MacDonald, pp. 97–98.
31. Ibid., pp. 258–59; and Barrett, *Automobile and Urban Transit*, pp. 97–98.
32. Davis, *Conspicuous Production*, chap. 7.

33. Middleton, "Goodbye to Interurbans," p. 41. See also Jensen, *American Heritage History,* p. 252.

34. Hilton and Due, p. 15. See also Jensen, p. 252.

35. Hilton and Due, pp. 18–19.

36. Jensen, p. 252.

37. Hilton and Due, p. 23.

38. Ibid.

39. Ibid., pp. 3–15.

40. Ibid., pp. 41–42.

41. Ibid., p. 197.

42. Jensen, p. 257.

43. Ibid., pp. 33–34.

44. Middleton, "Goodbye to Interurbans," pp. 37–38, 67–68. See also Hilton and Due, pp. 38–41.

45. Chandler and Salsbury, *Pierre S. duPont,* p. 614; and Hilton and Due, p. 35.

46. Crump, *Big Red Cars,* pp. 42–45. See also Crump, *Henry Huntington,* p. 11.

47. Crump, *Henry Huntington,* pp. 12–14.

48. Crump, *Big Red Cars,* p. 44.

49. Donaldson and Myers, *Rails through Orange Groves,* pp. 107, 114. See also Crump, *Big Red Cars,* pp. 44–45; and Myers, "Pacific Electric Railway," p. 73.

50. Crump, *Henry Huntington,* p. 13.

51. Ibid., pp. 16–26.

52. Crump, *Big Red Cars,* pp. 203–10; and Hilton and Due, chap. 1.

CHAPTER 5: MOTORING FOR PROFIT

1. Childs, *Trucking and Public Interest*, pp. 38–39.

2. Ibid., pp. 33–37.

3. Yergin, *The Prize,* p. 171.

4. Ibid. See also Childs, pp. 9–10.

5. *America's Highways,* p. 98.

6. Hilton and Due, *Electric Interurban Railways,* p. 228.

7. Keeshin, *No Fears,* p. 19.

8. Childs, pp. 31–40.

9. Keeshin, p. 18.

10. Childs, pp. 16–17.

11. Hilton and Due, p. 236.

12. *America's Highways,* p. 108.

13. Ibid., p. 98.

14. Childs, p. 11.

15. Hilton and Due, p. 238.

16. *America's Highways,* p. 42. See also Childs, pp. 12–13.

17. *America's Highways,* p. 118.

18. *Commercial and Financial Chronicle,* January 3, 1920, p. 14.

19. Sayre, *Albert Baird Cummins,* pp. 489–506. See also Kolko, *Railroads and Regulation,* pp. 228–29.

20. Kolko, p. 230.

21. Childs, pp. 12–13.
22. *America's Highways,* pp. 102–3. See also Fuessle, "Pulling Main Street," p. 640.
23. MacDonald, "What Our Highways Mean."
24. Hilton and Due, p. 238.
25. Interview with Margaret Oberlin.
26. *America's Highways,* pp. 97–99.
27. Childs, p. 30.
28. *America's Highways,* p. 117.
29. *Illinois Public Utilities Commission v. Duke.*
30. *Frost v. Railroad Commission.*
31. Childs, p. 72.
32. MacDonald, "Commercial Vehicles."
33. Interstate Commerce Commission (ICC), *Interstate Commerce Commission Reports,* 70 ICC 224, 1921, p. 224.
34. Ibid., 67 ICC 760, 1921, p 760.
35. Ibid., 72 ICC 13, 1922, p. 13.
36. Ibid., 76 ICC 695, 1922, p. 695.
37. MacDonald, "Commercial Vehicles."
38. ICC, *Fortieth Annual Report of the Interstate Commerce Commission,* pp. 41–43.
39. Childs, p. 94.
40. ICC, *Motor Bus and Truck Operation,* p. 748.

CHAPTER 6: THE TROJAN HORSELESS CARRIAGE

1. Corbett, *Oklahoma's Highways.*
2. Bates, *Story of Congress,* pp. 442–43.
3. Seely, *American Highway System,* p. 58.
4. MacDonald, "What Our Highways Mean."
5. Chandler and Salsbury, *Pierre S. duPont,* p. 614. "Panama Canal": McCullough, *Path between the Seas,* p. 610.
6. U.S. House Committee on Roads, *Hearings on H.R. 63, H.R. 3252, H.R. 4971, H.R. 6133,* March 10, 1924.
7. *America's Highways,* pp. 103–6.
8. Seely, p. 52.
9. MacDonald, "What Our Highways Mean." See also Seely, p. 107.
10. Seely, pp. 54–59.
11. Long, *Roy D. Chapin,* pp. 30–32.
12. Seely, p. 61.
13. Ibid., p. 53.
14. Ibid.
15. Ibid.
16. The National Auto Road, although free when it was opened in 1806, began to charge tolls about 1830.
17. MacDonald, untitled 1923 radio address.
18. Dunn, *Miles to Go,* pp. 103–4. See also Richardson, *British Motor Industry,* p. 67.

19. Seely, p. 59.
20. Highway Education Board, "Program for Proceedings."
21. Dearing, *American Highway Policy*.
22. James, "Teaching Highway Economics," p. 236.
23. Highway Education Board.
24. Ibid., p. 41
25. Ibid. See also Chandler, p. 472; and Weisberger, *The Dream Maker*, p. 224.
26. *America's Highways*, p. 124.
27. Lewis, *Henry Ford*, p. 165.
28. Highway Education Board.
29. National Automobile Chamber of Commerce, *National Transportation Committee*.
30. St. Clair, *Motorization*, p. 141.
31. DeGregorio, *U.S. Presidents*, p. 537.
32. St. Clair, p. 141.
33. Interchange between Representative John Robsion of Kentucky and Thomas H. MacDonald; see House Committee on Roads, March 19, 1924.
34. MacDonald, "Commercial Vehicles."
35. Abandonments reported in annual reports of decisions of the Interstate Commerce Commission (ICC) from 1921 to 1925. MacDonald asserted in his "Commercial Vehicles" article that of 2,439 miles abandoned since 1920, 58 percent were mine and logging trackage abandoned "on account of exhaustion of the natural resources for the exploitation of which it was constructed," versus 4.3 percent given up because of motor competition. The ICC's published annual reports from 1921 through July 1925, the month before MacDonald's article appeared, show approximately 10 percent more mileage abandoned than does MacDonald's figure. Of the 2,771 miles abandoned, 34 percent stemmed from motor competition, versus 23 percent for exhaustion of mining operations. The remaining abandonments were for other reasons.
36. Dearing, *American Highway Policy*.
37. *Sproiles v Binford*, 380–83; and *Stephenson v Binford*, 269–72. See also Childs, *Trucking and Public Interest*, chap. 4.
38. MacDonald, "Highways and Railroads."
39. Testimony by MacDonald, before Interstate Commerce Commission. See also MacDonald's testimony before the Senate Commerce Committee.
40. U.S. Department of Commerce, *Statistical Abstract of the United States,* 1950, pp. 708–19.
41. Office of County Clerk, probate records, Bryan, Texas.
42. Ambrose, *Eisenhower,* vol. 2, p. 612.

CHAPTER 7: DERAILING THE TROLLEYS

1. Crump, *Big Red Cars,* p. 204. See also Davis, *Conspicuous Production,* p. 159.
2. Barrett, *Automobile and Urban Transit*, pp. 128–29.
3. Hilton and Due, *Electric Interurban Railways,* p. 226.

4. Advertisement by the Willys-Overland Company in *Ladies' Home Journal*, March 1917 (hereafter cited as Willys-Overland ad).

5. Hilton and Due, p. 237.

6. Testimony of Thomas H. MacDonald, U.S. House Committee on Roads, March 19, 1924.

7. St. Clair, *The Motorization of American Cities*.

8. Hilton and Due, p. 231.

9. Willys-Overland ad.

10. Interview with William A. Myers.

11. Crump, p. 203.

12. Barrett, "Public Policy and Private Choice," pp. 474, 497.

13. Flink, *Automobile Age,* pp. 362–63.

14. *U.S. v National City Lines,* trial transcripts, vol. 1, p. 429.

15. St. Clair, *Motorization,* p. 59. See also Kwitny, "Great Transportation Conspiracy," p. 18; and *U.S. v National City Lines* 186, F2d, 562, 565 (1951).

16. Sloan, *Years with General Motors,* p. 151.

17. Flink, p. 192.

18. Sloan, p. 282.

19. St. Clair, "Entrepreneurship and Automobile Industry," pp. 167–68.

20. Thompson, "American Passenger Train," pp. 10–13.

21. Kwitny, p. 18.

22. *U.S. v National City Lines,* trial transcripts, vol. 1, p. 442.

23. Ibid., p. 448.

24. Whitt, *Urban Elites,* p. 47.

25. Thompson, pp. 11–12; Kwitny, p. 14; and St. Clair, pp. 57–59.

26. Flink, p. 365.

27. Whitt, pp. 45–46.

28. St. Clair, *Motorization,* p. 59.

29. Ibid., pp. 58–59. See also, General Motors, *Transportation Products,* p. 40.

30. *U.S. v National City Lines,* trial transcripts, vol. 1, p. 518.

31. Ibid., p. 59.

32. Kwitny, p. 18.

33. Hilton and Due, pp. 199–203.

34. Hawes, *Utility Holding Companies,* sec. 2, pp. 14–15. See also St. Clair, *Motorization,* p. 111; and Kwitny, p. 15 .

35. Hawes, sec. 2, pp. 14–15.

36. St. Clair, *Motorization,* p. 60.

37. Ibid.

38. Schisgall, *Greyhound Story,* p. 32; "largest shareholder": Thompson, "American Passenger Train," p. 11.

39. *U.S. v National City Lines,* 186, F2d, 562 (1951).

40. Ibid.

41. Ibid.

42. Farrell, *Who Made Streetcars Go?*

43. *U.S. v National City Lines.*

44. Ibid.

45. Yago, *Decline of Transit,* p. 61.

46. *U.S. v National City Lines*.
47. St. Clair, *Motorization,* pp. 63–64.
48. Kwitny, p. 20.
49. St. Clair, *Motorization,* p. 66.
50. Ibid., pp. 65–66.
51. Kwitny, p. 20. In 1974, a U.S. Senate assistant counsel, Bradford C. Snell, recounted the conspiracy account before Senator Philip A. Hart's antitrust subcommittee, then investigating the auto and ground transportation industries. His story was part of a larger assault on General Motors, which included allegations of GM's collaboration with the Nazis in World War II and of GM's pressuring of railroads to accept diesel locomotives, which Snell claimed were less efficient than electric locomotives (U.S. Senate Committee on the Judiciary, Subcommittee on Antitrust and Monopoly, *American Ground Transport*).
52. Kwitny, p. 20.
53. Letter from B. F. Stadley, the secretary of Phillips Petroleum, to H. C. Grossman, the vice-president of General Motors, October 11, 1943, quoted in Yago, *Decline of Transit,* p. 60.
54. *U.S. v National City Lines*, trial transcripts, vol. 1, p. 639.
55. Yago, p. 61.
56. Kwitny, p. 21.
57. *U.S. v National City Lines*, trial transcripts, vol. 1, p. 565.
58. Ibid.
59. St. Clair, *Motorization,* p. 66.
60. Flink.
61. *U.S. v National City Lines*.
62. Ibid., vol. 1, p. 429. See also Kwitny.
63. Yago, p. 62.
64. Flink.
65. Hilton and Due, p. 245.
66. Ibid., p. 251.

CHAPTER 8: APPLYING THE BRAKES

1. Transcript of U.S. Senate Interstate Commerce Committee, *Hearings on S. 2793,* Feb. 1–8, 1932; "free for all": Childs, *Trucking,* p. 95.
2. Flink, *Automobile Age,* pp. 188–93.
3. Fuess, *Joseph B. Eastman,* p. 184.
4. "Unions and Railroads Ratify."
5. Flink, *Automobile Age,* p. 51.
6. Barnard, *Independent Man,* p. 8.
7. Nevins, *Ford: The Times,* p. 243.
8. Crawford, *Pressure Boys,* p. 250.
9. Seely, "Railroads," p. 46.
10. Childs, *Trucking,* part 3B.
11. Interstate Commerce Commission (ICC), *Fortieth Annual Report*, p. 42.
12. Childs, p. 94.

13. Ibid., pp. 90, 122.
14. Flink, p. 131.
15. Seely, p. 46.
16. Fuess, pp. 182–83.
17. Seely, p. 46. See also Fuess, p. 185; and Overbey, *Free Enterprise Alternative,* p. 19.
18. Seely, p. 52.
19. Ibid., p. 48.
20. Childs, p. 94.
21. ICC, *Coordination of Motor Transportation*, 182, 263, April 6, 1932.
22. Nevins, p. 245.
23. U.S. Senate Interstate Commerce Committee, *Hearings on S. 2793.*
24. Childs, p. 96.
25. Seely, p. 53.
26. ICC, *Coordination of Motor Transportation*, p. 263. The commission seemed in a quandary over the "practical difficulties" of regulating an industry composed of a very large number of small operators, just the opposite from the railroads. "Under these circumstances, we deem it wise to make haste slowly," the commission concluded (p. 263).
27. Childs, p. 96.
28. *Sproiles v Binford*, 286, U.S. 374, AT 385, 394.
29. Keeshin, *No Fears,* chap. 3.
30. Childs, p. 104.
31. Crawford, p. 260.
32. Ibid., p. 262.
33. Keeshin, chap. 3.
34. Finch, pp. 144–45; see also Davis, *New Deal Years,* p. 111.
35. Hoogenboom and Hoogenboom, *History of ICC*, p. 113.
36. Ibid., p. 118.
37. Davis, pp. 111–12.
38. Hoogenboom and Hoogenboom, p. 124. The National Transportation Committee also included among its members the financier Bernard Baruch and the one-time Democratic presidential candidate Al Smith.
39. Boardman, *Flappers, Bootleggers,* p. 7.
40. Flink, p. 212.
41. Foster, *Streetcar to Superhighway,* p. 125. See also Finch, *Highways to Heaven,* p. 143.
42. Heppenheimer, "Rise of Interstates," p. 9.
43. Seely, pp. 88–89. See also *America's Highways,* p. 123.
44. Mertz, p. 21.
45. "Only one": "Presidential Elections since 1789," pp. 81–89; "eastern financiers": Barone and Ujifusa, "American Politics," p. 1242.
46. "Boyhood zest": Freidel, *Franklin D. Roosevelt,* p. 410; "Ripley": Fusfeld, *Economic Thought,* pp. 27–28.
47. "Roosevelt Outlines."
48. Ibid.

49. Fusfeld, p. 239. See also "Roosevelt Outlines."
50. Wentworth and Flexner, *Dictionary of American Slang,* p. 50.

CHAPTER 9: HARD TIMES

1. Dunn, *Miles to Go,* pp. 33–34.
2. Nash, *Great Depression,* pp. 78–79.
3. Boardman, *Flappers, Bootleggers,* pp. 137–38.
4. Childs, *Trucking,* p. 107.
5. Ibid., p. 112.
6. Ibid., pp. 113–14. For the thirteen months ending in March 1935, the NRA received 4,445 complaints, dismissing most of them and taking only 43 to court.
7. Ibid., p. 115.
8. Childs, p. 128.
9. Fuess, *Joseph Eastman,* pp. 129, 322.
10. Mason, *Brandeis,* p. 86. See also Childs, p. 121.
11. Childs, p. 123.
12. Mason, p. 86.
13. Childs, p. 120.
14. Fuess.
15. Childs, p. 123.
16. Stone, *Interstate Commerce Commission,* p. 29.
17. Williams, *Rail-Motor Rate Competition,* p. 3.
18. Felton and Anderson, *Motor Carrier Industry,* p. 6.
19. Childs, p. 124.
20. Ibid., p. 131.
21. The act treated contract carriers lightly, requiring them simply to obtain operating permits, charge not more than stated rates, and work limited hours.
22. Dunn, *Miles to Go,* p. 33.
23. Hoogenboom and Hoogenboom, *History of the ICC,* p. 135.
24. Ibid.
25. Rose, *Interstate Highway Politics,* p. 4.
26. Fusfeld, *Economic Thought*, p. 132.
27. *America's Highways,* p. 124.
28. Ibid., p. 125.
29. Mertz, "Origins of Interstates," p. 25.
30. "What Editors Are Saying," citing editorials from the *Concord Tribune*, December 22, 1930; the *Washington Post*, September 30, 1930; and the *Findlay Courier*, October 4, 1930, among others.
31. *America's Highways,* p. 124.
32. Foster, *Streetcar to Superhighway,* pp. 125–26.
33. Rose, p. 2.
34. Martin, *Railroads Triumphant,* pp. 365–66; "Thought we were crazy": Sloan, *Years with General Motors,* p. 352.
35. Tugwell, *Roosevelt's Revolution*.

36. Seely, *American Highway System,* p. 84.
37. Heppenheimer, "Rise of the Interstates," p. 9.
38. International Chamber of Commerce, "Highway Administration," p. 104.
39. Mertz, p. 31.
40. "Cheapest Protection."
41. Mertz, p. 28.
42. Fusfeld, pp. 27–28.
43. Diary of Treasury Secretary Henry Morgenthau, entry for December 10, 1934, archives of Franklin D. Roosevelt Library, Hyde Park, N.Y.; and Ickes, *Secret Diary of Harold L. Ickes,* entry for December 13, 1934.
44. *America's Highways,* p. 136. Also interview with Terry Tondro.
45. Mertz, p. 28.
46. Frederick C. Horner, letter to Alfred Reeves.
47. *America's Highways,* p. 125.
48. Mertz, p. 32.
49. *America's Highways,* p. 125.
50. MacDonald, note 49. The historian Bruce Seely notes, "Significantly, every opponent of the bill had parroted the BPR's arguments" (*American Highway System,* p. 163).
51. U.S. House, *Toll Roads and Free Roads,* pp. vii–x, 1–7.
52. MacDonald, note 52.
53. The last-minute infusion came from a Public Works Administration grant and bond purchases by the Reconstruction Finance Corporation.
54. Patton, "Quick Way from Here," pp. 96–100; and Cupper, "To the Future," pp. 102–11. See also *America's Highways,* pp. 136–37; and Mertz, p. 41.
55. Mertz, p. 41.
56. Patton, *Open Road,* p. 100.

CHAPTER 10: A WAR ABROAD, A CONFLICT AT HOME

1. Mertz, "Origins of Interstates," p. 52.
2. "Auto freak" is the term that Dieter Lippert, the director of the Munich rapid transit system, used during a personal interview to describe Adolf Hitler.
3. Mertz, p. 52.
4. Stover, *Life and Decline,* p. 210.
5. Ibid., pp. 181–82. See also Martin, *Railroads Triumphant,* pp. 299–300.
6. Stover, p. 179.
7. St. Clair, *Motorization,* p. 139.
8. Martin, p. 371.
9. Casdorph, *Let the Good Times Roll,* p. 41.
10. Martin, p. 372. See also Stover, p. 184.
11. MacDonald, Speech to North Atlantic States.
12. Stover, p. 183.
13. Ads in national magazines, 1943, 1944.
14. Casdorph, p. 6.

15. Martin, p. 372.
16. Stover, p. 184.
17. Ibid., p. 183.
18. U.S. Department of Commerce, Bureau of the Census, *Historical Statistics, 1975,* p. 11. The 1920 census showed a nearly equal number of towns over and under twenty-five hundred people. During the next twenty years the more populous towns would grow by 40 percent; the more sparsely settled, by only 10 percent.
19. Rose, *Interstate Highway Politics,* p. 24.
20. Seely, *American Highway System,* p. 212.
21. Rose, pp. 39–40.
22. Ibid., p. 19.
23. St. Clair, pp. 120–21.
24. Rose, p. 19.
25. Ibid., pp. 19–20.
26. Mertz, pp. 69–71.
27. Ibid., pp. 73–74.
28. Leavitt, *Superhighway: Superhoax,* pp. 152–53.
29. In a January 1944 speech to the American Society for Civil Engineers, quoted in Mertz, p. 76.
30. Rose, p. 27.
31. Ibid.
32. Patton, *Open Road.*
33. Mayne, *Recovery of Europe,* pp. 30–31.
34. Price, *Marshall Plan,* p. 30. See also *Encyclopaedia Britannica*, vol. 9, p. 755.
35. Casdorph, pp. 117–20.
36. *America's Highways,* p. 154; "Levitt" and "Crosley": Dickson, *Timelines,* pp. 21, 14.
37. Boardman, p. 212.
38. *America's Highways,* p. 160.
39. Ibid. See also Rose, p. 31.
40. Stover, pp. 211–17; "GM": Saunders, *Railroad Mergers,* p. 62.
41. Stover, pp. 213–15.
42. Saunders, p. 70.
43. Stover, pp. 215–17. "Vista dome" cars had been conceptualized as early as the 1890s, when a *Scientific American* article let imaginations take flight. But a GM executive, Cyrus R. Osborn, conceived the modern domed car after riding in the cab of a diesel freight locomotive, watching the Colorado Rockies pass by through the cab's wraparound windows.
44. Stover, p. 219.
45. Sillcox, "Train-Truck Trouble," p. 9.
46. Stover, p. 237.
47. Ibid., pp. 267–68.
48. Heppenheimer, "Rise of Interstates," p. 10.
49. *America's Highways,* p. 167.
50. Ibid., pp. 166–69.

51. Ibid.
52. Mertz, p. 85.
53. Rose, p. 32.
54. Ibid., p. 34. Alfred Sloan, while GM's chairman, had founded NHUC in 1932.
55. Seely, p. 197.
56. Rose, pp. 41–42.
57. Ibid., p. 60; "few intimates": Patton, p. 146.
58. Mertz, p. 87, The principle that MacDonald espoused of guaranteeing replacement housing was not enshrined in federal law until 1978, when a bill sponsored by Senator Lowell P. Weicker, Jr., (R-Conn.) passed Congress.
59. Mertz, pp. 89–90.

CHAPTER 11: INTERSTATE SOCIALISM

1. Fisher, *Story of National Highway Users Conference,* p. 1.
2. Ibid., pp. 15–39.
3. Declaring that Washington had a "responsibility to build roads," NHUC demanded that general revenues, not fuel taxes, pay for the program.
4. Heppenheimer, "Rise of Interstates," p. 12.
5. Rose, *Interstate Highway Politics,* pp. 42–43. Among those signing on were fleet operators' associations, commercial carriers, oil companies, the American Automobile Association, the U.S. Chamber of Commerce, and Associated General Contractors of America, the trade association of road construction contractors.
6. Rose, pp. 48–49. The only ray of sunshine on the horizon was that Congress in 1952 had voted to spend $25 million out of its $550 million highway appropriations to pave the first of the interstate roads laid out in 1944.
7. Dickson, *Timelines,* pp. 60–83.
8. "peaks and valleys": Ambrose, *Eisenhower*, vol 2., p. 250.
9. Ibid., p. 250. See also Smart, "1919," pp. 18–25.
10. "Trusted aides": Rose, p. 70.
11. Rose, p. 71.
12. Ibid., p. 72.
13. Mertz, "Origins of Interstates," p. 109.
14. Lay, *Ways of the World,* p. 319.
15. Finch, *Highways to Heaven,* pp. 229–33. Sharing Moses's views was Bertram Tallamy, the influential head of the New York Thruway Authority and a future federal highway administrator.
16. Mosley, *Blood Relations,* pp. 226, 262, 286–91. "Idealistic mission": Schwartz, *Urban Freeways,* p. 428. Donated to the state of Delaware in 1924, the highway forms part of today's Route 13.
17. St. Clair, *Motorization,* p. 141.
18. *America's Highways,* p. 166.
19. Ambrose, p. 301.
20. "$50 Billion Roads Planned," p. 1.

21. Egan, "Eisenhower Bids," recounting remark by Governor Howard Pyle of Arizona.

22. Ibid.

23. Ibid. Robert Moses took credit for getting Eisenhower to use the $50 billion figure. Within months, however, the administration had scaled that down to $27 billion dollars, and the $50 billion estimate was never used again. See Caro, *Power Broker,* p. 921.

24. Ambrose, p. 251; "federal budget": Heppenheimer, p. 11. See also Eisenhower, *Mandate for Change,* p. 650.

25. Mertz, pp. 112, 118.

26. Egan.

27. "Business is Ready."

28. Fleeson, "$50 Billion More," p. 1.

29. *New York Times,* July 13, 14, 15, 1954, p. 1; and *Life,* July 19, 1954, pp. 75–80.

30. Seely, *American Highway System,* p. 219.

31. "special assistant": Seely, p. 214.

32. Schwartz, p. 495; car descriptions: Finch, pp. 203–8.

33. Finch, p. 225.

34. Lay.

35. Mertz, pp. 115–19; Rose, p. 74; Schwartz, p. 431.

36. Rose, pp. 75–77; "Truckers would pay": Eisenhower's February 22, 1955, message to Congress, Hearings of the Roads Subcommittee, Senate Public Works Committee, Feb. 1955, p. 1046.

37. Dickson, pp. 87–92.

38. "radical ideas": Hagerty, p. 137.

39. Mertz, p. 122.

40. *America's Highways,* p. 173. "banker's bill": *America's Highways,* p. 173.

41. Kahn, "Political Change in America," p. 150.

42. Rose, p. 79.

43. Rose, pp. 80–84.

44. U.S. Senate Committee on Public Works, *Hearings on S. 1160*, pp. 942–43.

45. MacDonald, U.S. Senate testimony cited in statement by William A. Bresnahan, assistant general manager of the American Trucking Association, ibid., p. 954.

46. Schwartz, p. 433. A majority of the committee hailed from rural states and predictably warmed to a bill continuing the traditional formula; see Kahn, pp. 150–53. The bill simply increased the gas tax one cent and boosted the federal share from 60 to 90 percent, but left state-federal control sharing untouched.

47. Schwartz, p. 434.

48. U.S. House Committee on Public Works, *Hearings on H.R. 4260*, p. 1258.

49. Leavitt, *Superhighways: Superhoax*, p. 45.

50. Seely, p. 216.

51. Rose, p. 83.

52. Dickson, p. 88.
53. Mertz, p. 141.
54. Rose, pp. 63–64.
55. Eisenhower, p. 649.
56. Rose, p. 89.
57. House Committee, *Hearing on H.R. 8836*, p. 224.
58. Among dozens of groups testifying before the House Ways and Means Committee hearing on H.R 8836, February 14–21, 1956.
59. Testimony as the president of the Automobile Manufacturers' Association before the Senate; see U.S. Senate Committee on Public Works, *Hearings on S. 1160*, p. 486.
60. Testimony of Andrew J. Sordoni, AAA President; see U.S. House Committee on Public Works, *Hearings on H.R. 4260*, p. 1276.
61. Testimony of AAA before U.S. House Ways and Means Committee, *Hearings on H.R. 8836*, February 14, 1956, p. 446.
62. Kahn, p. 156.
63. Rose, p. 82.
64. Schwartz, p. 435.
65. Ibid., p. 498.
66. Moynihan, "New Roads and Urban Chaos," p. 13.
67. Schwartz, pp. 435, 498.
68. The American Trucking Associations had lobbied so hard against this provision in Fallon's 1955 bill that House leaders Sam Rayburn and John McCormack credited the bill's failure to that group's efforts.
69. Kahn, pp. 154–55.
70. Ibid., p. 155.
71. Ibid., pp. 158–59.
72. Seely, pp. 214–15.
73. Rose, p. 85. The bill the House passed on April 27, 1956, by 388 to 19, swept the issues of turnpike reimbursement and tax equity under the rug, to minimize dissident votes.
74. Congressional Quarterly, *Congress and the Nation*, pp. 530–31. The final product required truckers to pay a three-cent-a-pound hike for rubber, a new three-cent tax on retreads, and a 2 percent additional excise tax on new vehicles. Congress agreed in principle to reimburse states for the cost of building toll roads, which now would be linked into the interstate system, but deferred a decision on just which ones would qualify.
75. Rose, p. 85; statement issued by William Norrlag, Jr., the general manager of the Central Motor Freight Association, in March 1956.
76. Rose, pp. 97–98.
77. Ibid., p. 100.
78. Leavitt, pp. 187–88.
79. Ambrose, p. 547. See also Schwartz, pp. 444–47.

CHAPTER 12: A NEW AMERICA

1. Finch, *Highways to Heaven,* p. 227. To strengthen the roads, the standard four- to five-inch road thicknesses would be doubled, atop a prepared roadbed as much as fifty inches deep.

2. Figures of the National Highway Users Conference, cited in Mowbray, *Road to Ruin,* p. 14.

3. The American Road Builders Association succeeded the League of American Wheelmen, founded in 1880 to lobby for good roads on behalf of bicyclists.

4. The National Highway Users' Conference claimed that its umbrella sheltered some three thousand organizations. The American Trucking Associations' lobbying affiliate, for instance, donated between $1,000 and $3,000 each to such friendly congressmen as George Fallon, John Blatnik, and John C. Kluczynski (Leavitt, *Superhighways: Superhoax*).

5. Leavitt, photograph preceding p. 115.

6. Ibid., p. 122.

7. Dickson, *Timelines,* pp. 105–10.

8. Ibid., pp. 128–31.

9. Ibid., p. 135.

10. Mitchell, "Thirty Years," p. 88.

11. Patton, *Open Road,* p. 147.

12. Leavitt, pp. 260–62.

13. Patton, p. 147.

14. Ibid.

15. Yergin, *The Prize,* p. 551.

16. Dickson, pp. 103–15.

17. *America's Highways,* p. 283.

18. "thirteen years": Mertz and Ritter, "Building the Interstate," p. 15; "$41 billion": Leavitt, p. 45.

19. Gans, *The Levittowners*; "Federal Housing Administration": Fishman, *Bourgeois Utopias*. See also Kaplan, *Dream Deferred*.

20. Jackson, *Crabgrass Frontier,* p. 207.

21. Halberstam, *The Reckoning,* p. 349.

22. "On the Interstate," pp. 12–13.

23. Burck, "Truckers Roll," pp. 75–85.

24. Yergin, p. 552.

25. Finch, pp. 237–38.

26. Patton, pp. 197–98.

27. Yergin, p. 551.

28. Patton, pp. 194-98.

29. U.S. Department of Transportation, *Consideration of Archaeology*, pp. 28, 30, 33.

30. Salsbury, *No Way to Run,* p. 33. See also Martin, *Railroads Triumphant,* p. 377.

31. Lyon, *To Hell in a Day Coach*.

32. Orenstein, *United States Railroad Policy,* pp. 64–65. See also Stover, *Life and Decline,* p. 231.

33. Lyon, p. 243.
34. Salsbury, p. 33.
35. Martin, pp. 379–80. See also Lyon, pp. 203–4.
36. Lyon, p. 188. Rails had carried canal boats on "piggyback" cars a century earlier and had hauled farmers' produce wagons in the 1880s. But modern truckers had fought piggybacking, fearing it would allow one mode to merge the speed of rail with the flexibility of trucks.
37. Ibid., p. 201.
38. Ibid. See also Stover, pp. 263–66.
39. *America's Highways,* p. 257; "Less than half": Gottmann, *Megalopolis,* p. 650.
40. Lyon, pp. 202–3. The Erie-Lackawanna and the Baltimore and Ohio each pleaded nolo contendere to rebate charges and paid a thousand-dollar fine.
41. U.S. Senate Committee on Interstate and Foreign Commerce, *Problems of the Railroads,* vol. 2, p. 833.
42. Ibid., p. 969.
43. Hoogenboom and Hoogenboom, *History of the ICC,* pp. 155–56.
44. Lyon, pp. 196–97. Section 15a (3) was added to Part I of the Interstate Commerce Act to provide the following:

> In a proceeding involving competition between carriers of different modes of transportation subject to this Act, the Commission, in determining whether a rate is lower than a reasonable minimum rate, shall consider the facts and circumstances attending the movement of the traffic by the carrier or carriers to which the rate is applicable. Rates of a carrier shall not be held up to a particular level to protect the traffic of any other mode of transportation, giving due consideration to the objectives of the national transportation policy declared in this Act.

45. Lyon, p. 211.
46. Scott, *Railroad Development Programs,* pp. 166, 116, 143. From 1954 to 1964, fourteen railroads serving Texas attracted 4,400 firms worth $2 billion and employing 84,000 people.
47. Ibid., p. 117.
48. Lyon, p. 183.
49. Ibid., p. 185.
50. Ibid., pp. 187–88.

CHAPTER 13: TROUBLE IN PARADISE

1. Mertz and Ritter, "Building the Interstate," pp. 123–24.
2. Minard, "Symposium Experts Cite Region's Needs."
3. Ibid.
4. Mertz and Ritter, pp. 12–13.
5. Johnson, "Commentary on My Years."
6. Mertz and Ritter, p. 19.

7. Ibid., p. 25.
8. Ambrose, *Eisenhower the President,* p. 528.
9. *America's Highways,* pp. 478–79.
10. Mertz and Ritter, pp. 31–33.
11. *America's Highways,* p. 317.
12. Mowbray, *Road to Ruin,* p. 181.
13. Ibid., p. 183.
14. Leavitt, *Superhighway: Superhoax*, p. 179.
15. Mowbray, p. 133.
16. Kahn, "Political Change in America," p. 150. The author notes that AASHO backed the BPR initiative, to "secure the widest support in Congress for interstates." See also Schwartz, "Urban Freeways."
17. Mertz and Ritter, p. 83.
18. Ibid., pp. 35–37.
19. Ibid., p. 72.
20. Mertz and Ritter, p. 80.
21. Ibid., p. 54; "Associated General Contractors": Leavitt, p. 150.
22. Congress directed the secretary of commerce to work with state highway departments and report their findings to Congress.
23. *America's Highways,* p. 295. See also Small, Winston, and Evans, *Road Work,* pp. 4–5.
24. Mertz and Ritter, p. 82. Congress also required that after 1965, "comprehensive planning" must precede any interstate project in a city of more than fifty thousand people. The *Engineering News Record* moaned that resultant delays for citizen input would mean the program, scheduled for completion by 1973, would not lay its last asphalt until 1981 (Mertz and Ritter, p. 91). See also Federal Highway Administration, "Improvement Status."
25. Mertz and Ritter, p. 79, citing the testimony of J. C. Womack, a Californian, before the House Subcommittee on Roads, April 1962.
26. Mertz and Ritter, pp. 95–96.
27. Ibid., p. 137.
28. Mowbray, p. 24. Later that year, LBJ tried to rein in highway spending by setting $2.2 billion aside until inflation eased. The howls of angry critics trimmed his freeze to $600 million.
29. U.S. House Committee on Public Works, *Hearings before the Special Subcommittee*, p. 170.
30. Ibid., pp. 6–71.
31. Mowbray, p. 15, citing figures from the National Highway Users Conference. See also Mowbray, p. 102.
32. Ibid., p. 101.
33. Leavitt, p. 265.
34. Mowbray, p. 187.
35. Ibid., p. 189.
36. Stover, p. 226.
37. Ibid., p. 231.

38. Lyon, *To Hell in a Day Coach,* p. 195; "New York Thruway": Douglas, *All Aboard,* p. 388.

39. Lyon, p. 217. Since 1940 Congress had encouraged lines to stay afloat by merging, but solvent railways understandably wanted no part of weaker lines.

40. Martin, *Railroads Triumphant,* pp. 382–83.

41. Kendrick, "Urban Transportation Policy," p. 131.

42. Congress in 1962 agreed to reimburse relocation payments paid by states but did not require states to make such payments. In 1968—by which time the interstates were three-quarters finished—Congress agreed to guarantee such payments to relocatees.

43. Leavitt, p. 5.

44. *America's Highways,* January 1968.

45. Mowbray, p. 201.

46. Ibid., p. 101.

47. Ibid., p. 180.

48. Mowbray, p. 35.

49. Mertz and Ritter, p. 162.

50. Leavitt, p. 186.

51. Mertz and Ritter, pp. 159–60. To add insult to injury, LBJ had had the audacity to name a newsman to head the highway program and a lawyer to captain the DOT.

52. Ibid., p. 159.

53. Ibid., p. 160.

54. Ibid., p. 161.

55. Leavitt, p. 233. Leavitt contends that by reaching far out into the countryside, a superhighway draws more property into the urban land market, while demand remains fixed, thus reducing average land values.

56. Mowbray, pp. 36–37.

57. Dunn, *Miles to Go,* pp. 123–24; "Tip O'Neill": Leavitt, p. 58.

58. Dunn, p. 124.

59. Ibid., p. 123.

60. Leavitt, p. 93. Leavitt details a generation-long battle for public transit against entrenched highway interests, against the backdrop of colonial rule then exercised by Congress over the District of Columbia.

61. Leavitt, pp. 89–93. James Dunn, in *Miles to Go,* reports that by 1970, freeway revolts were brewing in Hartford, Chicago, Shreveport, Baltimore, Boston, New York City, Cleveland, Philadelphia, Providence, San Francisco, Seattle, and Washington, D.C.

62. Leavitt, p. 190.

63. Mowbray, p. 204.

64. Hilton, *Federal Transit Subsidies,* pp. 98–99. Cities with rail transit were largely those that had bought out a private system.

65. Cudahy, *Cash, Tokens,* pp. 180–82.

66. Ibid., p. 183.

67. Ibid., p. 187.

68. Mertz and Ritter, pp. 54, 89; Johnson, "A Commentary."
69. Mertz and Ritter, p. 148.
70. Ibid., p. 57.
71. Ibid., p. 92. See also Flink, *Automobile Age,* p. 378.
72. Flink, p. 379. The money was allocated as part of the Urban Mass Transit Act. In 1962, President Kennedy had supported an effort, blocked successfully by the highway-motor complex, to funnel $500 million a year to rail rapid transit.
73. Dunn, p. 125.
74. Burby, *Great American Motion Sickness,* pp. 315–17. Actually, as early as 1969, the National Auto Dealers Association had told a Senate hearing, "It is imperative that public transportation play a more vital role in the future if we expect to make any headway with our urban problems of congestion, poverty, pollution and employment." But NADA's president made it clear that highway funds should not be tapped to pay for it (U.S. Senate Committee on Banking and Currency, *Hearings on Bills to Amend the Urban Mass Transportation Act of 1964,* pp. 400–401.
75. Burby, pp. 306–7.
76. Ibid., pp. 310–11.
77. Ibid., pp. 312–13. Volpe had apparently done well to secure a five-year delay. Burby reports that the Nixon administration had wanted a two-year extension, principally to allow time to strategize how to kill it completely.
78. Burby, pp. 313–14.
79. Flink, p. 379; "Such cities": Cudahy, p. 201. Congress appropriated $133 million for mass transit purposes.
80. Cudahy, p. 221.
81. Dunn, p. 125.
82. Mertz and Ritter, p. 207. See also Yergin, *The Prize,* pp. 615–17.
83. Flink, p. 373.
84. Dunn, p. 125.
85. Mertz and Ritter, p. 213.
86. Fischler, *Moving Millions,* p. 225.
87. Flink, p. 379.
88. Mitchell, "30 Years," p. 81.
89. Dunn, p. 125.
90. Patton, *Open Road,* p. 269.
91. Ibid., p. 271.
92. A dozen cities, including Baltimore, Miami, and Atlanta, took up the offer in the next two years to build subways. Smaller cities—Buffalo, Sacramento, San Jose, and Minneapolis, among them—built surface-level light rail systems akin to the old interurbans. See Finch, *Highways to Heaven,* p. 337.
93. Small, Winston, and Evans, pp. 4–5.
94. Fischler, pp. 224–25.

CHAPTER 14: THE UNSHACKLING

1. "62 to 1": Wilner, "User Charges"; Saunders, *Railroad Mergers,* p. 334. The other prime example was Great Britain, the nation whose laws and customs America most closely followed from its inception.

2. Patton, *Open Road,* p. 269.

3. Association of American Railroads (AAR), "Railroad Facts," pp. 29–32.

4. Martin, *Railroads Triumphant,* p. 345. See also, Dunn, *Miles to Go,* p. 41.

5. Dunn, pp. 40–42.

6. Amtrak, *Source Book.*

7. "How to Trim Amtrak," pp. 28–29.

8. Hilton, *Amtrak,* p. 78, quoting the Norfolk and Western Railway president, John P. Fishwick.

9. Martin, p. 129.

10. Ibid., p. 131.

11. Saunders, *Railroad Mergers,* p. 330. The Penn Central had lost as much as $237 million a year in operating revenues, even disregarding fixed costs.

12. Ibid., pp. 295–98.

13. Ibid., p. 299.

14. Ibid., p. 300.

15. Ibid., p. 305.

16. Ibid., pp. 307, 324.

17. Conrail's predecessors were the bankrupt Ann Arbor Railroad, the Central Railroad of New Jersey, the Erie Lackawanna Railway, the Lehigh and Hudson River Railway, the Lehigh Valley Railroad, the Penn Central Transportation Company, and the Reading Company.

18. Loving, "Conrail Is Still Seeking," p. 120. The Railroad Revitalization and Regulatory Reform Act of 1976 insured railroads' control by giving the industry six of eleven seats on Conrail's board of directors.

19. U.S. Congress, Congressional Budget Office, "Economic Viability of Conrail," p. 4.

20. Labich, "Blessings by the Truckload," p. 139.

21. Loving, p. 120.

22. Saunders, pp. 319–321.

23. Dunn, pp. 43–44. Congress passed the Regional Rail Reorganization Act, commonly dubbed the "3R Act," in 1973, setting up the U.S. Railway Association to reorganize the bankrupt rails. The Railroad Revitalization and Regulatory Reform Act of 1976 (the "4R Act") provided the means for the USRA to subsidize Conrail.

24. Dunn, pp. 44–45. The Railroad Revitalization and Regulatory Reform Act of 1976 instructed the ICC to keep hands off any railroad increase or decrease in rates of 7 percent or less and to accommodate the railroads' desire for peak-period and seasonal rate alterations. See also Felton and Anderson, *Regulation and Deregulation,* p. 38.

25. Saunders, pp. 308, 322.

26. Keeler, *Railroads, Freight,* p. 33. Members of the Washington establishment were not unanimous in their support of Amtrak and Conrail. President

Carter tried to trim Amtrak's budget by nearly half and to dismantle Conrail as a deficit-cutting measure. Congress beat down the latter proposal and held Amtrak cuts to 13 percent. See Yago, *Decline of Transit*. See also Dunn, p. 41; and Hilton, p. 79.

27. Felton, pp. 144–45.
28. U.S. House Committee on Public Works, Subcommittee on Surface Transportation, Regulation of Ground Transportation in Denver, Colorado, pp. 133–35; "Truckers Roll toward Deregulation," p. 76. See also Labich, "Blessings by the Truckload," p. 138.
29. Keeler, p. 29.
30. Stone, *Interstate Commerce Commission,* pp. 89–90.
31. Congress said the ICC should consider no railroad rate too high unless the railway had "market dominance" over the particular traffic. The commission interpreted *market dominance* in such a way to justify denying most requests for railroad rate hikes. Lawmakers also abolished the principle that railroads were a quasi-utility that had to continue money-losing routes and carry commodities, such as the mails, below cost.
32. Felton, p. 39.
33. Ibid.
34. Stone, p. 188.
35. Ibid., p. 115.
36. Ibid., p. 138.
37. Keeler, p. 82.
38. Stone, p. 92. The commissioner was Betty Jo Christian.
39. Ibid., p. 115.
40. Orenstein, *United States Railroad Policy,* p. 65; Staggers description: *Congressional Directory*, p. 188. See also Keeler, pp. 98–99.
41. "Economic Viability of Conrail," pp. 5–7.
42. Keeler, pp. 99, 105.
43. Felton, pp. 144, 150. The Motor Carrier Act of 1980 let truckers increase or decrease their rates within a "zone of reasonableness," which at the outset meant 10 percent up or down.
44. Ibid., pp. 144–48. Under the Motor Carrier Act of 1935, an applicant for operating authority had to prove that existing rail and road carriers could not service the traffic adequately. The 1980 act shifted the burden of proof to the existing carriers. The price of the carriers' new freedom was to curb the time-honored rate bureaus that railroads and truckers had relied on. The rate bureaus would have violated antitrust laws had their carriers not themselves been regulated. Once road and rail could compete openly, the bureaus—which some feel may have kept rates unreasonably high—had to go.
45. Martin, p. 392.
46. Keeler, p. 99.
47. Ibid., p. 105.
48. Stone, p. 116. The Staggers bill, while termed deregulation legislation, actually freed up about two-thirds of all railroad rate-setting from regulation.

49. Keeler, p. 107. A 4 percent rate of return jumped to 5 percent in 1981. See also Stone, p. 130.
50. Stone, p. 90.
51. Keeler, p. 41.
52. "Economic Viability of Conrail," pp. xiii, 5–7. The Northeast Rail Service Act of 1981 (NERSA) relaxed the abandonment policies.
53. Martin, p. 303.
54. Stone, p. 137.

CHAPTER 15: SAME GAME, NEW RULES

1. Wilner, "Railroads and Productivity," p. 36.
2. Ibid., p. 31.
3. Interview with Frank Wilner.
4. Ibid.
5. Harper, "Fading Railroads," p. 22.
6. Wilner, "Railroads and the Marketplace," p. 27; Association of American Railroads (AAR), "Railroad Facts."
7. Wilner, "Railroads and Productivity," p. 9; AAR, "Railroad Facts."
8. Tully, "Comeback Ahead." Also "Railroad Facts," pp. 29, 55.
9. Interview with Frank Wilner.
10. Wilner, "Railroads and the Marketplace," p. 36.
11. Tully.
12. Wilner, "Railroads and Productivity," p. 37.
13. Bryant, "St. Johnsbury," p. D17.
14. McCarthy, "Highway Safety Implications." See also Kaufman, "Truckers Split"; and Schulz, "Railroads Only Hurt Themselves." Since Congress has jurisdiction over only a fraction of the roadways that trucks travel, the ATA has fought the battle for LCVs in state legislatures across the country. A dozen or more states already allow the longer rigs.
15. Wilner, "Railroads and the Marketplace," p. 33.
16. Wilner, "Railroads and Productivity," p. 28
17. "Railroad Facts," p. 42.
18. Borlaug Phillips and McCutchen, "Economic Regulation," p. 323.
19. Khalaf, "Walter Was Very Creative." See also "Railroad Facts," p. 3.
20. Interview with Walter Rich, November 5, 1992.
21. Amtrak, *1992 Annual Report*, p. 7.
22. Ibid., and interview with Clifford Black, April 27, 1993.
23. Dao, "Amtrak's Envious Look," p. Bl.
24. Amtrak, "Amtrak All Aboard." See also other Amtrak entries.
25. "A Decade of Riding the Rails," p. 81.
26. Travels and interviews aboard Amtrak's "Lake Shore Limited" and "Pioneer" routes, May 19–25, 1993.
27. "Federal Transportation Funding," pp. 2, 16.
28. "USA Snapshots."
29. Passell, "Transit Green," p. 5.
30. Zamichow and Perlman, "$1.23 Billion Grant," p. 1.

CHAPTER 16: TAKING STOCK

1.   Lines spoken by Danny DeVito in *Other People's Money*.
2.   *Ladies' Home Journal*, pp. 46–47.
3.   Gifford, "Interstate Highway System," pp. 319–22.
4.   Quote contained in reply to author's letter of inquiry to Senator Gore, February 16, 1993.
5.   Patton, *Open Road*, p. 271.
6.   As of this writing, the federal gasoline tax is 18.4 cents a gallon.
7.   Bailey, "Making the Car Pay," p. 1. The author's study of Minneapolis roads concluded that removing the portion of local property taxes that pay for roads would require a 17.5 percent increase in gas taxes.
8.   MacKenzie, "Going Rate," p. 9.
9.   Small, Winston, and Evans, *Road Work*, p. 57.
10. Campaign for New Transportation Priorities, "Transportation and Tax Policy," p. 4. See also MacKenzie, p. 9.
11. "Highway Statistics, 1989," p. 41. And the costs could be even higher. One California engineer, Stanley Hart, who has studied the amount such ancillary costs add to Pasadena's tax bill, believes these figures extrapolated to America as a whole would yield a tax burden of $60 billion dollars. See Hart, "Huge City Subsidies."
12. National Association of Railroad Passengers, *Urban and Suburban Transportation*, p. 5; MacKenzie, pp. 10–11; Chafee, "Driving Home."
13. "13 percent": MacKenzie, p. 16.
14. MacKenzie, p. 17.
15. Ibid.; *Urban and Suburban Transportation*, p. 2; Ravenel, "Designing Defense," p. 46; Yergin, *The Prize*, p. 775.
16. Chafee, p. 22.
17. Views on enrichment of suburbs from interview with William Klein.
18. Interview with Gary Washburn.
19. Page, "Surface Transportation."
20. Observations from author's driving on freeways in greater Los Angeles during October 1991.
21. Texas Transportation Institute, "Roadway Congestion."
22. General Accounting Office, *Traffic Congestion*, pp. 63–64.
23. French, "Efficiency and Equity." See also MacKenzie, p. 15.
24. Morris, "Getting from Here to There."
25. MacKenzie, p. 13. Figures are in 1989 dollars.
26. Chafee, p. 22.
27. Eno Foundation for Transportation, "Transportation in America," pp. 23, 33.
28. *The Fact Book 1993*, p. 80.
29. MacKenzie, p. 19.
30. Ibid. The $130 billion total is broken down as follows: $58.1 billion—productivity losses; $38.3 billion—property damages; $24.9 billion—auto insurance (payments); $13.4 billion—uncompensated economic losses; $12.6 billion—medical expenses; $15.7 billion—legal, court, and administrative

costs; $2.4 billion—lost time; $2 billion—travel delays; $900 million—government emergency services (These figures are from a study prepared by the Urban Institute for the Federal Highway Administration).

31. Interview with Shaun Mooney; and *The Fact Book 1993*, p. 16.
32. Morris.

CHAPTER 17: TECHNOLOGY TO THE RESCUE?

1. Gartner and Reiss, "Congestion Control"; "Cars That Drive Themselves," p. 40.
2. Olszewski and Turner, "New Approaches."
3. Small, Winston, and Evans, *Road Work*, p. 89; and Small, "Urban Traffic Congestion," p. 8.
4. "Relieving Gridlock."
5. Maykuth, "Technology Paving Way."
6. Truelove, "Strategies for Gaining." In regions where the cost of electronic monitoring is not justified, government could require commuters to display prepaid windshield cards.
7. Decorla-Souza and Kane, "Peak Period Tolls."
8. "Cars are Smarter"; and interview with Kent Taylor, and test demonstration. Travtek is a partnership of General Motors, the AAA, the Federal Highway Administration, the Florida Department of Transportation, and the City of Orlando. Also, the author received a demonstration of the system operated by the Los Angeles Department of Transportation in October 1991.
9. "Robo-Roads."
10. "Cars That Drive Themselves," p. 90.
11. Fehr, "Area Traffic Control," p. 7.
12. "Technology Not Prime Barrier."
13. Hyman, "Pavement, Bridge," p. 157.
14. Kamin and Washburn, "Personal Transit Still Must," p. 12.
15. Sloane, "Peering Back into Future," p. 2.
16. Fabian, "Automated People Movers."
17. Maney, "Fiber Optics to Break,'," p. 15.
18. Arthur, "How to Give Up," pp. 25–29.
19. Crane, "Computer Commuters," pp. 26–47.
20. Interview with Jean-Loup L'Espuissas.
21. Ride on X2000 from New Haven, Connecticut, to Washington, D.C., April 26 and 30, 1993.
22. Vranich, "High Speed Hopes Soar," p. 30.
23. Material from Republic Locomotive, Greenville, South Carolina.
24. Test demonstration in Emsland, Germany, on June 25, 1992.
25. Vranich, *Supertrains*, pp. 90–91.
26. Information gained from meetings with Sam Tabuchi, president, and Jim Taylor, vice-president, of Maglev, Inc., during March 1991 and March 1992.
27. Observations from author's visit to Transrapid's test site in Emsland, Germany, June 26, 1992.

28. Wald, "Clean Air Laws."
29. Lane, "Clinton Orders Purchase."
30. "Natural Gas Gets Crowning."
31. Faiola, "New Pump at Florida."
32. Adler, "Big 3 Close."
33. Bishop, "Details Unveiled."
34. Wald, "Going beyond Batteries."
35. Stipp, "GM and Utility Mount."
36. Wald, "Imagining the Electric-Car."
37. Salpukas, "Satellite System Helps."
38. Wilner, "Railroads and Productivity," p. 19.
39. Wilner, "Railroads and the Marketplace," p. 33
40. Towle, "Pena Touts Conversion Plan."
41. Sims, "Arms Makers Vie."

CHAPTER 18: SINKING OR SWIMMING IN A GLOBAL ECONOMY

1. Seely, "A Republic Bound Together," p. 39.
2. Kay, "Paved with Good Intentions."
3. Cassidy, "Great Decisions are Made."
4. Hepler, "On the Roads Again." See also "Transportation Infrastructure—Better Tools Needed for Making Decisions on Using ISTEA Funds Flexibly."
5. Cantor, "Highway Construction: Its Impact." The author cautions that a dollar spent on highways is a dollar taken away from other programs, so the loss to those has to be balanced against the gain to the economy from new roads.
6. Aschauer, "Transportation Spending."
7. Keveney, "Solo Drivers May Pay." While a third of commuters participated in van and car pools in 1980, this dropped off to little more than a fifth a decade later, in part because of generous employer subsidies. See Sims, "Motorists Are Still Shunning."
8. Replogle, "Making Suburbs Sustainable."
9. McCarthy and Tay, "Road Pricing in Singapore."
10. Casavant and Lenzi, "Economic Analysis."
11. Dance, "Why American Roads," pp. 13–16. Typically, builders of U.S. superhighways lay 4 inches of asphalt atop 12 inches of concrete on 2 to 3 feet of compacted original soil. Contrast that to Germany, which covers its roads with 3 inches of special asphalt atop a 4- to 6-inch asphalt base above 10 inches of gravel drainage on top of 4 inches of asphalt separation, which itself overlays 4 to 6 feet of backfilled new soil. European road builders add innovative polymers to asphalt and mix new additives to concrete. Novaphalt, used widely by Europeans since 1976, costs only 4 percent to 8 percent more than traditional asphalt but lengthens pavement life from 50 to 100 percent.
12. Van Voorst, "Why America Has," pp. 64–65.
13. Osborne, "Reinventing Government," p. 277; and Donahue, *Privatization Decision,* pp. 216–17.

14. Weiman, "Road Work Ahead," pp. 42–48.
15. "Pay as You Drive."
16. Gomez-Ibanez et al., "Prospects for Private."
17. Project proposals on file in the California Department of Transportation, Sacramento, California.
18. Freeman and Aldcroft, *Transport in Victorian Britain*, p. 15.
19. Interviews with Ralf Ratzenberger and Dieter Lippert.
20. Interview with Jean-Loup L'Espuissas.
21. Interview with Rudiger Wenk
22. Interview with Francis Fabre.
23. Interviews with David Bayliss, David Hollings, and Robert Shelton.
24. Interviews with David Hollings and Robert Shelton.
25. Interview with David Bayliss.
26. Pitcher, "Better Understanding," p. 15.
27. The University of Michigan Researcher Andrzej S. Nowak wired interstate bridges with computerized weighing devices and found 150 overweight trucks out of 7,000 "weighed," some exceeding the legal limit by fifty thousand pounds. See Cain, "Heavy Rigs Ruining Roads," p. D1.
28. Pitcher. See also Randall, "Truckers Are Facing."
29. Elmer-Dewitt, "Take a Trip," pp. 51–56. See also Morris, "Getting from Here to There."
30. "The World's Largest Industrial Corporations," p. 184.

BIBLIOGRAPHY

Abrams, Charles. *Forbidden Neighbors*. New York: Harper & Brothers, 1955.

Ambrose, Stephen L. *Eisenhower the President*, vols. 1 and 2. New York: Simon & Schuster, 1984.

American Automobile Association. "The Beginning of the Automobile and the American Automobile Association." *White Rose Motorist*, September 1961.

American Petroleum Institute. "What Editors Are Saying About Gasoline Taxes." Washington, D.C.: American Petroleum Institute, 1931.

America's Highways, 1776–1976. Washington, D.C.: Department of Transportation, Federal Highway Administration, 1976.

"America's Information Highway: A Hitch-hiker's Guide." *The Economist*, January 7, 1994, p. 35.

Amtrak. "Amtrak All Aboard." Washington, D.C.: National Railroad Passenger Corporation, 1992.

————. *1992 Annual Report*. Washington, D.C.: National Railroad Passenger Corporation, 1992.

————. *Source Book*. Washington, D.C.: National Railroad Passenger Corporation, 1991.

"Armed Ship Bill Beaten." *New York Times*, March 5, 1917, p. 1.

Arthur, Charles. "How to Give Up Going to Work." *New Scientist*, October 24, 1992, p. 25.

Aschauer, David. "Transportation Spending and Economic Growth." Washington, D.C.: American Public Transit Association, September 1991.

Associated Press. "Mass Transit." April 15, 1991.

Association of American Railroads. "Railroad Facts." Washington, D.C.: Association of American Railroads, 1992.

Bailey, John. "Making the Car Pay Its Way: The Case of Minneapolis Roads." Minneapolis, Minn.: Institute for Local Self-reliance, 1992.

Bailey, Stephen K. *The New Congress*. New York: St. Martin's, 1966.

Baker, Ray Stannard. *Woodrow Wilson*. New York: Doubleday, Doran, 1937.

Bardou, Jean-Pierre. *The Automobile Revolution: The Impact of an Industry*. Chapel Hill: University of North Carolina Press, 1982.

Barger, Harold. *The Transportation Industries 1889–1946: A Study of Output Employment and Productivity*. Salem, N.H.: Arno, 1975.

Barnard, Harry. *Independent Man: The Life of Senator James Couzens*. New York: Scribner's, 1958.

Barnes, Fred. "Planes, Migraines, and Automobiles." *Business Month,* August 1990, p. 13.

Barone, Michael, and Grant Ujifusa. "The Almanac of American Politics 1992." Washington, D.C.: National Journal, 1992.

Barrett, Paul. *The Automobile and Urban Transit: The Formation of Public Policy in Chicago, 1900–1930*. Philadelphia: Temple University Press, 1983.

———. "Public Policy and Private Choice: Mass Transit and the Automobile in Chicago between the Wars." *Business History Review* 59 (Winter 1975).

Bates, Ernest Sutherland. *The Story of Congress—1789–1935*. New York: Harper & Brothers, 1936.

Beard, Charles, and Mary Beard. *The Rise of American Civilization,* vol. 2. New York: Macmillan, 1927.

Belasco, Warren James. *The Road from Autocamp to Motel, 1910–45*. Cambridge, Mass.: MIT Press, 1979.

Bishop, Jerry E. "Details Unveiled on Battery Built for Electric Car." *Wall Street Journal*, April 9, 1993.

"Board Establishes System for Loans." *New York Times,* February 9, 1932.

Boardman, Barrington. *Flappers, Bootleggers, "Typhoid Mary," & The Bomb. An Anecdotal History of the United States from 1923–1945*. New York: Harper & Row, 1988.

Bonavia, Michael R. *The Nationalisation of British Transport: The Early History of the British Transport Commission*. New York: Macmillan, 1987.

"Boosting U.S. Highway IQs Requires Varied Sciences." *Signal,* April 1993.

Bourke-White, Margaret. "The Long, Long Road." *Life,* July 19, 1954, pp. 75–80.

Brindley, John E. *History of Road Legislation in Iowa*. Des Moines: State Historical Society of Iowa, 1912.

Brough, James. *The Ford Dynasty: An American Story*. New York: Doubleday, 1977.

"Build Roads." *Engineering News-Record,* July 19, 1917.

Burby, John. *The Great American Motion Sickness—Or Why You Can't Get There from Here*. Boston: Little, Brown, 1971.

Burck, Charles G. "Truckers Roll toward Deregulation." *Fortune,* December 18, 1978, p. 75.

Burt, Olive. *The Story of American Railroads and How They Helped Build a Nation*. New York: John Day, 1969.

"Business is Ready." *New York Times,* February 15, 1954, p. 1.

Cable, Mary. *Avenue of the Presidents*. Boston: Houghton Mifflin, 1969.

Cain, Stephen. "'Heavy Rigs Ruining Roads,' Study Says." *Ann Arbor News,* August 15, 1991, p. D1.

California Department of Transportation. 1992 project proposals on file, Sacramento, Calif.

Campaign for New Transportation Priorities. "Transportation and Tax Policy." Washington, D.C.: National Association of Railroad Passengers, 1991.

Cantor, David J. "Highway Construction: Its Impact on the Economy." *Congressional Research Service,* no. 93-21E (January 6, 1993).

————. "Transportation Infrastructure and Manufacturing Costs of Production." *Congressional Research Service,* no. 93-319E (March 12, 1993).

Caro, Robert A. *The Power Broker: Robert Moses and the Fall of New York.* New York: Vintage, 1975.

"Cars Are Smarter with Computerized Dashboard Map." *Washington Times,* November 12, 1991.

"Cars That Drive Themselves." *Omni,* April 1993.

Carson, Clarence B. *Throttling the Railroads.* Indianapolis: Liberty Fund, 1971.

Casavant, Kenneth L., and Jerry Lenzi. "An Economic Analysis of the Appropriate Fee and Fine Structure for Overloaded Vehicles: Economic Incentive to Overload versus Road Damage Caused by Overloading." Paper presented at World Conference on Transportation Research, Lyon, France, June 1992.

Casdorph, Paul D. *Let the Good Times Roll: Life at Home in America During World War II.* New York: Paragon House, 1989.

Cassidy, William B. "Great Decisions Are Made Playing the MPO Game." *Transport Topics,* February 15, 1993.

Chafee, Sen. John H. "Driving Home a New Transportation Policy." *EPA Journal* 19 (September/October 1992): 21.

Chalmers, David M. *Neither Socialism nor Monopoly: Theodore Roosevelt and the Decision to Regulate the Railroads.* Philadelphia: Lippincott, 1976.

Chandler, Alfred D., Jr., ed. *The Railroads: The Nation's First Big Business.* Salem, N.H.: Arno, 1981.

Chandler, Alfred D., Jr., and Stephen Salsbury. *Pierre S. duPont and the Making of the Modern Corporation.* New York: Harper & Row, 1971.

Cheape, Charles W. *Moving the Masses: Urban Public Transit in New York, Boston and Philadelphia.* Cambridge, Mass.: Harvard University Press, 1980.

Chepesiuk, Ron. "Highways Get Smart." *Sky,* March 1991, p. 25.

Childs, Willliam R. *Trucking and the Public Interest: The Emergence of Federal Regulation 1914–1940.* Knoxville: University of Tennessee Press, 1985.

Chrysler Corporation. *The Story of an American Company.* Detroit: Chrysler Corporation, 1955.

Coit, Margaret. *Mr. Baruch: The Man, the Myth, the Eighty Years.* Boston: Houghton Mifflin, 1957.

Commercial and Financial Chronicle, January 3, 1920, p. 14.

Conant, Michael. *Railroad Mergers and Abandonments.* Berkeley: University of California Press, 1964.

Condit, Carl W. *The Port of New York: A History of the Rail and Terminal System from the Beginnings to Pennsylvania Station.* Chicago: University of Chicago Press, 1980.

Congressional Directory. Washington, D.C.: GPO, 1967.

Congressional Quarterly Annual. Washington, D.C.: GPO, 1954.

Connecticut State Register and Manual. Hartford, Conn.: Office of the Secretary of State, 1973.

Corbett, William Paul. "Oklahoma's Highways: Indian Trails to Urban Expressways." Ph.D. diss., Oklahoma State University, 1982.

Crane, Robert. "Computer Commuters." *Government Executive*, March 1993, p. 26.

Crawford, Kenneth G. *The Pressure Boys: The Inside Story of Lobbying in America.* Salem, N.H.: Arno, 1974.

Crump, Spencer. *Henry Huntington and the Pacific Electric: A Pictorial Album.* Glendale, Calif.: Trans-Anglo Books, 1978.

———. *Ride the Big Red Cars.* Glendale, Calif.: Trans-Anglo Books, 1962.

Cudahy, Brian J. *Destination Loop: The Story of Rapid Transit, Railroading in and around Chicago.* Chicago: Greene Press, 1982.

———. *Cash, Tokens and Transfers: A History of Urban Mass Transit in North America.* New York: Fordham University Press, 1990.

Cupper, Dan. "To the Future." *American Heritage,* May/June 1990.

Dance, Betsy. "Why American Roads All Go to Pot." *Washington Monthly,* November 1991, p. 13.

Dao, James. "Amtrak's Envious Look at Post Office." *New York Times,* May 13, 1992.

———. "Passenger Tax Set at Three Airports for Transit Plan." *New York Times,* July 24, 1992.

Davis, Donald Finlay. *Conspicuous Production: Automobiles and Elites in Detroit, 1899–1933.* Philadelphia: Temple University Press, 1988.

Davis, Kenneth Kulp. *Administrative Law.* St. Paul, Minn.: West, 1959.

Davis, Kenneth S. *The New Deal Years, 1933–1937.* New York: Random House, 1979.

Dearing, Charles L. *American Highway Policy.* Washington, D.C.: Brookings Institution, 1941.

"A Decade of Riding the Rails." *New York Times,* January 4, 1993, p. 8.

Decorla-Souza, Patrick, and Anthony Kane. "Peak Period Tolls: Precepts and Prospects." *Transportation* 46 (1992): 293.

DeGregorio, William A. *The Complete Book of U.S. Presidents.* Avenal, N.J.: Wings Books, 1984.

DeParle, Jason. "West Virginia Students Still Riding into the Future." *New York Times,* August 25, 1991.

Dickson, Paul. *Timelines.* New York: Addison-Wesley, 1990.

Dixon, Frank Haigh. *Railroads and Government: Their Relations in the United States, 1910–1921.* New York: Scribner's, 1922.

Donahue, John D. *The Privatization Decision: Public Ends, Private Means.* New York: Basic Books, 1989.

Donaldson, Stephen E., and William A. Myers. *Rails through the Orange Groves.* Glendale, Calif.: Trans-Anglo Books, 1989.

Douglas, George H. *All Aboard.* New York: Paragon House, 1992.

Dreiser, Theodore A. *A Hoosier Holiday.* New York: Lane, 1916.

Drury, George H. "TRAINS Rides the TGV: Like a Jet About to Take Off," *TRAINS,* April 1989, p. 53.

Dulles, Foster Rhea. *Americans Abroad: Two Centuries of European Travel.* Ann Arbor: University of Michigan Press, 1964.

Dunn, James A., Jr. "Group Politics and Governing the Automobiles in France: The Politics of Highway Finance." Unpublished research paper delivered to Northeast Political Science Association, Philadelphia, November 1991.

——. *Miles to Go: European and American Transportation Policies*. Cambridge, Mass.: MIT Press, 1981.

——. "Public Transportation in the Provinces: The Partnership of Public Money and Private Management in France." Unpublished research paper delivered to Urban Affairs Association, Cleveland, Ohio, April 29–May 2, 1992.

Eckenrode, H. J., and Pocahontas Wight Edmunds. *E. H. Harriman: The Little Giant of Wall Street*. Salem, N.H.: Arno, 1981.

"Education for Highway Engineering and Highway Transport." Second National Conference, Highway Education Board, Washington, D.C., October 26–28, 1922.

Egan, Leo. "Eisenhower Bids States Join U.S." *New York Times*, July 13, 1954, p. 1.

——. "Governors Oppose U.S. Aid." *New York Times*, July 14, 1954, p. 1.

——. "Business Is Ready to Start Uprising." *New York Times*, July 15, 1954, p. 1.

"The Eight Fastest Railways in the World." *International Railway Traveler*, May/June 1992.

Eisenhower, Dwight. *Mandate for Change*. New York: New American Library, 1963.

——. "Special Message to the Congress Regarding the National Highway Program," February 22, 1955.

Ellis, Edward Robb. *Echoes of Distant Thunder: Life in the United States 1914–1918*. New York: Coward, McCann & Geoghegan, 1975.

Elmer-Dewitt, Peter. "Take a Trip into the Future on the Electronic Superhighway." *Time*, April 12, 1993, p. 50.

Encyclopaedia Britannica. Chicago: Encyclopaedia Britannica, 1978.

Eno Foundation for Transportation. "Transportation in America: A Statistical Analysis of Transportation in the United States." Westport, Conn.: Eno Foundation for Transportation, May 1990.

Eustis, John R. "The Banner Year of Tours Begins." *Independent*, April 5, 1919, p. 36.

Fabian, Lawrence. "Automated People Movers and Their Technical Requirements." Paper presented at World Conference on Transportation Research, Lyon, France, June 1992.

Faiola, Anthony. "New Pump at Florida Shell Serves Up Gas Au Naturel." *Journal of Commerce*, March 9, 1993.

Faith, Nicholas. *The World the Railways Made*. New York: Carroll & Graf, 1990.

Farrell, Michael R. *Who Made All Our Streetcars Go? The Story of Rail Transit in Baltimore*. Baltimore: Baltimore NRHS Publications, 1973.

"Federal Transportation Funding: Selected Programs Fiscal Years 1980–1993." *Congressional Research Services*, February 28, 1993.

Fehr, Stephen C. "Area Traffic Control Goes Video." *Washington Post*, October 16, 1991.

Fellmeth, Robert C. *The Interstate Commerce Omission: The Public Interest and the ICC*. New York: Grossman, 1970.

Felton, John Richard, and Dale G. Anderson, eds. *Regulation and Deregulation of the Motor Carrier Industry*. Ames: Iowa State University Press, 1989.

"$50 Billion Roads Planned." *Washington Post*, July 13, 1954, p. 1.

Finch, Christopher. *Highways to Heaven*. New York: HarperCollins, 1992.

Fischler, Stanley I. *Moving Millions*. New York: Harper & Row, 1979.

Fisher, Yule. *The Story of the National Highway Users Conference*. Washington, D.C.: National Highway Users Conference, 1973.

Fishman, Robert. *Bourgeois Utopias*. New York: Basic Books, 1989.

Fleeson, Doris. "$50 Billion More for Highways." *Washington Star*, July 14, 1954, p. 1.

Flink, James J. *The Automobile Age*. Cambridge, Mass.: MIT Press, 1988.

Ford Motor Company. *Freedom of the American Road*. Dearborn, Mich.: Ford Motor Company, 1956.

"For a Century, a Book to Build a Dream On." *Hartford Courant*, January 26, 1993, p. 1.

Foster, Mark S. *From Streetcar to Superhighway: American City Planners and Urban Transportation, 1900–1940*. Philadelphia: Temple University Press, 1981.

Freeman, Michael J., and Derek H. Aldcroft, eds. *Transport in Victorian Britain*. Manchester, England: Manchester University Press, 1988.

Freidel, Frank. *Franklin D. Roosevelt: Launching the New Deal*. Boston: Little, Brown, 1973.

French, Mark. "Efficiency and Equity of a Gasoline Tax Increase." Finance and Economics Discussion Series, no. 33. Washington D.C.: Federal Reserve Board, July 1988.

Friedlander, Ann F., and Richard H. Spady. *Freight Transportation Regulation: Equity, Efficiency and Competition in the Rail and Trucking Industries*. Cambridge, Mass.: MIT Press, 1980.

Fuess, Claude Moore. *Joseph B. Eastman: Servant of the People*. New York: Columbia University Press, 1952.

Fuessle, Newton. "Pulling Main Street Out of the Mud." *Outlook*, August 16, 1922.

Fusfeld, R. *The Economic Thought of Franklin D. Roosevelt and the Origins of the New Deal*. New York: Columbia University Press, 1954.

Gans, Herbert J. *The Levittowners*. New York: Pantheon, 1966.

Gartner, Nathan H., and Robert A. Reiss. "Congestion Control in a Freeway Corridor: A Simulation Study." Paper presented at World Conference on Transportation Research, Lyon, France, June 1992.

"Gasoline: Its Dispensing Stations Can Be Made Sightly." *Building Age*, January 1928.

General Motors. *The First Seventy-five Years of Transportation Products*. Princeton, N.J.: Automobile Quarterly Publications, 1983.

Gifford, Jonathan L. "The Innovation of the Interstate Highway System." *Transportation Research* 18A (1984), p. 4.

Goddard, Stephen B. "The New Haven Railroad: A Case Study of an Industry Disease." Unpublished bachelor's thesis Bates College, 1963.

Gomez-Ibanez, José A., Arnold M. Howitt, John R. Meyer, and Allan D. Wallis. "The Prospects for Private Rail Transit: Lessons from Three Case Studies." Final Report to Urban Mass Transportation Administration, December 1991.

Gomez-Ibanez, José A., and John R. Meyer. "Toll Roads and Private Concessions in France and Spain." Paper presented to John F. Kennedy School of Government, Harvard University, 1992.

Gottmann, Jean. *Megalopolis*. New York: Twentieth Century Fund, 1961.

Gould, Lewis L. *Reform and Regulation: American Politics, 1900–1916*. New York: Wiley, 1978.

Gould, Stephen. "U.S. Telecommunications Infrastructure: Projected Future Evolution." *Congressional Research Service*, February 3, 1993.

Green, Constance McLaughlin. *Washington: Capital City, 1879–1950*. Princeton, N.J.: Princeton University Press, 1963.

Hagerty, James C. *The Diary of James C. Hagerty: Eisenhower in Mid-Course*. Bloomington: Indiana University Press, 1983.

———. "Roosevelt Outlines Six-Point Rail Plan." *New York Times*, September 18, 1932, p. 1.

Halberstam, David. *The Reckoning*. New York: Morrow, 1986.

Hamilton, Dane. "J. B. Hunt Designs Container in Bid to Enter Long-Haul Auto Market." *Journal of Commerce*, February 18, 1993.

———. "Truckers Accelerate Bid to Increase Speed Limit." *Journal of Commerce*, May 11, 1993.

Harper, Edwin L. "The Myth of Fading Railroads." *Journal of Commerce*, May 18, 1993.

Harris, Frank W. "Do Our Highways Need More Railways?" *Western Highways Builder*, July 1930.

Harrod, Steven. "Death Wish: The Good Roads Trains Impact on American Transportation Policy." Unpublished paper submitted in partial fulfillment of master's degree at Massachusetts Institute of Technology, 1992.

Hart, Stanley. "Huge City Subsidies for Autos, Trucks." *California Transit League*, July–September, 1986, p. 1.

Hau, Timothy D. "Congestion Charging Mechanisms: An Evaluation of Current Practice." Paper presented at World Conference on Transportation Research, Lyon, France, June 1992.

Hawes, Douglas W. *Utility Holding Companies*. New York: Clark Boardman, 1987.

Hazard, John L. *Managing National Transportation Policy*. Westport, Conn.: Eno Foundation for Transportation, 1988.

Hepler, Heather. "On the Roads Again." *American City & County*, December 1993.

Heppenheimer, T. A. "The Rise of the Interstates." *Invention & Technology*, Fall 1991.

"High-Tech Transport." *Governing*, December 1990.

Highway Education Board. "Highway Education Board: Its Members and Work." Washington, D.C.: Highway Education Board, September 20, 1932.

———. *Program for Proceedings of Second National Conference on Education for Highway Engineering and Highway Transportation*. Washington, D.C.: Highway Education Board, October 26–28, 1922.

"Highway Statistics, 1989." Federal Highway Administration, U.S. Department of Transportation, FHWA-PL-90-003.

Hilton, George W. *Amtrak: The National Railroad Passenger Corporation*. Washington, D.C.: American Enterprise Institute for Public Policy Research, 1980.

————. *Federal Transit Subsidies: The Urban Mass Transportation Assistance Program*. Washington, D.C.: American Enterprise Institute for Public Policy Research, 1974.

Hilton, George W., and John F. Due. *The Electric Interurban Railways in America*. Stanford, Calif.: Stanford University Press, 1960.

Hindley, Geoffrey. *A History of Roads*. London: Peter Davies, 1972.

Hofsommer, Don. *The Southern Pacific, 1901–1985*. College Station: Texas A & M University Press, 1986.

Hofstadter, Richard. *The American Political Tradition—And the Men Who Made It*. New York: Knopf, 1967.

Holbrook, Stewart H. *The Age of the Moguls*. Garden City, N.Y.: Doubleday, 1953.

————. *The Story of American Railroads*. New York: Crown, 1947.

Hoogenboom, Ari, and Olive Hoogenboom. *A History of the ICC: From Panacea to Palliative*. New York: Norton, 1976.

Hornbeck, J. F. "Highway Privatization and ISTEA: Economic Policy and Financing Issues." *Congressional Research Service,* December 1, 1992.

Horner, Frederick C. Letter to Alfred Reeves. Scheveningen, Holland, June 25, 1938. From Thomas H. MacDonald Archives, Texas A & M University, College Station.

"How to Trim Amtrak without Getting Caught." *Business Week*, December 4, 1978, pp. 28–29.

Hoyner, Dan. "Metropolitan Chicago Almanac." *Chicago Sun Times*, 1991.

Hyman, William A. "Pavement, Bridge, Safety and Congestion Management Systems: A Need for a Clear Federal Vision." *Transportation Quarterly* 47 (April 1993).

Ickes, Harold L. *The Secret Diary of Harold L. Ickes: The First 100 Days, 1933–1936*. New York: Simon & Schuster, 1954.

"Inauguration Day Story as It Grew." *Hartford Times,* March 5, 1917, p. 15.

Ingraham, Joseph C. "Vast Traffic Study Planned." *New York Times,* February 13, 1954, p. 1.

"Inside DOT." Federal Department of Transportation Memorandum, May 10, 1991.

Insurance Information Institute. *The Fact Book 1993*. New York: Insurance Information Institute, 1993.

International Chamber of Commerce. 'Highway Administration and Finance in 15 Countries." Paris: International Chamber of Commerce, 1936.

Interstate Commerce Act of 1887.

"Interstate Commerce Bill Becomes a Law." *New York Times,* February 5, 1887, p. 1.

Interstate Commerce Commission. *Coordination of Motor Transportation,* 182 ICC 263, April 6, 1932.

————. *Fortieth Annual Report of the Interstate Commerce Commission*. Washington, D.C.: GPO, 1926.

————. *Interstate Commerce Commission Reports,* 162, 1910.

————. *Interstate Commerce Commission Reports,* 70 ICC 224, 1921.

————. *Interstate Commerce Commission Reports,* 67 ICC 760, 1921.

————. *Interstate Commerce Commission Reports,* 72 ICC 13, 1922.

————. *Interstate Commerce Commission Reports,* 76 ICC 695, 1922.

————. "Joint Freight Tariff of Northern Pacific Railway Company." July 25, 1904. Interstate Commerce Commission Records, box 731, vol. 2, National Records Center, Suitland, Md.

————. *Motor Bus and Truck Operation,* 140 ICC 685, 1928.

Itzkoff, Donald M. *Off the Track: The Decline of the Intercity Passenger Train in the United States.* Westport, Conn.: Greenwood Press, 1985.

Jackson, Kenneth T. *Crabgrass Frontier: The Suburbanization of the United States.* New York: Oxford University Press, 1985.

James, Stephen. "Teaching Highway Economics and Safety to the Youth of the Nation." Washington, D.C.: Highway Education Board, Convention Publication, 1923.

Jensen, Oliver. *The American Heritage History of Railroads in America.* New York: American Heritage, 1975.

Jerome, John. *The Death of the Automobile: The Fatal Effect of the Golden Era, 1955–1970.* New York: Norton, 1972.

Johnson, Alfred E. "A Commentary on My Years in Washington." *American Highways,* October 1972.

Johnson, Gerald W. *Woodrow Wilson.* New York: Harper & Brothers, 1944.

Josephson, Matthew. *The Robber Barons: The Great American Capitalists 1901–1961.* San Diego, Calif.: Harcourt Brace, 1934.

Jouzaitis, Carol. "The Data Highway On Its Way." *Chicago Tribune,* May 10, 1993.

Joy, Henry B. "The Traveler and the Automobile." *Outlook,* April 25, 1917.

Kahn, Ronald C. "Political Change in America: Highway Politics and Reactive Policymaking." In *Interstates: Public Values and Private Power in American Politics,* ed. J. David Greenstone. Chicago: University of Chicago Press, 1982.

Kamin, Blair, and Gary Washburn. "Personal Transit Still Must Prove Its Worth." *Chicago Tribune,* June 23, 1991, p. 12

Kaplan, Samuel. *The Dream Deferred: People, Politics and Planning in Suburbia.* San Francisco: Seabury Press, 1976.

Kapor, Mitchell, and Jerry Berman. "A Superhighway through the Wasteland." *New York Times,* November 24, 1993.

Karr, Ronald Dale. *Lost Railroads of New England.* Pepperell, Mass.: Branch Line Press, 1989.

Kaufman, Lawrence H. "Truckers Split on Issue of Big Rigs, Poll Shows." *Journal of Commerce,* April 8, 1991.

Kay, Jane Holtz. "Paved with Good Intentions." *The Nation,* August 3, 1992.

Keeler, Theodore E. *Railroads, Freight and Public Policy.* Washington, D.C.: Brookings Institution, 1982.

Keeshin, John Lewis. *No Fears, Hidden Tears: A Memoir of Four Score Years.* Chicago: Castle-Pierce Press, 1983.

Kelley, Ben. *The Pavers and the Paved.* New York: Donald W. Brown, 1971.

Kendrick, Frank J. "Urban Transportation Policy: Politics, Planning and People." In *Urban Problems and Public Policy,* ed. Robert L. Likneberry and Louis H. Mansotti. Lexington, Mass.: Lexington Books, 1975.

Keveney, Bill. "Solo Drivers May Pay." *Hartford Courant,* February 28, 1993, p. 1.

Khalaf, Roula. "Walter Was Very Creative." *Fortune,* August 5, 1991.

Kinsey, E. R. "Report on Rapid Transit for St. Louis." St. Louis: City of St. Louis, 1926.

Klein, Maury. "A Hell of a Way to Run a Railroad." *Audacity*, Fall 1992, pp. 22–31.

Kolko, Gabriel. *Railroads and Regulation 1877–1916*. Princeton, N.J.: Princeton University Press, 1965.

Krohe, James, Jr. "Daley's Trolley." *Chicago Reader*, October 18, 1991, p. 1.

Krukowski, John. "RAP Trims Road Cost by Ten Percent." *Highway and Heavy Construction Magazine*, May 20, 1991.

Kwitny, Jonathan. "The Great Transportation Conspiracy." *Harper's*, February 1981, p. 14.

Labich, Kenneth. "Blessings by the Truckload." *Fortune*, November 11, 1985.

Laing, Hamilton. "The Transcontinental Game: Motoring Over Our Longest Road." *Sunset*, February 1917, p. 73.

Lane, Ed. "Clinton Orders Purchase of 35,000 Alternative-Fuel Vehicles." *Inside DOT & Transportation Week*, February 26, 1993, p. 3.

Latham, George E. "The Automobile and Automobiling." *Munsey's*, May 1903.

Lave, Charles. "Transit Subsidies: The Help That Failed." *Washington Post*, June 10, 1991.

Lay, M. G. *Ways of the World*. Camden, N.J.: Rutgers University Press, 1992.

League of American Wheelmen Bulletin and Good Roads Magazine, January 24, 1896.

Leavitt, Helen. *Superhighway: Superhoax*. New York: Doubleday, 1970.

Lelyveld, Michael S. "Motor Carriers Offer to Buy Mass. Turnpike." *Journal of Commerce*, October 29, 1991.

Levey, Irving L. *Condemnation in U.S.A.* New York: Clark Boardman, 1969.

Lewis, David L. *The Automobile and American Culture*. Ann Arbor: University of Michigan Press, 1986.

———. *The Public Image of Henry Ford*. Detroit: Wayne State University Press, 1976.

Lincoln Highway Association. *The Lincoln Highway; The Story of a Crusade That Made Transportation History*. New York: Dodd, Mead, 1935.

Link, Arthur S., ed. *Papers of Woodrow Wilson*. Princeton, N.J.: Princeton University Press, 1982.

———. *Woodrow Wilson: Campaigns for Progressivism and Peace, 1916–1917*. Princeton, N.J.: Princeton University Press, 1954.

———. *Woodrow Wilson and the Progressive Era, 1910–1917*. New York: Harper & Brothers, 1954.

Long, J. C. *Roy D. Chapin*. Detroit: self-published, 1945.

Loving, Rush, Jr. "Conrail Is Still Seeking the Route to Profitability." *Fortune*, March 13, 1978, p. 120.

Lyon, Peter. *To Hell in a Day Coach*. Philadelphia: Lippincott, 1967.

MacAvoy, Paul W. *The Economic Effects of Regulation: The Trunk-Line Railroad Cartels and the Interstate Commerce Commission Before 1900*. Cambridge, Mass.: MIT Press, 1965.

MacDonald, Forrest. *Insull*. Chicago: University of Chicago Press, 1962.

MacDonald, Thomas H. Address to American Association of State Highway Officials' Fourteenth Annual Meeting, 1923.

———. "Commercial Vehicles on Free Highways." *Journal of Land and Public Utility Economics*, August 1925.

———. Fourteen-volume informal compilation of speeches. Washington, D.C.: Department of Transportation Library.

———. "Highways and Railroads." *Scientific American*, April 1932.

———. Radio address aired nationally, 1923. Fourteen-volume compilation of speeches. Washington, D.C.: Department of Transportation Library.

———. "What Our Highways Mean to Us." *Trade Winds,* February 1923.

MacKenzie, James J. "The Going Rate: What It Really Costs to Drive." Washington, D.C.: World Resources Institute, June 1992.

Maney, Kevin. "Fiber Optics to Break Open the Data Bank." *USA Today*, February 19, 1993.

Martin, Albro. *Enterprise Denied*. New York: Columbia University Press, 1971.

———. *Railroads Triumphant*. New York: Oxford University Press, 1992.

Martin, Hugo. "Elevated Line Appears Headed for Long Haul in Permit Process." *Los Angeles Times*, January 3, 1993.

Marx, Leo. *The Machine in the Garden*. New York: Oxford University Press, 1964.

Mason, Alpheus Thomas. *Brandeis: A Free Man's Life*. New York: Viking, 1946.

Mayer, Martin. *The Builders*. New York: W. W. Norton, 1978.

Maykuth, Andrew. "Technology Paving Way for Cars to Zip Past Tollbooth." *Philadelphia Inquirer*, September 24, 1991.

Mayne, Richard. *The Recovery of Europe: From Devastation to Unity*. New York: Harper & Row, 1970.

McCarthy, Patrick. "Highway Safety Implications of Expanded Use of Longer Combination Vehicles (LCVs)." Paper presented at World Conference on Transportation Research, Lyon, France, June 1992.

McCarthy, Patrick, and Richard Tay. "Road Pricing in Singapore: Too Much of a Good Thing?" Unpublished paper presented at World Conference on Transportation Research, Lyon, France, June 1992.

McCullough, David. *The Path between the Seas: The Creation of the Panama Canal, 1870–1914*. New York: Simon & Schuster, 1977.

McKay, John. *Tramways and Trolleys: The Rise of Urban Mass Transportation in Europe*. Princeton, N.J.: Princeton University Press, 1976.

Mercer, Lloyd J. *Railroads and Land Grant Policy: A Study in Government Intervention*. San Diego, Calif.: Academic Press, 1982.

Mertz, Lee. "Origins of the Interstates." Unpublished paper prepared for colleagues in Federal Highway Administration, 1987.

Mertz, W. L., and Joyce Ritter. "Building the Interstate, 1956–1974." Unpublished paper prepared for colleagues in Federal Highway Administration, 1974.

Meyer, John R. *The Economics of Competition in the Transportation Industries*. Cambridge, Mass.: Harvard University Press, 1959.

Meyer, John R., and José A. Gomez-Ibanez. *Transit and Cities*. Cambridge, Mass.: Harvard University Press, 1981.

Middleton, William D. "Gems of Symmetry and Convenience." *American Heritage*, February 1973.

———. "Goodbye to the Interurbans—Or Is It Hello Again?" *American Heritage*, April 1966.

————. *The Time of the Trolley.* Waukesha, Wis.: Kalmbach, 1967.

Miller, John Anderson. *Fares, Please! From Horse-Cars to Streamliners.* New York: Appleton-Century, 1941.

Miller, Julie. "Now Arriving: Costliest Plans for Commuter Lines Since 1970." *New York Times,* February 21, 1993.

Minard, Ralph. "Symposium Experts Cite Region's Needs." *Hartford Times,* September 10, 1957, p. 1.

Mitchell, John G. "30 Years on Ike's Autobahns." *Audubon*, November 1986.

Morgenthau, Henry. Diary entry by Secretary of the Treasury Henry Morgenthau, December 10, 1934. Franklin D. Roosevelt Archives, Hyde Park, N.Y.

Morris, David. "Getting from Here to There: Building a Rational Transportation System." Minneapolis, Minn.: Institute for Local Self-reliance, 1992.

Morris, Edmund. *The Rise of Theodore Roosevelt.* New York: Coward, McCann & Geoghegan, 1979.

Mosley, Leonard. *Blood Relations: The Rise and Fall of the duPonts of Delaware.* New York: Atheneum, 1980.

"Movement of Highway Trailers by Rail." Interstate Commerce Commission Reports, case no. 31375. Washington, D.C.: GPO, 1954.

Mowbray, A. Q. *Road to Ruin: A Critical View of the Federal Highway Program.* Philadelphia: Lippincott, 1968.

Mowry, George E. *The Era of Theodore Roosevelt and the Birth of Modern America.* New York: Harper & Row, 1958.

Moynihan, Daniel Patrick. "New Roads and Urban Chaos." *The Reporter,* April 14, 1960, p. 13.

Mumford, Lewis. *The Highway and the City.* New York: Harcourt, Brace & World, 1963.

Myers, William A. "The Big Red Cars of the Pacific Electric Railway." In *From Horse Car to Big Red Car to Mass Rapid Transit: A Century of Progress*, ed. Thomas H. Shanks. Virginia Beach, Va.: Donning, 1991.

Nash, Gerald D. *The Great Depression and World War II: Organizing America, 1933–1945.* New York: St. Martin's, 1979.

Nash, Jay Robert. *Makers and Breakers of Chicago.* Chicago: Academy Press, 1985.

National Association of Railroad Passengers, Campaign for New Transportation Priorities. *Urban and Suburban Transportation: Programs and Policies for More Liveable Cities.* Washington, D.C.: National Association of Railroad Passengers, 1991.

National Automobile Chamber of Commerce. *Report to the National Transportation Committee.* Washington, D.C.: National Automobile Chamber of Commerce, 1923.

National Geographic Society. *The Builders.* Washington, D.C.: National Geographic Society, 1992.

"Natural Gas Gets Crowning Touch." *Chicago Tribune*, May 24, 1993.

Nevins, Allan. *Ford: The Times, the Man, the Company.* New York: Scribner's, 1954.

Norman, Henry, M.P. "The Coming of the Automobile." *World's Work*, April 1903.

"Of Grants and Greed." *Sunday Oregonian,* May 23, 1993, p. 1.

Office of the County Clerk. Probate records of estate of Thomas MacDonald, Bryan, Texas.

Olszewski, Piotr, and David J. Turner. "New Approaches to the Problem of Urban Traffic Congestion in Singapore." Paper presented at World Conference on Transportation Research, Lyon, France, June 1992.

"On the Interstate: A City of the Mind." *Time,* June 3, 1985.

"Opening Gun in Battle for Cloture." *Hartford Times,* March 6, 1917, p. 1.

Orenstein, Jeffrey. *United States Railroad Policy: Uncle Sam at the Throttle.* Chicago: Nelson-Hall, 1990.

Osborne, David. "Reinventing Government." In *Mandate for Change,* ed. Will Marshall and Martin Schram. New York: Berkley, 1993.

Overbey, Daniel L. *Railroads: The Free Enterprise Alternative.* Westport, Conn.: Quorum Books, 1982.

Owen, Wilfred. "The Outlook for Highway Transportation." *American Highways,* April 1950.

———. "Problems and Implications of the National Highway Program." *American Highways,* July 1950.

Passell, Peter. "Transit Green, Gridlock Blues." *New York Times,* October 30, 1991.

———. "Cheapest Protection of Nature May Lie in Taxes." *New York Times,* November 24, 1992, p. C1.

Patton, Phil. *Open Road: A Celebration of the American Highway.* New York: Simon & Schuster, 1986.

———. "A Quick Way from Here to There Was Also a Frolic." *Smithsonian,* October 1990.

"Pay as You Drive." *The Economist,* February 11, 1989.

Phillips, C. W. Speech delivered at the annual meeting of the American Association of State Highway Officials, New York City, 1947.

Pisarski, Alan E. "Commuting in America: A National Report on Commuting Patterns and Trends." Westport, Conn.: Eno Foundation for Transportation, 1987.

Pitcher, Robert C. "A Better Understanding of 'The Railroads' Self-interest." Washington, D.C.: American Trucking Association, 1991.

Pitt, David E. "Transit Agency Wants to End Airport Express." *New York Times,* October 22, 1989.

Plowden, William. *The Motorcar in Politics, 1896–1970.* London: Bodley Head, 1971.

Pomeroy, Earl. *In Search of the Golden West: The Tourist in Western America.* New York: Knopf, 1957.

Price, Harry B. *The Marshall Plan and Its Meaning.* Ithaca, N.Y.: Cornell University Press, 1955.

Rae, John B. *American Automobile Manufacturers: The First Forty Years.* Philadelphia: Chilton, 1959.

"Railroads and Wagon Roads." *Good Roads,* January 1892, pp. 39–42.

Railway Gazette, February 1891.

Randall, Eric D. "Truckers Are Facing a Rough Road." *USA Today,* March 4, 1993.

Ravenel, Earl. *Designing Defense for a New World Order*. Washington, D.C.: Cato Institute, 1991.

"Relieving Gridlock." *Journal of Commerce*, January 14, 1992.

Replogle, Michael. "Making Suburbs Sustainable: Linking Land Use and Transportation." Paper presented at World Conference on Transportation Research, Lyon, France, June 1992.

Richardson, Kenneth. *British Motor Industry*. London: Archon, 1977.

Rifkin, Glenn. "Smart Plans for Clogged Roads." *New York Times*, November 20, 1991.

Ripley, William Z. *Railroads: Finance and Organization*. New York: Longmans, Green, 1915.

Robyn, Dorothy. *Braking the Special Interests: Trucking Deregulation and the Politics of Policy Reform*. Chicago: University of Chicago Press, 1987.

Rose, Mark. *Interstate Highway Politics*. Lawrence: Regents Press of Kansas, 1979.

Rowland, T. H. *Roman Transport in the North of England*. London: Howe Brothers.

St. Clair, David J. "Entrepreneurship and the Automobile Industry." Unpublished Ph.D. diss., University of Utah, 1979.

———. *The Motorization of American Cities*. Westport, Conn.: Praeger, 1986.

Salpukas, Agis. "Satellite System Helps Trucks Stay in Touch." *New York Times*, June 5, 1991.

Salsbury, Stephen. *No Way to Run a Railroad: The Untold Story of the Penn Central Crisis*. New York: McGraw-Hill, 1982.

Sandburg, Carl. *Complete Poems of Carl Sandburg*. New York: Harcourt Brace Jovanovich, 1969.

"The Sanitary Dining Car." *Literary Digest*, October 10, 1914, p. 683.

Saunders, Richard. *The Railroad Mergers and the Coming of Conrail*. Westport, Conn.: Greenwood Press, 1978.

Sayre, Ralph. "Albert Baird Cummins and the Progressive Movement in Iowa." Unpublished Ph.D. diss., Columbia University, 1958.

Schissgall, Oscar. *The Greyhound Story: From Hibbing to Everywhere*. Chicago: J. G. Ferguson, 1985.

Schulz, John D. "Railroads Only Hurt Themselves by Fighting LCVs, ATA Chief Charges." *Traffic World*, April 10, 1991.

Schwartz, Gary T. "Urban Freeways." *Southern California Law Review*, March 1976.

Scott, Roy V. *Railroad Development Programs in the Twentieth Century*. Ames: Iowa State University Press, 1985.

Seely, Bruce E. *Building the American Highway System: Engineers as Policy Makers*. Philadelphia: Temple University Press, 1987.

———. "Railroads, Good Roads and Motor Vehicles: Managing Technological Change." *Railroad History Bulletin* 155 (Autumn 1986).

———. "A Republic Bound Together." *Wilson Quarterly* 17 (Winter 1993): 19.

Shanks, Thomas H., ed. *From Horse Car to Big Red Car to Mass Rapid Transit: A Century of Progress*. Virginia Beach, Va.: Donning, 1991.

Sharfman, I. L. *The Interstate Commerce Commission: A Study in Administrative Law and Procedure*. New York: Commonwealth Fund, 1931.

Sharp, Richard G., and Martha B. Lawrence. "Computerization Takes Hold." *Railway Age,* March 1993.

Sillcox, L. K. "Train-Truck Trouble." Paper delivered to Harvard University's Graduate School of Business Administration, December 8, 1950.

Sims, Calvin. "Arms Makers Vie to Build Rail Car." *New York Times*, May 8, 1993.

———. "Motorists Are Still Shunning Car Pools: They Want To Be Alone." *New York Times*, November 4, 1991.

Sloan, Alfred P., Jr. *My Years with General Motors*. New York: Doubleday, 1964.

Sloane, Todd. "Peering Back into the Future for a New Way to Move Masses." *City & State*, April 22, 1991.

Small, Kenneth A. "Urban Traffic Congestion: A New Approach to the Gordian Knot." *Brookings Review* Spring 1993.

Small, Kenneth A., Clifford Winston, and Carol A. Evans. *Road Work: A New Highway Pricing and Investment Policy*. Washington, D.C.: Brookings Institution, 1989.

Smart, Vaughn. "1919: The Interstate Expedition." *Constructor*, August 1973.

Smith, Adam. *An Inquiry into the Nature and Causes of the Wealth of Nations*. 1776. Reprint. Chicago: Encyclopaedia Britannica, 1985.

Smith, Page. *America Enters the World*. New York: McGraw-Hill, 1985.

Stipp, David. "GM and Utility Mount Charts on Electric Cars." *Wall Street Journal*, May 19, 1993.

Stone, Richard D. *The Interstate Commerce Commission and the Railroad Industry: A History of Regulatory Policy*. Westport, Conn.: Praeger, 1991.

Stone, Roy. "Road Building to Be Taught in Common Country Schools." *League of American Wheelmen Bulletin and Good Roads,* August 14, 1896.

Stopher, Peter. "Financing Transportation Investments in the United States: Past Practice and Current Trends." Paper presented at World Conference on Transportation Research, Lyon, France, June 1992.

Stover, John F. *American Railroads*. Chicago: University of Chicago Press, 1961.

———. *The Life and Decline of the American Railroad*. New York: Oxford University Press, 1970.

Suplee, Curt. "Robo-roads: Making Highways 'Smart.'" *Washington Post,* May 27, 1991.

Tebbel, John, and Mary Ellen Zuckerman. *The Magazine in America*. New York: Oxford University Press, 1991.

"Technology Not Prime Barrier to Smart Roads." *Engineering Times*, August 1991.

Texas Transportation Institute. "Roadway Congestion in Major Urbanized Areas 1982–1987." College Station: Texas Transportation Institute and U.S. Federal Highway Administration, 1989.

Thompson, Gregory Lee. "The American Passenger Train in the Motor Age: Archival and Econometric Analyses of Explanations for the Decline in California." Unpublished Ph.D. diss., University of California–Irvine, 1987.

Towle, Michael D. "Pena Touts Conversion Plan." *Fort Worth Star-Telegram*, April 16, 1993.

"Transportation and Tax Policy." Washington, D.C.: Campaign for New Transportation Priorities, 1991.

Transportation Research Board. "Critical Issues in Transportation for the 1990s." *TR News*, November/December 1991.

Truelove, Paul. "Strategies for Gaining Political Acceptance for Urban Road Pricing." Paper presented at World Conference on Transportation Research, Lyon, France, June 1992.

Tuchman, Barbara W. *The Zimmerman Telegram.* New York: Ballantine, Macmillan, 1958.

Tugwell, Rexford. *Roosevelt's Revolution the First Year: A Personal Perspective.* New York: Macmillan, 1977.

Tully, Shawn. "Comeback Ahead for Railroads." *Fortune*, June 17, 1991.

"Unions and Roads Ratify Agreement." *New York Times,* February 1, 1932, p. 1.

Upham, Charles. "Car Shortage and Its Relation to Highway Work." *Engineering News-Record*, December 13, 1917.

U.S. Congress. Congressional Budget Office. "Economic Viability of Conrail." August 1986.

U.S. Department of Commerce, Bureau of the Census. *Historical Statistics of the U.S., 1975.* Washington, D.C.: GPO, 1975.

————. *Statistical Abstract of the United States.* Washington, D.C.: GPO, 1950.

U.S. Department of Transportation. *America's Highways, 1776–1976.* Washington, D.C.: GPO, 1976.

————. *Daily News Summary.* Washington, D.C.: Department of Transportation, 1991.

————. *Daily News Summary.* Washington, D.C.: Department of Transportation, 1992.

————. *Daily News Summary.* Washington, D.C.: Department of Transportation, 1993.

————. *Daily News Summary.* Washington, D.C.: Department of Transportation, 1994.

————. Office of Environmental Policy. *The Consideration of Archaeology and Paleontology in the Federal Aid Highway Program.* Washington, D.C.: GPO, January 1979.

U.S. Federal Highway Administration. *Highway Statistics, 1989.* FHWA-PL-90-003. Washington, D.C.: GPO, 1989.

U.S. General Accounting Office. *Transportation Infrastructure: Better Tools Needed for Making Decisions on Using ISTEA Funds Flexibly.* Washington, D.C.: GPO, October 1993.

U.S. House. *Federal Aid to Good Roads.* 62d Cong., 3d sess., 1915. H. Doc. 1510.

————. *Toll Roads and Free Roads.* 76th Cong., 1st sess., 1939. H. Doc. 272.

U.S. House Committee on Public Works. *Hearings before the Special Subcommittee of the House Committee on Public Works,* 90th Cong., 1st sess., 23 May 1967.

U.S. House Committee on Public Works. *Hearings on H.R. 4260,* 84th Cong., 1st sess., 1955.

U.S. House Committee on Public Works, Subcommittee on Surface Transportation. *Regulation of Ground Transportation in Denver, Colorado: Hearing before the Committee on Public Works, Subcommittee on Surface Transportation.* 96th Cong., 1st sess., 21 August 1979.

U.S. House Committee on Public Works and Transportation. *Surface Transportation Bills: Hearings before the Committee on Public Works and Transportation.* 102d Cong., 1st sess., 1991.

U.S. House Committee on Public Works and Transportation, Subcommittee on Surface Transportation. *Deregulating Surface Transportation in Harrisburg, Pennsylvania: Hearing before the Committee on Public Works and Transportation, Subcommittee on Surface Transportation.* 96th Cong., 1st sess., 27 October 1979.

U.S. House Committee on Roads. *Hearings on H.R. 63,* 68th Cong., 2d sess., 19 March 1924.

———. *Hearings on H.R. 3232,* 68th Cong., 2d sess., 19 March 1924.

———. *Hearings on H.R. 4971,* 68th Cong., 2d sess., 19 March 1924.

———. *Hearings on H.R. 6133,* 68th Cong., 2d sess., 19 March 1924.

U.S. House Ways and Means Committee. *Hearings on H.R. 8836,* 84th Cong., 2d sess., 1956.

U.S. Interstate Commerce Commission. Bureau of Transportation Economics and Statistics. *Interstate Commerce Commission Activities 1887–1937.* Washington, D.C.: GPO, 1975.

U.S. Senate Committee on Banking and Currency. *Hearings on Bills to Amend the Urban Mass Transportation Act of 1964.* 90th Cong., 1st sess., 1967.

———. *Urban Mass Transportation Bills: Hearings before the Committee on Banking and Currency.* 91st Cong., 1st sess., 1969.

U.S. Senate Committee on Interstate and Foreign Commerce. *Problems of the Railroads: Hearings before the Committee on Interstate and Foreign Commerce,* vol. 2. 85th Cong., 2d sess., 1958.

U.S. Senate Committee on Interstate and Foreign Commerce, Subcommittee on Surface Transportation. 87th Cong., 1st sess., 1961.

U.S. Senate Committee on the Judiciary, Subcommittee on Antitrust and Monopoly. *American Ground Transport: Hearings before the Committee on the Judiciary, Subcommittee on Antitrust and Monopoly.* 93d Cong., 2d sess., 1974.

U.S. Senate Committee on Public Works. *Hearings on S. 1048,* 84th Cong., 1st sess., 21 February 1955.

———. *Hearings on S. 1072,* 84th Cong., 1st sess., 21 February 1955.

———. *Hearings on S. 1160,* 84th Cong., 1st sess., 21 February 1955.

———. *Hearings on S. 1573,* 84th Cong., 1st sess., 21 February 1955.

U.S. Senate Interstate Commerce Committee. *A Bill to Regulate Motor Carriers: Hearings on S. 2793,* 72d Cong., 2d sess., 1932.

"USA Snapshots." *USA Today,* August 5, 1991.

Van Voorst, Bruce. "Why America Has So Many Potholes." *Time,* May 4, 1992, p. 64.

Vranich, Joseph. "High Speed Hopes Soar." *Railway Age,* May 1992.

———. *Supertrains: Solutions to America's Transportation Gridlock.* New York: St. Martin's, 1991.

Wald, Matthew L. "Clean Air Laws Push Big 3 to Cooperate on Electric Car." *New York Times,* April 14, 1993.

———. "Going Beyond Batteries to Power Electric Cars." *New York Times,* March 3, 1993.

———. "Imagining the Electric-Car Future." *New York Times,* April 28, 1993.

Ward, James A. *Railroads and the Character of America, 1820–1887*. Knoxville: University of Tennessee Press, 1986.

Warner, Sam Bass, Jr. *Streetcar Suburbs*. Cambridge, Mass.: Harvard University Press, 1978.

Weiman, Clark. "Road Work Ahead: How to Solve the Infrastructure Crisis." *Technology Review* 96 (January 1993).

Weisberger, Bernard A. *The Dream Maker: William C. Durant, Founder of General Motors*. Boston: Little, Brown, 1979.

Weiss, Stewart. "Suddenly the Street Is Hot to Get Aboard Conrail." *Business Week,* January 13, 1986.

Welty, Gus. "Roadway for the 21st Century." *Railway Age*, March 1993.

Wentworth, Harold, and Stuart Berg Flexner, eds. *Dictionary of American Slang*. New York: Crowell, 1975.

White, John H., Jr. "Changing Trains." *Invention & Technology*, Spring/Summer 1991, p. 35.

White, William Allen. *Autobiography of William Allen White*. New York: Macmillan, 1946.

Whitt, J. Allen. *Urban Elites and Mass Transportation*. Princeton, N.J.: Princeton University Press, 1982.

Williams, Ernest W., Jr. *The Regulation of Rail-Motor Rate Competition*. New York: Harper & Brothers, 1951.

Willys-Overland Company. "Advertisement." *Ladies' Home Journal*, March 1917, p. 46.

Wilner, Frank N. "Railroads and the Marketplace." Washington, D.C.: Association of American Railroads, 1987.

———. "Railroads and Productivity." Washington, D.C.: Association of American Railroads, 1991.

———. "User Charges and Transportation Efficiency." Washington, D.C.: Association of American Railroads, 1990.

"Wilson Sounds a Solemn Note." *New York Times,* March 6, 1917, p. 1.

Wolman, Harold, and George Reigeluth. *Financing Urban Public Transportation: The U.S. and Europe*. New Brunswick, N.J.: Transaction Books, 1980.

Wood, Robert C. *Suburbia: Its People and Their Politics*. New York: Houghton Mifflin, 1958.

"The World's Largest Industrial Corporations." *Fortune,* July 27, 1993, p. 184.

Wright, J. Patrick. *On a Clear Day You Can See General Motors*. Grosse Pointe, Mich.: Wright Enterprises, 1979.

Yago, Glenn. *The Decline of Transit: Urban Transportation in German and U.S. Cities, 1900–1970*. New York: Cambridge University Press, 1984.

Yergin, Daniel. *The Prize: The Epic Quest for Oil, Money and Power*. New York: Simon & Schuster, 1991.

Young, Andrew D. *The St. Louis Streetcar Story*. Glendale, Calif.: Interurban Press, 1988.

Young, Andrew D., and Eugene F. Provenzo, Jr. *The History of the St. Louis Car Company "Quality Shops."* Burbank, Calif. Howell-North, 1978.

Zamichow, Nora, and Jeffrey A. Perlman. "$1.23 Billion Grant to Clear Way for Third Subway Segment." *Los Angeles Times*, May 14, 1993, p. 1.

INTERVIEWS

•————————————————•

Allsop, Richard. Interview by author. London, England, June 8, 1992.

Amtrak personnel. Interview by author. Aboard Lake Shore Limited, Michigan, May 20, 1993.

Bayliss, David, director of planning, London Underground. Interview by author. London, England, June 8, 1992.

Black, R. Clifford, public affairs director. Interview by author. Washington, D.C., April 27, 1993, and several subsequent telephone interviews.

Boghani, Ashok B., director, Arthur D. Little consultants. Interview by author. Lyon, France, July 2, 1992.

Byrne, Julie, chief of on-board services. Interview by author. Aboard X-2000 train from New Haven to Washington, April 26, 1993.

Capon, Ross, director of the National Association of Railroad Passengers. Interview by author. Washington, D.C., April 27, 1993.

Deffke, Hermann. Interview by author. Bonn, Germany, June 25, 1992.

Dunn, Dr. James, chair, Department of Political Science, Rutgers University at Camden, N.J. Numerous telephone interviews by author, 1991–1992.

Endo, Goro, senior transportation engineeer, California Department of Transportation. Interview and demonstration ride by author. Los Angeles, October 10, 1991.

Evans, Dr. Diana, Trinity College, Hartford, Conn. Numerous interviews by author, 1990–1992.

Fabre, Francis. Interview by author. Brussels, Belgium, June 10, 1992.

Furst, Rudiger, engineeer, Industrieanlagen Betriebsgesellschaft. Interview by author and demonstration ride on Maglev train. Emsland, Germany, June 26, 1992.

Gomez-Ibanez, Dr. José A., John F. Kennedy School of Government, Harvard University. Interview by author. Cambridge, Mass., October 1990, and several subsequent telephone interviews.

Hollings, David, and Robert Sheldon, transport consultants. Interview by author. London, England, June 8, 1992.

Joseph, Steven, director of T-2000. Interview by author. London, England, June 8, 1992.

Kinsella, James H. Interview by author. Hartford, Conn., October 12, 1989.

Klein, William, research director, American Planning Association, Chicago. Telephone interview by author. June 16, 1993.

Knickenberg, Joachim, and Michael Robler, Deutsche Bundesbahn. Interview by author. Frankfurt, Germany, June 24, 1992.

Larned, Larry, historian, Connecticut Department of Transportation. Interview by author. Wethersfield, Conn., January 1990, and subsequent telephone interviews.

LeCaille, Jean, director, French Union Routière. Interview by author. Paris, France, June 12, 1992.

L'Espuissas, Jean Loup, and Jacques Rabouel, representatives of French National Railways. Interview by author. Paris, France, June 12, 1992.

Lippert, Dieter, director, Munich rapid transit system. Interview by author. Munich, Germany, June 23, 1992.

Mejia, Mariana, assistant information officer, California Department of Transportation. Telephone interview by author. October 7, 1991.

Mooney, Shaun, senior vice president and economist, Insurance Information Institute, New York. Telephone interview by author. June 16, 1993.

Myers, William A. Interview by author. Rosemead, Calif., October 10, 1991.

Oberlin, Margaret. Telephone interview, June 5, 1990.

Ratzenberger, Ralf. Interview by author. Munich, Germany, June 23, 1992.

Rich, Walter, president, Delaware Otsego Corporation, and William Matteson, vice president. Interview by author. Cooperstown, N.Y., November 5, 1992.

Schackies, Siegbert, East Europe and USSR officer, Federal Highway Administration. Interview by author. Washington, D.C., March 1992.

Tabuchi, Sam, president, Maglev, Inc., and James Taylor, vice president. Interviews by author. Orlando, Fla., March 1991, March 1992.

Taylor, Kent, research and development director, American Automobile Association. Interview by author. Heathrow, Fla., March 30, 1992.

Tondro, Prof. Terry, University of Connecticut School of Law, Hartford. Telephone interview by author. November 21, 1992.

Turner, Frank. Telephone interview by author. March 7, 1990.

Wackers, Manfred, president, Transrapid International, and Robert Budell, his assistant. Interviews by author. Munich Germany, June 23, 1992.

Washburn, Gary, columnist for *Chicago Tribune*. Telephone interview by author. September 1991.

Weingroff, Richard, information liaison specialist, Federal Highway Administration. Numerous personal and telephone interviews by author, 1990–1994.

Wenk, Rudiger. Interview by author. Brussels, Belgium, June 10, 1992.

Wilner, Frank N., assistant vice president, Association of American Railroads. Interview by author, Washington, D. C., April 27, 1993 and numerous subsequent telephone interviews.

LEGAL CASES

•────────────────────────────────•

City of Spokane et al. v Northern Pacific Railroad et al., I.C.C. Reports 162 (1910).

Frost & Frost Trucking Co. v Railroad Commission of California, 271 US 582, 599–600 (1926).

Illinois Public Utilities Commission et al. v Duke Cartage Company, 266 US 570, 577 (1925).

Munn v Illinois, 94 US 113 (1876).

Sproiles v Binford, 286 US 374, 380–383 (1932).

Stephenson v Binford, 287 US 251, 269–72 (1932).

U.S. v National City Lines, 186 F2d 562 (1951).

U.S. v National City Lines, court transcripts of trial testimony. Docket #9943-53, vol. 1, pp. 429 et seq. National Archives and Federal Record Center, Chicago.

Wabash, St. Louis and Pacific Railway Co. v Illinois, 118 US 557 (1886).

ACKNOWLEDGMENTS

By the early 1960s, the competition from Connecticut's new interstate highways had forced the proud New York, New Haven, and Hartford railroads into bankruptcy. Then an undergraduate at Bates College, I explored this topic in a senior economics thesis and developed a fascination with the struggle between road and rail that would lead me back to the nineteenth century. Bates economics department chair Ralph Chances and his colleagues deserve thanks for helping spark my early interest.

I discovered, as an urban newspaperman and a Congressional aide during the balance of the 1960s, that the heralded interstates seemed to cause, especially in the cities, more problems than they solved. But marrying, raising a family, and pursuing a law career would intervene before I could continue my inquiry. Picking up the thread in 1988, I came to realize that the powerful lobby that made the interstates possible was not a post–World War II phenomenon as was conventionally assumed, but had been carefully constructed and nurtured after World War I and had clashed with the railroads in open and guerilla war ever since.

In the next six years of unearthing and telling this tale, I acquired many debts. First of all, I thank my family for standing by this effort. My wife and best friend, Patty Goddard, repeatedly made me refocus on this epic saga during my wanderings by imploring, "It's the story, stupid!" My son Brad Goddard and daughter, Chelsey Goddard, assisted as able clipping services from Virginia and Chicago. And the fact this book was published at all is a tribute to my multi-faceted son Taegan Goddard, who offered unstinting and insightful counsel in areas ranging from policy analysis and data organization to copyediting and marketing and roused his father from despair in the bad times.

My partner, Cynthia Blair, offered consistent support while quietly holding up my end of our law practice when necessary. Law student Sandra

Cheffetz was invaluable in researching and production, and Nancy Miller and Madeleine Quirion applied their computer and office skills ably in helping produce this manuscript.

Several dozen individuals have been generous in offering me their time and counsel to help me understand the fields of American road and rail travel through interviews, answers to inquiries, confirming (or denying) that I was on the right track, and reading parts of the manuscript. Two merit thanks above all others: Richard Weingroff, a Federal Highway Administration writer with a trenchant wit, argued the highway case persuasively in the face of my criticisms and went the extra mile to supply me with material and critique my thesis. Dr. James Dunn, a Rutgers University political scientist, was among the earliest to see merit in this project and enhanced it through offering me encouragement and contacts.

I also credit Frank Wilner of the Association of American Railroads, Ross Capon of the National Association of Railroad Passengers, and Cliff Black of Amtrak, for so ably advancing the railroad perspective; Amtrak personnel on the Lake Shore Limited and Pioneer routes for being forthcoming about life on the rails; William Klein of the American Planning Association, Shaun Mooney of the Insurance Information Institute, and Margaret Oberlin, Thomas MacDonald's daughter; John Doyle of the American Trucking Association; veteran trucker J. R. Halladay; Professor Terry Tondro of the University of Connecticut Law School; and transportation columnists Bill Keveney of the *Hartford Courant,* Gary Washburn of the *Chicago Tribune,* and Mark Stein of the *Los Angeles Times.*

I am indebted to many fine academics, who through little-noticed but important, often skillfully written works, have lit my way down the dark tunnel I've followed the last several years. And others who helped came from many walks of life. Thanks go to: Larry Larned, James Kinsella, and Diana Evans in Hartford; Siegbert Schacknies in Washington, D.C.; Walter Rich and Bill Matteson in Cooperstown, New York; Sam Tabuchi and Jim Taylor in Orlando; Kent Taylor in Heathrow, Florida; Bill Myers and Goro Endo in Los Angeles; Richard Allsop, Steven Joseph, David Bayliss, and David Hollings in London; Jean-Loup L'Espuissas, Jacques Rabouël, and Jean LaCaille in Paris; Tony Gomez-Ibanez and Alan Altshuler in Cambridge; Francis Fabre and Rudiger Wenk in Brussels; Ralf Ratzenberger, Dieter Lippert, Manfred Wackers, and Robert Budell in Munich; Joachim Knickenberg and Michael RöBler in Frankfurt; Hermann Deffke in Bonn; Rudiger Furst in Emsland, Germany; and officials of and participants in the World Conference on Transportation Research in 1992 in Lyon, France.

Numerous individuals have been kind enough to read sections of this manuscript or offer helpful comment. Among them are my brothers Ralph Goddard and Harvey Goddard and my sister, Marian Mullet; Bill Keveney, Richard Weingroff, Frank Wilner, Barbara Hellenga, Professor Tom Grant, Bob Halladay, Suzanne Zack, James Gorman, George Graves, Pam Leucke, Bob Dean, Dave Icikson, Kenny Rogers, Bob Hall, Steve Harrod, Art Lipman, Ed French, John Chapin, and Bill Breetz. Their insights and suggestions for improving this manuscript are gratefully acknowledged.

I also wish to thank officials at a number of libraries and archives for helping pave the way, so to speak, for this book. To the staff of the Hartford Public Library, which I am privileged to serve as board president, I am grateful for a steady stream of information, suggestions and encouragement. Also I acknowledge the staffs of the New York Public Library, the Los Angeles Public Library, the Connecticut State Library, the Chicago Public Library, and the Franklin Delano Roosevelt Archives in Hyde Park, New York; the Joseph Eastman Archives at Amherst College; the Sterling and Mudd Libraries at Yale University; the Widener, Baker, and Kennedy School Libraries at Harvard University; the Washington University Library in St. Louis; the Library of Congress; the Federal Department of Transportation Library; the National Archives; the Connecticut Department of Transportation library; the library of L'École des Ponts et Chaussées in Paris; and National Records Centers in Suitland, Maryland, and Chicago.

The expertise and tenacity of my agent, John Ware, have been instrumental in enabling me to publish this book. Steven Fraser, my editor at Basic Books and an accomplished historian, saw value in this heretofore untold saga of road and rail and contributed an unerring sense of structure to the work. I owe gratitude as well to others at Basic Books: Matt Shine, who shepherded a million and one production details; Sharon Sharp, for her incisive copyediting; Linda Carbone, Mike Mueller, Justin McShea, and Gary Murphy.

INDEX